OSTRO

For my two loves,
Norihiko & Haruki

OSTRO

The pleasure that comes from slowing down and cooking with simple ingredients.

plum.   Julia Busuttil Nishimura   Pan Macmillan Australia

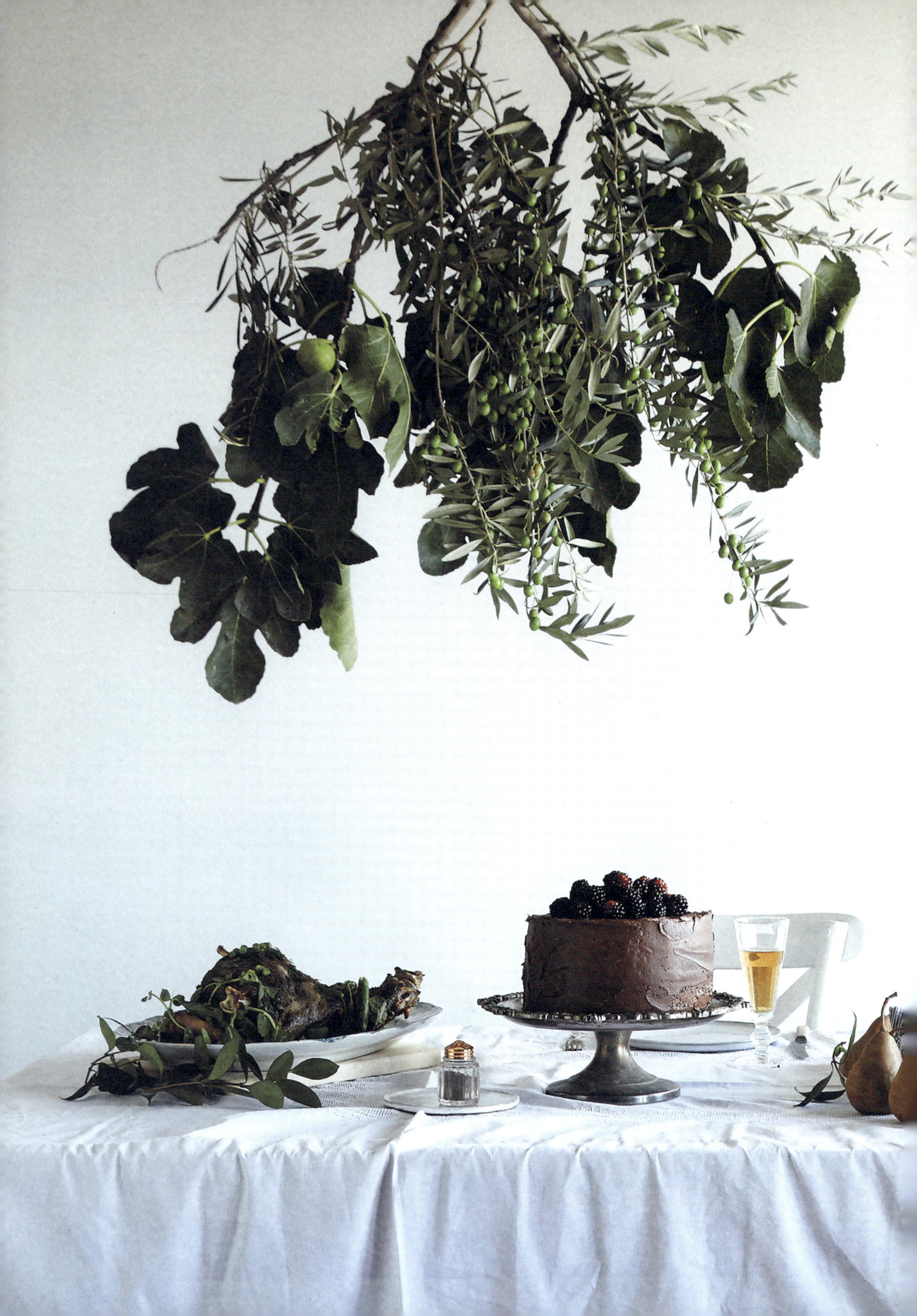

CONTENTS

Introduction ... 6
Cook's Notes ... 12

Bread and Pizza ... 17
Vegetables ... 45
Soup ... 83
Pasta and Grains ... 107
Seafood and Meat ... 153
Biscuits, Loaves and Cakes ... 193
Dessert ... 227

Acknowledgements ... 266
Index ... 268

INTRODUCTION

My cooking isn't terribly fancy – I make simple food that is comforting and generous in spirit. My approach to food favours intuition over strict rules and is about using your hands, rushing a little less and savouring the details. Cooking and eating can too easily become hurried and meaningless activities, where instead they can be treated as important daily rituals, in which the actual making of food is a celebration. By taking some time to think about how you will cook a particular ingredient, or how a recipe can be adjusted to suit what is in season or available in your area, you become more connected to the food and its origins and purpose in your meal.

Growing up, food was, of course, a means of sustenance, but – as is so often the case within migrant communities – for my family it was also a way of preserving memories and maintaining a connection to Malta, their home in the Mediterranean before they immigrated to Australia. The food my mum would cook, and the stories she would tell me about the way her mother used to cook, still follow me around in the kitchen and influence the way I think about food. The pleasure that comes from cooking with simple ingredients, the satisfaction to be gained from repurposing scraps to create an entirely new meal and the rewards that come when you are patient with your food are all things I learned from a very young age.

My time spent living and working in Italy when I was in my early twenties only strengthened my love for uncomplicated food. I learned how to make and cook pasta, and that every meal is worthy of a celebration. I lived on a property near a town called Orbetello, between the sea and the rolling hills so synonymous with Tuscany. I witnessed such thoughtfulness in selecting ingredients for the family meals, which significantly influenced my growth as a cook. I was touched by the questions that would be asked before ingredients were decided upon: *What is good today? Where has it come from? How long has it been here?* It reflected the trust placed in the person selling you the produce – often they knew what you wanted even before you did. Many times we would go somewhere with the intention of buying zucchini, but they weren't at their best that day so we would come home with ripe eggplant instead. This completely altered the way I thought about food. It sounds like a cliché to say it was life changing, but it was – I found a sense of clarity.

I've always felt so comfortable in Italy. Speaking the language helps, of course, but I'm certain there's more to it than that. The generosity expressed through food and the care taken with the small details – it always feels so familiar. I am so grateful to the Agostini family, who I worked for. They play such an important role in this book. They inspired me endlessly, just by being.

I started writing notes on food and cooking when I was young – reading as much as I could, writing as I cooked and sharing my ideas. For a long time, it was mostly scribble in a notebook. And then it moved online, as most of the world did. I started Ostro when I was in Italy as a space for sharing my recipes and thoughts. *Ostro* is the Italian name for the southerly Mediterranean wind and the word also shares roots with the etymology of the name *Australia*. To me, it represents my Maltese heritage, my other home in Italy, as well as the here and now in Australia.

I've always liked to accompany my recipes with a gathering of thoughts on the ways in which a particular dish sits in that exact time or moment. Sometimes a recipe's origins will be deeply rooted in family, or it may have arrived after seeing what was ready to be picked in the garden. However they come about, my recipes are merely guides, which I hope you adapt and make your own.

Although I know it is not always possible, I am a strong believer in supporting local producers and makers. Buying your food from knowledgeable people, and talking to them about it, means that you usually get the best of what's on offer in that particular season and the conversation can bring another layer of appreciation to your food. It also puts you in a pretty good position to create something that simply tastes really good.

If you have access to a local farmers' market, it is a wonderful opportunity to see what is truly in season and to speak to the people who are growing and caring for the produce. While they might not have the thing you were looking for, that can force you to be more creative and reactive as a cook.

I choose to cook food that is understated, so starting with good-quality produce is paramount. I cook this type of food because it doesn't have to be 'special'. It's not food that needs to be placed on a pedestal or admired from afar; it is food that slowly weaves its way into the fabric of your daily life – food for living and sharing.

Cooking a slow braise or making fresh pasta should not be an arduous task; it should be what makes the eating so enjoyable. For me, it is as much of a pleasure to make as it is to eat. I think, in part, it is because I love the serenity that preparing food brings me. It has a grounding quality. And I don't just get that when making food that requires time and patience, but from 'fast' food too. Just being in the kitchen, even making the simplest thing, can become part of something bigger. While I never forget that the end goal is to have a meal on the table, it can be so much more, too.

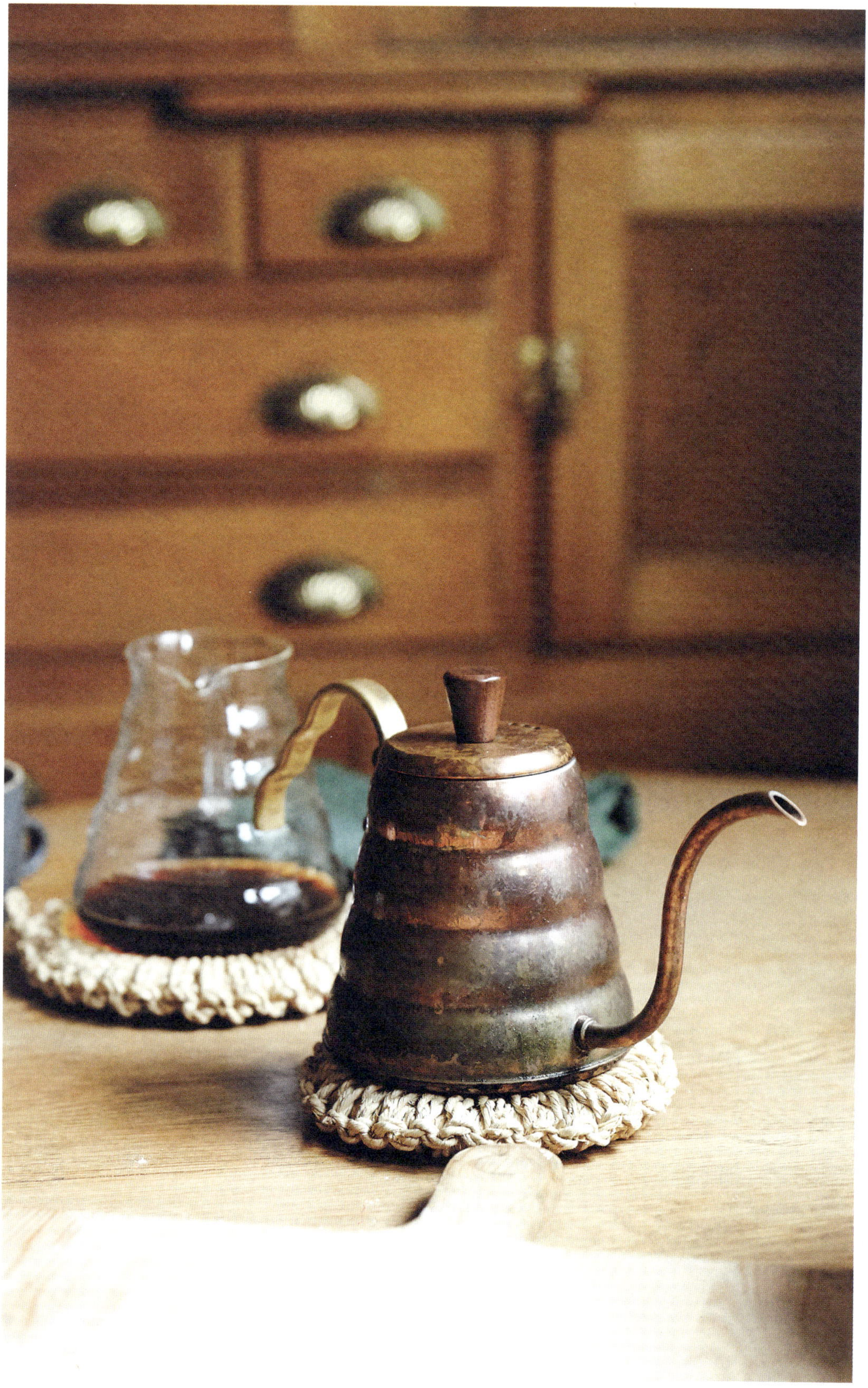

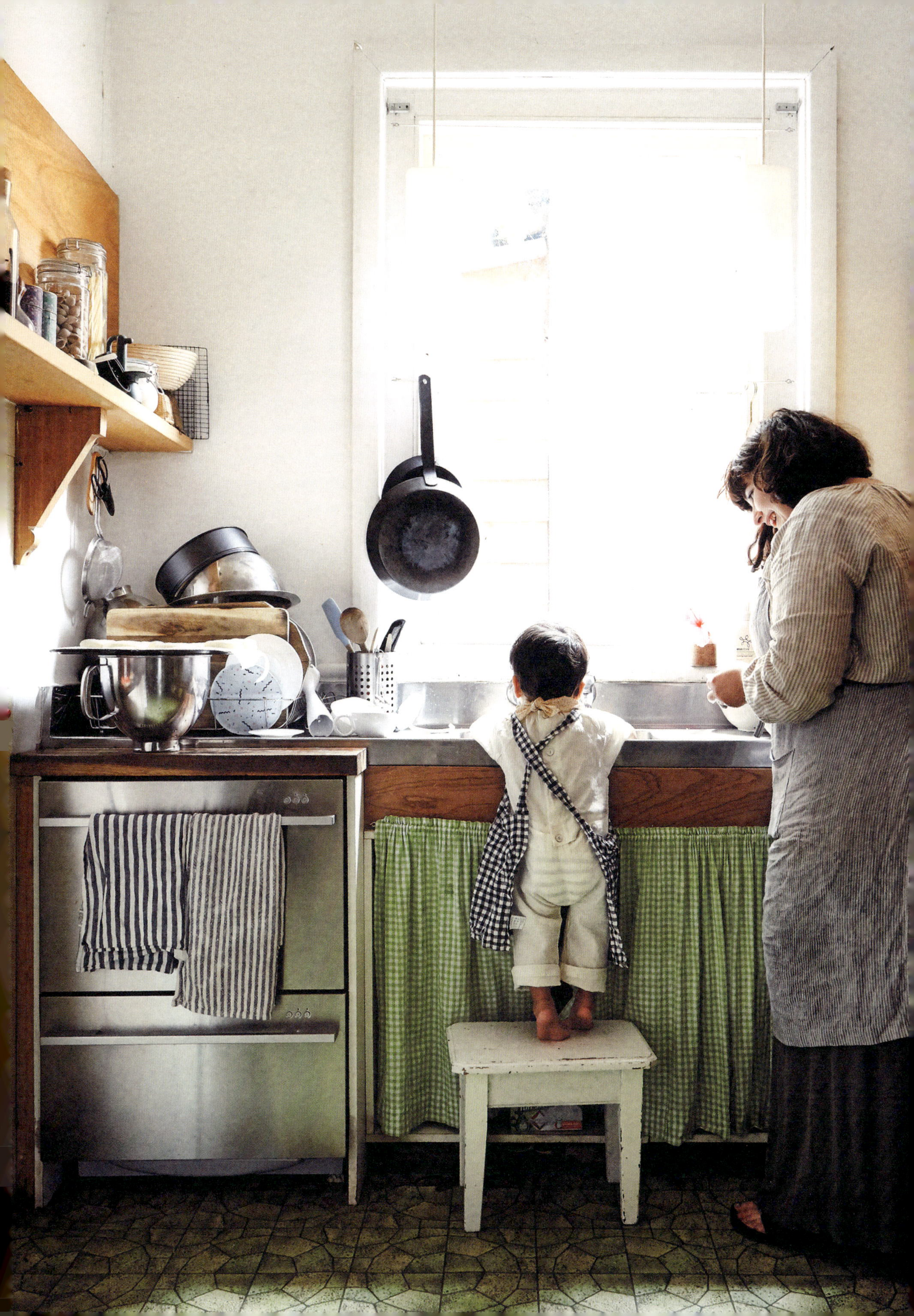

I do own a few electric kitchen appliances, such as an ice-cream churn and a mixer, but I really want to encourage you to avoid turning to machines if the only reason is to save a little time. For the few minutes you might gain, you lose the opportunity to really feel – in the most literal sense – what you are cooking. Take pasta-making, for example. While I do give measurements in my recipes, every type of flour is different and may require more or less water to bring the dough together. When you make pasta by hand, you will know exactly when it is the right texture – this is much harder if you prepare the dough in a food processor. When I make my walnut sauce, being able to dip my finger into the mortar is so important for testing the flavour and consistency. Your hands bring warmth and allow you to feel and connect with the food. Although it may sound like I'm just being romantic, it is really the most basic and accessible way to cook, and I think we have been fooled into thinking that we need expensive 'tools' to make nice food. I would argue that we don't and that for the most part, food tastes better without them. My preference is to rely on my hands as much as I can, as it gives me more freedom.

We visit Japan quite frequently, since my husband, Nori, is Japanese. I remember once staying with our friends in the countryside, a few hours from Tokyo. They desperately wanted to eat fresh pasta and I was more than happy to oblige. I set off to the local supermarket to see what I could find. I settled on my very favourite pasta, orecchiette – which needs only flour and water – and managed to find some herbs that I could use in a sauce. I didn't need any specific equipment and instead, we all sat around the dinner table drinking sake and making the pasta by hand. The pasta not only tasted wonderful, but cost very little too.

This act of sitting around a table together preparing a meal is, to me, the essence of cooking. And this is where a lot of meal preparation takes place in our home – around the dinner table. It is a large oak table, well worn but sturdy and so familiar. It is where I roll out fresh pasta, where I sit down to pod peas and beans, and where I knead bread. The dining room has the best light in the house and it is a communal space where our little family congregates – myself, Nori and our son, Haruki. Sharing meals together is so important – it is time to talk, listen and enjoy each other's company. Of course, we spend a lot of time together in the actual kitchen, too. Nori is an amazing cook who has taught me so much – not just about Japanese food, but about patience, respect and care for food. The way he carefully chops, and gently washes and attends to the rice – it's all love. Watching him cook, or better still, cooking together, is really the greatest pleasure. The small rituals – not only cooking, but making coffee every morning, buying our produce at the market or sharing a meal as a family – are what punctuate our days and ground us.

Here in this book, I hope you will find recipes that bring you great joy to prepare and eat. There are many recipes that you can settle in to – really get to know – for leisurely cooking on the weekend or a day off. But there are also recipes that take very little time to prepare – your anthem for reliable meals during the week. Regardless of when you make them, all of my recipes highlight the gratification of using simple ingredients to create delicious food. They are yours for the taking – a suggestion on how to cook and eat – with room for your own tweak or addition. If your garlic is strong and sharp, perhaps you will add less. Or maybe your sage leaves are less perfumed than usual, so you will throw in a few extra. For this reason, it is important to taste or smell everything – the raw ingredients and your dish as it's cooking. The recipes give measurements and detailed instructions, but relying on your own senses and intuition in the moment will give you the best results. I hope some of my daily rituals become yours, too.

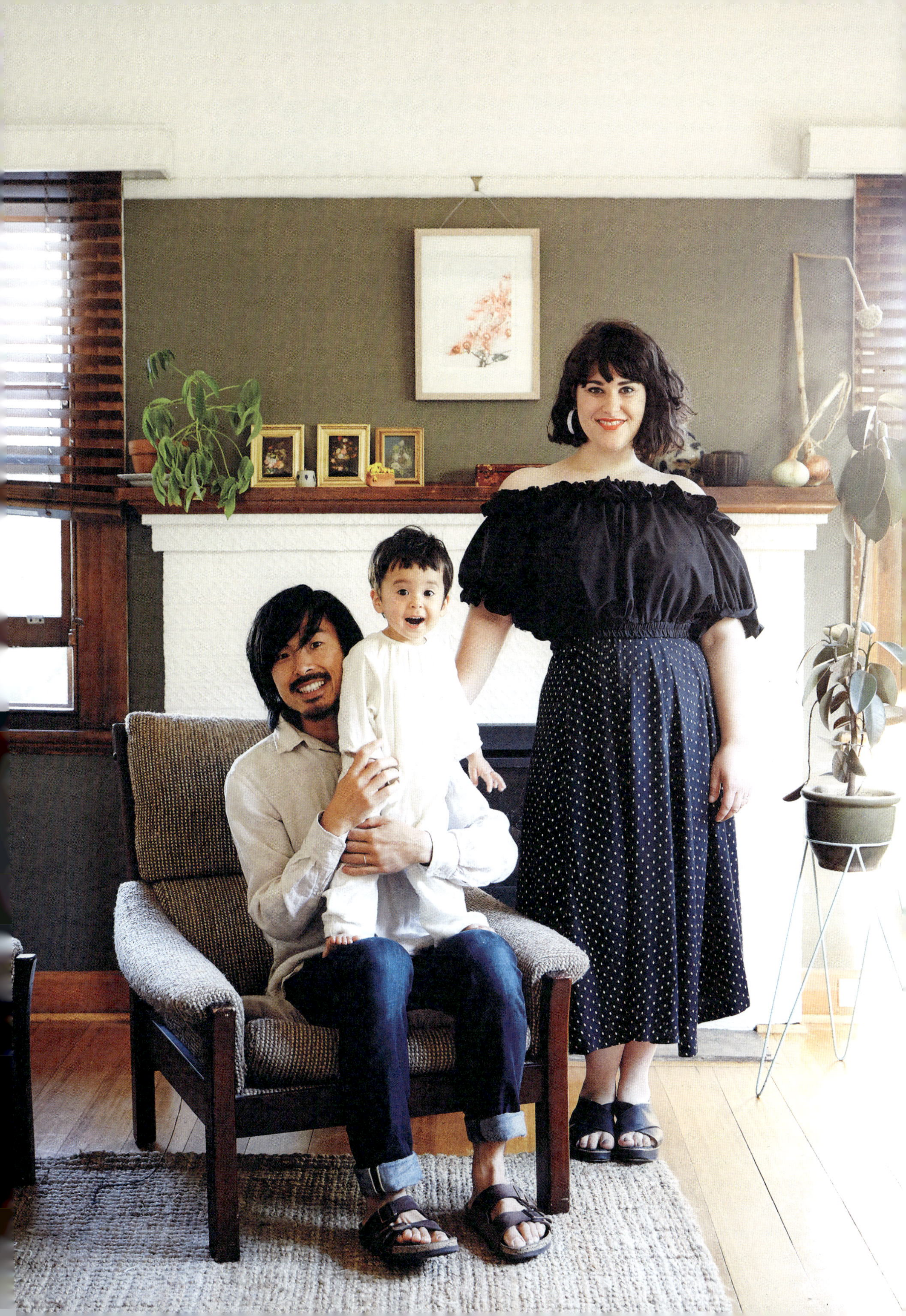

COOK'S NOTES

Cream

I prefer to use pure cream. It is free of additives, such as thickeners and gelatine, and is really versatile. If you can't find it, substitute with thickened cream.

Deep-frying

I prefer to deep-fry in a heavy-based saucepan rather than a bench-top deep-fryer. I find you can get the same result with much less oil and it is easily regulated with a thermometer.

Eggs

I always use organic free-range eggs. It is one of the things I never compromise on. Buy a brand of eggs you trust – you can look up the density of hens per hectare with a quick online search, so it's worthwhile doing a little research before paying good money for eggs that aren't as they claim. I use 'extra-large' eggs in my cooking, weighing an average of 60 g per egg.

Flour

In many of my recipes, I suggest using a specific type of flour. Tipo 00 is a finely milled flour that's ideal for making pasta. Tipo 0 is a little coarser than 00, but still finer than all-purpose plain flour. It is great for breads, certain focaccia and doughnuts.

Semolina flour or *semola di grano duro rimacinata* is durum wheat that has been finely milled. It is a wonderful, amber-coloured flour, perfect for creating the right texture in certain pasta shapes. Semolina flour is more textured than tipo 00 and plain flour, but by no means coarse. You should be able to find it at most Italian grocers, or at good speciality supermarkets. Some of the more common brands are De Cecco, Divella, Caputo and Molini Pizzuti; look for '*farina preparato per pasta fatta in casa*' on the label. If unavailable, simply substitute with tipo 00 or all-purpose plain flour, although the pasta will have a softer texture compared to pasta made with semolina flour. For dusting, fine semolina can be used instead.

Herbs

Fresh herbs bring so much life to food. I always have some growing in pots, no matter where I am.

Legumes and beans

It is important to sort beans and legumes before using them. Often there are very hard or dried ones that you don't want to keep, and sometimes you can find small stones, especially in lentils. I tip them onto a bench and have a bowl at the ready, sliding the good ones into the bowl and discarding anything undesirable.

I almost always soak my legumes and beans in plenty of cold water overnight, just at room temperature. I then drain and rinse them thoroughly before cooking.

Olive oil

I always use extra-virgin olive oil, even in cakes. There are some very good Australian-produced olive oils, which are so lovely to use. Depending on the season, we rotate between Australian, Italian and Spanish.

Oven temperatures

All cooking temperatures given are for a conventional oven. If you have a fan-forced oven, drop the cooking temperature by 10–20°C (check your oven manual).

Parmesan and pecorino

Although there are many types available, when a recipe calls for parmesan, my choice is Parmigiano Reggiano, which is produced in a very select few cities in northern Italy. It is usually made with a mixture of skim and whole cow's milk and is wonderfully nutty and salty. Sometimes I will use Grana Padano, which is similar to Parmigiano Reggiano, but produced around the Po Valley – spanning a much larger area than where Parmigiano Reggiano is made. While many people believe that Grana Padano is simply the cheaper, and therefore inferior, sibling to Parmigiano Reggiano, it is only less expensive because there are more producers. Grana Padano is a little less intense, made only with skim milk, and is great when you don't want to overpower your dish. Both cheeses are aged for varying amounts of time and can be found at good delis and food stores. A little really goes a long way, so buy the good stuff, if you can. It lasts a long time in the fridge so think of it as an investment.

Pecorino is made from ewe's milk and is made in several regions all over Italy. The most famous cheeses are Pecorino Romano and Pecorino Sardo, mostly produced in Sardinia and sometimes in the region of Lazio and the province of Grosetto, in Tuscany, very close to where I lived. Romano is quite salty and strong, whereas Sardo is rich and nutty, making it suitable for dishes where you don't want the cheese to overpower, such as pesto alla genovese. Pecorino Toscano is one of my favourite types; however, here in Australia, Romano and Sardo are the most common.

Pasta

When using store-bought pasta, try to buy the best you can afford, made from durum wheat. Although good-quality pasta is becoming increasingly available from supermarkets, usually the best ones are found in specialty grocers or shops. The suggested portion size for dried pasta is around 80 g per person.

When making pasta from scratch, it is really useful to have a wooden surface to work on. Wood, being a natural material, has warmth and provides good friction, especially for rolling out dough. It is particularly important when making hand-shaped pasta, such as gnochetti, orecchiette and pici. Of course if you don't have a wooden surface, your regular bench is perfectly fine.

Always rest your dough at room temperature for at least 30 minutes, wrapped tightly with a damp cloth or plastic wrap so it doesn't dry out. After the dough has rested, it is best made, cooked and eaten as soon as possible.

Generously salt the water the pasta is going to cook in. Do this once the water has come to a rolling boil. I suggest around 2 ½ teaspoons of salt per litre of water. Cooking pasta in salty water is important. No matter how delicious your sauce is, if the pasta water isn't salty enough you will never end up with a perfectly seasoned dish.

Give the pasta a stir as soon as it's in the boiling water, then leave it to cook according to the instructions or until al dente.

I almost always add the pasta to the sauce, and not the other way around. By having the pan with the sauce ready on the heat, the pasta can be drained and tipped into the pan, ready to be coated with the sauce.

If using store-bought pasta, I usually take 1–2 minutes off the suggested cooking time if I am going to finish cooking it in the pan with the sauce. Keep the cooking water when you drain the pasta (a pasta pot with a built-in drainer is handy but not vital). It is starchy, salty and full of flavour, and a ladle or two should usually be added to the sauce to finish the dish. It can help to loosen a sauce or thicken one.

Have everyone ready to eat as soon as the pasta is ready. Pasta, especially fresh pasta, is best served and eaten immediately.

Seasoning

Seasoning is very important. I season at certain points as I cook and then again before serving. I usually only season with sea salt flakes and rarely with black pepper. It's easy to automatically reach for both, but while salt enhances the flavour of most foods pepper can overpower. When I do use pepper, it is always freshly ground and used thoughtfully.

Tomatoes

Store tomatoes on your kitchen bench rather than in the fridge. If a recipe calls for fresh tomatoes, only make that dish when tomatoes are very much in season. It is better to wait for summer than to use watery, pale, insipid tomatoes that have been grown in a shed somewhere. That goes for everything, really – buy in-season and local, where possible.

Yeast

I use active dry yeast for all my recipes. It usually provides very reliable results and is easily found in most food stores, regardless of your location.

OSTRO

Day 1

- ✓ Ricciarelli
- ✓ Oat biscuits
- · Orange hazelnut shortbread
- ✓ Lemon olive oil cake
- ✓ Chocolate cake
- · Sardines - pine nuts, fennel, orange
- · School prawns - fennel salt
- · Lamb shoulder - peas + aioli
- · Lamb meatballs
- ✓ Honey ice cream

Day 2

- ✱ Braised lamb w chickpeas
- · Veal cotoletta
- ✱ Apple hazelnut cake
- · Ricotta tortelloni *anyh*
- · Squid - nduja

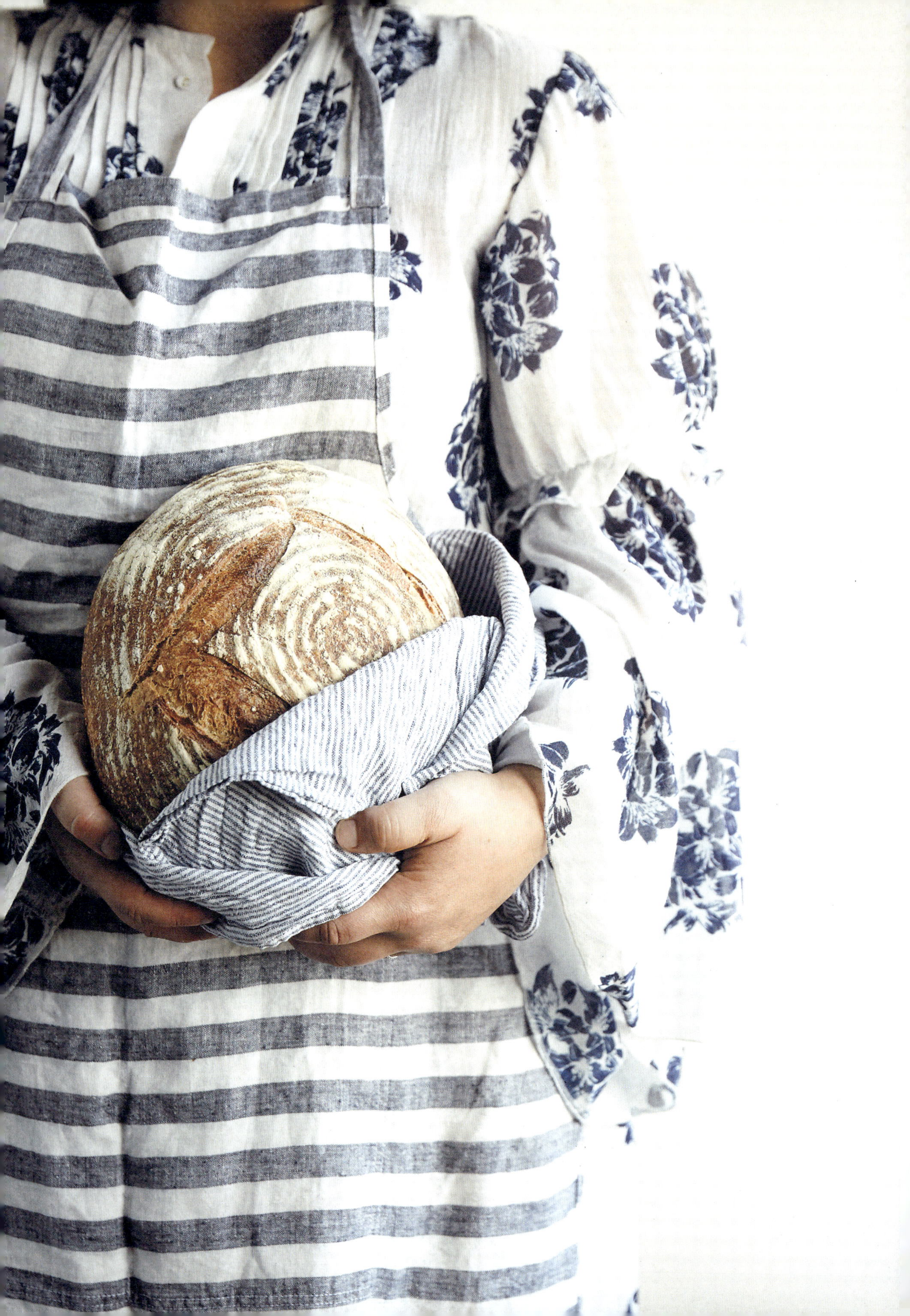

BREAD AND PIZZA

❦

I am in constant awe of the beauty that can arise from the simplest ingredients. There are few transformations more dramatic and gratifying than when you combine flour, water and very few other ingredients, and they come together into a bread or pastry dough that really has endless uses. For bread dough, a yeast or a natural leaven is usually added too, and, while I don't go into naturally leavened breads here (a rather large topic that I feel deserves more space than a single chapter), I have included recipes that are all tied together by their use of flour or bread. They are very simple to make and require little active preparation time. The nutty and floral aromas of bread or pizza baking will fill your kitchen — incentive enough to set aside an hour or two.

CROSTINI OF ANCHOVY, BUTTER AND MOZZARELLA

SERVES 6–8

I first encountered these divine crostini while I was working in a beautifully small town in southern Tuscany, perched between the coast and the hills. While this style of crostini isn't particularly unique to this area, they are still popular, nonetheless. And why wouldn't they be? Creamy Italian butter, milky mozzarella and the salty hit from the anchovies – you really must try them for yourself. We would prepare them as a snack before dinner, usually on the weekends when we had more time to spend in the kitchen. The crostini would come out piping hot and be devoured within minutes. If you can find Italian butter, it's well worth using here as it is super creamy and has a subtle sweetness – plus, it usually comes in the most gorgeous packaging.

1 baguette, cut into 1 cm slices

30 g unsalted butter, softened

12 anchovy fillets, cut into thirds

250 g buffalo mozzarella, cut into 5 mm slices

Preheat the oven to 180°C.

Arrange the bread on a baking tray and spread each slice with a little butter. Drape a piece of anchovy over each, then top with a slice of mozzarella.

Bake for 12–15 minutes until the bread is golden and the mozzarella is bubbling but not coloured. Allow to cool ever so briefly, just a minute – barely two – and serve.

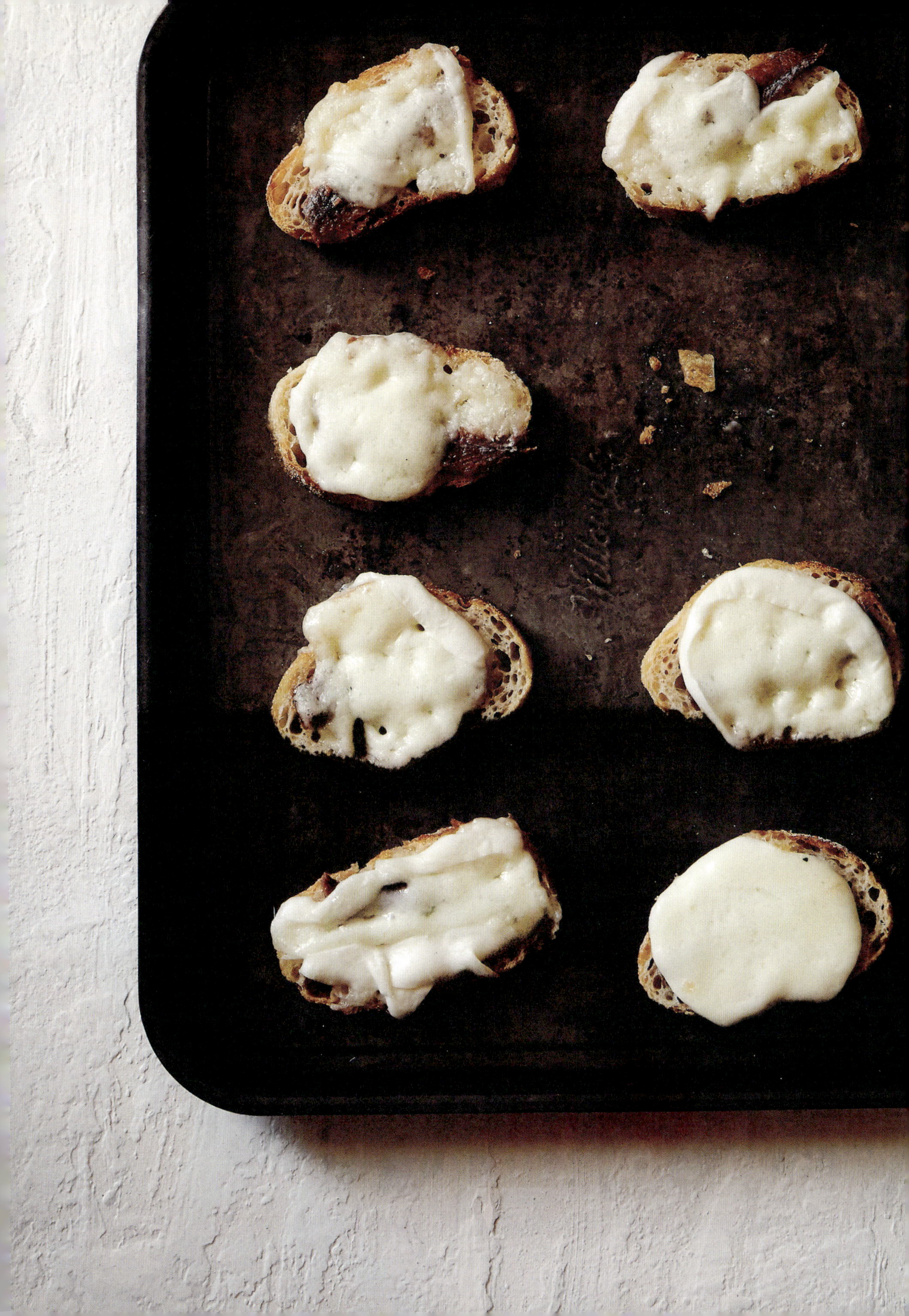

CROSTINI OF ZUCCHINI AND BASIL

❦ SERVES 6 ❦

By cooking slowly over a low heat, the zucchini here becomes lovely and sweet, without losing its structure. As well as being beautiful on garlicky toasts, this mixture makes a wonderful pasta sauce – stirred through with some ricotta – or a simple side dish for roasted or barbecued meats. Although crostini means 'small toasts', I often like to make them a little larger, so have suggested ciabatta – but of course you could use slices of baguette instead, which would make a perfect snack to serve with drinks. If you have zucchini flowers, they make for a pretty garnish. The small zucchini from the flowers can also be used – simply halve them and add to the pan along with the diced zucchini.

4 zucchini (about 900 g in total), cut in half lengthways, deseeded and cut into 1 cm pieces

2 French shallots, finely diced

small bunch of basil, trimmed, plus extra leaves to serve

2 tablespoons extra-virgin olive oil, plus extra for drizzling

sea salt

6 × 1.5 cm slices of ciabatta or other crusty bread

1 garlic clove, cut in half

handful of mint leaves, roughly chopped

small pinch of dried chilli flakes (optional)

Place the zucchini in a large frying pan. Add the shallots and the basil, stalks and all. Drizzle with the olive oil and season with a generous pinch of salt. Place the frying pan over a low heat and stir so that everything is well coated with the oil and salt.

Cook gently for 25–30 minutes, stirring occasionally, until the zucchini is tender and just beginning to collapse. Adjust the seasoning if necessary and allow to cool, removing the stalks.

Meanwhile, preheat a grill to hot. Drizzle a little olive oil over the slices of bread and arrange on a baking tray. Place under the grill and toast for 2–3 minutes, flipping the slices halfway, until golden on both sides. Rub the oiled side of the toasts with the cut side of the garlic clove, rubbing no more than twice on each slice, as the raw garlic can be overpowering.

Top the toasts with the cooled zucchini mixture, the extra basil leaves and the mint. If desired, serve with a drizzle of olive oil and a sprinkle of dried chilli flakes.

PICTURED ON PAGE 22

CROSTINI OF CANNELLINI BEANS, BLACK OLIVES AND MINT

SERVES 6

These crostini are wonderfully moreish and packed full of flavour – the creaminess of the white beans paired with the salty olives is one of my favourite combinations. I like to have some sort of pre-cooked bean or pulse in the fridge, at the ready for when I need to make a quick snack like this one. You can, of course, use beans from a can, just be sure to rinse them. I prefer to use dry-cured black olives, which have been cured in layers of salt for several weeks rather than brine. Their texture is meatier than brined olives and they have a unique flavour. You can usually find dry-cured olives in the deli section of Italian supermarkets. If they're unavailable, substitute another black olive.

large handful of mint leaves

40 g pitted dry-cured black olives, roughly chopped

finely grated zest and juice of ½ lemon

1 tablespoon extra-virgin olive oil, plus extra for drizzling

sea salt and black pepper

6 × 1.5 cm slices of ciabatta or other crusty bread

1 garlic clove, cut in half

CREAMY WHITE BEANS

2 garlic cloves, peeled

250 g canned or cooked cannellini beans, drained and rinsed (see Note)

100 ml vegetable stock (see recipe page 104)

sea salt and black pepper

2 tablespoons extra-virgin olive oil

To make the beans, lightly crush each garlic clove using the heel of your knife. Place the garlic in a small saucepan with the beans and vegetable stock. Season with salt and pepper and simmer over a low heat for 10 minutes. Roughly mash the beans and garlic together using the back of a fork and drizzle in the olive oil. Set aside to cool. The beans will continue to absorb liquid as they cool, so don't strain.

While the beans are cooling, add the mint to the chopped olives and continue to chop, mixing the mint and olives together. Transfer to a small bowl and stir in the lemon zest and juice and the olive oil. Season to taste and set aside.

Preheat a grill to hot. Drizzle a little olive oil over the slices of bread and arrange on a baking tray. Place under the grill and toast for 2–3 minutes, flipping the slices halfway, until golden on both sides. Rub the oiled side of the toasts with the cut side of the garlic clove, rubbing no more than twice on each slice, as the raw garlic can be overpowering.

Top the crostini with a generous spoonful of the creamy white beans and then a little of the olive mixture. Serve immediately.

NOTE: If cooking the beans yourself, soak 110 g dried cannellini beans in cold water overnight then cook in boiling water for 45–60 minutes or until tender. The time taken to cook will depend on the beans themselves. Older beans will take longer, so keep checking from the 45 minute mark.

PICTURED ON PAGE 23

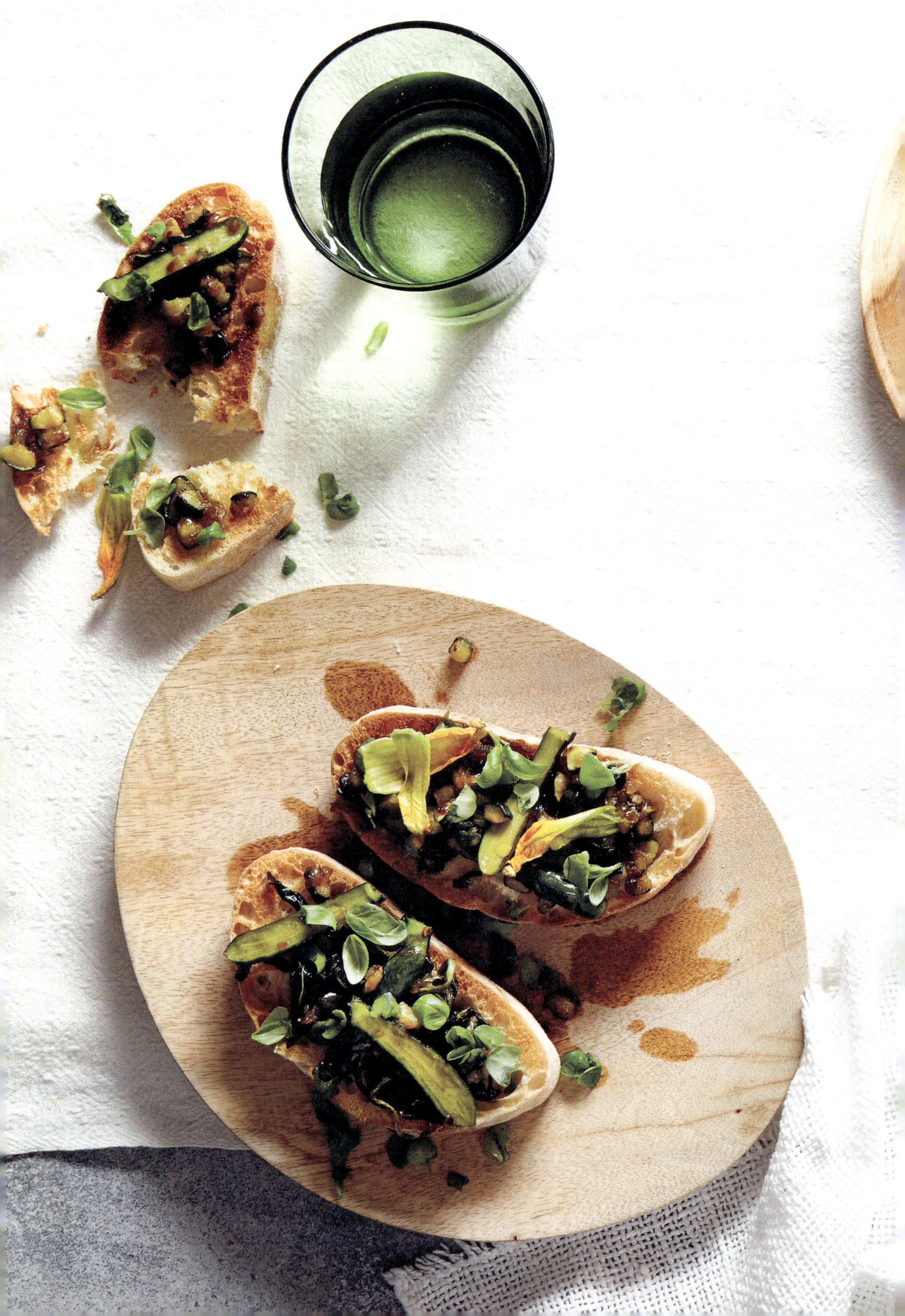

LEFT TO RIGHT: Crostini of zucchini and basil (page 20) and Crostini of cannellini beans, black olives and mint (page 21)

HOMEMADE RICOTTA WITH SEED CRACKERS AND HONEY

SERVES 8–10 AS A STARTER

One of my earliest food memories is making Maltese *irkotta*. I think I was perhaps four, and the vivid memory of collecting seawater is strong in my mind. I can still picture the ice-cream tub we used to collect the salty water and the cheese baskets sitting on the sink. My father immigrated to Australia from Malta in the early 1960s. My mum's parents were Maltese too, so it's safe to say we ate *irkotta* a lot, along with other Maltese staples like broad beans, capers, peas and rabbit. These foods kept us tied to Malta and still, when I make ricotta, I feel like it's somehow part of something a little bigger.

Ricotta is traditionally made with whey, which can be tricky to get. I've adapted the recipe to use mostly milk, which gives you similar results. The nutty seed crackers are the perfect accompaniment to the creamy ricotta, and they can be devoured just as soon as they've cooled down.

100 g (¾ cup) pumpkin seeds

2 tablespoons linseeds

70 g sunflower seeds

100 g (⅔ cup) plain flour

½ teaspoon baking powder

2 tablespoons sesame seeds

generous pinch of sea salt

honey, to serve

HOMEMADE RICOTTA

2 litres full-cream milk (preferably unhomogenised)

400 ml pure cream

pinch of sea salt

2 tablespoons lemon juice

130 g (½ cup) plain yoghurt

To make the ricotta, combine the milk, cream and salt in a large saucepan. Bring to the boil over a medium heat. As soon as the milk comes to the boil, add the lemon juice and yoghurt and reduce the heat so that the mixture is barely simmering. Keep at this temperature for 2 minutes, stirring very gently, being careful not to break the curds. Reduce to the lowest heat and continue cooking, without stirring, for 2–3 minutes. Turn off the heat and cool completely without disturbing the curds. Strain the curds from the liquid into a small cheesecloth- or muslin-lined strainer, or into cheese baskets if you have them. The longer you leave the ricotta to strain, the firmer the curds will be. If you prefer a softer curd, transfer the ricotta from the strainer after 10 minutes. For a firmer cheese, leave the ricotta to strain for at least 30 minutes. Transfer the strained curds to an airtight container. This recipe makes about 650 g – you won't quite need all of it for this dish, but it will keep in the refrigerator for up to 3 days.

For the crackers, preheat the oven to 180°C. Line two baking trays with baking paper or baking sheets.

Pound the pumpkin seeds, linseeds and sunflower seeds using a mortar and pestle or blitz in a food processor until finely ground. Transfer to a mixing bowl and add the flour, baking powder, sesame seeds and salt. Mix in about 100 ml of water, enough to make a firm but workable dough. Tip onto a clean work surface and knead for 5 minutes or until smooth, adding a little flour if the dough is too sticky. Roll into a ball, cover with a damp cloth or plastic wrap and rest in the fridge for 30 minutes.

Roll the dough out to 3 mm thick and cut into rounds using a 4 cm circle cutter. Re-roll the scraps of dough and repeat. Transfer to the prepared trays, leaving some space in between each cracker as they will spread a little. Bake for 10–12 minutes, until just golden. Allow to cool then serve topped with the ricotta and drizzled with honey. The crackers will keep in an airtight container for up to a week.

PICTURED ON PAGE 27

BREAD AND PIZZA 25

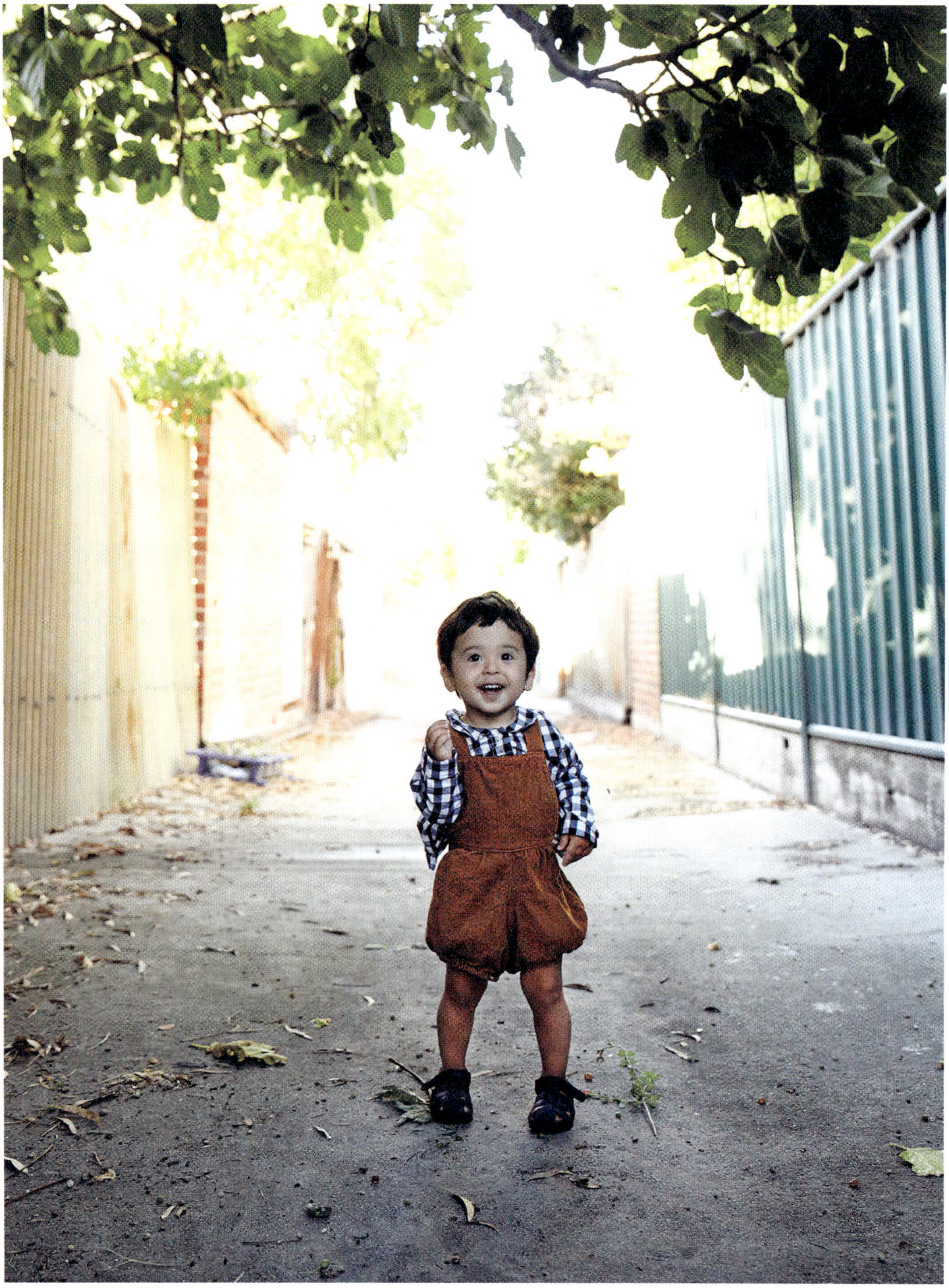

Homemade ricotta with seed crackers and honey (page 24)

ROSEMARY GRISSINI

MAKES ABOUT 60

Grissini are perfect to begin a meal, served simply on their own, or as I like to, with some thinly sliced prosciutto at the table for guests to wrap around each length. My favourite addition to the dough is fresh rosemary, but fennel seeds or fresh thyme are also lovely. This recipe makes a rather large batch, but the grissini keep well for 3–5 days in an airtight container.

7 g active dry yeast

1 teaspoon caster sugar

1 teaspoon sea salt, plus extra for sprinkling

200 ml lukewarm water

2 tablespoons rosemary leaves, finely chopped

300 g tipo 0 flour, plus extra for dusting

70 ml extra-virgin olive oil, plus extra for brushing

Mix together the yeast, sugar, salt and water in a large bowl. Set aside for 10 minutes or until the mixture is foaming.

Add the rosemary to the yeast mixture, along with the flour and olive oil. Mix with a wooden spoon or your hand until the dough begins to come together, then turn out onto a lightly floured work surface and knead for 5 minutes or until smooth and elastic. Transfer to a lightly oiled bowl and cover with a cloth or plastic wrap. Set aside in a warm place to rise for 1½ hours or until the dough has doubled in size.

Preheat the oven to 180°C. Lightly grease two baking trays with olive oil.

Knock the air from the dough and turn out onto a lightly floured work surface. Roll the dough out into a large rectangle, about 1 cm thick. Cut into strips 5 cm long and 1 cm wide. Using your hands, roll each strip into a long, thin shape. I like them quite thin, but if you prefer them a little fatter just roll them so. Arrange the grissini on the prepared trays, allowing a little space for them to spread. You will need to cook them in batches as they won't all fit on the two trays.

Brush the grissini with oil and sprinkle with sea salt. Bake for 10–12 minutes, until golden and crisp. Repeat with any remaining dough. Allow to cool and store in an airtight container for 3–5 days.

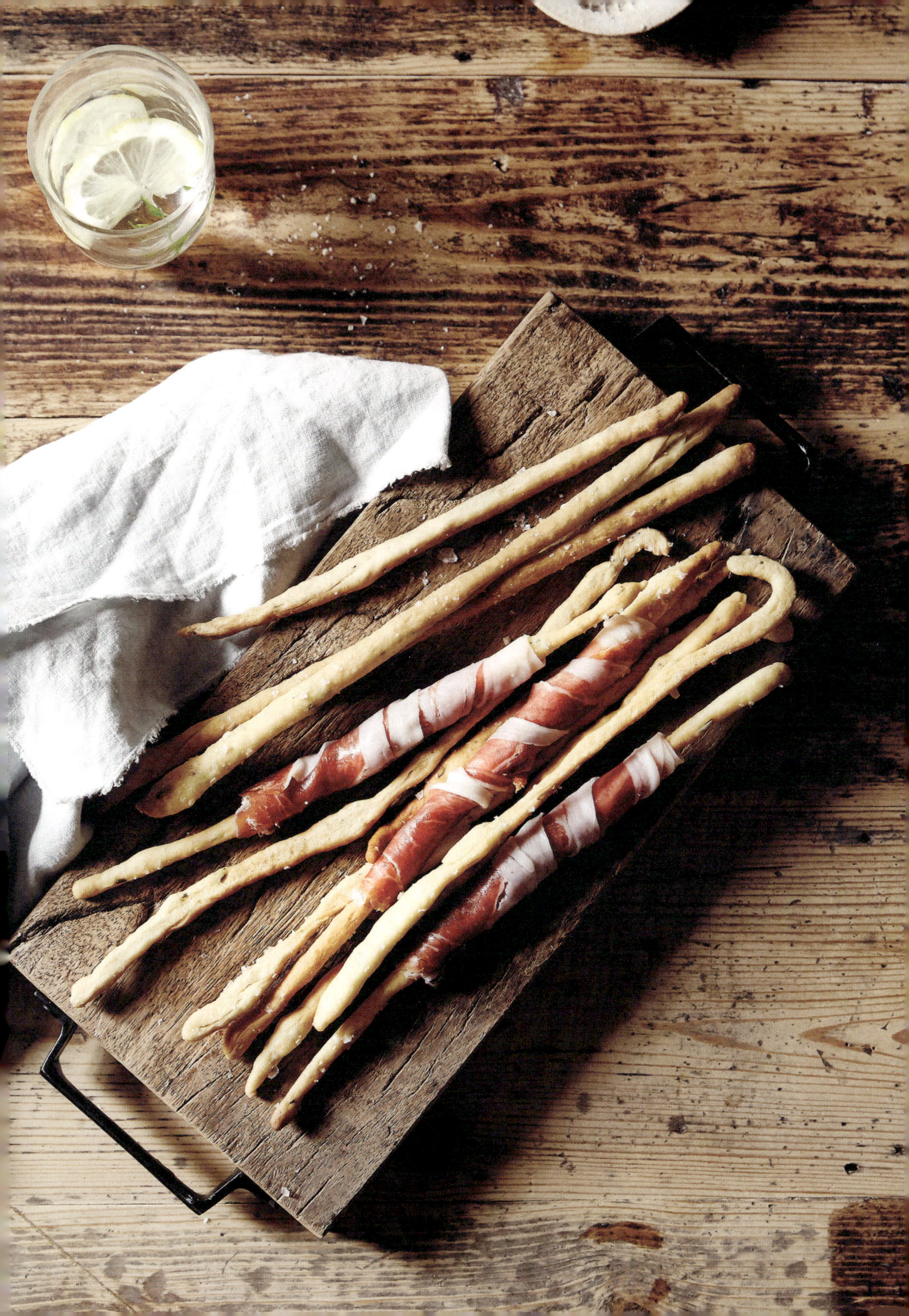

SOFT CHEESE FOCACCIA

MAKES TWO 20 CM ROUND FOCACCIA

This focaccia, called *focaccia col formaggio*, which hails from Liguria in Italy's north, is more like a stuffed flatbread than the fluffy and bread-like focaccia we're used to. Made with an unleavened dough that's rolled out so thin you should be able to read the newspaper through it and filled with creamy stracchino cheese, it is really delicious. Although the cheese can be a little tricky to find outside of Italy, it is well worth the search, and many specialty Italian delis do stock it. As well as getting the dough paper thin, the resting time is key, as it will make the dough easier to work with. Tipo 0 flour is preferable for this dough, and if you can find the Manitoba variety, even better, but if it is not available you can use plain flour – you just need to take extra care when rolling out the dough to avoid tears, although a few tears here and there are more than fine.

200 g tipo 0 flour

45 ml extra-virgin olive oil, plus extra for drizzling

100 ml lukewarm water

350 g stracchino (see Note)

sea salt

To make the dough, place the flour on a clean work surface and make a well in the centre. Pour the olive oil into the middle and then slowly pour in the water, mixing the flour into the middle with your hand as you pour. Slowly the dough will come together. It should be soft but not sticky. Knead for 5 minutes or until smooth. Transfer to a lightly oiled bowl and cover with a cloth or plastic wrap. Set aside to rest for 2 hours in the fridge.

Preheat the oven to 220°C. Lightly grease a 20 cm round baking tray.

Tip the dough out onto a lightly floured work surface and divide it into four equal-sized pieces. Re-cover three of the pieces and set aside. Roll the dough out into a round that is as thin as you can roll it without tearing – it should cover the entire tray. Take half of the cheese and break off pieces, dotting them evenly over the base of the focaccia. Now, take another piece of dough and repeat the rolling process, then drape over the top of the cheese. Using your rolling pin, roll around the edge of the tray to trim away any of the dough overhang. Pinch a few holes in the top layer of the dough, gently press out any air, then seal the focaccia by pressing around the edges. Drizzle generously with olive oil and sprinkle with salt. Bake for around 10 minutes, until golden and crisp. Cut into large pieces and serve.

Repeat with the remaining dough and cheese.

NOTE: Stracchino is a soft, creamy cow's milk cheese available from good Italian delis. If it's unavailable, you can substitute fresh mozzarella, which will need to be drained of excess moisture, or another soft melting cheese.

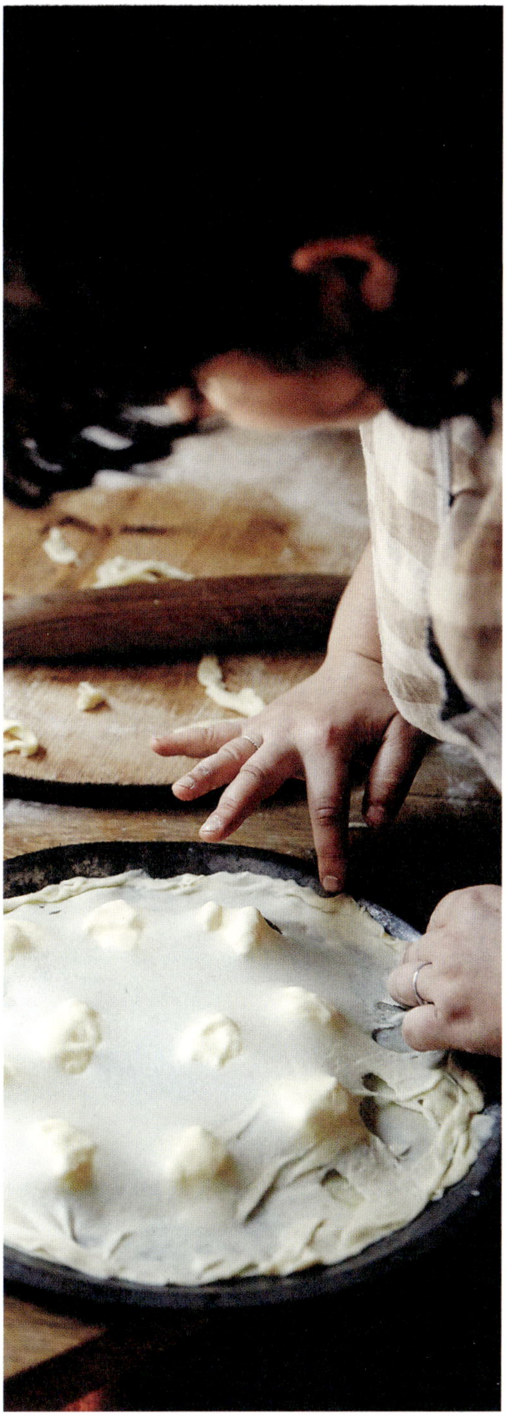

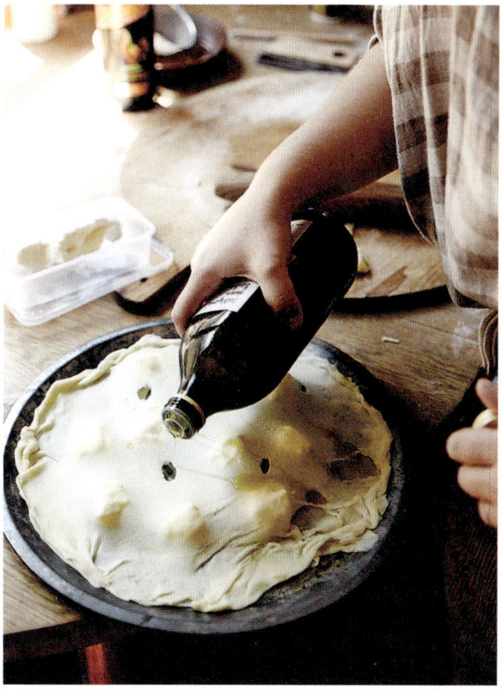

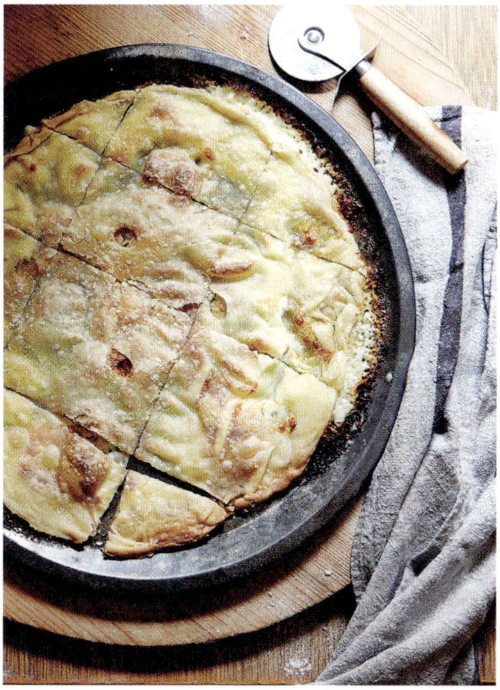

OLIVE OIL FOCACCIA

MAKES ONE 20 CM × 30 CM FOCACCIA

When I lived in Italy, I worked as a nanny in the afternoons, but during the day I would keep myself busy by cooking lunch for the family and preparing the morning tea for the workers at the property where I lived. Most mornings it would be olive oil focaccia sliced horizontally and stuffed with paper-thin slices of mortadella or with slices of mozzarella and tomato and basil – a quick, delicious fix indeed. I've also included some suggestions at the end of the recipe for some of my favourite toppings for this beautiful bread. Sometimes I cook them in a wood-fired oven, which is a great option if you have one, but a regular oven works well too. I've suggested a rectangular shape for the bread below, but it's really up to you.

350 g tipo 00 flour, plus extra for dusting

1 teaspoon sea salt, plus extra for sprinkling

1 teaspoon caster sugar

7 g active dry yeast

60 ml (¼ cup) extra-virgin olive oil, plus extra for drizzling

200 ml lukewarm water

Preheat the oven to 180°C. Line a 20 cm × 30 cm baking tray with lightly oiled baking paper.

In a large bowl, combine the flour, salt, sugar and yeast. Pour in the olive oil and, in a steady stream, slowly add the water and stir until a shaggy dough forms. Turn out onto a clean work surface and, using your hands, bring the dough together and knead for 5 minutes or until you have a smooth dough that is soft but not sticky. Add a little extra flour if it is sticking to the bench. Transfer to a lightly oiled bowl and cover with a cloth or plastic wrap. Set aside in a warm place to rise for 30 minutes or until the dough has doubled in size.

Knock the air from the dough and turn out onto a lightly floured work surface. Using your hands or a rolling pin, stretch the dough out into a rectangle approximately 20 cm × 30 cm. It really doesn't have to be a perfect rectangle and, in fact, I prefer a more organic shape. Transfer the focaccia to the prepared baking tray and make small dimple-like indentations in the surface of the focaccia using your fingers. If you wish to top the focaccia (see overleaf), now is the time to do so. Drizzle very generously with olive oil and sprinkle with sea salt. Allow to rise in a warm place for another 15 minutes.

RECIPE CONTINUED OVERLEAF ⟶

Bake for 20–25 minutes or until golden.

BREAD AND PIZZA 33

RECIPE CONTINUED ⟶

TOPPINGS

For **cherry tomato focaccia**, simply scatter 250 g of cherry tomatoes over the dough, then drizzle with olive oil and scatter over some salt before baking.

For **pumpkin, rosemary and onion focaccia**, cut 150 g of pumpkin into 2 cm pieces and arrange on a baking tray. Drizzle with 1 tablespoon of olive oil, season with salt and roast in a 180°C oven for 20–25 minutes, until golden and cooked through. Fry 2 thinly sliced onions, 2 roughly chopped garlic cloves and 1 tablespoon of roughly chopped rosemary leaves in 2 tablespoons of olive oil in a large frying pan over a low heat for 10–15 minutes or until soft. Allow to cool. Scatter the onion mixture and roasted pumpkin over the focaccia dough before baking.

PICTURED ON PAGES 36–7

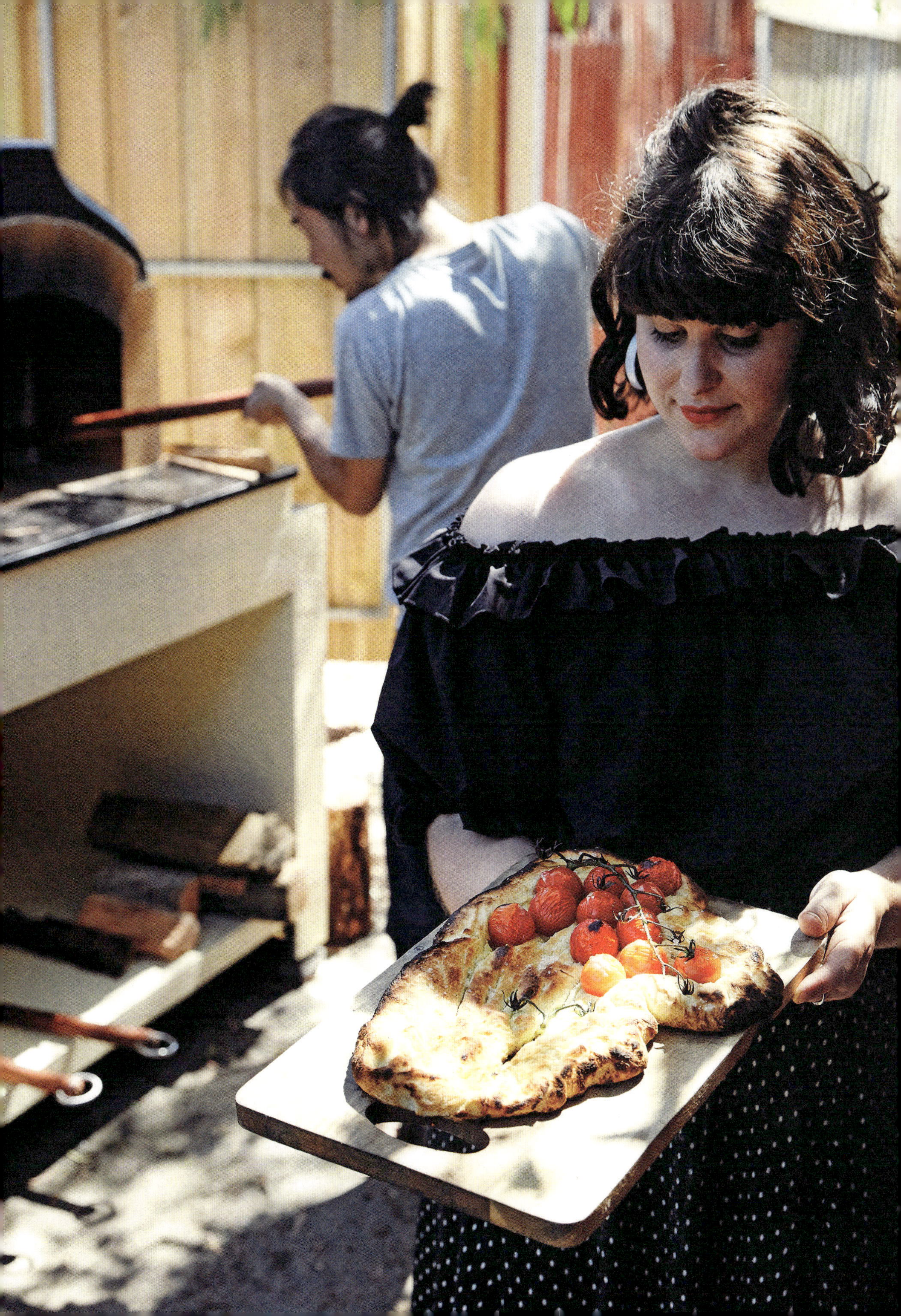

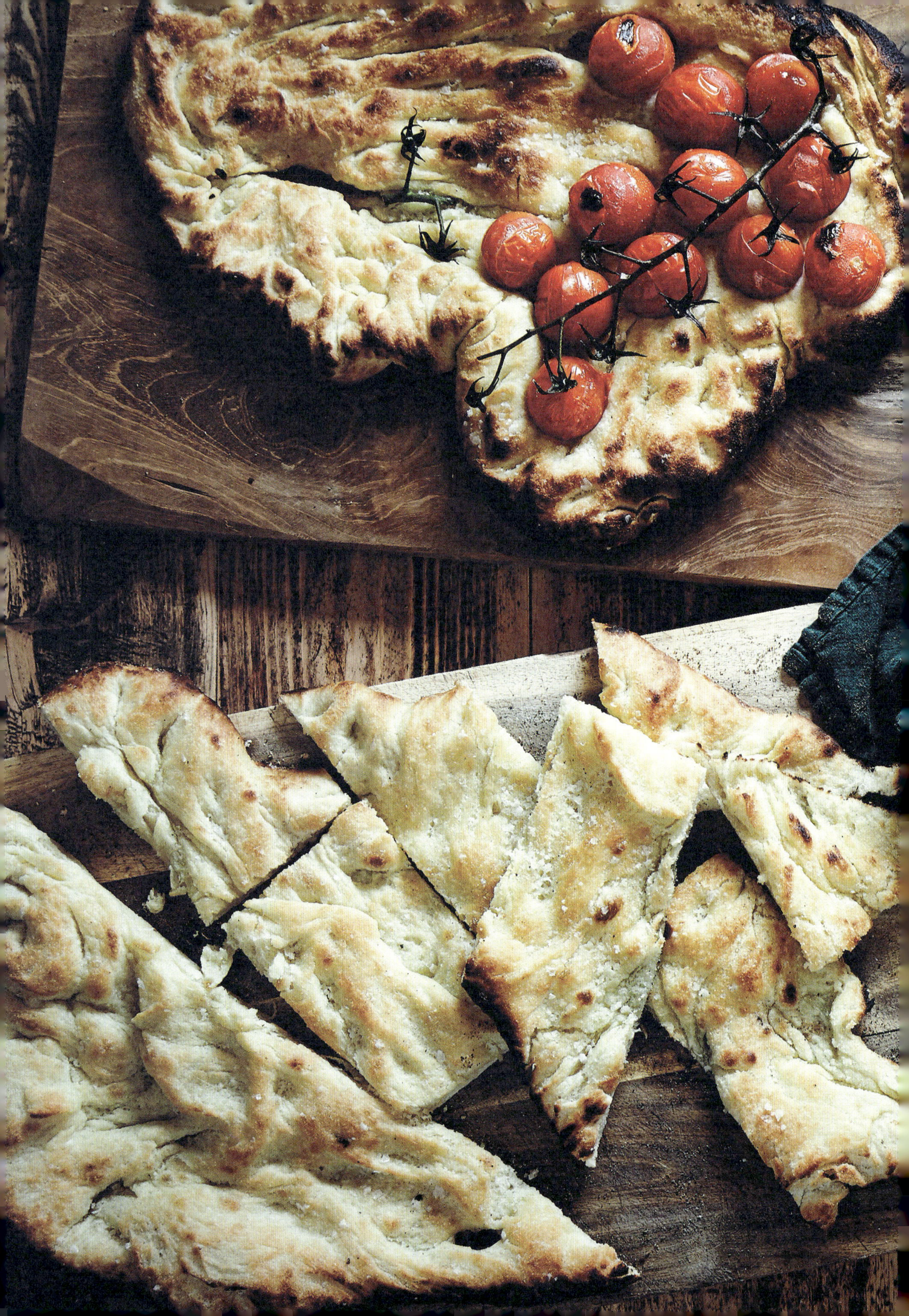

CLOCKWISE FROM TOP LEFT: *Cherry tomato focaccia (page 34),
Pumpkin, rosemary and onion focaccia (page 34) and Olive oil focaccia (page 32)*

PIZZA FOUR WAYS

MAKES FOUR 20 CM PIZZAS

There are few things that give me greater pleasure in the kitchen than the coming together of flour, water and yeast to create something special like pizza. It may be the child in me that is amused by the living nature of yeast, but when you see the dough slowly rising it is rather exciting.

Making pizza at home is relatively simple, it just requires a little planning and some care at the end of proving to ensure the precious lightness of the dough isn't lost. I use a pizza stone and preheat it in the oven for at least 45 minutes, but a preheated baking tray will work well, too. If I'm *really* lucky, I'll borrow a pizza oven, which cooks them very quickly – perfect for entertaining. Overleaf, you will find some of the ways I like to eat my pizza, but I'm sure you will have your own favourite toppings – just remember, less really is more and using fewer toppings is a good way to avoid a soggy base, which is often a problem with home-cooked pizza.

500 g strong bread flour or tipo 0 flour, plus extra for dusting

7 g active dry yeast

2 teaspoons sea salt

2 tablespoons extra-virgin olive oil, plus extra for drizzling

250 ml (1 cup) lukewarm water

semolina, for dusting

In a large bowl, mix the flour, yeast and salt together. Make a well in the centre and pour in the oil and water. Using your hand or a wooden spoon, mix until a shaggy dough comes together. Turn out onto a lightly floured work surface and knead rather vigorously for 10 minutes, until it becomes smooth and elastic. Shape the dough into a ball and transfer to a large oiled bowl. Drizzle some more oil over the dough, cover with a cloth or plastic wrap and set aside in a warm place to rise for 1 hour or until doubled in size. Knock back the dough, cover again and place in the fridge to rise for 12–24 hours.

Preheat the oven to its hottest setting (about 280°C) and place a pizza stone or 20 cm round baking tray in the oven to preheat. If using a pizza stone, it will need to be placed in a cold oven to avoid cracking. If using a tray, place it in the oven to preheat for 45 minutes before cooking your pizza.

Tip the dough out onto a generously floured work surface and divide it into four pieces. Using your hands, gently stretch and push each piece of dough into a 20 cm circle. Start by pressing down around 2 cm from the edge to create a crust, then slowly stretch the dough. Allow to rest for 20 minutes before topping.

Generously dust a flat tray or pizza peel (see Note) with semolina and gently place your pizza base onto the tray or peel. Top with your chosen toppings and transfer the pizza to the preheated stone or tray – careful, it will be blisteringly hot! Cook for 8–10 minutes until the base is puffy and the edges begin to bubble. Transfer to a board, topping with other ingredients if required, then cut and serve.

NOTE: A pizza peel is a large, flat tray with a long handle used to transfer pizza. They're available from most cooking supply shops, but a completely flat tray will work just as well. The easiest way to transfer the pizza to the hot stone in the oven is to make sure that your tray or peel is generously dusted with semolina. Once you're ready to transfer your topped pizza, open the oven and pull out the shelf that's holding the preheated stone or tray. Line up the peel or tray and in two or three short, fast shakes, guide the pizza onto the stone.

RECIPE CONTINUED OVERLEAF ⟶

BREAD AND PIZZA 39

RECIPE CONTINUED →

CHICORY, PROVOLONE AND SALAMI PIZZA

Provolone is a wonderful cow's milk cheese that's great on pizza because it melts really well. It usually comes in *dolce* or *picante* styles, the former being much milder than the sharper, aged variety. Choose whichever suits your tastes, although I tend to go for the milder variety for pizza. The bitterness of the chicory balances out the richness nicely here. Try to avoid super-processed salami that comes in a uniform log – look for salami that is a bit motley and homemade looking, as they are usually the most flavourful. Also, make sure the slices aren't too thin, otherwise they get too crisp and can burn during cooking.

1 tablespoon extra-virgin olive oil, plus extra for drizzling

100 g chicory, roughly chopped

1 garlic clove, finely chopped

juice of ½ lemon

sea salt

50 g mozzarella, grated

100 g provolone, grated

6 slices of salami

Heat the olive oil in a frying pan over a low–medium heat and add the chicory. Stir and cook for 1–2 minutes or until just collapsed. Add the garlic and lemon juice and cook for another 30 seconds. Season to taste and set aside to cool. Scatter the mozzarella and provolone over the pizza base and arrange the chicory and salami on top. Cook the pizza as instructed on page 38.

PICTURED ON PAGE 43

PIZZA MARGHERITA

If we're making pizza at home when tomatoes are in season and they're all sweet and juicy, I usually skip making a proper tomato sauce and just squeeze the super-ripe tomatoes over the base. This turns into its own sauce during cooking. You could also drape prosciutto over the pizza once it's out of the oven for something extra special. A large spoonful of the fresh tomato sauce on page 141 or the winter tomato sauce on page 142 would also be a wonderful base for this pizza. If you're using a sauce instead of the fresh tomatoes, spread it over the base before adding the cheese.

150 g buffalo mozzarella or fior di latte, roughly torn

100 g very ripe cherry tomatoes, cut in half

sea salt

10 basil leaves, plus extra to serve (optional)

extra-virgin olive oil, for drizzling

Distribute half the cheese over the pizza base. Scatter over the cherry tomatoes, squeezing the juices onto the pizza as you go. Season to taste, top with half of the basil leaves and drizzle with a little olive oil. Cook the pizza as instructed on page 38, then top with the remaining cheese and basil.

PICTURED ON PAGE 43

TALEGGIO AND POTATO PIZZA

Taleggio is a pretty funky cheese with a pungent aroma. It comes from the north of Italy and is one of my absolute favourites. One New Year's Eve, in Ancona, I had a slice of taleggio and potato pizza from a pizzeria I wish I could remember the name of. I'm not sure if it was just because it was New Year's Eve and I was in Italy for the first time as a wide-eyed eighteen year old, but gosh, it was the best slice of pizza I ever ate! Here is my version …

100 g taleggio

50 g mozzarella, grated

1 rosemary sprig, leaves picked and finely chopped

½ potato, thinly sliced on a mandoline

extra-virgin olive oil, for drizzling

sea salt

Tear off pieces of the taleggio and distribute over the pizza base. Sprinkle with the mozzarella and rosemary. Arrange a layer of potato over the top, drizzle with olive oil and scatter with salt. Cook the pizza as instructed on page 38.

PICTURED ON PAGE 42

BUFFALO MOZZARELLA, GUANCIALE AND ZUCCHINI PIZZA

Guanciale (cured pork jowl) is rich and fatty. Used sparingly, it brings with it a lovely sweetness. I adore it on pizza, especially with buffalo mozzarella and zucchini. If unavailable, substitute pancetta.

150 g buffalo mozzarella, roughly torn

50 g guanciale, thinly sliced

4 paper-thin slices of zucchini (use a mandoline)

sea salt

10 basil leaves

extra-virgin olive oil, for drizzling

Distribute half of the mozzarella over the pizza base and drape the guanciale and zucchini over the top. Season to taste, top with half of the basil leaves and drizzle with a little olive oil. Cook the pizza as instructed on page 38, then top with the remaining cheese and basil.

PICTURED ON PAGE 42

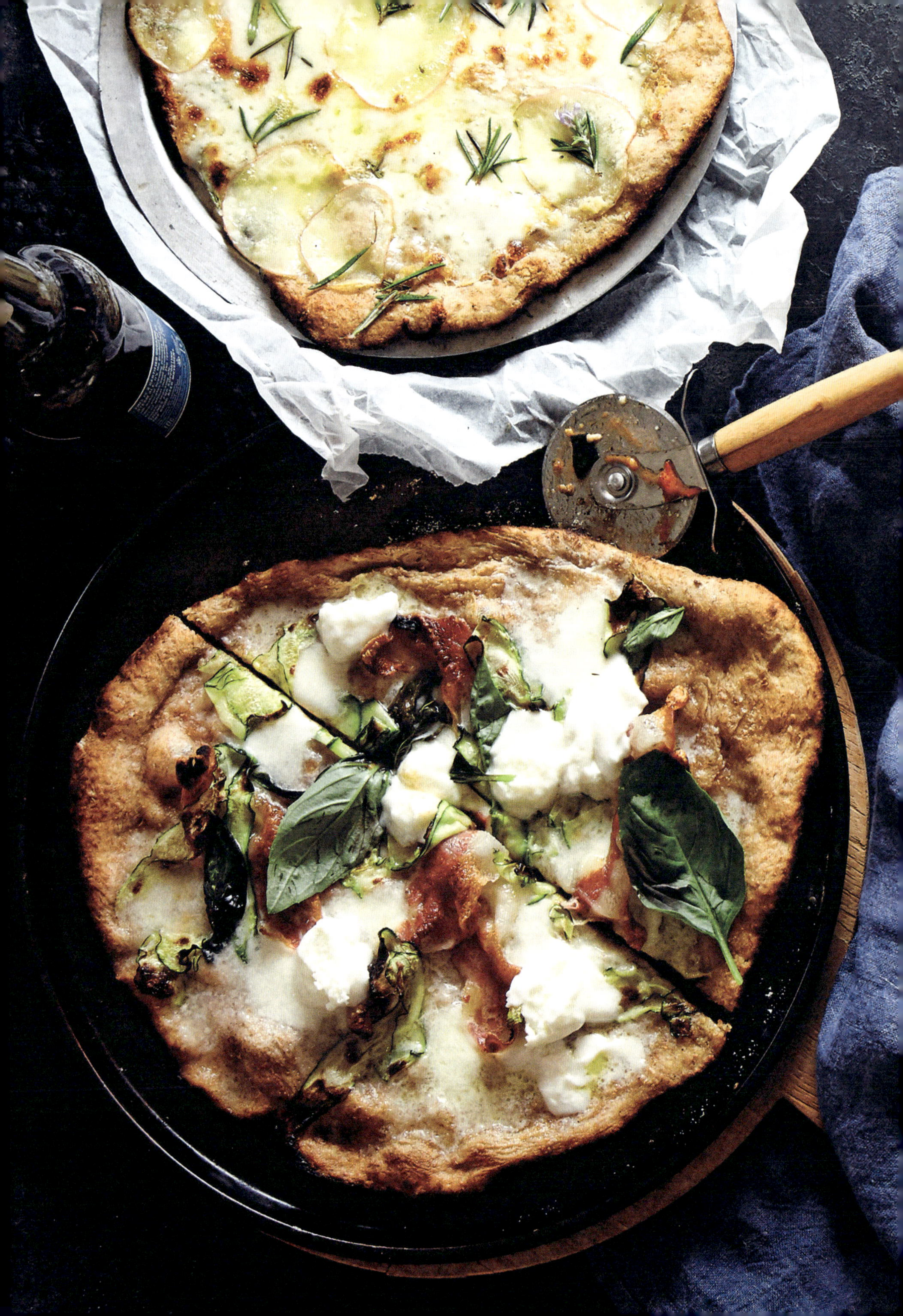

CLOCKWISE FROM TOP LEFT: Taleggio and potato pizza (page 41), Chicory, provolone and salami pizza (page 40), Pizza margherita (page 40) and Buffalo mozzarella, guanciale and zucchini pizza (page 41)

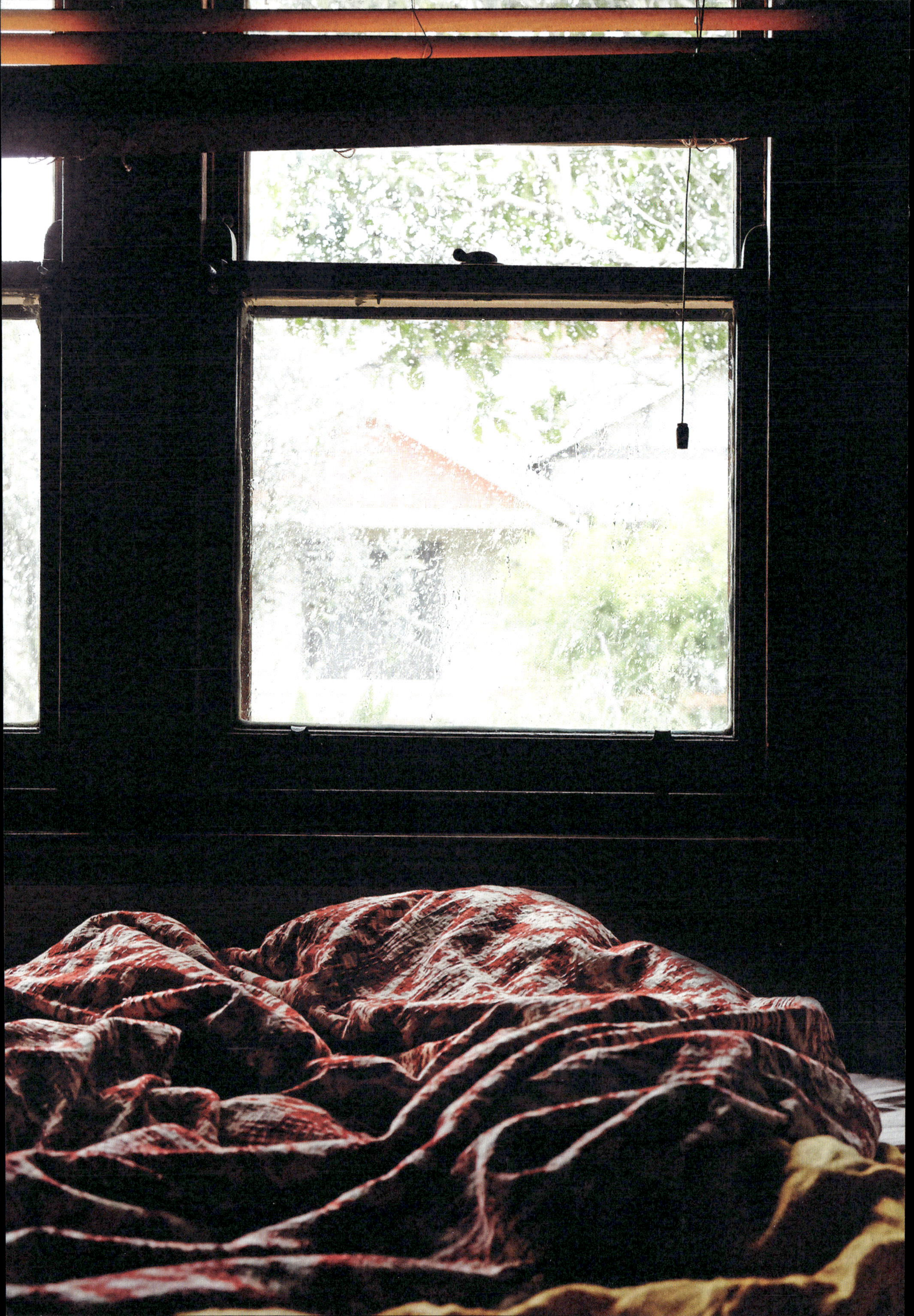

VEGETABLES

Every weekend, I leave the farmers' market with baskets overflowing with the freshest vegetables and fruits. We eat a lot of plant-based meals in our house – in fact, they make up the majority of our food. Vegetables can accompany other meals, as they so often do, but they can also be the main event at the dinner table. The time of year and what is available at the market dictates how we eat. And the ingredients that are in season are usually the most affordable, too. In this chapter you will find recipes that celebrate those small and joyful windows when particular ingredients are at their best.

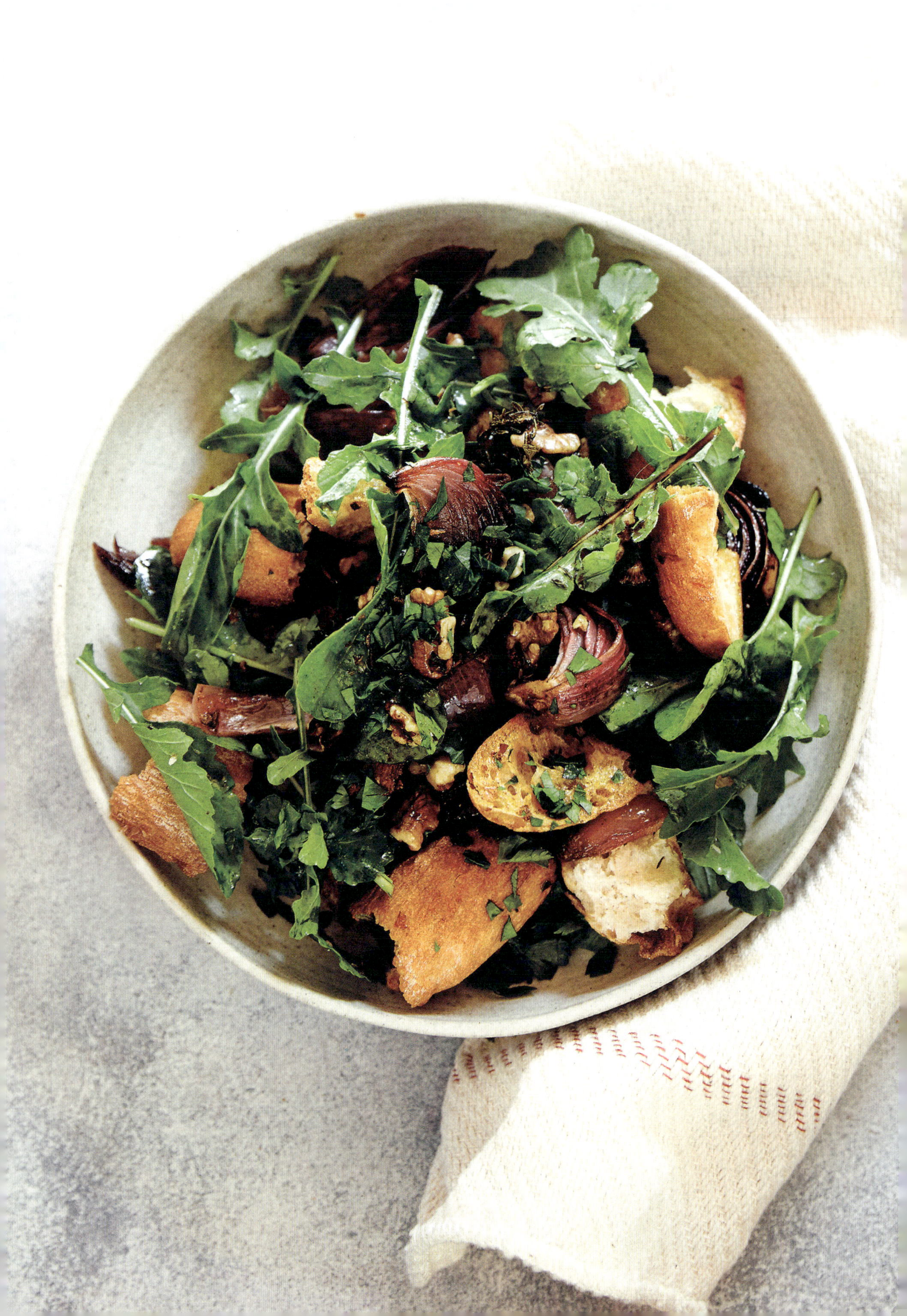

ROASTED ONION AND BREAD SALAD

SERVES 4 AS A SIDE

This is a hearty salad and a great way to use up stale bread. The onions really are the star of this dish, thanks to a long, slow roast in the oven. I like to use peppery wild rocket here, but you can throw in any leafy green that you prefer.

2 large red onions, each cut into 8 segments

2 tablespoons extra-virgin olive oil, plus extra if needed

1 tablespoon balsamic vinegar, plus extra if needed

3 thyme sprigs

sea salt

2–3 slices of day-old sourdough or crusty bread (about 150 g), torn into 3 pieces

30 g (¼ cup) walnuts

handful of flat-leaf parsley leaves, roughly chopped

50 g wild rocket

Preheat the oven to 170°C.

Place the onion in a small bowl with the olive oil, balsamic vinegar and thyme. Season with salt and toss the onion so it is well coated. Arrange in a small baking dish or tray and bake for 1–1½ hours until golden and caramelised, stirring every so often to ensure it doesn't burn. Set aside to cool.

Arrange the bread on a baking tray. Bake for 10–15 minutes until toasted and golden.

Meanwhile, lightly toast the walnuts in a dry frying pan over a low–medium heat for 1–2 minutes until just coloured.

Combine the onion and bread in a large bowl and toss so the bread soaks up some of the dressing. Add the parsley and rocket and mix well. Check the balance between the oil and vinegar in the dressing and drizzle with a little extra olive oil and vinegar as needed. Season to taste with salt and serve.

ZUCCHINI AND MINT SALAD

SERVES 4–6 AS A SIDE

I like to make this salad in peak summer, when zucchini are growing prolifically and different heirloom varieties are available at local markets. It is a classic combination – zucchini, mint and chilli – which benefits from the creaminess of the buffalo mozzarella.

25 g (¼ cup) flaked almonds

5 zucchini (about 1 kg in total), sliced into ribbons using a peeler or mandoline

1 small red chilli, thinly sliced

large handful of mint leaves, torn

300 g buffalo mozzarella, torn

2 tablespoons extra-virgin olive oil

juice of ½ lemon

sea salt

Toast the almonds in a small, dry frying pan over a low heat until just coloured. Set aside to cool.

Combine the zucchini, chilli, mint and almonds in a large bowl. Add the mozzarella then drizzle over the olive oil and lemon juice and gently toss everything to combine. Season to taste and serve immediately.

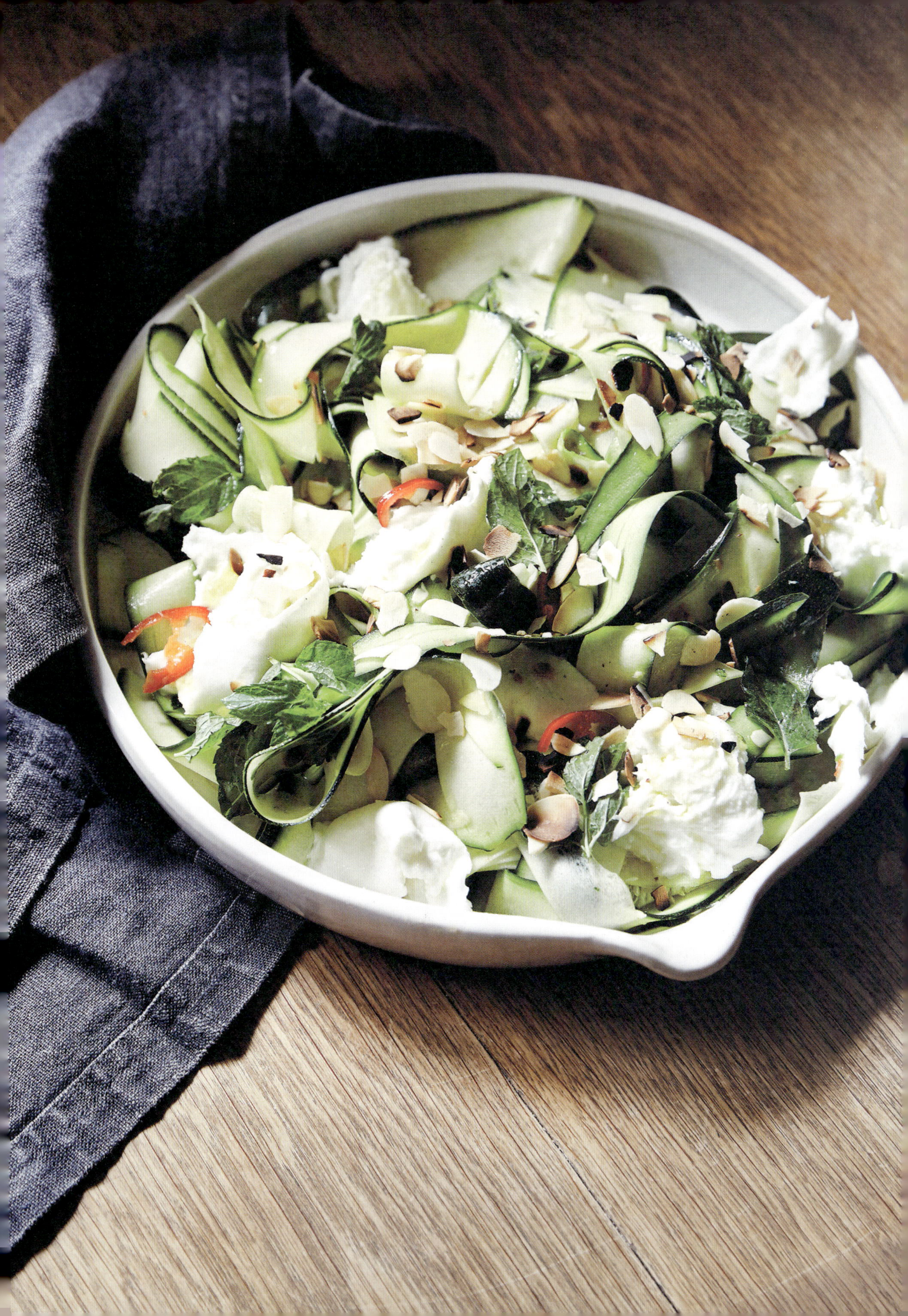

BABY BEETROOTS WITH BURRATA AND WALNUTS

SERVES 4 AS A SIDE

Burrata is the most beautiful fresh cheese – a mozzarella exterior with a soft centre made from cream and stretched curds. Serve the burrata whole and pierce it at the table to reveal the oozy centre which, thanks to the beetroots, will become iridescent pink. If you can't find baby beets, you can use normal ones – just cook them for about 1 hour and then cut them into 3 cm wedges.

2 bunches of baby beetroots (about 500 g), trimmed

1 tablespoon extra-virgin olive oil, plus extra for drizzling

50 g (½ cup) walnuts

small bunch of mint, leaves picked and roughly torn

sea salt

1 × 200 g burrata

Preheat the oven to 180°C.

Place the beetroots on a piece of aluminium foil large enough to make a parcel. Drizzle with the olive oil and wrap in the foil. Bake for 40–45 minutes or until tender when pierced with a knife. Allow to cool, then peel the skin away using a knife. (Wear gloves if you want to avoid having the beetroot stain your skin.) Halve each beetroot, leaving smaller ones whole, and place in a bowl.

Meanwhile, scatter the walnuts on a baking tray and toast in the oven for around 10 minutes. Set aside to cool, then add to the beetroots along with the mint. Season to taste and drizzle with a little extra olive oil. Transfer to a serving dish and top with the burrata.

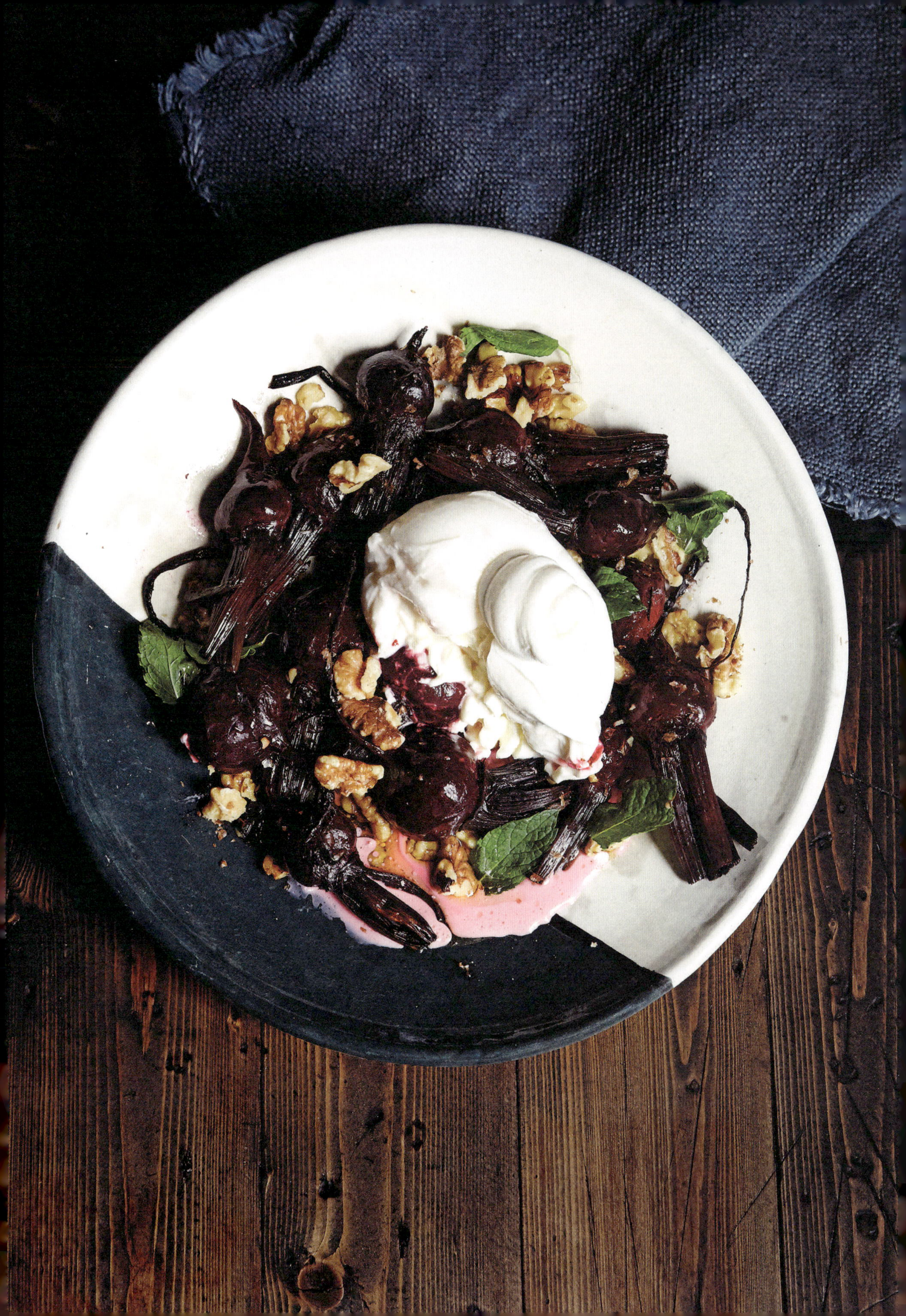

ROASTED BROCCOLI WITH LEMON, GARLIC AND ANCHOVY CRUMBS

· SERVES 4 ·

The wonderful pairing of broccoli with anchovy and breadcrumbs is well known and loved in Italy, especially in Puglia, where it's often eaten with pasta. In this dish, I roast the broccoli with lemon and garlic and top it with flavour-packed anchovy crumbs. I usually collect all the stale bits of bread throughout the week and make a big batch of breadcrumbs, so there's always some in an airtight container in the cupboard should the need for crunch arise.

1–2 slices of day-old crusty bread, (about 60 g) cut into 3 cm pieces

2 heads of broccoli (about 700 g in total), cut into large florets and stalks peeled and cut into pieces

1 head of garlic, sliced horizontally

80 ml (⅓ cup) extra-virgin olive oil

1 lemon, quartered

4 anchovy fillets

finely grated pecorino, to serve

Preheat the oven to 200°C.

Spread the bread pieces onto a baking tray and bake for 15–20 minutes until completely dried out. Roll over the bread with a rolling pin to break it into crumbs. I like quite a rough crumb, some smaller bits too – you want a bit of texture here. Alternatively, pulse the bread in a food processor.

Arrange the broccoli, including the trimmed stalks, and the garlic in a large roasting pan. Top with 2 tablespoons of olive oil and the lemon quarters, squeezing the juice into the pan as you add them. Mix so that everything's nicely coated. Bake for 25–30 minutes, turning halfway through, until the broccoli is tender and coloured.

Meanwhile, warm the remaining olive oil in a small frying pan over a low heat. Add the anchovies and cook for 2–3 minutes until they have melted into the oil. Increase the heat to medium, add the breadcrumbs and fry for 2–3 minutes until golden and crunchy. Set aside to cool.

Arrange the roasted broccoli on a large serving dish along with any garlic or juices from the pan. Scatter generously with pecorino and top with the anchovy breadcrumbs. Serve immediately.

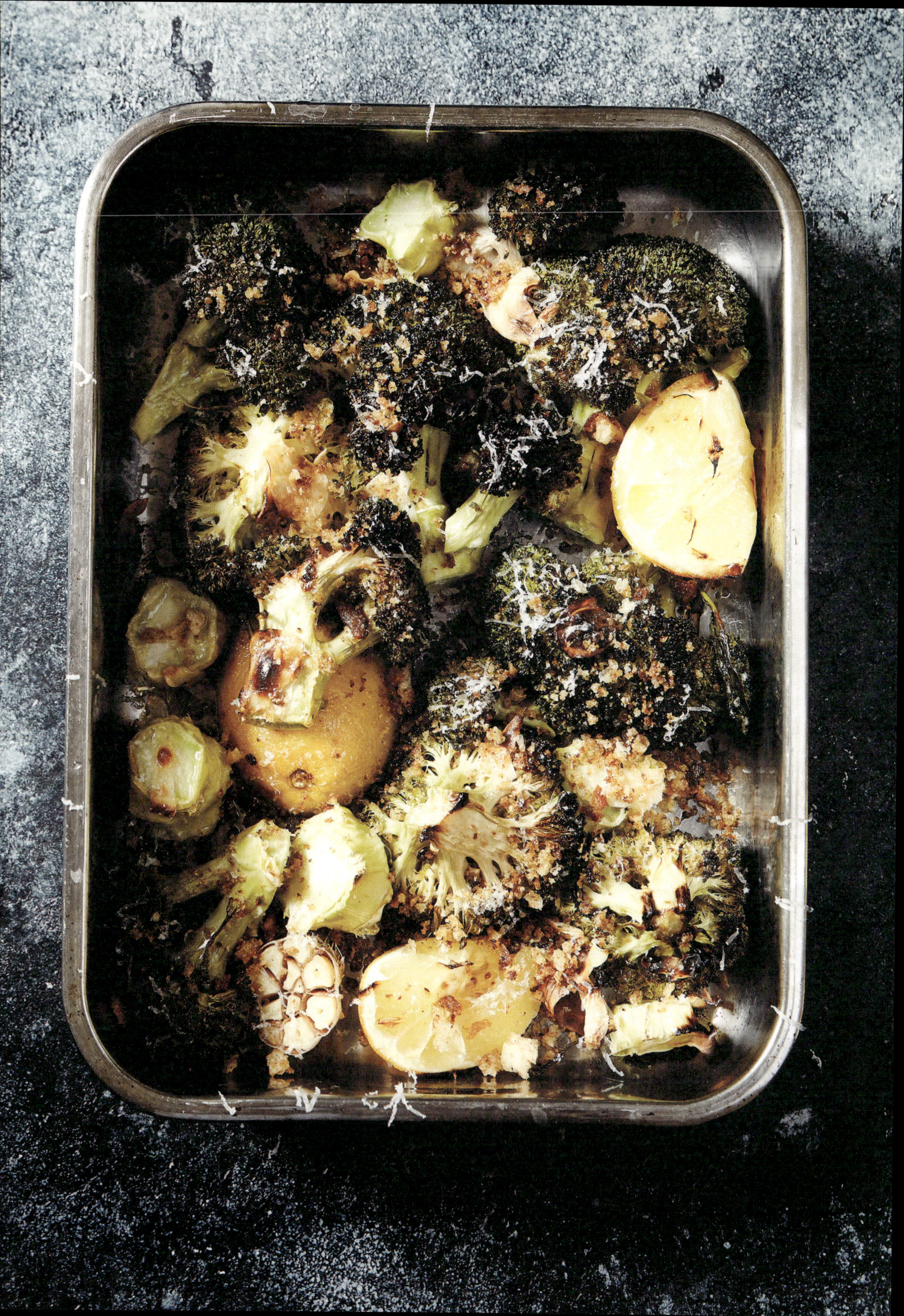

ROAST POTATOES WITH TOMATO AND ANCHOVIES

SERVES 4 AS A SIDE

This is my absolute favourite way to eat roast potatoes, and something we used to make often when I lived in Italy. The potatoes are crisp and soft all at once, the tomatoes burst open to release their wonderful juices and the anchovies melt away, giving the whole dish a subtle saltiness. Three ingredients that really come alive when combined. I like to use a mixture of red and yellow cherry tomatoes, but whatever you have to hand is fine.

700 g small kipfler potatoes or other waxy potato, scrubbed and cut in half lengthways

250 g cherry tomatoes

8 anchovy fillets

1 tablespoon extra-virgin olive oil

sea salt

Preheat the oven to 180°C.

Arrange the potatoes in a large roasting pan. Scatter the cherry tomatoes over and drape the anchovies on top. Drizzle with the olive oil and season with a little salt, keeping in mind that the anchovies will provide much of the salt required.

Roast for about 45 minutes, until the potatoes are crisp and the tomatoes are bursting from their skins.

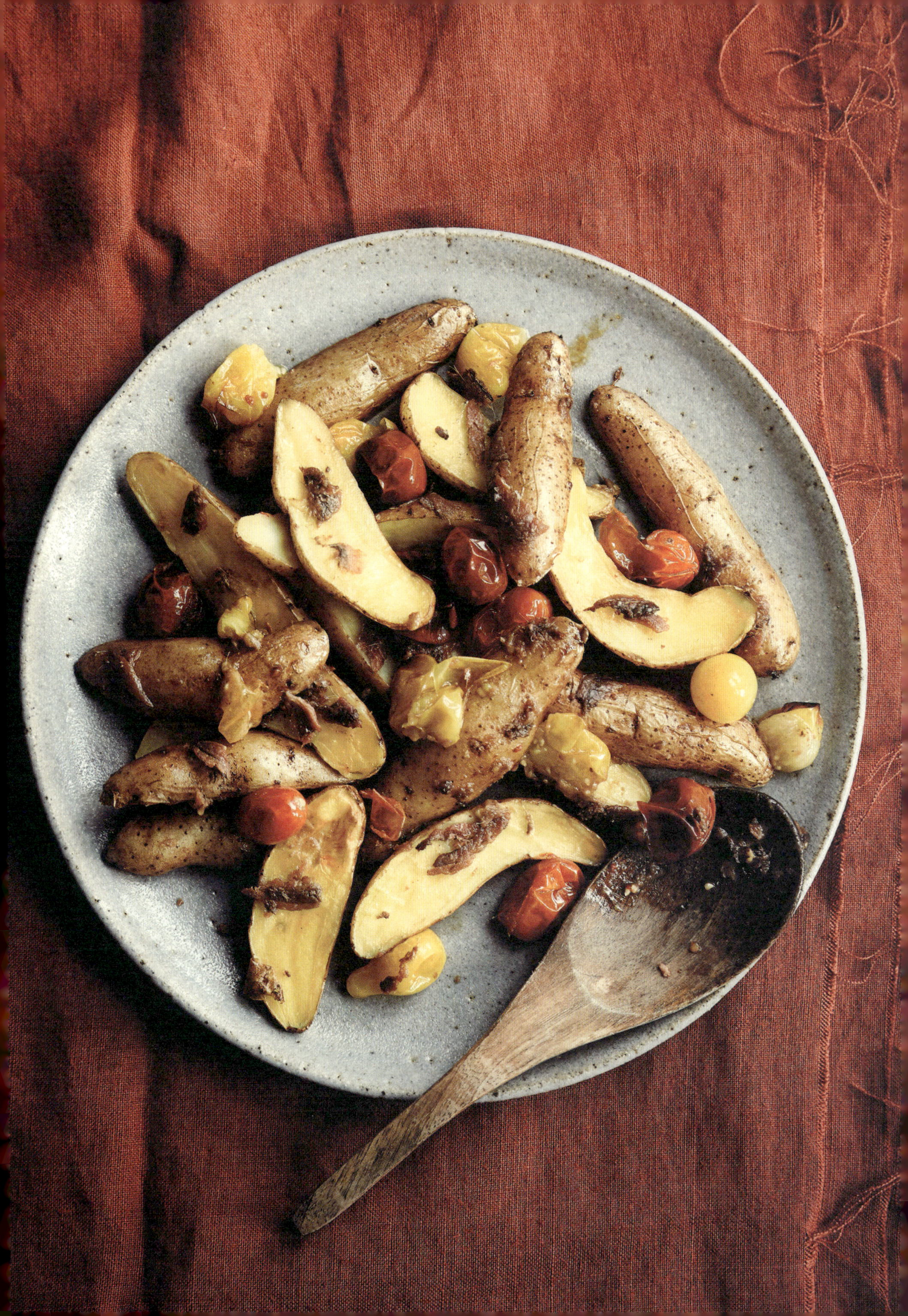

MUSHROOM AND BARLEY PIE

SERVES 8

This is a pie for autumn, when the days are shortening and you feel like a hearty pie with beautifully buttery pastry. A variety of mushrooms will give this pie a great depth of flavour and don't be afraid to use varieties you might usually associate with other cuisines – oyster, enoki and shiitake mushrooms are all great in this recipe in small quantities, as well as Swiss brown and chestnut mushrooms.

Feel free to use a good-quality store-bought puff pastry for this pie, but if you have the time, do give the rough puff a go. While it still takes some time, it is nowhere near as laborious as regular puff. It can be made in advance – it will last a few days in the fridge – and when the pie comes out of the oven and you see all the layers in your pastry, I think you will feel proud of your efforts.

---

1 egg, lightly beaten

ROUGH PUFF PASTRY

350 g plain flour

pinch of sea salt

350 g chilled unsalted butter, cut into cubes

about 80 ml (⅓ cup) iced water

MUSHROOM AND BARLEY FILLING

100 g pearl barley

60 g butter

2 leeks, white and light green parts only, finely sliced and washed

sea salt

100 g cavolo nero, tough stems removed, leaves washed thoroughly and roughly chopped

60 ml (¼ cup) extra-virgin olive oil, plus extra if needed

900 g mixed mushrooms, cleaned and larger mushrooms chopped

2 garlic cloves, finely chopped

handful of tarragon leaves, finely chopped

handful of flat-leaf parsley leaves, finely chopped

finely grated zest of 1 lemon

150 g crème fraîche

black pepper, to taste

To make the pastry, tip the flour onto a clean work surface and sprinkle with the salt. Add the butter and toss through the flour. Using a metal pastry scraper or a knife, cut the butter into the flour until the mixture resembles coarse breadcrumbs. There should be larger pieces of butter too, so don't overwork it at this stage. Sprinkle with iced water, one tablespoon at a time, until the dough just comes together, using your hands or a pastry scraper to bring it all together. I find I usually need around 80 ml (⅓ cup), but just go by how the pastry feels – some flours need more or less water. It still should be a little shaggy with visible pieces of butter. Shape the pastry into a flattish rectangle, cover with a damp cloth or plastic wrap and refrigerate for at least 30 minutes.

Remove the pastry from the fridge and, on a lightly floured work surface, roll the dough into a 10 cm × 30 cm rectangle that's about 1 cm thick, continuing to dust your work surface with a little more flour if the dough is too sticky. Bring the short ends of the dough into the middle, and then fold in half where the short ends meet, almost like a book. Wrap the pastry and chill again for 30 minutes. Repeat the rolling, folding and chilling process two more times. Refrigerate until needed, removing it from the fridge 10 minutes before using.

Preheat the oven to 180°C. Line a baking tray with baking paper.

For the mushroom filling, cook the pearl barley in a saucepan of boiling water for 20–25 minutes until just cooked, but still al dente. Drain, rinse and set aside to cool. In a large frying pan, heat the butter over a low–medium heat and, when foaming, add the leeks with a pinch of salt and sauté for 5 minutes or until soft. Add the cavolo nero and continue to cook for 3-4 minutes or until just wilted. Transfer the leeks and cavolo nero to a large bowl and set aside. Increase the heat to medium and add the olive oil. Add the mushrooms and cook for 8–10 minutes until the mushrooms have collapsed slightly, but are still holding their shape. Stir in the garlic

RECIPE CONTINUED OVERLEAF ⟶

VEGETABLES 57

RECIPE CONTINUED •—→

and cook for another minute. (Depending on how big your pan is, you may need to cook the mushrooms in batches as I do.) Transfer the mushrooms to the bowl with the leeks, then add the tarragon, parsley, lemon zest, crème fraîche and the pearl barley. Season to taste, then stir well to ensure everything is well combined.

Divide the pastry dough into two. Roll each piece into a 40 cm × 20 cm rectangle. Place one piece of pastry onto the prepared baking tray and arrange the filling on top, leaving a 1 cm border of pastry all the way around. Whisk 1 teaspoon of water into the egg, and brush around the pastry border. Top with the second piece of pastry, gently press down on the edges to seal, then brush the top of the pie with the remaining egg wash. Using a very sharp knife, make shallow diagonal slashes in the top of the pastry to make a diamond pattern. Try not to cut all the way through. This is just to give the pie a beautiful finish and encourage it to puff up during baking, but some deeper cuts won't hurt. Bake in the oven for 45 minutes or until the pastry is puffy and golden.

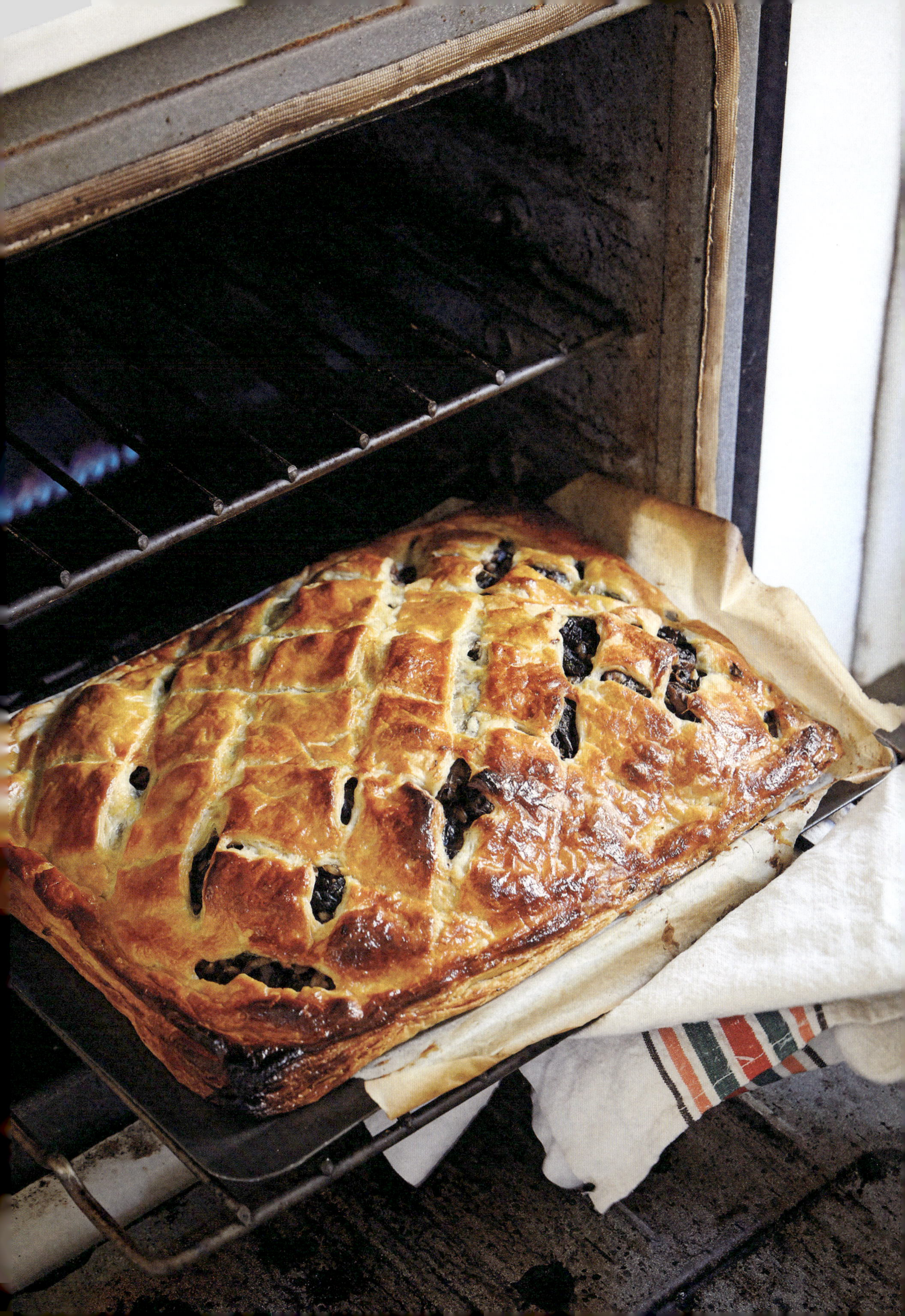

GREENS PIE

· SERVES 6 ·

This is a take on my Auntie Mary's ricotta pie, which she made for my sister and me when we arrived in Malta for the first time. We had docked into the port of Valletta after a rather long train trip from Rome to Sicily, and then a boat from Sicily to Malta. It was nearly eleven o'clock at night by the time we arrived at her house, just a few days before Christmas, and waiting for us was a still-warm ricotta pie and roasted rabbit. We'd never met Auntie Mary before, but I instantly felt at home. I've added greens to this pie, and sneaked some cheddar cheese into the pastry, which is not Maltese at all, but very delicious nonetheless.

1 tablespoon extra-virgin olive oil

2 leeks, white and light green parts only, finely sliced and washed

3 garlic cloves, finely sliced

sea salt

600 g leafy greens, such as cavolo nero, spinach and silverbeet, tough stems removed, leaves washed thoroughly and left damp

150 g fresh full-fat ricotta

100 ml pure cream

2 eggs, lightly beaten

finely grated zest of 1 lemon

pinch of freshly grated nutmeg

black pepper

CHEDDAR SHORTCRUST PASTRY

300 g plain flour

100 g cheddar cheese, grated

pinch of sea salt

200 g chilled unsalted butter, cut into cubes

about 60 ml (¼ cup) iced water

To make the pastry, combine the flour, cheese and salt in a bowl. Add the butter, and rub into the flour using your fingertips until it resembles coarse breadcrumbs. Drizzle in enough iced water, a tablespoon at a time, to bring the dough together using your hands. Divide the dough in two and flatten into squares. Cover with plastic wrap and refrigerate for at least 30 minutes.

Preheat the oven to 180°C. Line a baking tray with baking paper.

Heat the olive oil in a frying pan over a low heat. Add the leek, garlic and a pinch of salt and sauté for about 10 minutes until soft and translucent. Set aside in a large bowl.

Place the damp greens in a large saucepan and cook for 3–4 minutes over a low heat, stirring occasionally, until just wilted. Set aside to cool, then squeeze any moisture from the greens. Roughly chop and add to the bowl with the leek.

Combine the ricotta, cream, most of the egg (leaving a little to make an egg wash for the pastry), lemon zest and nutmeg in a small bowl and mix until smooth. Add to the greens and leek mixture and stir to combine well. Season to taste and set aside.

Remove the dough from the fridge and allow to rest at room temperature for 10 minutes. Roll each piece into a 25 cm square. Place one piece of pastry on the prepared baking tray and arrange the filling on top, leaving a 1 cm border of pastry all the way around. Whisk 1 teaspoon of water into the remaining egg to make a wash, and brush around the border of pastry. Top with the second piece of dough, trim any excess, then pinch the edges together to seal, marking with your index finger to create a crimped effect. Brush the top of the pie with the remaining egg wash and poke a hole in the centre of the pie using a small, sharp knife to allow steam to escape during cooking. Bake for 45–50 minutes until golden and cooked through. Serve warm or at room temperature.

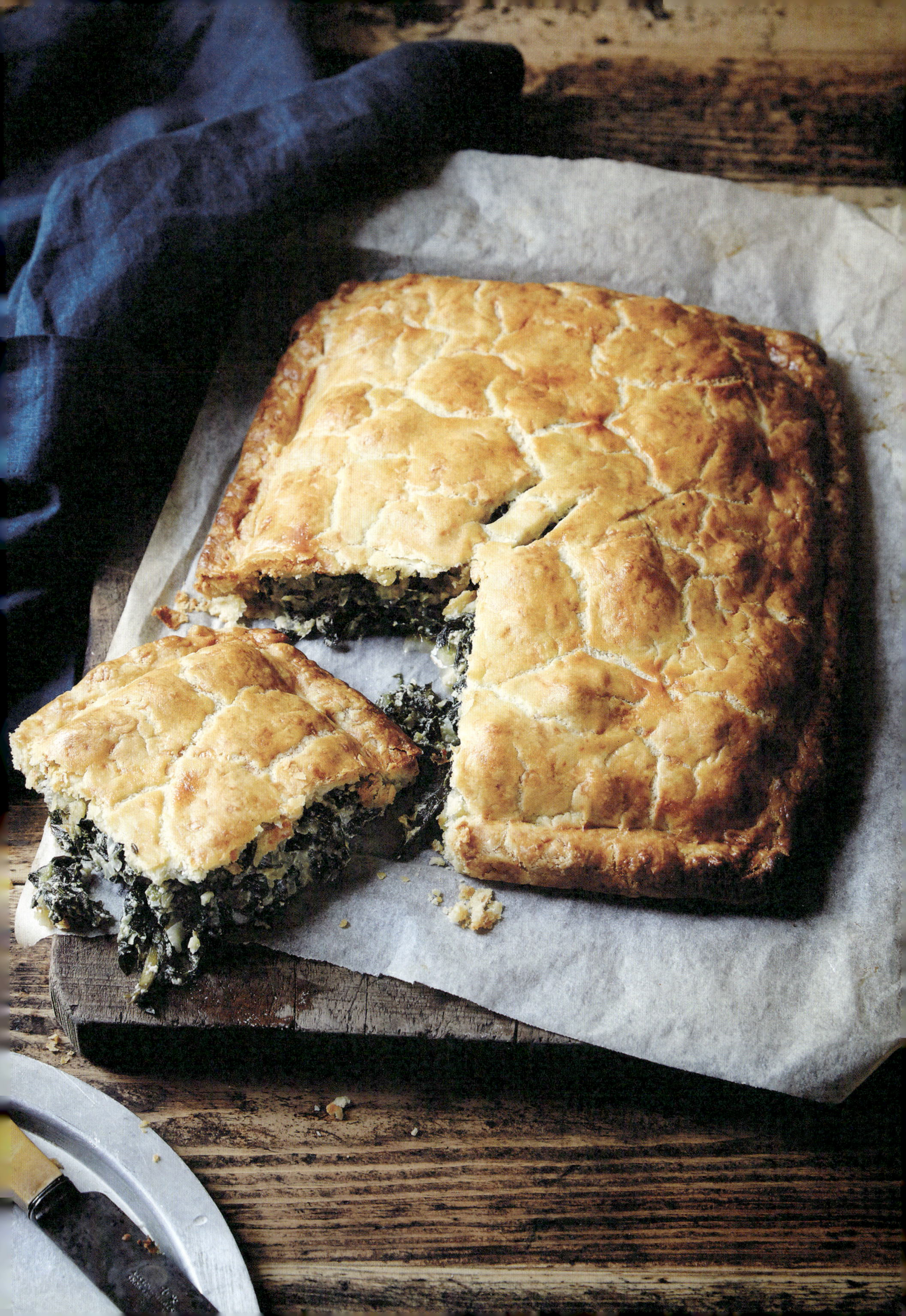

ROASTED PEPPERS WITH BASIL AND CAPERS

SERVES 4 AS A SIDE

These peppers are so wonderful in summer, and they're great to keep in the fridge as an easy accompaniment to a main meal or for spooning onto grilled bread rubbed with garlic for a snack. I usually use red capsicums, but a mixture of red and yellow is also lovely. I prefer not to use green capsicums as I find they lack the sweetness and are far too bitter.

6 red capsicums, or a mixture of red and yellow

30 g salted capers, rinsed

handful of basil leaves, plus extra to serve

2 tablespoons extra-virgin olive oil, plus extra to serve

1 tablespoon red wine vinegar

sea salt

Preheat the oven to 200°C.

Arrange the capsicums in a roasting pan and bake for about 1 hour, turning them over halfway through cooking, until they have collapsed and the skins have blackened. Transfer to a bowl and cover with plastic wrap, or do as I do and place them in a large saucepan covered with a tea towel and then the lid to trap the steam. The aim is to let the capsicums sweat so the skin peels away easily.

When the capsicums are cool enough to touch but still quite warm, remove the skin from the flesh – it should just peel away. Discard the skin, stalks and seeds, and drain to remove any excess liquid. Try to keep the capsicums in as large pieces as possible. Place the capsicums in a non-reactive (ceramic or glass) container and add the remaining ingredients. Mix gently with your hands, season to taste, and allow to sit for at least 15 minutes before serving. Drizzle with olive oil and serve with extra basil leaves on top.

NOTE: I usually prepare these roasted peppers in advance and store them in the fridge, where they'll keep in a non-reactive airtight container for up to 1 week. They are best brought to room temperature before serving. I like to arrange them on a plate and scatter with some fresh basil leaves.

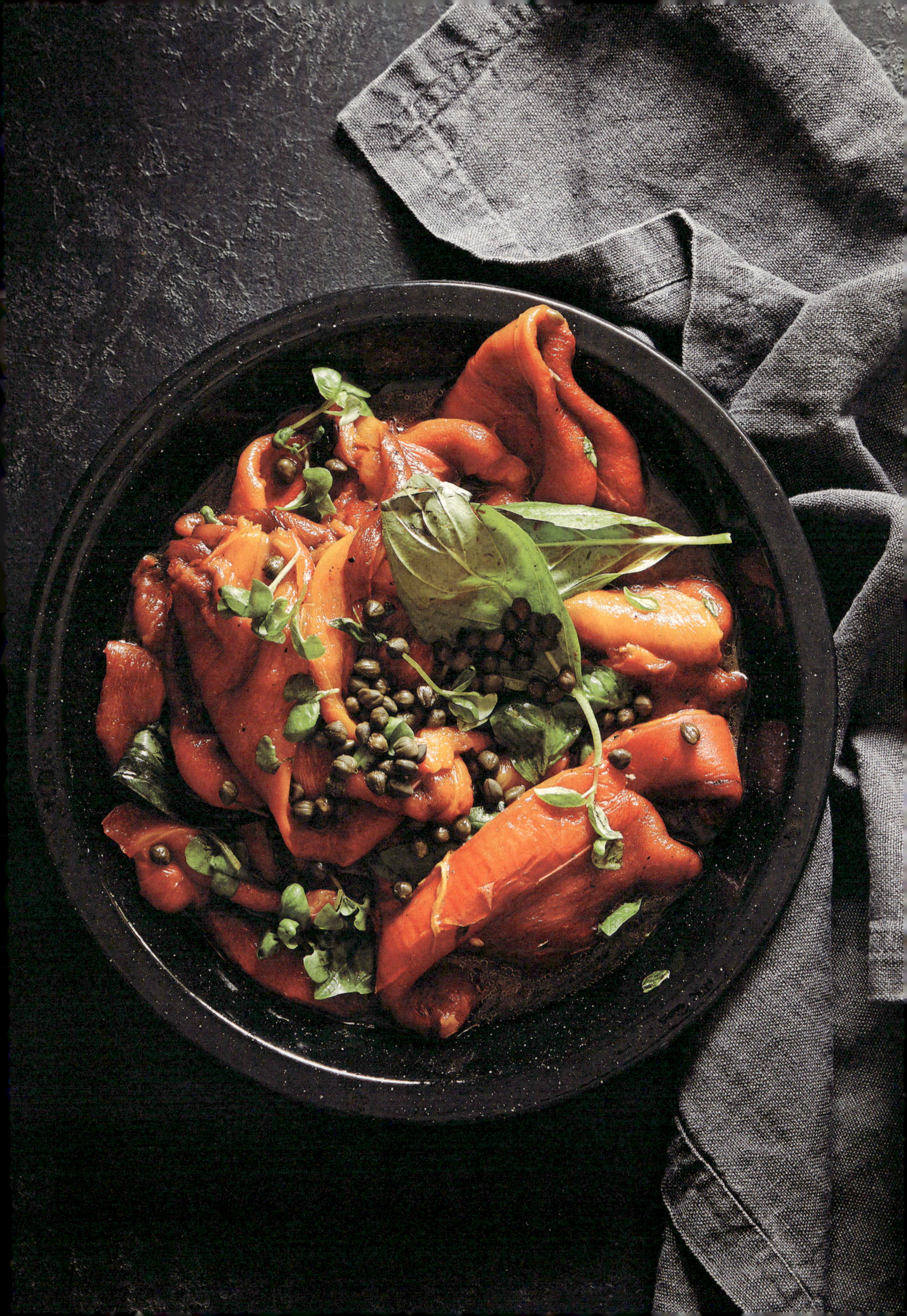

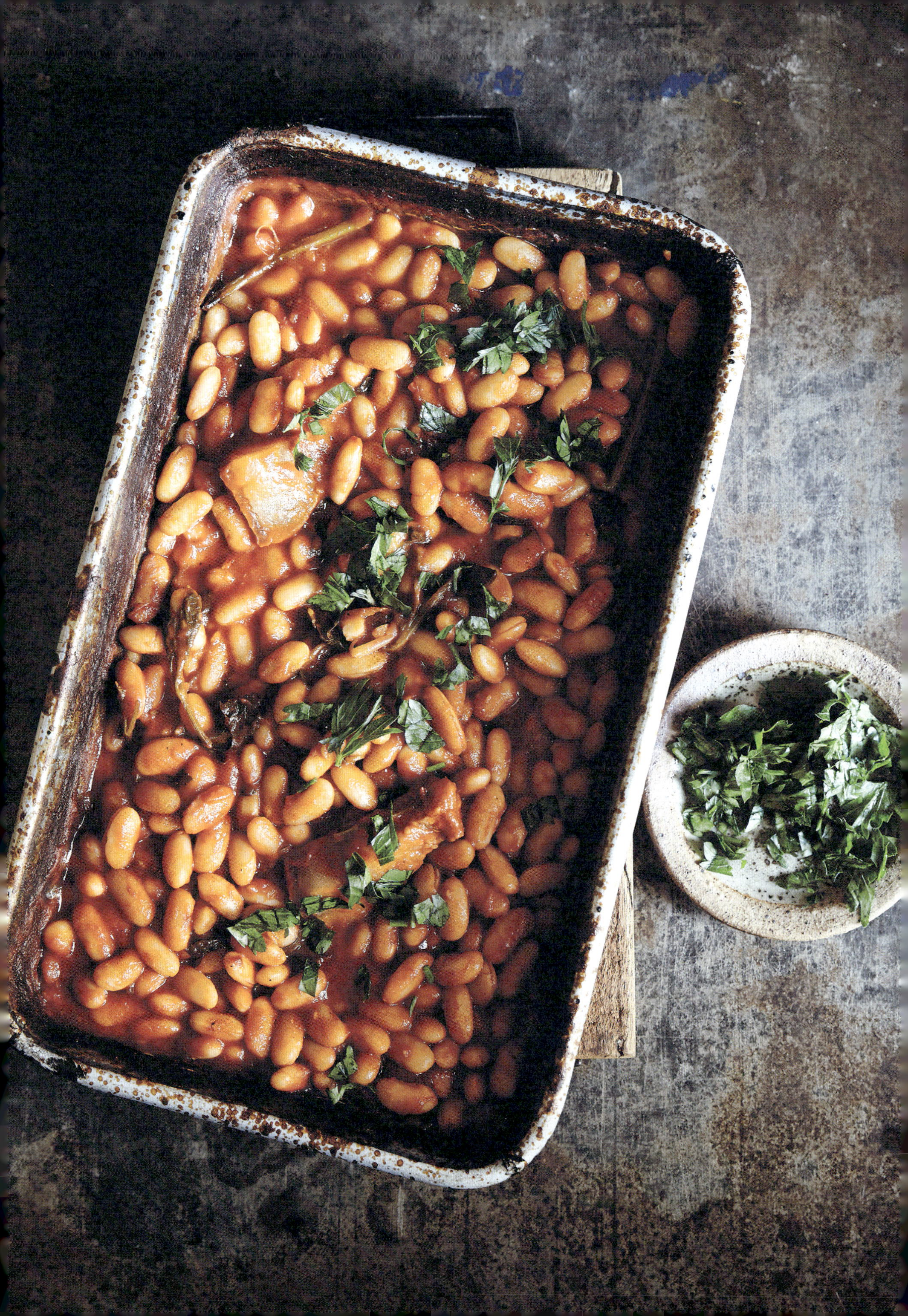

SLOW BAKED BEANS

SERVES 4–6

When you think of baked beans, it's hard not to think of them coming from a can – but as a child, it was never that way for me. It's not only simple to make your own baked beans, but they are far more delicious than anything you can buy. Although they take a while to make, most of that time is just the beans slowly cooking away in the oven, needing only a little stir every so often. The beans are perfect on hot buttered sourdough for breakfast, or heated in a pan with a few eggs dropped in to poach in the sauce.

400 g dried cannellini beans

1 fresh bay leaf

2 garlic cloves, peeled

1 dried chilli (optional)

500 g tomato passata

1 × 60 g piece of guanciale or pancetta

3 flat-leaf parsley sprigs, roughly torn, stalks and all, plus an extra handful of roughly chopped leaves to serve

1 rosemary sprig

½ teaspoon smoked paprika

1 teaspoon fennel seeds

sea salt

extra-virgin olive oil, for drizzling

Soak the cannellini beans in a large bowl of cold water overnight. Drain and rinse thoroughly.

Preheat the oven to 160°C.

Place the beans in a large saucepan with the bay leaf, garlic and chilli, if using. Cover with cold water and bring to the boil over a high heat. Keep at a rolling boil and cook for 30 minutes. Drain, leaving the bay leaf, chilli and garlic in with the beans. Transfer to an ovenproof casserole dish or cast iron pot with a lid. Add the passata, guanciale or pancetta, flat-leaf parsley stalks, rosemary, paprika, fennel seeds and 400 ml of water. Season to taste. Bake, covered with a tight-fitting lid or tin foil, for 2½–3 hours until the beans are tender and the sauce is thick and rich. Check on the beans every 30 minutes or so, giving them a stir and topping up with a little water if needed.

Serve drizzled with olive oil and scattered with parsley leaves.

NOTE: This recipe is easily made suitable for vegetarians – just omit the guanciale or pancetta.

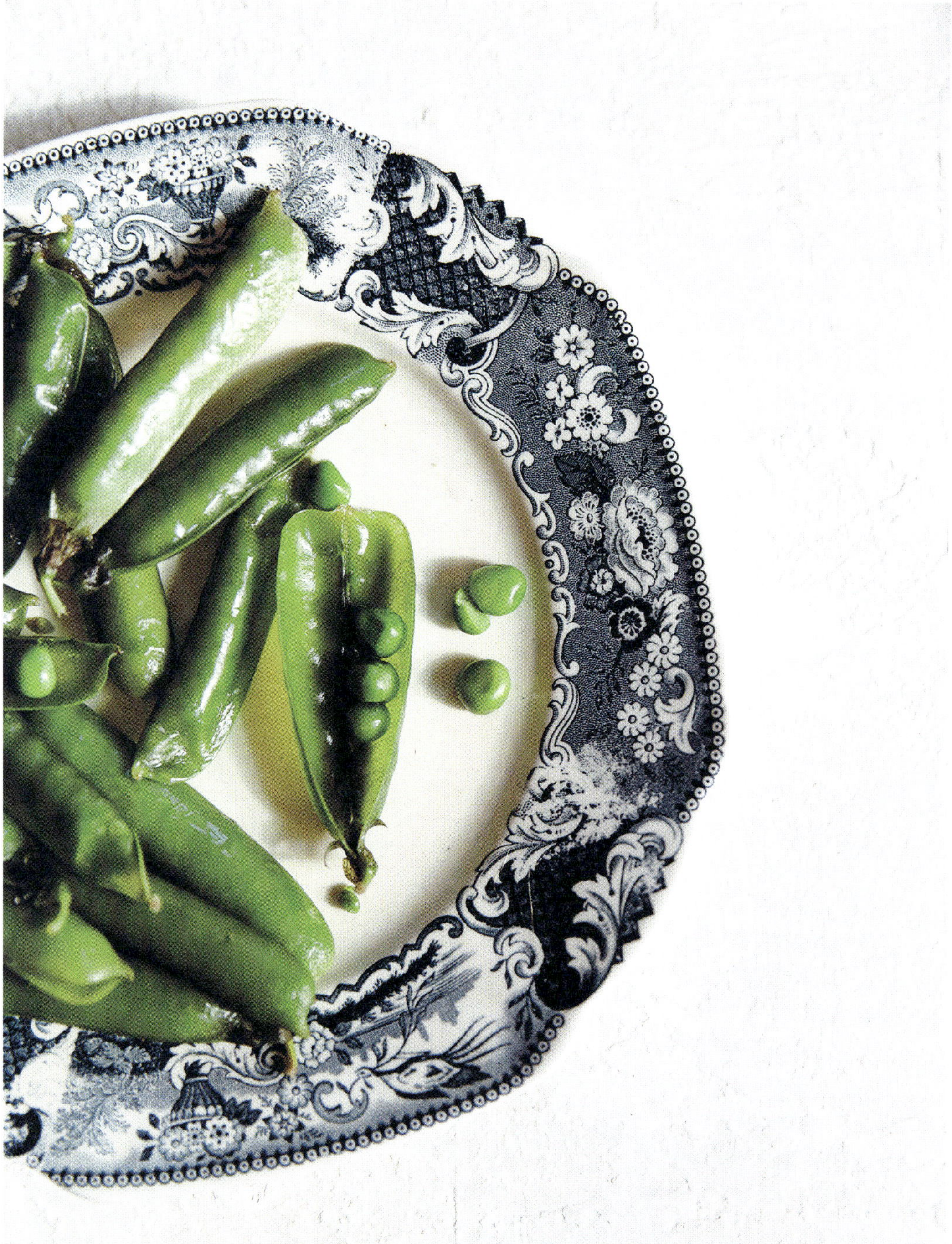

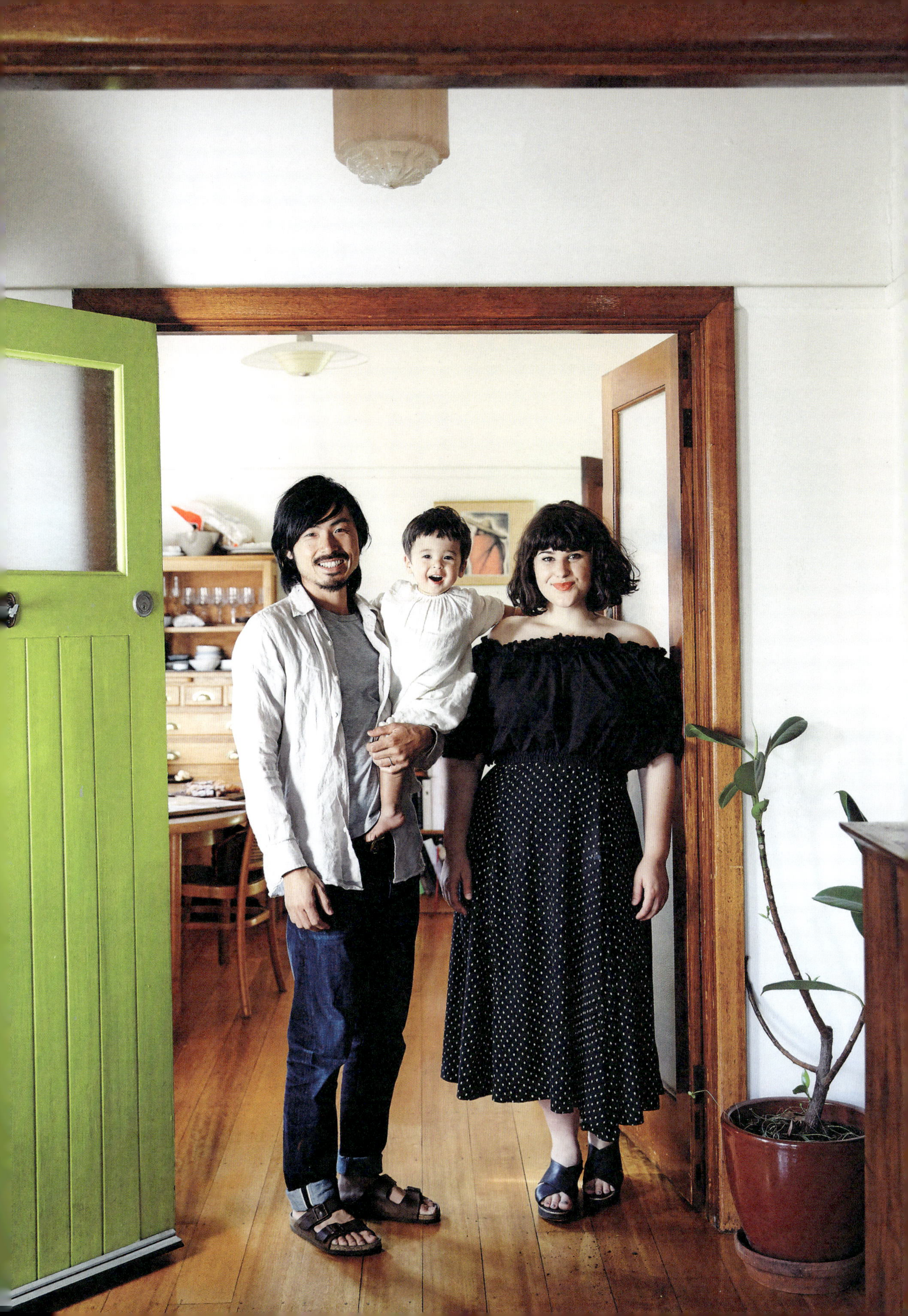

ROASTED CAULIFLOWER AND WHEAT SALAD

SERVES 4–6

I adore the combination of cauliflower and tahini, so this salad gets a solid workout during the week at our house. It's nourishing and substantial enough to be its own meal. Also, it's a hardy salad that won't go soggy, so any leftovers can be packed away and eaten for lunch the following day.

50 g (⅓ cup) blanched whole almonds

1 large head of cauliflower (about 1 kg), cut into florets

1 tablespoon extra-virgin olive oil

pinch of sea salt

150 g whole wheat grains (see Note)

small bunch of mint, leaves picked and roughly chopped

small bunch of flat-leaf parsley, leaves picked and roughly chopped

6 pitted prunes, roughly chopped

1 tablespoon salted capers, rinsed

TAHINI DRESSING

2 tablespoons tahini

60 ml (¼ cup) extra-virgin olive oil

1 tablespoon apple cider vinegar

sea salt

Preheat the oven to 180°C.

Arrange the almonds on a baking tray and roast in the oven for about 10 minutes or until just golden. Transfer to a large mixing bowl. Arrange the cauliflower on the tray. Drizzle with the olive oil and season with the salt. Roast for about 45 minutes or until tender and golden. Transfer to the bowl with the almonds.

Meanwhile, cook the wheat in a saucepan of boiling water over a medium–high heat for 30–35 minutes until al dente. Drain and set aside to cool.

For the dressing, whisk the tahini, olive oil and vinegar together. Add a little water to thin if necessary – it should be thick but pourable. Season to taste.

Add the mint, parsley, prunes, capers and wheat to the mixing bowl and stir to combine. Arrange the salad in a serving bowl and drizzle with the dressing.

NOTE: Wheat grains are whole grains from the wheat plant – they look similar to barley or spelt grains. While typically milled into flour, the whole grain can be used as a substitute for barley, rice or other grains. You can buy them from health-food shops and grocers that have bulk bins of dry goods. If unavailable, you can substitute farro, barley, freekeh or even brown rice; just be sure to adjust your cooking time to suit, as they take a little less time.

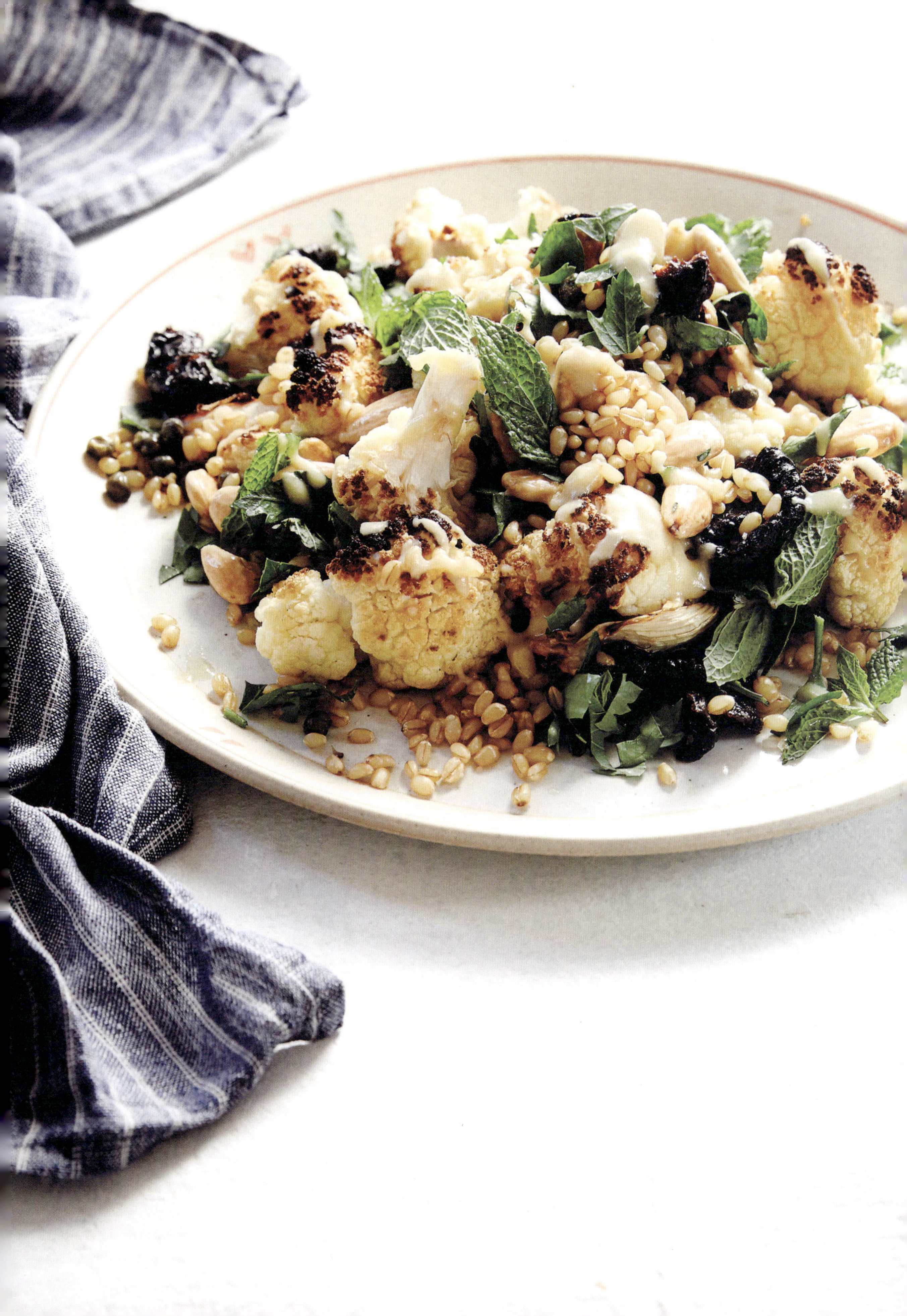

HOUSE SALAD

SERVES 4

Our house salad is a staple on our dinner table, especially when we need something crunchy and fresh to accompany a rich meal in winter. It has everything: texture from the fennel and celery, bitterness from the leaves and sweetness from the raisins. Feel free to add extras like toasted nuts, seeds or shaved parmesan.

150 g mixed salad leaves, such as radicchio, mâche, baby spinach, rocket, beetroot leaves and chicory, larger leaves torn

1 celery stalk, thinly sliced

1 small fennel bulb, thinly sliced and fronds chopped

large handful of flat-leaf parsley leaves

50 g raisins

2 tablespoons extra-virgin olive oil

juice of ½ lemon

sea salt

Place the salad leaves in a large bowl. Add the celery and the fennel bulb and fronds, along with the parsley and raisins. Mix to combine.

Whisk the olive oil and lemon juice in a small bowl and season to taste. Just before serving, drizzle the salad with the dressing.

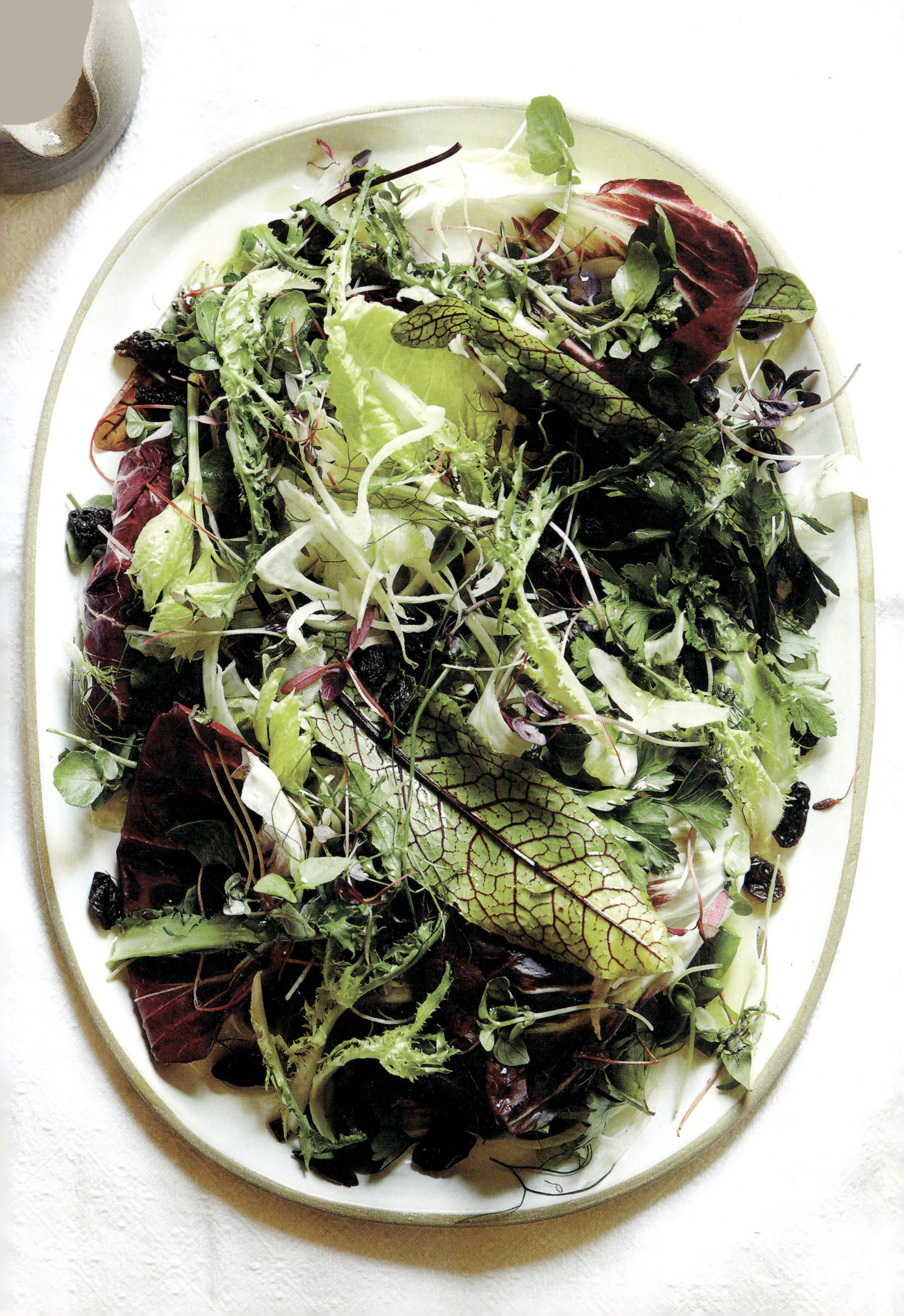

TOMATO AND RED ONION SALAD

SERVES 4–6

A refreshing salad for when tomatoes are at their best, in late January and February. A mixture of smaller and larger heirloom varieties will make this salad pop – there isn't much for the tomatoes to hide behind, so avoid pale and tasteless ones. Tarragon works really well in this salad. It has similar licorice properties to basil, which is, of course, a more than fine substitute.

1 small red onion, finely sliced

sea salt

1 kg mixed tomatoes

small handful of tarragon leaves, roughly chopped

2 tablespoons extra-virgin olive oil

1 tablespoon red wine vinegar

Mix the onion with 1 teaspoon of sea salt in a small bowl. Use your hands to really get the salt in there – this will help to subdue the sharpness of the raw onion. Set aside for 10 minutes, then squeeze out any excess moisture and transfer to a large bowl.

Cut any large tomatoes into quarters, halve the smaller ones and leave any very small ones whole. Add the tomato to the onion along with the tarragon and gently mix everything together to combine.

Whisk the olive oil and vinegar together with a generous pinch of salt. Pour the dressing over the salad and serve.

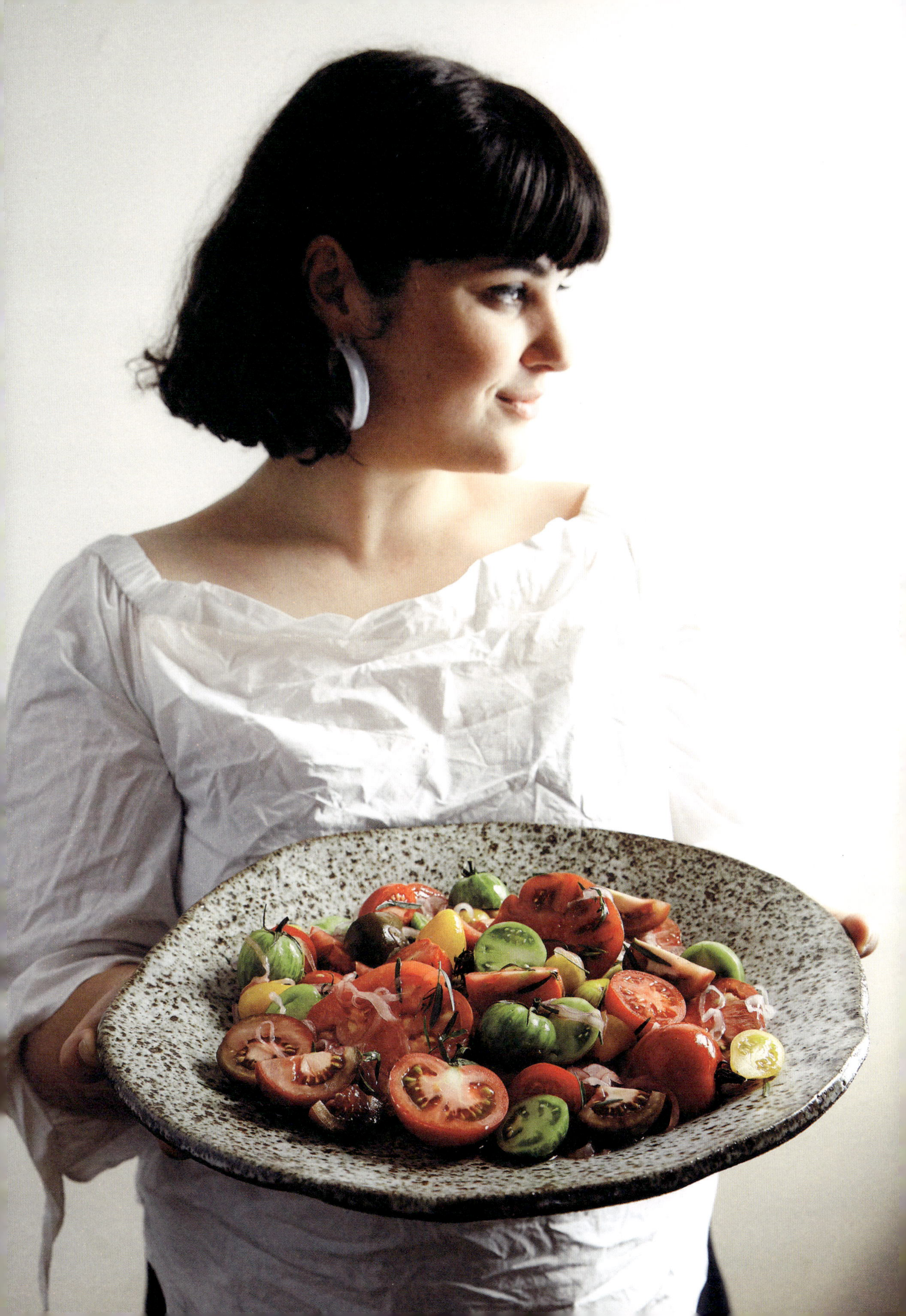

A DEPENDABLE CABBAGE SALAD

SERVES 4–6

This refreshing cabbage salad is well loved in our family. It's barely a recipe, and there is lots of room for interpretation. Blanched peas could be added, different herbs, fresh chilli – adapt it to suit your style and preference.

40 g (½ cup) flaked almonds

¼ white cabbage, finely shredded

large handful of flat-leaf parsley leaves, torn

large handful of basil leaves, torn

large handful of mint leaves, torn

50 g parmesan, shaved

60 ml (¼ cup) extra-virgin olive oil

juice of 1 lemon

1 tablespoon good-quality mayonnaise (see Caper Mayonnaise recipe page 164, but omit the capers if desired)

2 tablespoons plain yoghurt

sea salt

Toast the almonds in a small, dry frying pan over a low heat until just coloured. Set aside to cool.

Combine the cabbage, herbs, parmesan and two-thirds of the almonds in a large bowl.

Whisk together the olive oil, lemon juice, mayonnaise and yoghurt in a small bowl. Drizzle over the salad and use your hands to mix it well. Season to taste and scatter with the remaining almonds before serving.

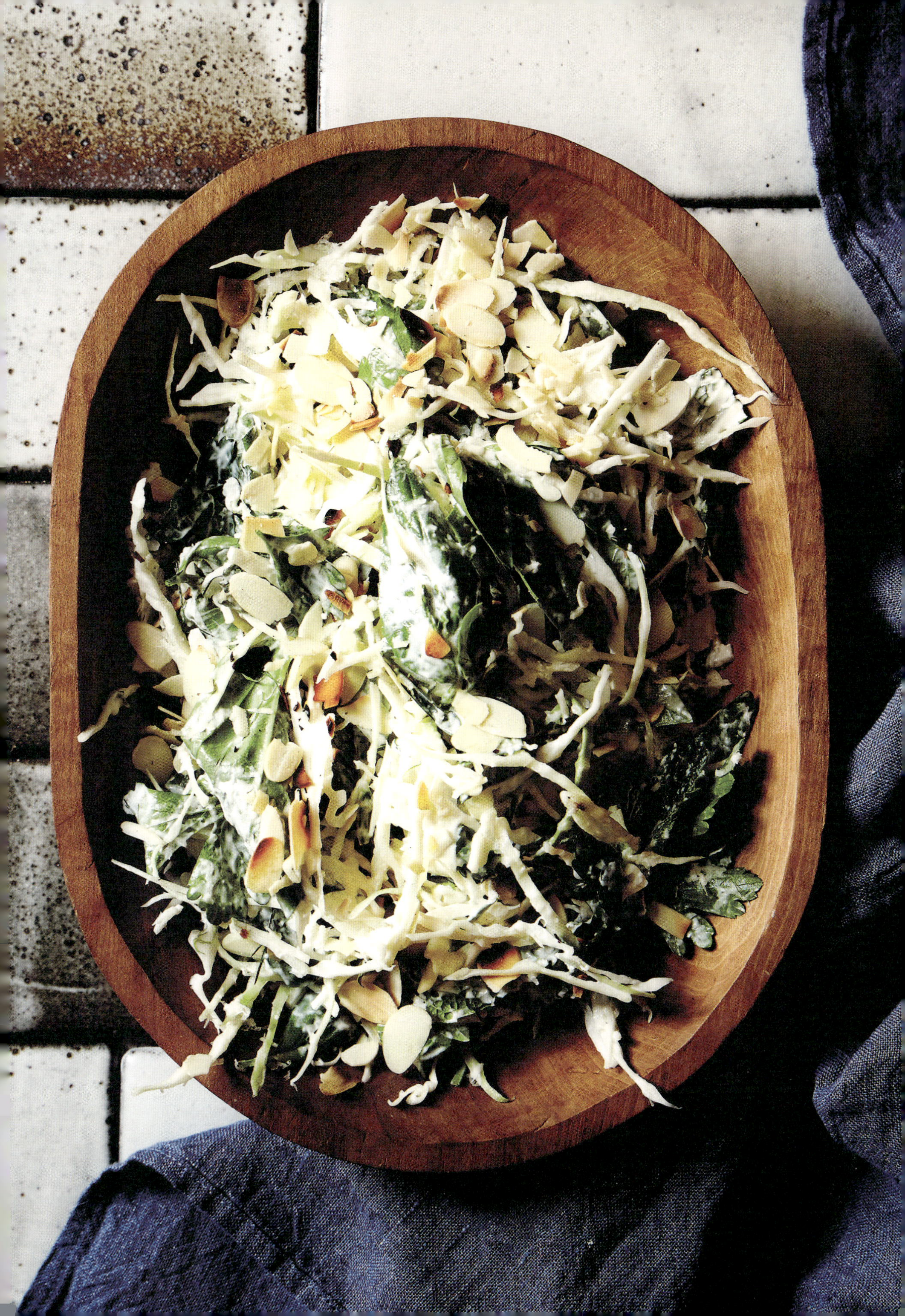

FIGS WITH HONEY AND LABNEH

SERVES 4

Labneh is yoghurt that has been strained to remove the whey, which results in a lovely thick, creamy texture, while retaining the distinctive sour taste of yoghurt. It is perfect in this simple salad, acting as a base for the figs, almonds and basil. I like to make a larger batch, as it lasts well in the fridge – this recipe makes the required amount for the salad, but feel free to double the recipe and hang 1 kg of yoghurt so that you have leftovers. Choose figs that are ripe, but not too soft.

500 g plain yoghurt

30 g (⅓ cup) flaked almonds

6–8 figs (about 300 g in total), cut in half or into quarters

10 basil leaves

HONEY DRESSING

1 tablespoon extra-virgin olive oil, plus extra if needed

1 tablespoon honey, plus extra if needed

sea salt and black pepper

To make the labneh, line a sieve with a clean piece of muslin or cheesecloth. Spoon in the yoghurt, then bring the edges of the muslin together and tie with some string to secure. It should resemble a sack. To hang, you can either suspend the tied-up yoghurt from a hook or similar, or tie the ends of the muslin to a long wooden spoon and prop up with some tall jars. Place a bowl underneath to catch the whey. The thickness of the labneh will depend on how long you leave it to strain. I prefer it to be not too firm for this salad, so I leave it for just 3–4 hours at room temperature, but if you want it to be thick, leave it to strain overnight in the fridge. Unwrap the cloth and transfer the labneh to an airtight container. The labneh will keep in the fridge for up to 1 week.

Toast the almonds in a small, dry frying pan over a low heat until just coloured. Set aside to cool.

Spoon the labneh onto a serving plate and arrange the figs on top. Sprinkle with the almonds and basil leaves.

To make the dressing, whisk the olive oil and honey in a small bowl until combined. Taste for balance, adding a little more honey or olive oil if needed, and season to taste. Drizzle over the salad and serve.

VEGETABLES 76

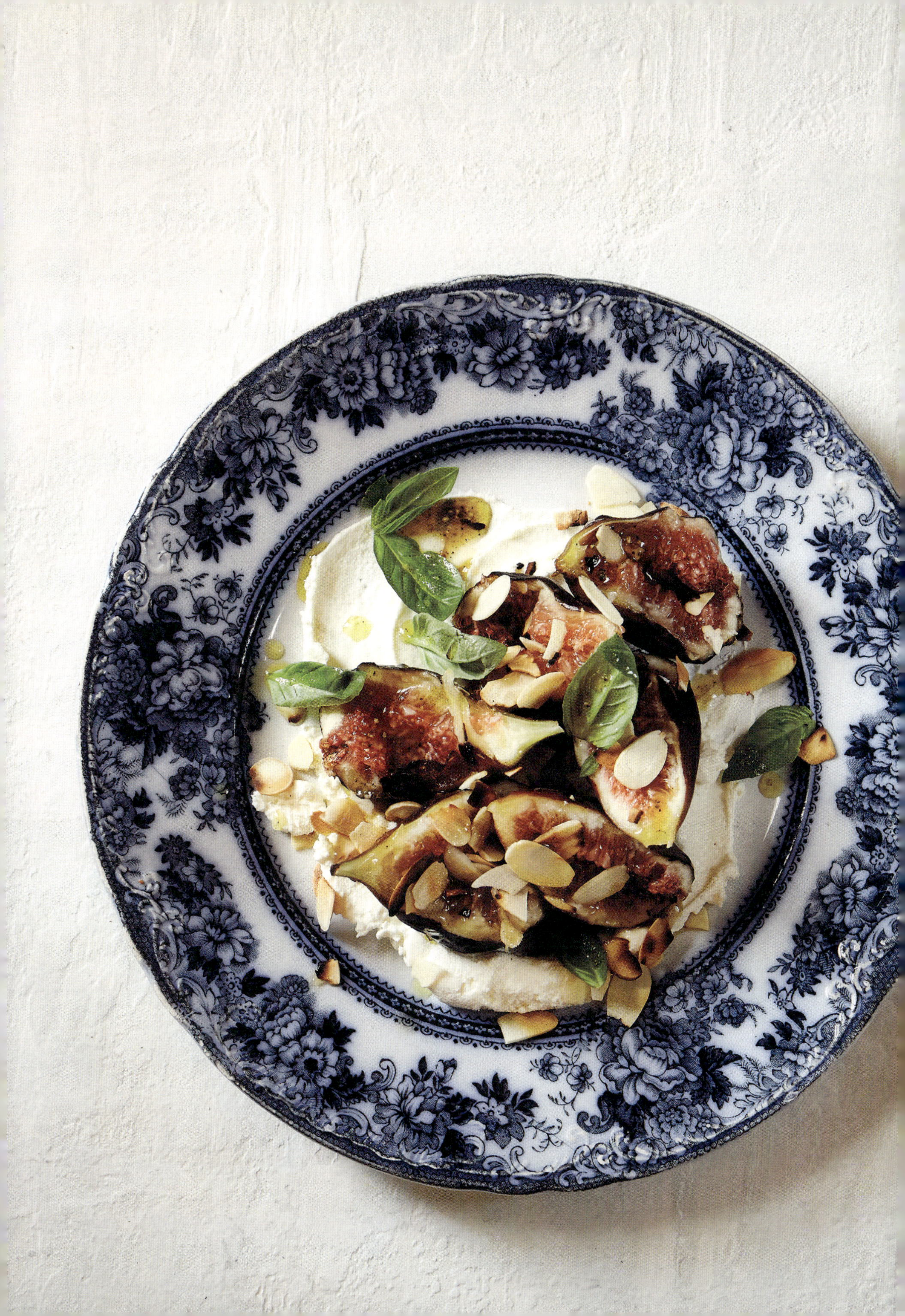

POTATO, LEEK AND MOZZARELLA PIE

SERVES 6–8

Made for sharing, this pie is real comfort food and it often finds its way onto our table. The olive oil pastry is really simple to prepare and crisps up wonderfully in the oven, while the inside becomes all perfumed and melty. Because of the olive oil, the pastry can be a little tricky to roll out perfectly, but that's almost part of its beauty. We always have some mozzarella in our fridge (the hard kind that keeps really well), just in case I want to make this pie – my standby when we want something hearty and filling. You could substitute the mozzarella for another melting cheese, such as fontina or asiago, and also add things like olives or anchovies for a real kick.

1 kg nicola or other waxy potatoes

1 tablespoon extra-virgin olive oil

15 g unsalted butter

2 leeks, white and light green parts only, finely sliced and washed

sea salt

1½ tablespoons finely chopped woody herbs (I like to use 2 teaspoons each of three different herbs, such as marjoram, sage, oregano, thyme or rosemary)

small bunch of flat-leaf parsley, leaves picked and roughly chopped

½ teaspoon dried chilli flakes

250 g mozzarella, cut into 2 cm chunks

1 egg, lightly beaten

OLIVE OIL PASTRY

400 g plain flour

pinch of sea salt

60 g chilled butter, cut into cubes

60 ml (¼ cup) extra-virgin olive oil

about 100 ml iced water

To make the pastry, combine the flour and salt in a large bowl. Add the butter, and rub into the flour using your fingertips until you have coarse crumbs. Pour in the olive oil and mix in enough iced water, a tablespoon at a time, until it comes together into a soft but not sticky dough. Turn out onto a clean work surface and bring the pastry together, gently kneading until a smooth dough has formed. Cover with a damp cloth or plastic wrap and refrigerate for at least 30 minutes.

Place the potatoes in a large saucepan and cover with cold water. Bring to the boil and cook over a medium–high heat for 25–30 minutes until just tender. Drain and set aside until cool enough to handle, then cut into 1–2 cm thick slices. Place in a large bowl and set aside.

Preheat the oven to 180°C. Line a baking tray with baking paper.

Heat the olive oil and butter in a large frying pan over a low heat. Add the leek and a pinch of salt and sauté for 5 minutes until softened and beginning to caramelise. Stir in the herbs and chilli flakes. Add to the potatoes along with the mozzarella and gently combine to coat. Season to taste.

Divide the pastry dough in two and, on a lightly floured work surface, roll one piece into a circle shape about 30 cm wide and about 5 mm thick. Place on the prepared baking tray and arrange the potato mixture on top, leaving a 1 cm border of pastry all the way around. Whisk 1 teaspoon of water into the egg to make a wash, and brush around the pastry border. Roll out the second piece of pastry to about the same size and shape (although it can be a little thinner). Lay over the top and seal the edges with your fingers in a rough crimping action. Brush the top of the pie with the remaining egg wash and poke a hole in the centre of the pie using a small, sharp knife to allow steam to escape during cooking. Bake for 30–35 minutes until the pastry is crisp and golden. Serve warm.

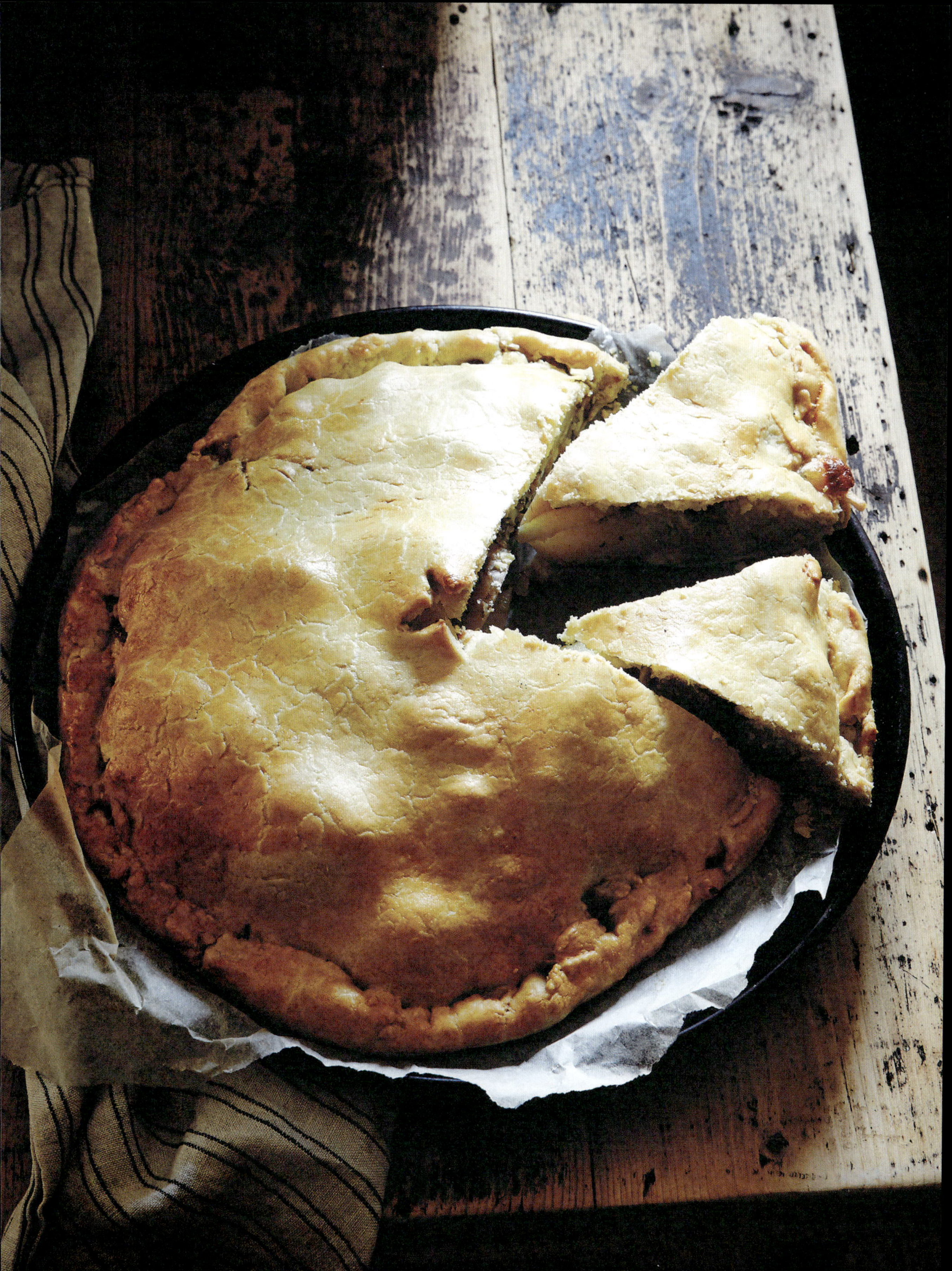

CHEESE AND ONION PIE

SERVES 6

Onions cooked slowly and gently bring the most amazing flavour to this pie – a subtle natural sweetness that cuts through the rich cheeses. I like to make this for picnics as it travels really well and is delicious cold. The pastry is rather delicate to work with, so be extra gentle when rolling it out. But rips and tears can be easily fixed with scrap pieces of dough, and I think the more homemade it looks, the better.

2½ tablespoons extra-virgin olive oil

3 onions, finely sliced

3 thyme sprigs, leaves picked

3 garlic cloves, roughly chopped

sea salt

2½ tablespoons pure cream

2 eggs

100 g fontina, broken into pieces

150 g asiago, grated

70 g provolone, grated

handful of flat-leaf parsley leaves, finely chopped

SOUR CREAM PASTRY

300 g plain flour

pinch of sea salt

50 g chilled butter, cut into 2 cm cubes

2½ tablespoons extra-virgin olive oil

60 g (¼ cup) sour cream

about 60 ml (¼ cup) iced water

To make the pastry, combine the flour and salt in a large bowl. Add the butter and rub into the flour using your fingertips until you have coarse crumbs. Pour in the olive oil and sour cream and incorporate using a spoon or your hands. Mix in enough iced water, a tablespoon at a time, until the dough just comes together. Form into a flat discs, cover with plastic wrap and refrigerate for at least 30 minutes.

Preheat the oven to 180°C. Line a baking tray with baking paper.

Heat the olive oil in a large pan over a very low heat. Add the onion, thyme, garlic and a pinch of salt and cook for 20–30 minutes, stirring often, until the onion is a light golden colour. Transfer to a large bowl.

Whisk the cream with one of the eggs in a small bowl. Add to the onions along with the cheeses and parsley. Season to taste (remember the cheeses will be fairly salty) and mix well.

On a lightly floured work surface, roll the pasty into a rough circle shape about 30 cm wide and about 5 mm thick, patching up any holes or tears as you go. Place on the prepared baking tray and pile the cheese into the middle of the pastry, leaving at least a 5 cm border of pastry all the way around. Trim any excess pastry.

Beat the remaining egg with 1 teaspoon of water. Working with a small section at a time, fold the edges over towards the middle, pleating the pastry as you work your way around the circle. Squeeze the edges together as you go, using a little of the egg wash if necessary. Brush the pastry with the remaining egg wash and bake for 45 minutes until the pastry and cheese are golden.

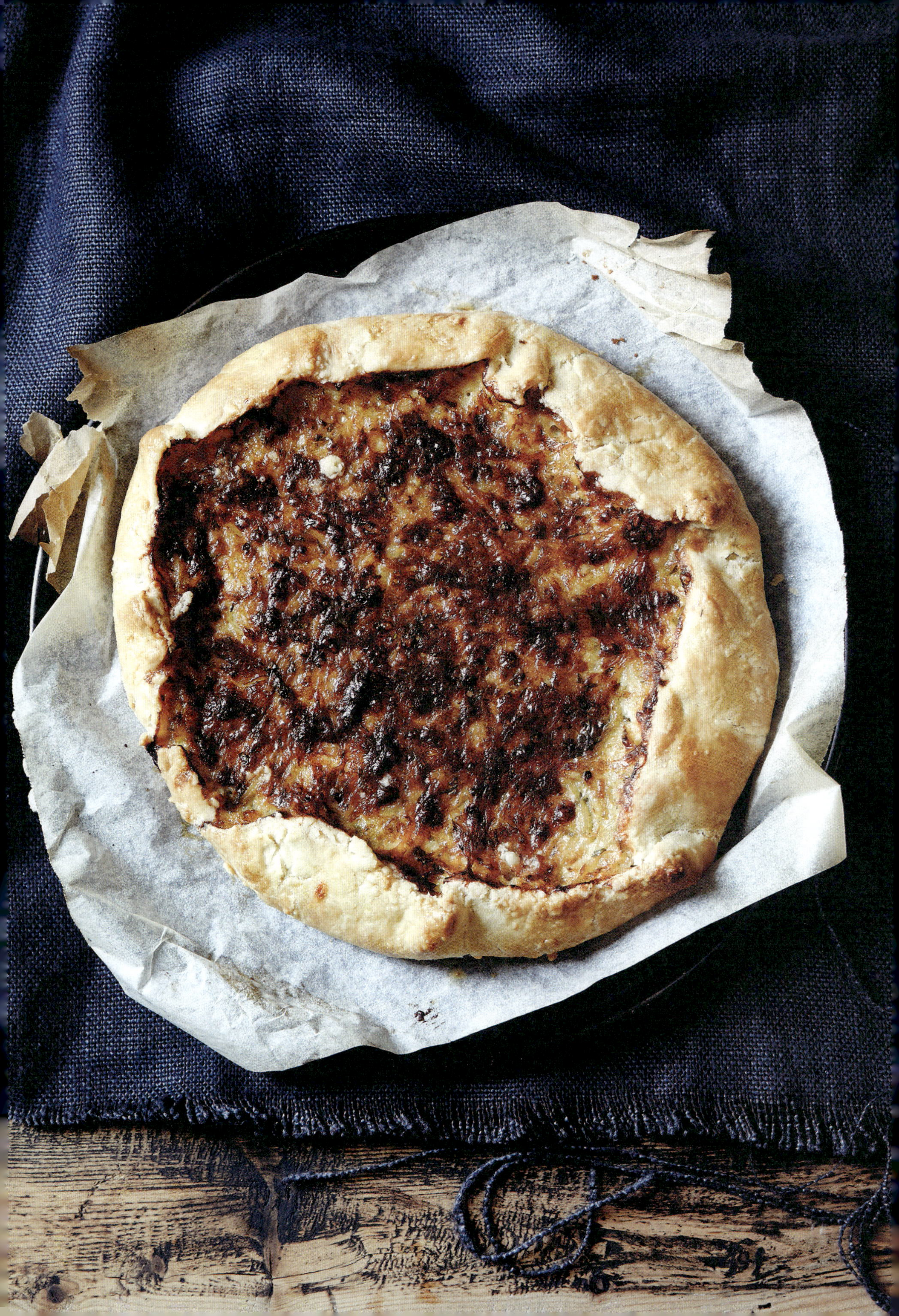

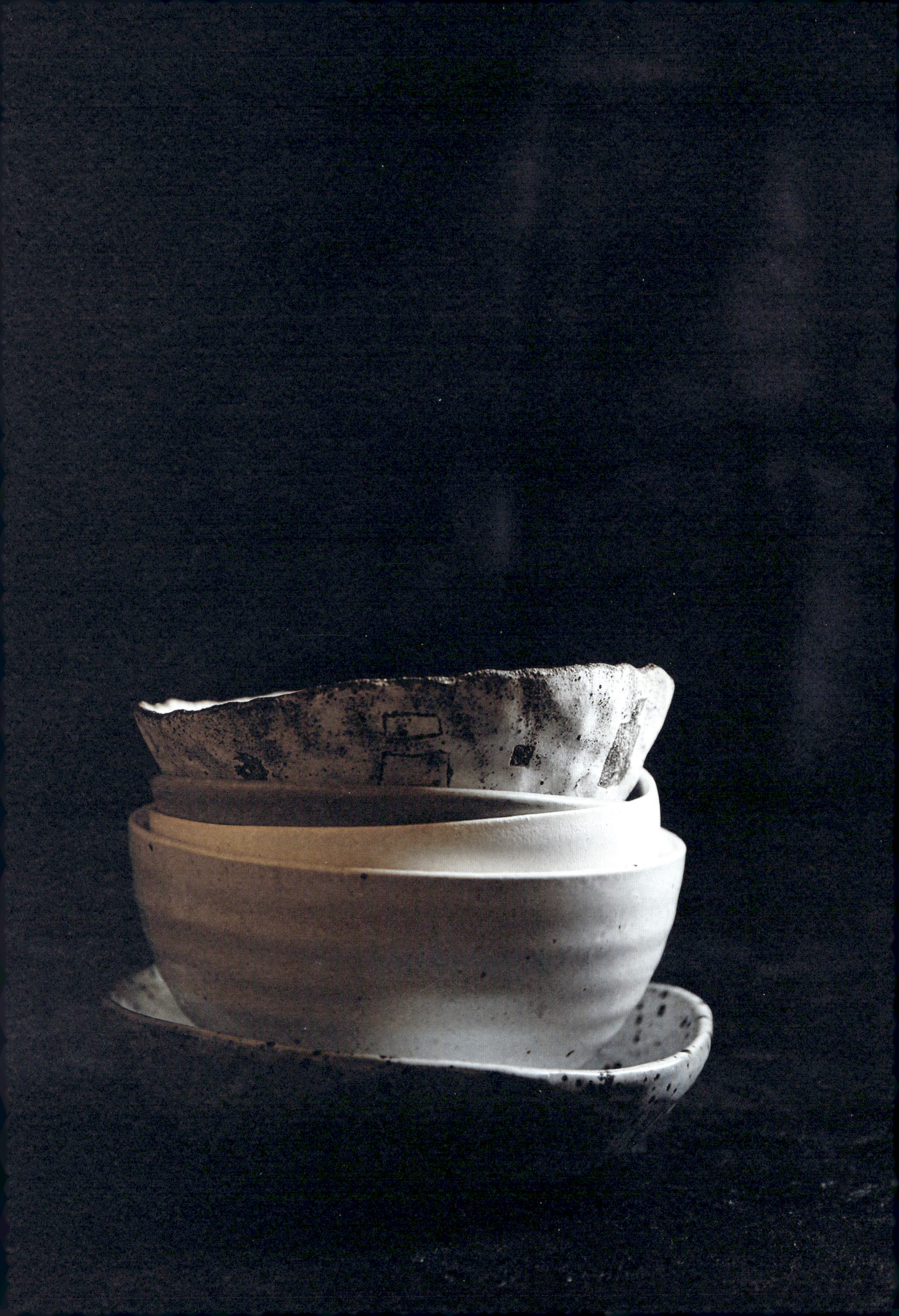

SOUP

Soup is the epitome of comfort food and, year round, it's something I love to cook and eat. Although simple to make, their flavours can be complex and enriched with the addition of homemade broth to give depth and nourishment. A soup bubbling away on the stove in the afternoon yields the promise of a hearty and satisfying meal to come, something that rarely fails to deliver. While soups certainly bring much-needed gratification in the winter time, they can be equally satisfying during the warmer months, and can be made with minimal fuss and effort.

RIBOLLITA

SERVES 6–8

Literally meaning 'reboiled', *ribollita* is a traditional Tuscan soup. Thick and robust, brimming with beans, cavolo nero and bread – it is hands down my very favourite soup. Ribollita never disappoints, and always satisfies. While studying in Florence, I was taught to make this soup by my landlord, Daniela. My recipe has evolved a little since then, so I am sure you will make it your own too. Just be sure to take your time when sautéing the aromatics, and use day-old crusty bread and the best quality olive oil you can afford for that final drizzle. You can use vegetable stock, or even water, instead of chicken stock – just be sure to adjust the seasoning accordingly.

1 tablespoon extra-virgin olive oil, plus extra for drizzling

120 g flat pancetta, cut into lardons

1 carrot, finely diced

2 celery stalks, finely diced

1 onion, finely diced

3 garlic cloves, roughly chopped

2 fresh bay leaves

½ teaspoon dried chilli flakes

sea salt

500 ml (2 cups) chicken stock (see recipe page 105), plus extra if needed

1 × 800 g can whole peeled tomatoes

1 bunch of cavolo nero, tough stems removed, leaves washed thoroughly and roughly chopped

250 g canned or cooked cannellini beans, drained and rinsed (see note on page 21)

4–6 slices of day-old crusty bread (about 300 g in total), roughly torn

grated parmesan, to serve (optional)

Heat the olive oil in a large saucepan over a low–medium heat. Add the pancetta, carrot, celery, onion, garlic, bay leaves, chilli flakes and a pinch of salt and sauté for 10–15 minutes, stirring occasionally, until soft and fragrant.

Add the stock, 500 ml (2 cups) of water and the tomatoes. Leave to simmer for 20–30 minutes, partially covered with a lid and stirring occasionally. It should still be quite broth-like at this stage, so top up with more stock or water if needed. Add the cavolo nero and the beans to the soup and cook for a further 15 minutes.

Add the bread to the soup, making sure the pieces are submerged. At this point, the soup will be really thick, so if you like your soup with a bit more liquid, add some more stock or water. Cook for just a few minutes or until the bread has softened, then season with salt.

Ladle the soup into bowls and serve with a generous grating of parmesan, if using, and a drizzle of olive oil.

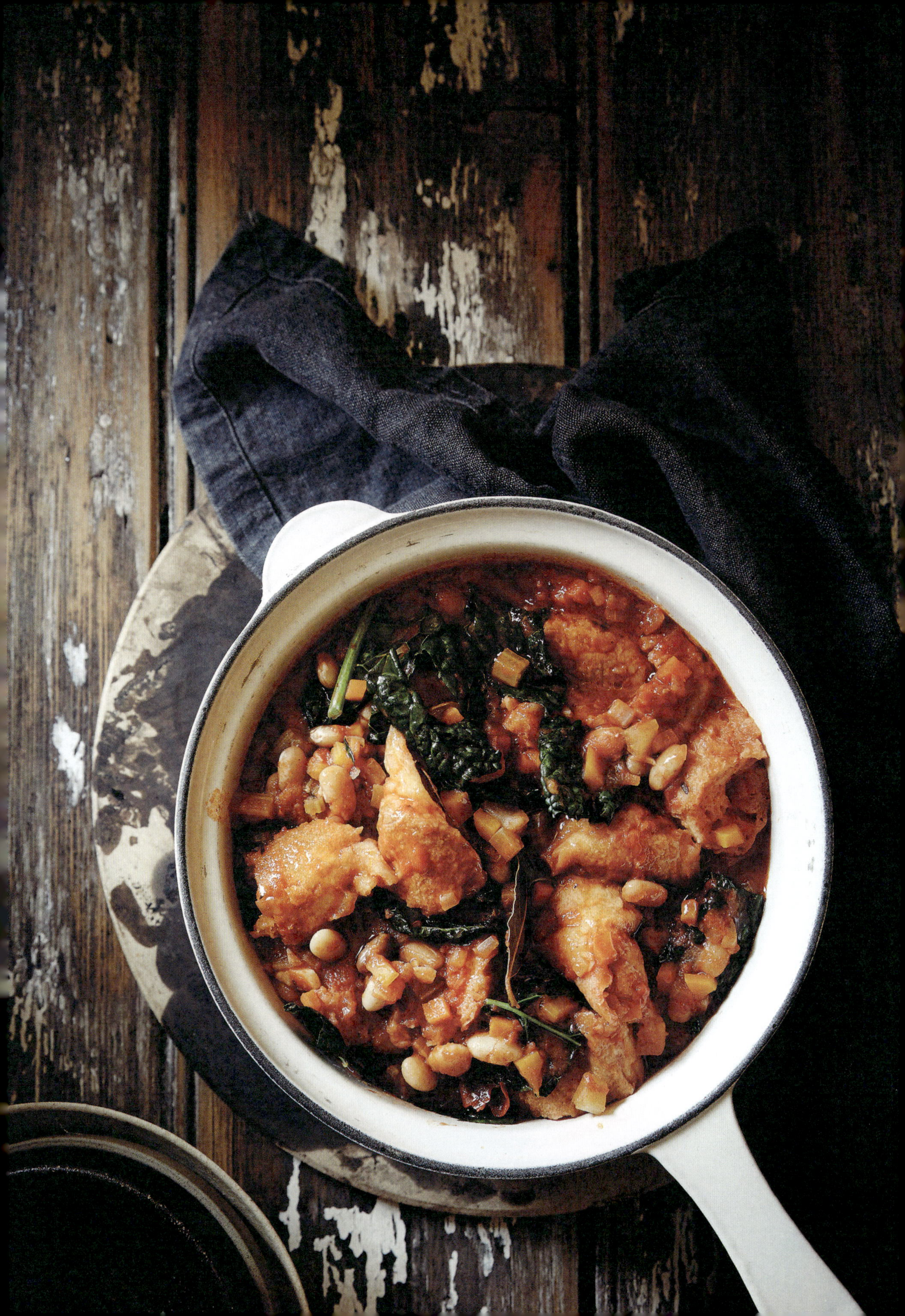

CHICKEN BROTH WITH WHEAT AND SPRING VEGETABLES

· ❦ SERVES 4 ❦ ·

With its beautiful broad beans, peas and nutty wheat grain, this broth is a lovely way to celebrate spring. Feel free to substitute the wheat for other grains, such as spelt, buckwheat or farro. Similarly, use whichever vegetables are in season; just be sure to keep an eye on them and adjust the cooking times to suit.

200 g whole wheat grains (see note on page 68)

1 tablespoon extra-virgin olive oil

1 leek, white and light green parts only, finely sliced and washed

1 celery stalk, finely chopped

sea salt

2 garlic cloves, roughly chopped

1 litre chicken stock (see recipe page 105)

500 g skinless chicken thighs

150 g shelled broad beans

100 g shelled fresh peas

black pepper

HERB OIL

1 garlic clove, peeled

large handful of mint leaves

large handful of flat-leaf parsley leaves

juice of ½ lemon

about 100 ml extra-virgin olive oil

sea salt

For the herb oil, finely chop the garlic and herbs together on a board. Transfer to a small bowl, squeeze in the lemon juice and drizzle in enough olive oil to give the sauce a pourable consistency. Season with salt and set aside.

Cook the wheat in a saucepan of boiling water over a medium–high heat for 20–25 minutes or until al dente. Drain and set aside.

Meanwhile, heat the olive oil in a large saucepan over a low heat. Add the leek, celery and a pinch of salt and gently fry for 7–8 minutes until soft and translucent. Add the garlic and cook for another 1–2 minutes. Pour in the chicken stock and bring to the boil. Reduce to a simmer and add the chicken thighs. Poach the chicken for about 12 minutes until just cooked, then remove and set aside until cool enough to handle. Shred the chicken into large pieces and set aside until ready to use.

Bring a saucepan of water to the boil. Add the broad beans, boil for a few minutes, then drain and set aside to cool. Peel off and discard the outer layer of the beans.

Add the wheat to the simmering broth and cook for 5 minutes so the wheat takes on some of the broth flavour. Return the chicken to the broth and add the peas and broad beans. Simmer for 2–3 minutes or until the peas and broad beans are just cooked. Season to taste then serve immediately, topped with spoonfuls of the herb oil.

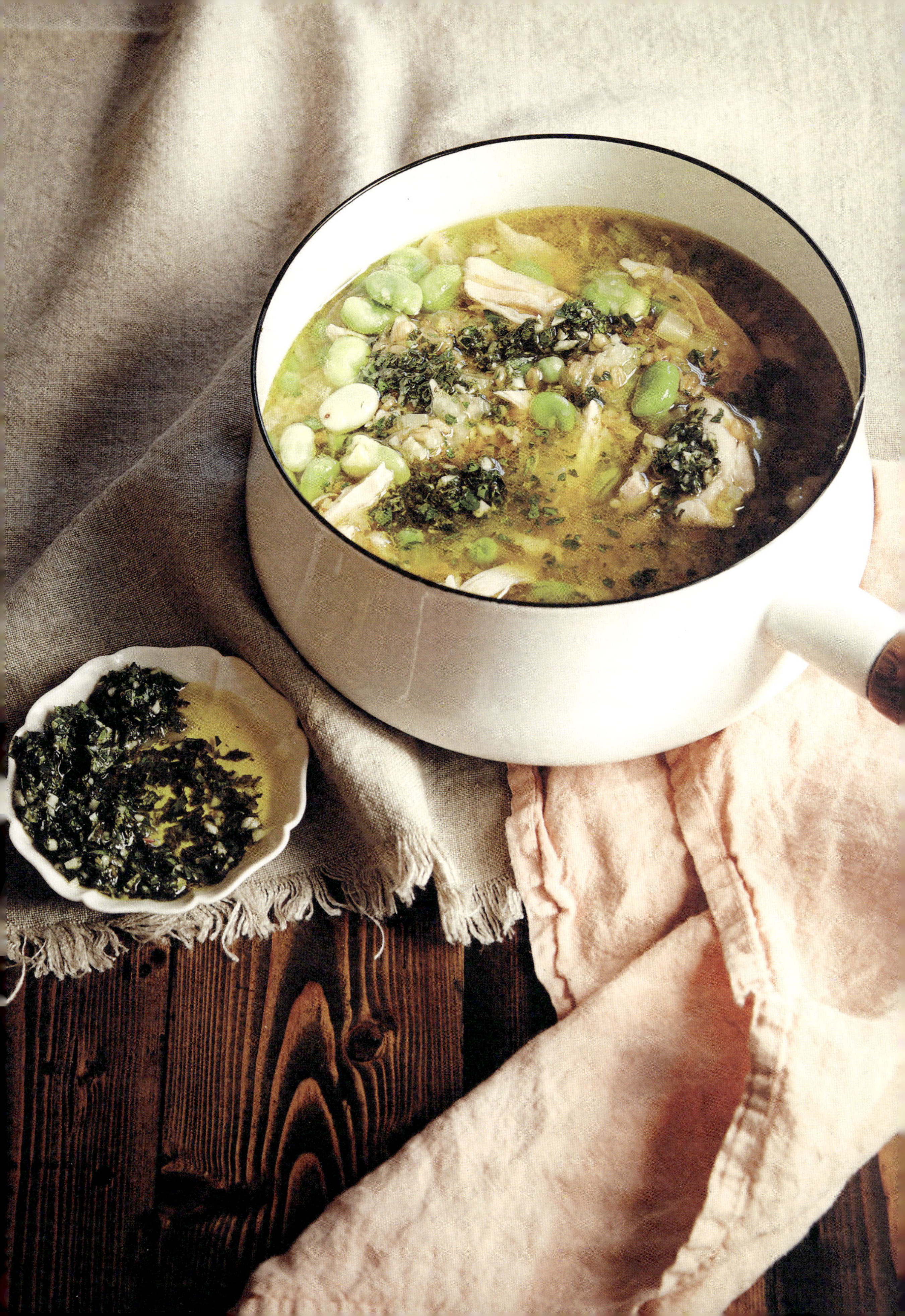

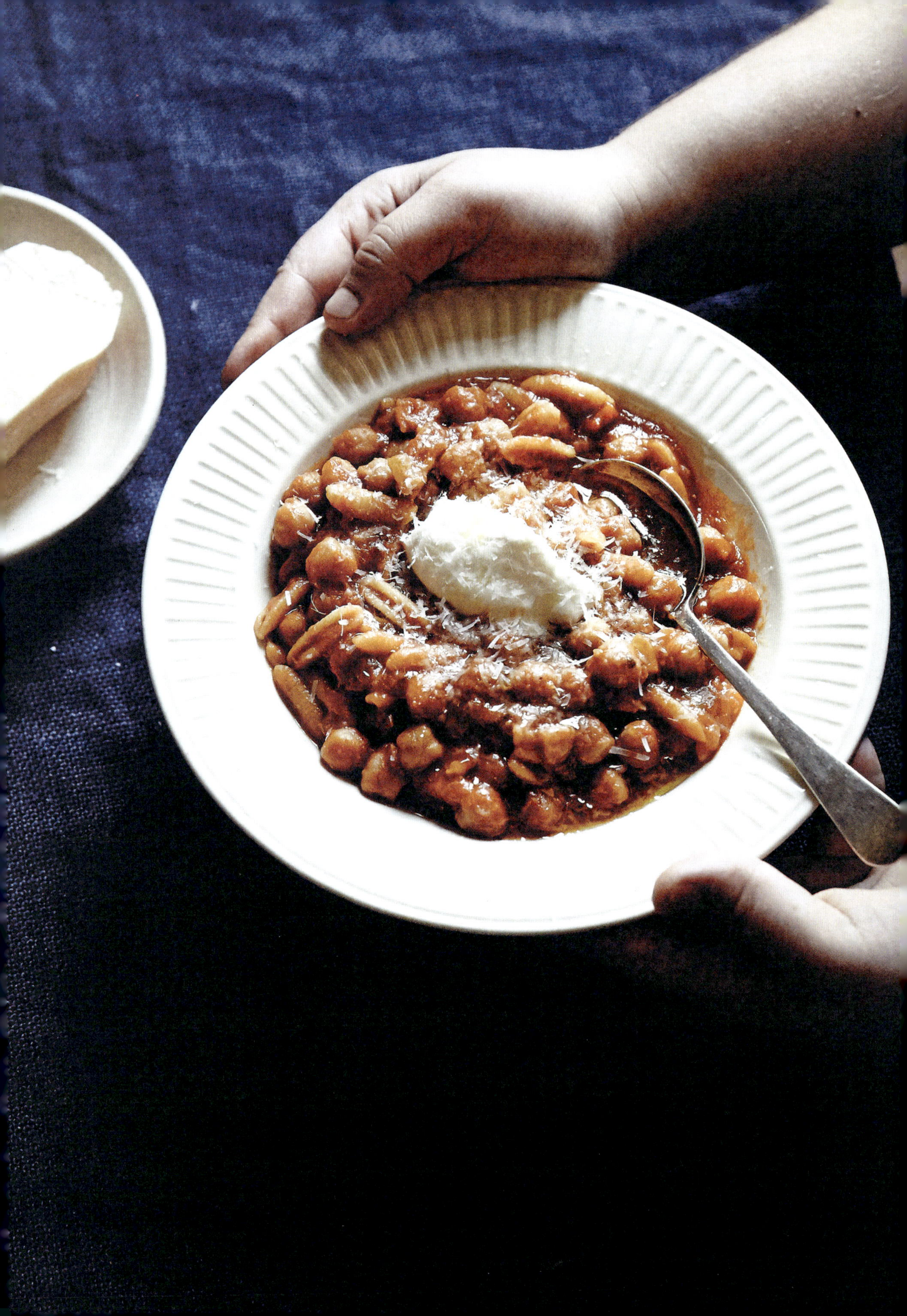

PASTA AND CHICKPEA SOUP

SERVES 4–6

This is my take on the classic *pasta e ceci*, which I am certain I almost entirely lived off when I was a rather poor student in Italy. While you can use canned chickpeas in this dish, I really think dried ones are the way to go here – they are, after all, the co-headlining act. Normally, some of the chickpeas are blended after cooking and added to the soup for creaminess, but on one occasion I decided to add some pumpkin and the addition has stuck – the pumpkin cooks down and becomes the thick, creamy element, which the blended chickpeas would usually provide. If you like, you can scoop out a cup or two of the chickpeas, blend until smooth and return it to the pot. The crème fraîche is a decadent but very delicious extra.

250 g dried chickpeas

1½ tablespoons extra-virgin olive oil, plus extra for drizzling

1 onion, finely chopped

1 celery stalk, roughly chopped

2 garlic cloves, peeled

sea salt

pinch of dried chilli flakes

2 rosemary sprigs

1 × 400 g can whole peeled tomatoes

1 litre chicken stock (see recipe page 105), vegetable stock (see recipe page 104) or water

350 g pumpkin, peeled and cut into 2 cm pieces

150 g short pasta, such as gnocchetti or ditalini

crème fraîche, to serve

grated parmesan, to serve

Place the chickpeas in a large bowl and cover with cold water to soak for at least 4 hours or overnight.

Heat the olive oil in a heavy-based saucepan over a low heat and add the onion, celery, garlic cloves and a pinch of salt. Cook for 10–15 minutes, stirring every minute or so, until soft and fragrant. Sprinkle in the chilli flakes and add the rosemary. Give everything a stir and cook for a further minute. Add in the tomatoes and turn the heat up to medium. Stir and simmer for 1–2 minutes.

Drain and rinse the chickpeas and add to the soup along with the stock or water and the pumpkin. Bring to the boil, then reduce the heat, cover and simmer for 1–1½ hours until the chickpeas are tender. Check the soup regularly, breaking up the pumpkin and tomatoes with the back of a wooden spoon and topping up with water if necessary. The soup should be very thick, so don't add too much water throughout the cooking – just enough to keep it from drying out. It shouldn't be at all broth-like.

When the chickpeas are tender, add the pasta and continue to simmer the soup for 10–12 minutes or until the pasta is al dente. Season to taste.

Remove and discard the rosemary stalks and serve the soup in bowls, topped with a dollop of crème fraîche, a scattering of parmesan and a good drizzle of nice extra-virgin olive oil.

BREAD AND ONION SOUP WITH GRUYERE

SERVES 6

When I was a child, I remember being so impressed by my mum being able to turn a pile of sliced onions into a soup as delicious and luxurious as this. Now that I fully understand the greatness of the brown onion, that awe is more a deep appreciation of a humble, yet vital, ingredient. This soup is my take on my mum's take on the classic French onion soup. I add the bread directly to the soup, cover it in cheese and then cook it all in the oven. Bring the bubbling soup to the table and serve it there for the full effect.

100 g butter, roughly chopped

2 kg onions, cut in half and very finely sliced

sea salt

70 ml brandy

1 teaspoon plain flour

1 litre beef stock (see recipe page 105)

1 fresh bay leaf

8 thyme sprigs

1–2 teaspoons red wine vinegar

black pepper

4–6 thick slices of day-old crusty bread

1 garlic clove, cut in half

3 thyme sprigs, leaves picked

220 g gruyere cheese, grated

Melt the butter in a large ovenproof saucepan over a medium heat. When the butter begins to foam, add the onion and a pinch of salt and stir to coat. Reduce to a low–medium heat and cook for 30–40 minutes, stirring occasionally, until the onions are caramelised and nicely golden. (You can do this in two batches if your pan isn't big enough.) Add the brandy and cook for a few minutes until the liquid has evaporated a little.

Preheat the oven to 180°C.

Combine the flour with a little of the stock and mix so there are no lumps. Add to the onions and cook for a minute or two, stirring constantly. Add the remaining stock, the bay leaf and 5 thyme sprigs and simmer for a further 20 minutes or until the soup is rich in colour. Add the red wine vinegar and season to taste (make sure you taste the soup before adding salt).

Rub each slice of bread with the cut side of the garlic clove. Arrange the bread over the soup, overlapping the slices a little if necessary. Pick the leaves from the remaining thyme sprigs. Sprinkle the bread with the thyme and cheese and bake for 10–15 minutes or until the cheese is bubbling and the edges of the bread are crunchy.

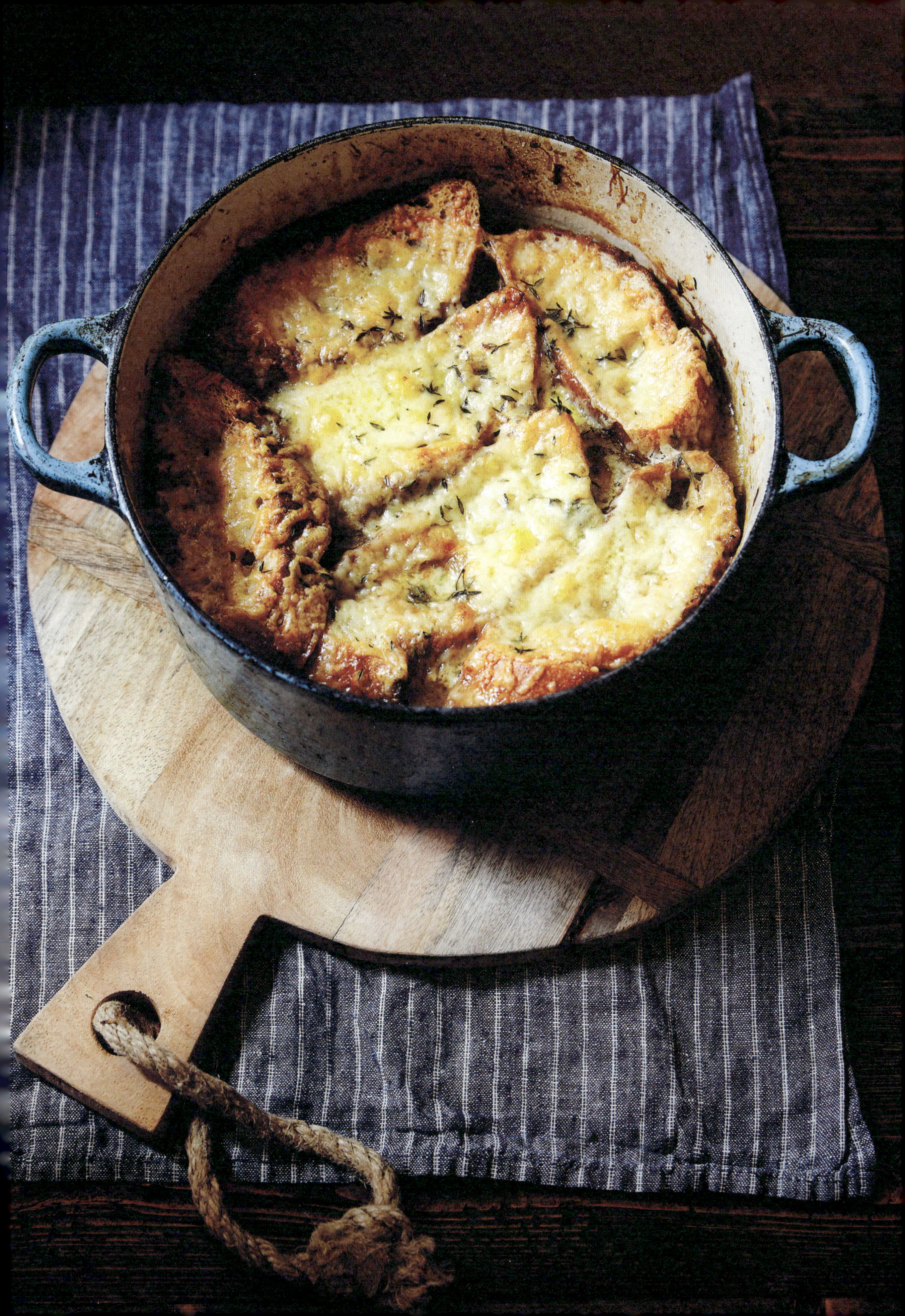

ALJOTTA – MY GRANDMOTHER'S FISH SOUP

SERVES 4–6

I only know it's her soup because when my mother taught me how to make it, every instruction would be prefaced with, 'Well, my mum would …'. I wish I had eaten my grandmother's soup as made by her, but it wasn't to be. Some details remain a little fuzzy – since she couldn't write, the recipe was never formally recorded. My mum recounts just observing my grandmother in the kitchen – blanching the tomatoes, making the broth, separating the meat from the bones. But I suppose that is what's so wonderful about food and memories – as a recipe changes hands and trickles down to the next generation, details blur and each maker is encouraged to use their own instincts and tastes. I've adapted this popular Maltese soup somewhat and made the stock separately, to avoid small bones in the soup. My mum suggested I reserve the meat from the fish I used to make the stock and add it to the soup at the end, because fish cooked on the bone is more giving of flavour – a wonderful piece of advice. I hope you make this recipe your own, too.

500 g roma tomatoes

2 tablespoons extra-virgin olive oil

1 onion, finely chopped

8 garlic cloves, finely chopped

sea salt

1.2 litres fish stock (see recipe page 104), plus any reserved meat from making the stock

125 g medium-grain rice

350 g skinless snapper fillets, cut into 3 cm pieces

large handful of mint leaves, finely chopped

large handful of flat-leaf parsley leaves, finely chopped

black pepper

lemon wedges, to serve

Score a cross in the base of each tomato using a sharp knife. Place in a saucepan or large heatproof bowl and cover with boiling water. Set aside for 5 minutes, then drain the tomatoes and remove the skins. Remove any tough stems from the insides of the tomatoes and roughly chop the flesh. Set aside.

In a large saucepan, heat the olive oil over a low–medium heat, add the onion, garlic and a pinch of salt and sauté for 10 minutes or until soft and translucent. Add the tomatoes and any juice to the pot and simmer for 2–3 minutes to amalgamate the aromatics and tomatoes. Add the stock and simmer for 10 minutes, stirring occasionally. Add the rice and cook for 8–10 minutes until al dente. Add the fish and continue to simmer for 3–4 minutes or until the fish is just cooked through. Stir in most of the mint and parsley, reserving some for serving, as well as any reserved meat from making the fish stock (if there is any). Season with salt and pepper and serve sprinkled with the remaining herbs and with wedges of lemon alongside.

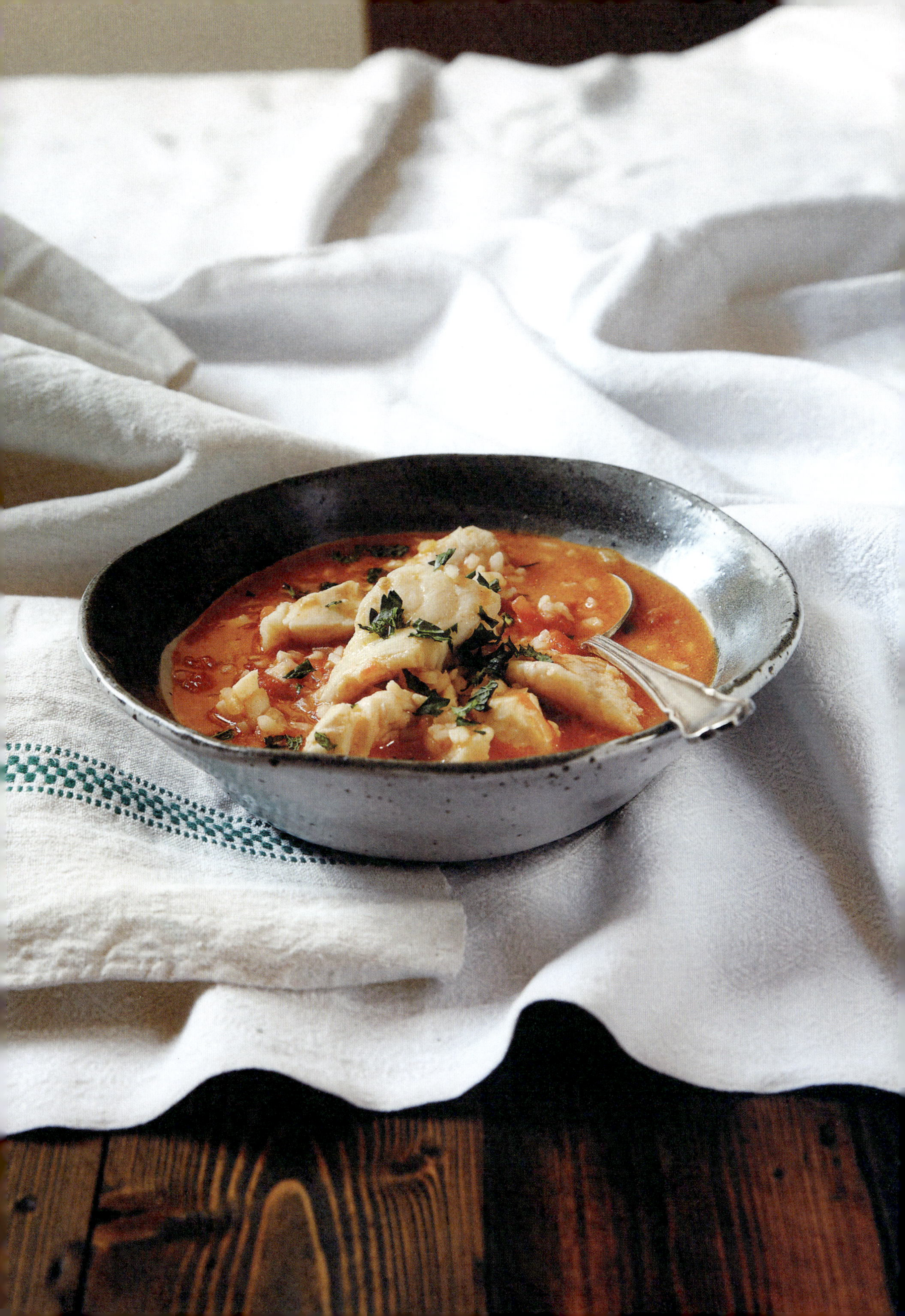

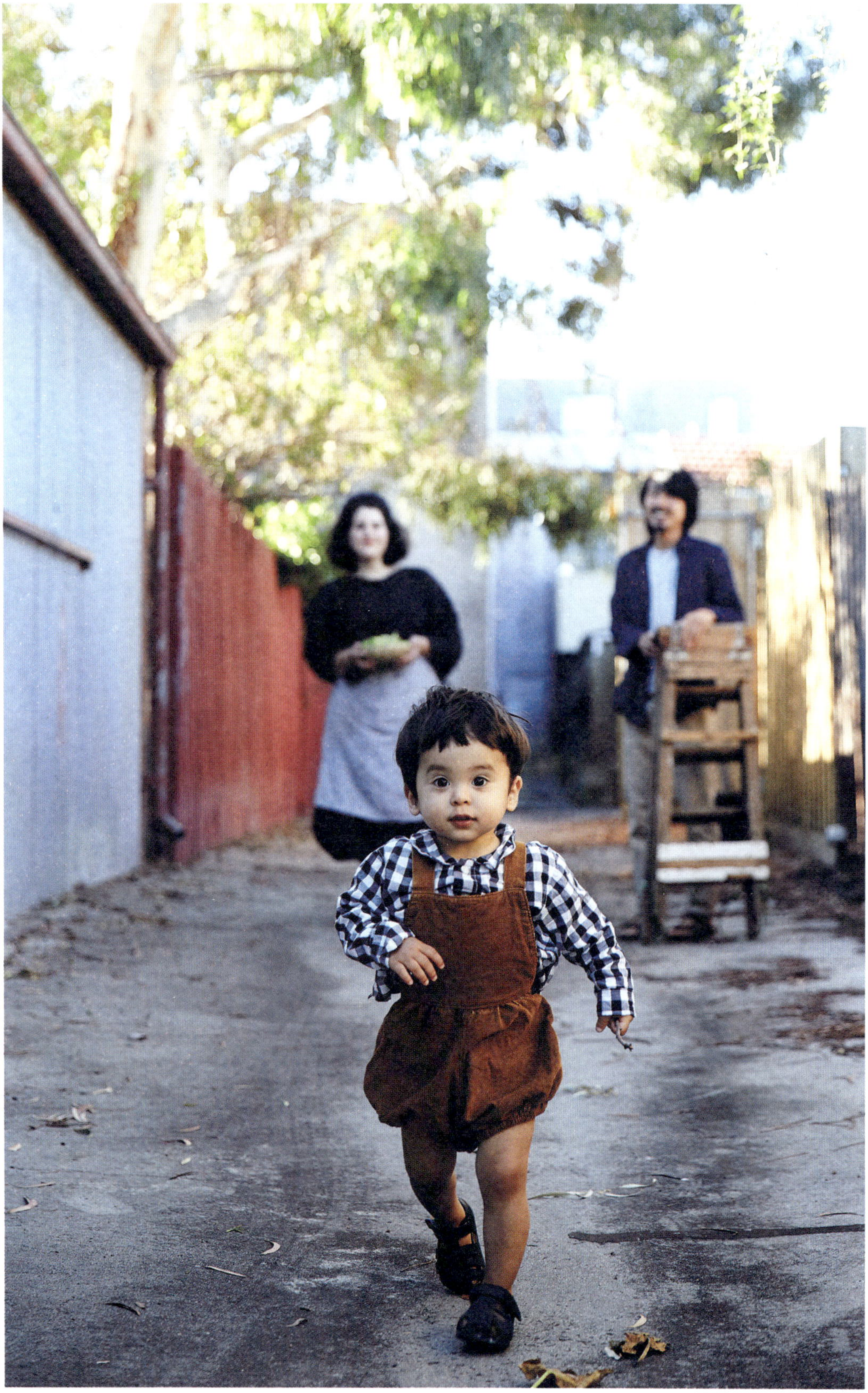

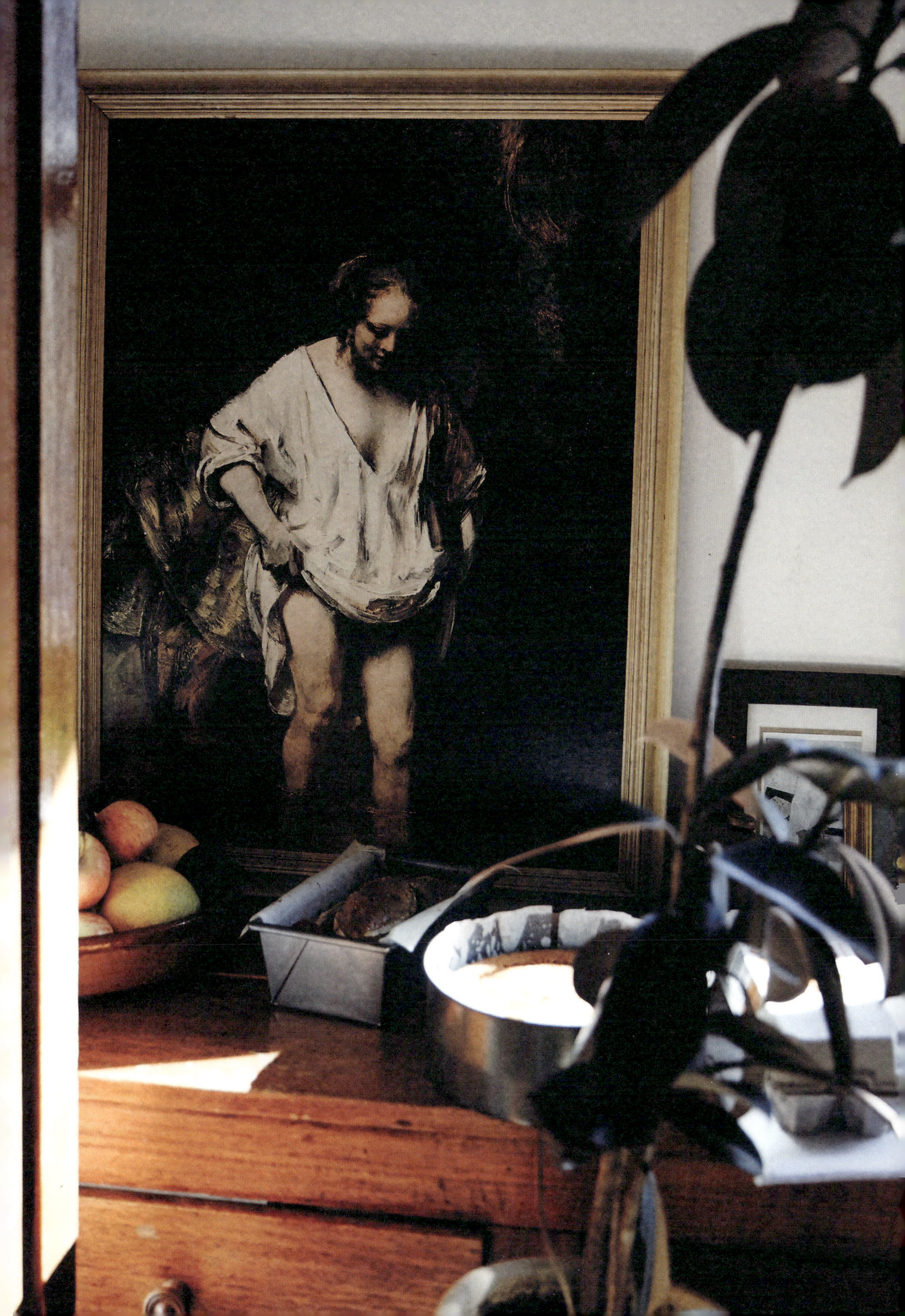

BARLEY, CAVOLO NERO AND BEEF BROTH

SERVES 4–6

Tough cuts of beef like shin, as I've used here, benefit from a long, slow cook. With a little love, they are the most flavourful and cost far less than the prime cuts. I like to use a dark beer in this broth, something like a stout or a dark ale, which adds lovely depth and richness. Sometimes, if I have them, I will add bones with marrow in them along with the meat, which gives the broth another layer of flavour.

25 g butter

2 tablespoons extra-virgin olive oil

2 onions, roughly chopped

sea salt

1 × 650 g boneless beef shin, cut into three pieces

250 ml (1 cup) dark beer, such as stout

200 g pearl barley

1 bunch of cavolo nero, tough stems removed, leaves washed thoroughly and roughly torn

black pepper

small handful of flat-leaf parsley leaves, roughly chopped

Melt the butter with half the olive oil in a large frying pan over a low heat. When the butter is foaming, add the onions and a pinch of salt and cook over a very low heat for 20–30 minutes, stirring occasionally, until soft and caramelised. Set aside.

Meanwhile, heat the remaining olive oil in a large saucepan over a medium–high heat. Add the pieces of beef and brown really well on all sides. Pour in the beer and bring to a simmer. Add 1.5 litres of water, bring to the boil then turn down the heat to low and simmer for about 3 hours or until the beef is tender. Check occasionally to ensure the beef is still covered, and top up with more water if necessary. Remove the beef, set aside until cool enough to handle, then shred into smaller pieces.

Meanwhile, add the pearl barley to the soup and simmer for 25–30 minutes, or until cooked. Add the cavolo nero along with the caramelised onions and shredded beef. Simmer for 4–5 minutes and season to taste. Ladle the soup into bowls and serve sprinkled with parsley.

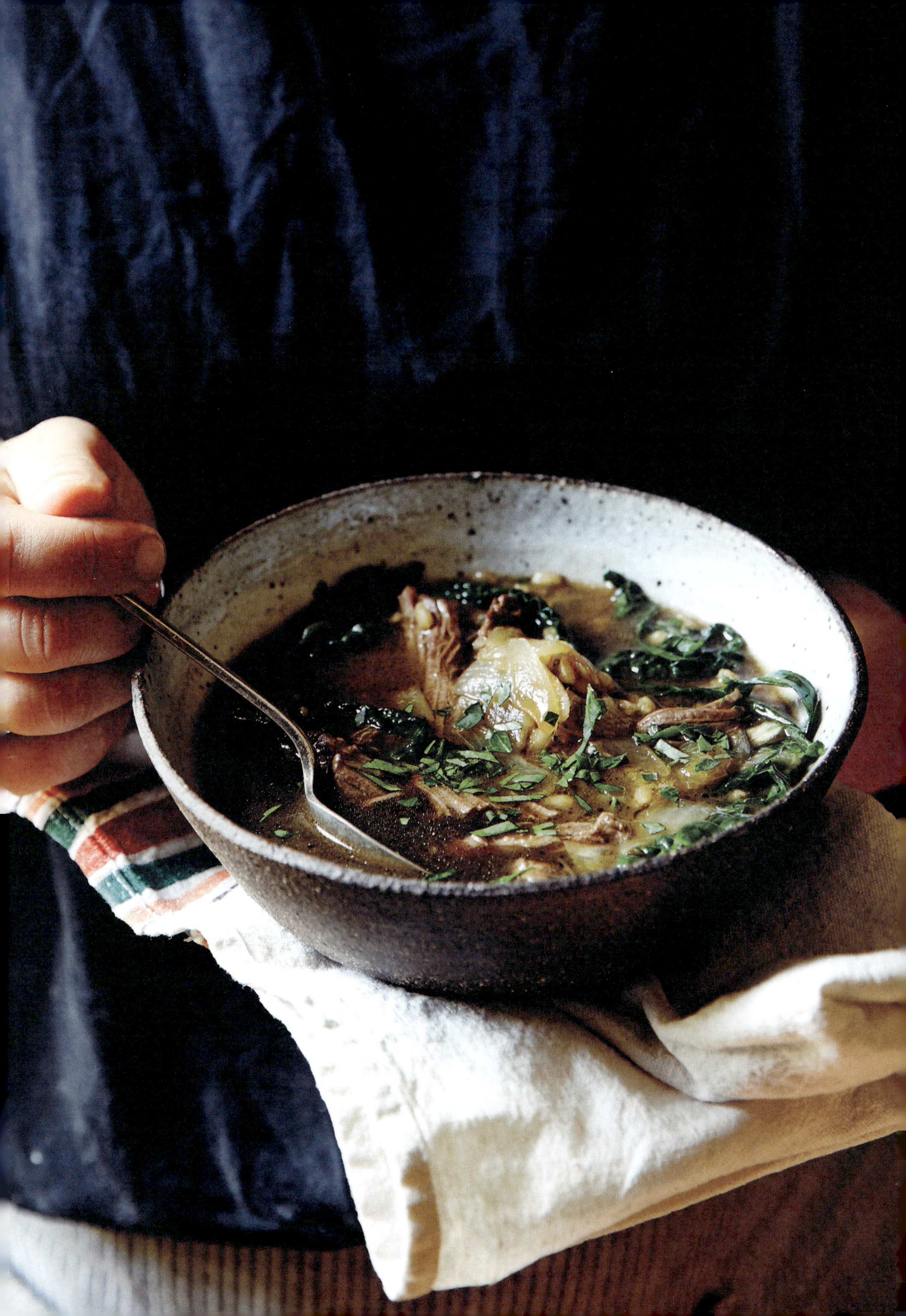

BORLOTTI BEAN SOUP WITH MALTAGLIATI

SERVES 4–6

Maltagliati, literally meaning 'poorly cut', are made from the offcuts of pasta dough left after preparing more precise shapes, such as tagliatelle or lasagne. I've included a recipe for a small quantity of pasta dough, in case you don't have any pasta scraps hanging around, or you can simply throw in 120 g of dried pasta, which will require a little longer cooking time. This soup is so nourishing and is made with basic ingredients, which are often in your kitchen. Before they are cooked, borlotti beans are beautifully patterned with streaks of magenta. They are a staple I unfailingly have at hand for their beauty and sustenance.

---

300 g dried borlotti beans

60 ml (¼ cup) extra-virgin olive oil, plus extra for drizzling

1 onion, finely chopped

1 celery stalk, finely chopped

1 carrot, finely chopped

sea salt

1 ripe tomato, roughly chopped

1 dried chilli

1 rosemary sprig

2 garlic cloves, roughly chopped

1.5 litres vegetable stock (see recipe page 104) or water

grated pecorino, to serve

MALTAGLIATI

about 100 g tipo 00 flour, plus extra for dusting

pinch of fine salt

1 egg

RECIPE CONTINUED OVERLEAF →

Place the borlotti beans in a large bowl and cover with cold water to soak for at least 6 hours or overnight.

To make the dough for the maltagliati, tip the flour and salt onto a clean work surface and make a well in the centre. Crack the egg into the middle and, using a fork, whisk gently to slowly incorporate the flour into the egg. When the mixture becomes too stiff to use the fork, use your hands to mix in as much flour as you need for a soft dough that isn't sticky but also not too dry. Flour can vary a lot, so you might not need all of it. Knead the dough for 8 minutes or until smooth and elastic. Cover with a damp cloth or plastic wrap and allow to rest at room temperature for at least 30 minutes.

On a lightly floured work surface, roll the dough out to a rough rectangle shape around 3 mm thick. Roll the dough through a pasta machine set to the widest setting, then roll again through the next two settings, dusting with a little flour between each roll if needed. Fold the dough back in on itself so it's a bit narrower than the width of the machine and use a rolling pin to flatten slightly. Set the machine back to the widest setting and roll back through the first three settings again, folding and flattening the pasta dough before each roll. The pasta should be strong now, and can be rolled through the narrower settings until the dough is your desired thickness. (Alternatively, because it is such a small amount of dough and the pasta doesn't need to be as thin as usual, you can just roll it out to about 2 mm thick using a long, thin rolling pin.) Cut the dough into rough 2 cm pieces. The less perfect the pasta shapes are, the better. Dust with a little flour and set aside while you make the soup.

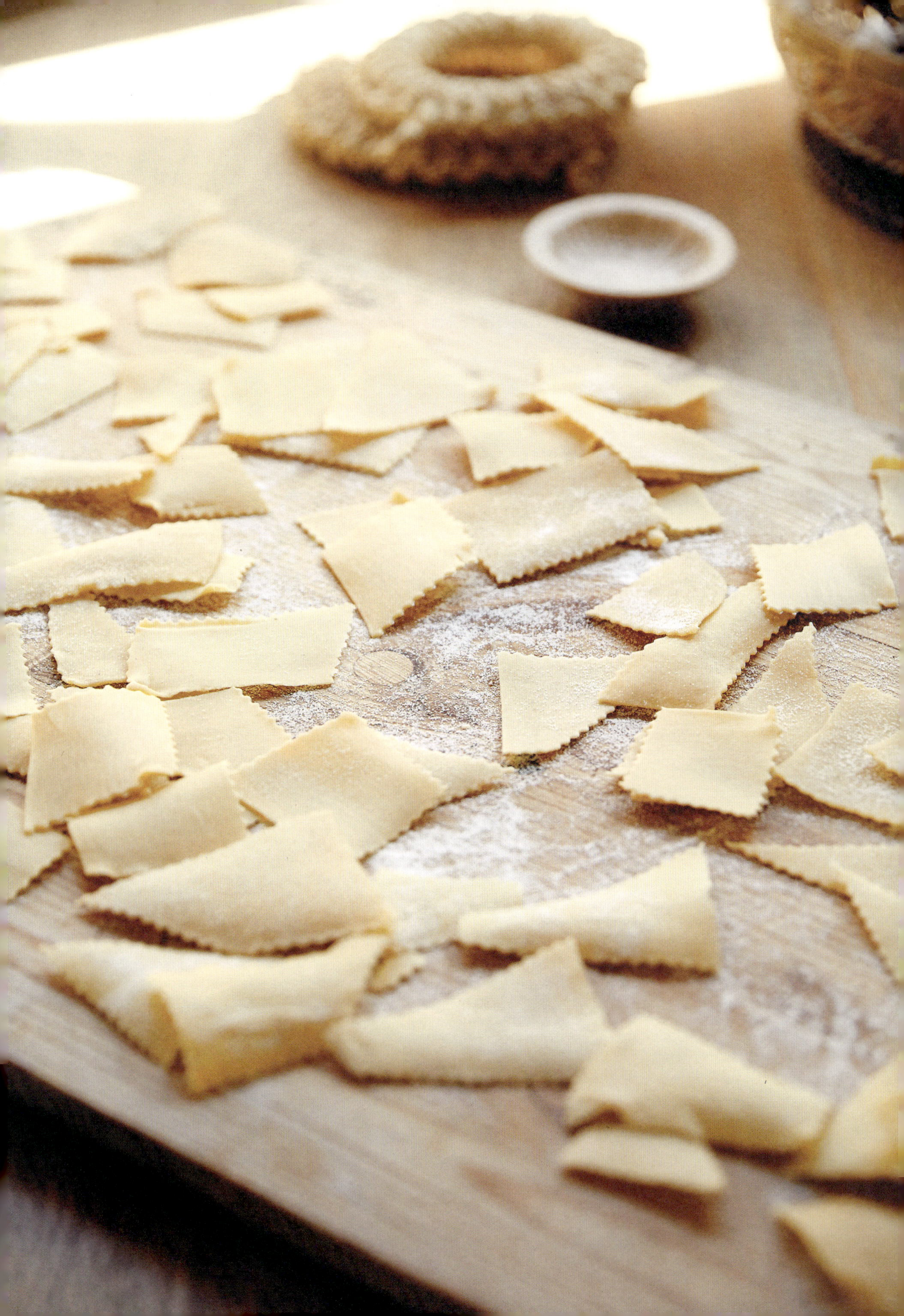

RECIPE CONTINUED •⟶

Heat the olive oil in a large saucepan over a low heat. Add the onion, celery, carrot and a pinch of salt and cook for 10–15 minutes until soft and translucent. Add the tomato, chilli, rosemary and garlic and stir to combine.

Drain and rinse the beans, then add them to the pan along with the stock or water. Simmer over a very low heat, with the lid half on, until the beans are tender. This usually takes 1 hour, but if the beans are older, it may take longer. When the beans are cooked, add the pasta. The starch from the pasta will thicken the soup a little more, so add more stock or water if needed (but keep in mind that this soup should be a bit more like a stew than a broth). Cook for 5 minutes or until the pasta is al dente, then season with salt. Ladle the soup into bowls and serve with a sprinkle with pecorino and a drizzle of extra-virgin olive oil.

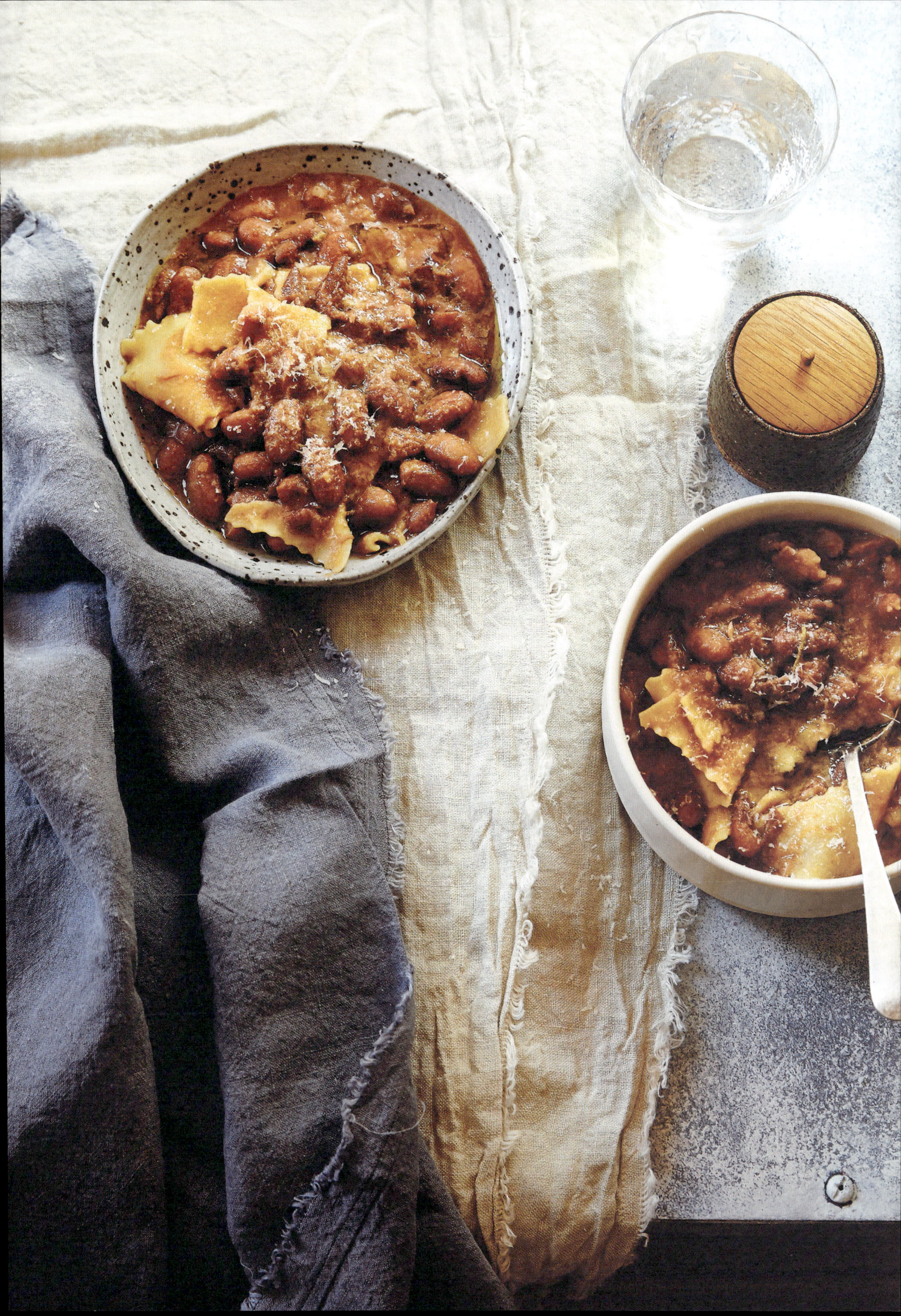

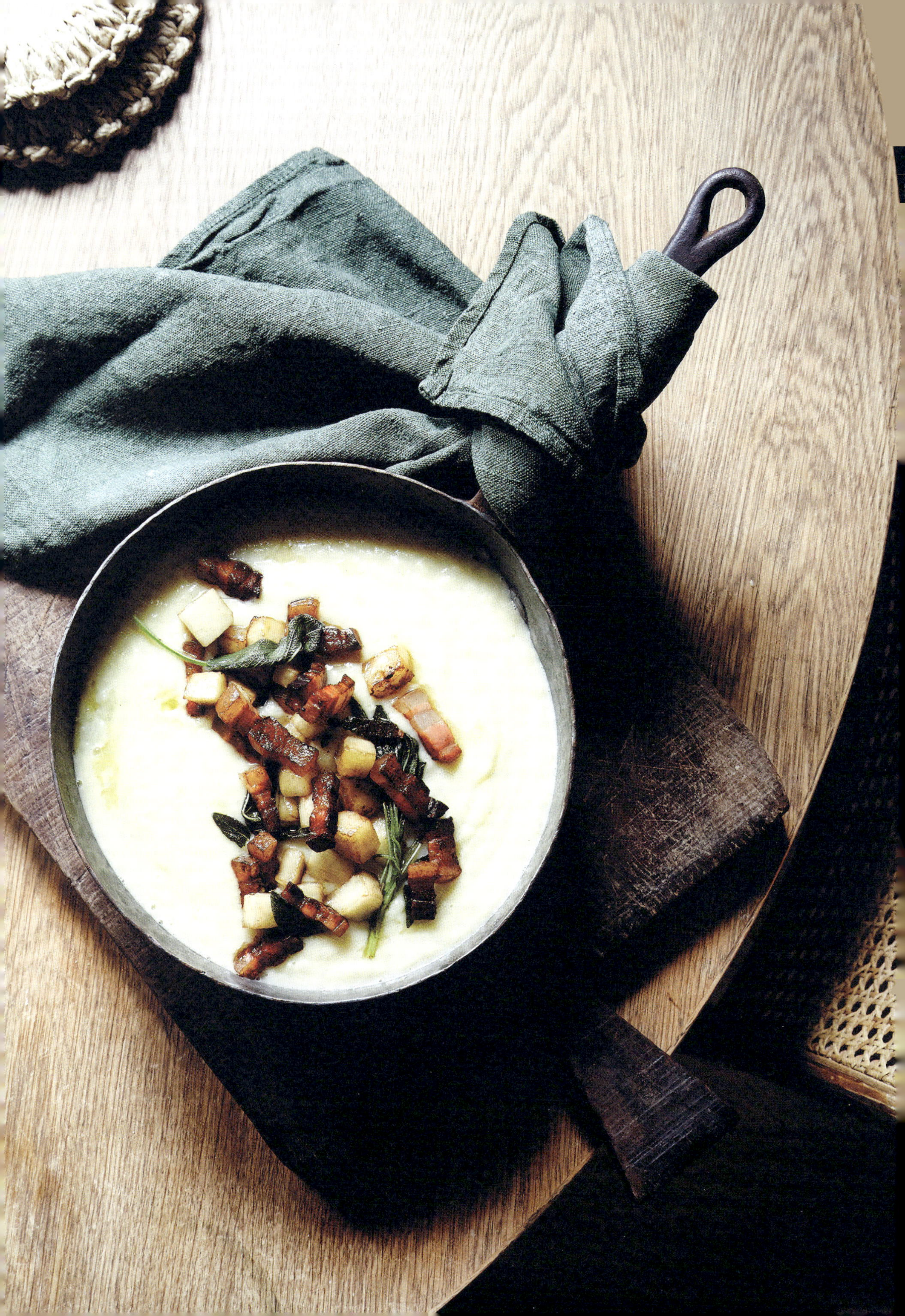

BUTTERY LEEK SOUP TOPPED WITH APPLE, PANCETTA AND SAGE

SERVES 4–6

Leeks cooked in butter really are a thing of beauty and the perfect start to a wonderfully creamy soup. This is an elegant soup – it's subtle in flavour and, although it's made with butter and cream, it's still light enough to eat a whole bowlful, and maybe more. You could, of course, serve the soup simply with an extra drizzle of cream and be completely satisfied, or do as I do and make it a little more special with the addition of salty pancetta, sweet apples and crispy sage.

50 g butter

6 large leeks, white and light green parts only, finely sliced and washed

2 garlic cloves, roughly chopped

sea salt

300 g potatoes, peeled and roughly chopped

1 litre vegetable stock (see recipe page 104) or chicken stock (see recipe page 105)

200 ml pure cream

APPLE, PANCETTA AND SAGE TOPPING

30 g butter

100 g flat pancetta, rind removed, cut into lardons

2 apples, peeled, cored and cut into 1 cm cubes

20 sage leaves

Melt the butter in a large saucepan over a low–medium heat. Add the leek, garlic and a pinch of salt and cook for 3–4 minutes, stirring often, until the leek is soft and sweet. Throw in the potato and cover with the stock. Bring to the boil, then reduce the heat and simmer, partly covered with a lid, for 30–35 minutes until the potatoes are cooked. Pour in the cream and cook for another 5 minutes. Transfer the soup to a food processor and blend until it is smooth and creamy (or use a hand-held blender to do this). Pour the soup back into the saucepan and keep warm over a very low heat (don't let it boil).

To make the topping, melt the butter in a small frying pan over a medium heat and add the pancetta and apples. Stirring often, cook for about 5 minutes until the pancetta has turned golden and the apples are cooked. Add the sage and cook for a minute to crisp.

Season the soup with salt and ladle into bowls. Serve topped with the apple, pancetta and sage.

VEGETABLE STOCK

Here is my recipe for basic vegetable stock, which can be used to enrich all kinds of dishes, especially soups. I much prefer to make my own stock as I can control the saltiness and make it exactly to my liking. The longer you simmer the stock, the stronger it will get. I prefer a more subtle broth, to complement rather than overpower the other ingredients in the dish. I definitely don't discard the vegetables I use in the stock – drizzle with olive oil and lemon juice and sprinkle with sea salt and you have a lovely supper, especially after a long day of cooking.

MAKES ABOUT 1.5 LITRES

3 celery stalks

2 carrots, peeled and cut in half

2 leeks, white and light green parts only, cut in half and washed

1 tomato, cut in half

1 onion, peeled

3 garlic cloves, peeled

4 black peppercorns

4 flat-leaf parsley stalks

2 fresh bay leaves

15 g dried porcini or shiitake mushrooms (optional)

sea salt

Place all the ingredients except the salt in a large stockpot and cover with enough cold water to submerge the vegetables (about 2 litres). Bring to the boil, then reduce to a low heat, cover and simmer for 1½–2 hours.

Strain through a muslin-lined sieve and season to taste. Discard the solids or keep for another use. Transfer the stock to an airtight container or zip-lock bags. The stock will keep in the fridge for up to 4 days or in the freezer for up to 3 months.

FISH STOCK

Making fish stock at home is extremely cost effective and is much more subtle in flavour than the store-bought ones usually are.
You should be able to buy whole fish bones with the heads still attached from your local fishmonger, usually for just a few dollars. I like to use snapper, but any white fish will do – just don't use anything too oily or strong-flavoured. Whatever fish you use, make sure it's really fresh as this will make all the difference. If the fish is too large for your pot, simply cut the carcass in half, or ask your fishmonger to do it for you.

MAKES ABOUT 1.2 LITRES

bones and head of 1 large white-fleshed fish, such as snapper or bass (about 1 kg in total)

1 onion, peeled and cut in half

1 carrot, peeled and cut in half

1 fresh bay leaf

5 black peppercorns

1 tomato, cut in half

3 flat-leaf parsley stalks

sea salt and black pepper

Place all the ingredients except the seasoning in a large stockpot and cover with 1.5 litres of cold water. Bring to the boil, then reduce to a low–medium heat and simmer with the lid half on for 20 minutes. Set aside to cool for 10 minutes.

Strain through a muslin-lined sieve. Pick any meat from the fish carcass and reserve for another use, and discard or reserve the rest of the solids. Season to taste and allow to cool completely. You can use the stock immediately or transfer it to an airtight container or zip-lock bags. The stock will keep in the fridge for up to 3 days or in the freezer for up to 3 months.

CHICKEN STOCK

Chicken stock is one of those staples that you find in most cupboards, fridges or freezers. Chicken stock made from scratch imparts the most wonderful depth of flavour to so many dishes. It takes very little effort, and while it requires some time simmering on the stove, it is rather low maintenance. You can substitute a whole bird for the frames and wings if you prefer. This will give you plenty of wonderfully poached chicken to use in other dishes.

MAKES ABOUT 3 LITRES

2 chicken frames

4 chicken wings

1 onion, peeled and cut in half

1 carrot, peeled and cut in half

1 celery stalk

3 garlic cloves, peeled

1 tomato, cut into quarters

1 fresh bay leaf

3 thyme sprigs

4 black peppercorns

generous pinch of sea salt

Place all the ingredients in a large stockpot and fill with enough cold water to cover everything by about 5 cm (about 4 litres). Bring to the boil, then reduce to a low–medium heat. Half cover with a lid and simmer for 3 hours, topping up with more water if needed and occasionally skimming any scum that rises to the surface, especially in the first 30 minutes when it will be most necessary.

Strain through a muslin-lined sieve and discard the solids or keep for another use. Allow to cool completely, then refrigerate overnight. Skim any fat that has risen to the surface and discard or set aside for cooking. You can use the stock immediately or transfer it to an airtight container or zip-lock bags. The stock will keep in the fridge for up to 3 days or in the freezer for up to 3 months.

BEEF STOCK

Beef stock is really handy to have on standby. By making it yourself, you can use good-quality bones to create a super-nourishing stock.

MAKES ABOUT 1.2 LITRES

1.5 kg beef bones

1 large onion, peeled and cut into quarters

2 carrots, roughly chopped

2 celery stalks, roughly chopped

4 garlic cloves

3 thyme sprigs

sea salt and black pepper

250 ml (1 cup) dry white wine

2 fresh bay leaves

4 flat-leaf parsley stalks

Preheat the oven to 180°C.

Arrange the beef bones, onion, carrot, celery, garlic and thyme in a roasting pan. Season with salt and pepper and roast for 1 hour or until the bones are golden and caramelised.

Transfer the bones and vegetables to a large stockpot and set aside. Pour the wine into the roasting pan, and place over a medium heat. Simmer for a few minutes, scraping the bottom of the pan with a wooden spoon so that you get all of the good caramelised bits off the base.

Pour the liquid into the stockpot and top up with 2 litres of water. Add the bay leaves and parsley stalks and simmer with the lid half on for 4–5 hours. During the first 30 minutes, skim off any scum that rises to the top and discard. If needed, top up the stock with more water during cooking.

Strain through a muslin-lined sieve and discard the solids or keep for another use. Allow to cool completely, then refrigerate overnight. Skim any fat that has risen to the surface and discard or set aside for cooking. You can use the stock immediately or transfer it to an airtight container or zip-lock bags. The stock will keep in the fridge for up to 3 days or in the freezer for up to 3 months.

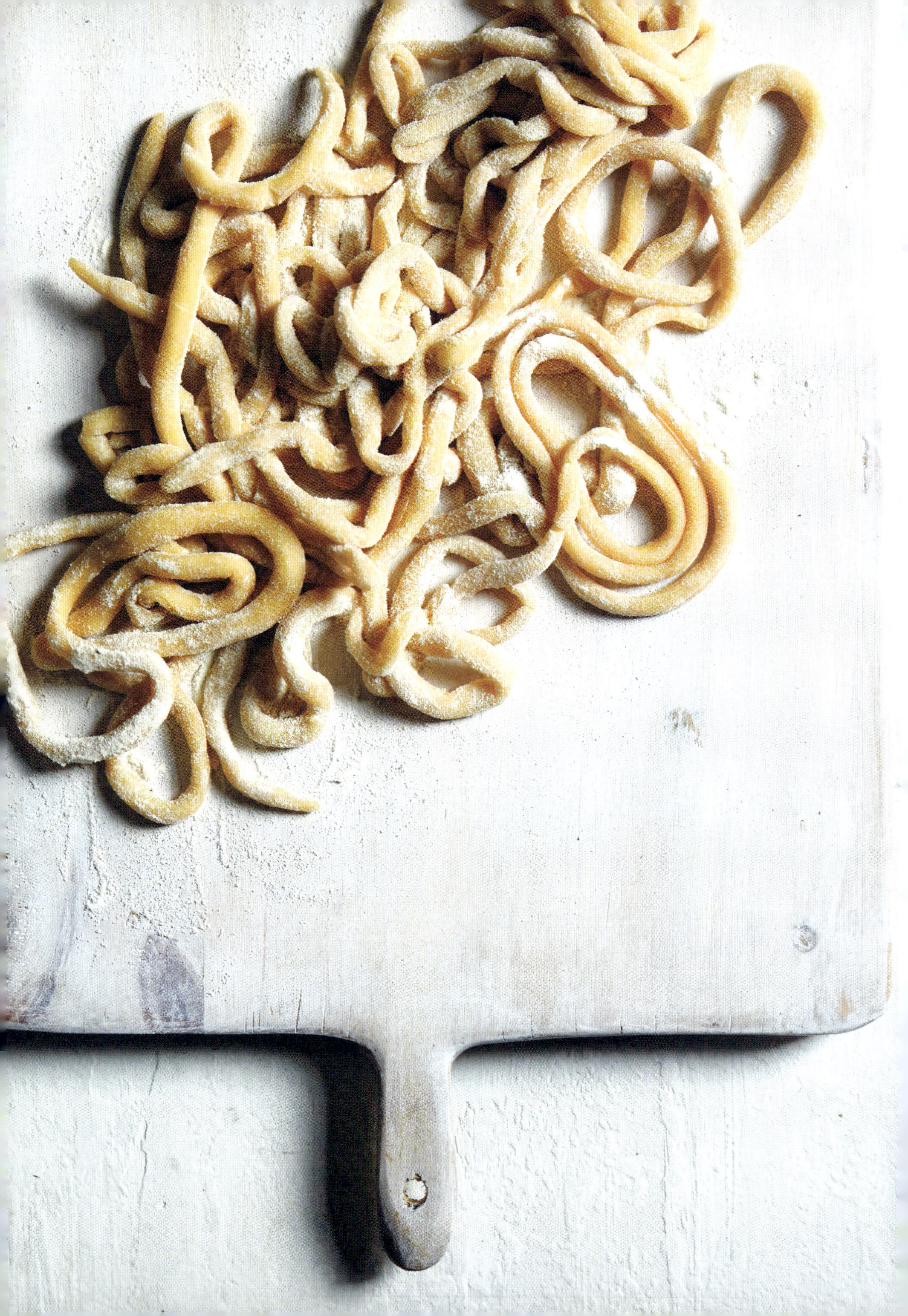

PASTA AND GRAINS

When I lived in Italy, each day was punctuated with a simple and pleasurable meal of pasta. It was sometimes polenta or another grain, but most often it was pasta. I could probably spend my whole life this way, too. I suppose I find the making of pasta rather restorative — the process forces me into a slow pace and allows me to indulge in quiet moments of thought. This chapter contains some of my very favourite recipes. I have suggested sauces to best suit the particular pasta shapes, but many of them are interchangeable. Making pasta by hand is not difficult, it just requires a little patience, instinct and a bit of practice. If you're short on time, good-quality dried pasta is a very fine alternative.

TROFIE WITH PESTO ALLA GENOVESE

SERVES 4–6

This is total comfort food and one of my favourite pasta dishes. I learned to make it many years ago with a friend, Giulio, who is from Ventimiglia, a town near Genoa where this pasta hails from. It has since become a staple in our home – something familiar to always fall back on, especially during summer when basil is abundant. Traditionally, this dish is paired with trofie, a short spiral pasta, which is relatively easy to make. If you'd prefer to use dried pasta, you can find trofie in many specialty Italian grocers, and if not, another short pasta like penne or fusilli would work too – you'll need about 400 g; just be sure to adjust the cooking time to suit, or cook the pasta separately and stir through with the pesto. Potato-wise, you want something that will hold its own, yet soften a little to help create some texture in the sauce – waxy potatoes are best for this. I like to use blue moon potatoes – which have an amazing purple skin and a wonderful texture – but nicola potatoes are delicious too.

250 g waxy potatoes, peeled, halved and cut into 2 cm slices

150 g green beans, trimmed and cut into 3 cm lengths

sea salt

extra-virgin olive oil, for drizzling

TROFIE

200 g tipo 00 flour

200 g semolina flour (see page 13), plus extra for dusting

generous pinch of sea salt

130–150 ml lukewarm water

BASIL PESTO

1 garlic clove, peeled

pinch of sea salt

bunch of basil, preferably small and sweet, leaves picked (about 30 g in total)

40 g (¼ cup) pine nuts

25 g (¼ cup) finely grated parmesan

25 g (¼ cup) finely grated good-quality pecorino (such as pecorino sardo)

about 60 ml (¼ cup) extra-virgin olive oil

To make the dough for the trofie, tip the flours onto a clean work surface. Add a generous three-fingered pinch of salt and mix with your hands. Make a well in the centre and slowly pour in the water, gradually drawing the flour into the water and mixing with your hands until you have a shaggy mass (you may need a little extra water to create the right consistency). Knead until it comes together into a smooth dough that is soft, but not sticky or too dry. Cover with a damp cloth or plastic wrap and allow to rest at room temperature for at least 30 minutes.

Divide the dough into four pieces. Cover three of the pieces and set aside. Roll the dough out into a rectangle about 1.5 mm thick. You can use a pasta machine or a rolling pin. You may need a little flour on your bench, but not too much, otherwise the dough will slide on your hands rather than roll when you're trying to shape it. Cut the dough into 2 cm squares. Take a square and place at the heel of your palm. Using your other palm, roll the dough into a spiral shape by rolling it towards your fingertips. This is best done on a wooden surface – so that the dough grips a little – but if you don't have a wooden bench, a large wooden cutting board will work well too. Roll the remaining squares into spirals, dust with a little extra semolina flour to stop them sticking together and set aside in a single layer. I usually lay the trofie on tea towels that have been generously dusted with semolina flour, which makes for an easy transfer into the pot. Repeat the rolling, cutting and rolling with the remaining pieces of dough.

RECIPE CONTINUED OVERLEAF ⟶

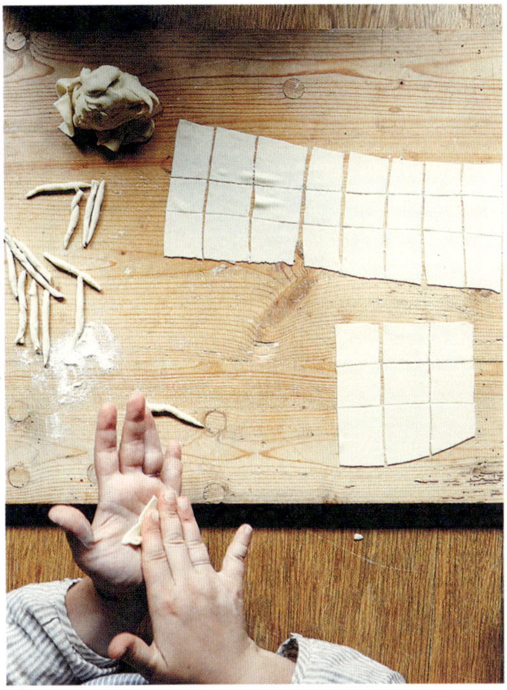

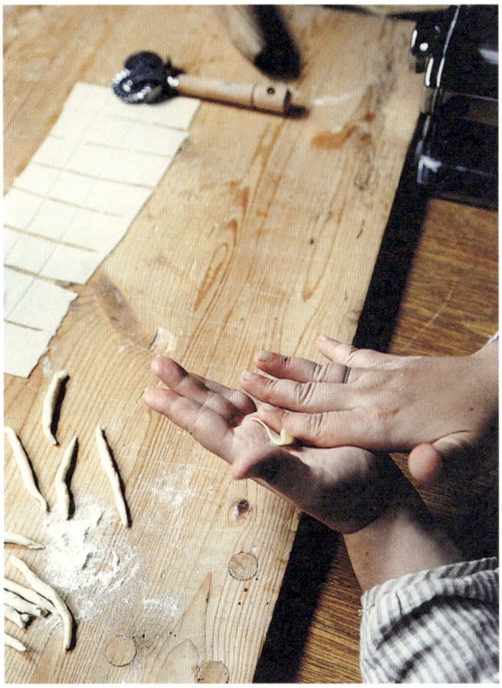

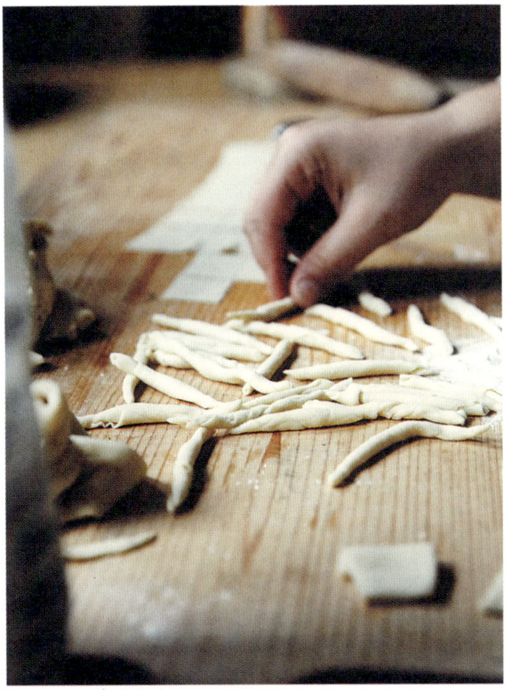

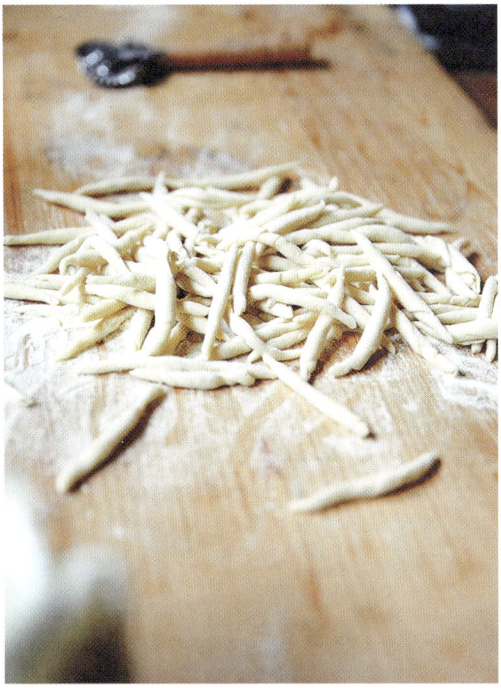

RECIPE CONTINUED ·⟶

To make the pesto, pound the garlic and salt using a mortar and pestle. Add the basil and crush in a circular motion. When a paste begins to form, add the pine nuts and pound. Stir in the parmesan and pecorino and drizzle in enough olive oil to thin the pesto to a dolloping texture. Alternatively, you can use a food processor; just be aware that the metal blades can quickly oxidise the basil leaves. Pulse everything except the oil and cheeses together, then drizzle in the oil while the motor is running, then stir in the cheeses by hand. Set aside.

Bring a large saucepan of salted water to the boil over a medium–high heat. Throw in the potatoes and boil for about 5 minutes, until firm but almost cooked. Add the pasta and beans and cook for 2–3 minutes until the pasta is al dente and the beans are cooked but still firm.

Drain, reserving some of the pasta water, and transfer the potatoes, beans and pasta to a large serving dish. Stir the pesto through, adding 60–125 ml (¼–½ cup) of pasta water as needed – enough to create a luxurious sauce. Be very gentle when stirring to avoid breaking the potatoes, as they can easily turn mushy at this point. Season to taste and serve with a drizzle of extra-virgin olive oil.

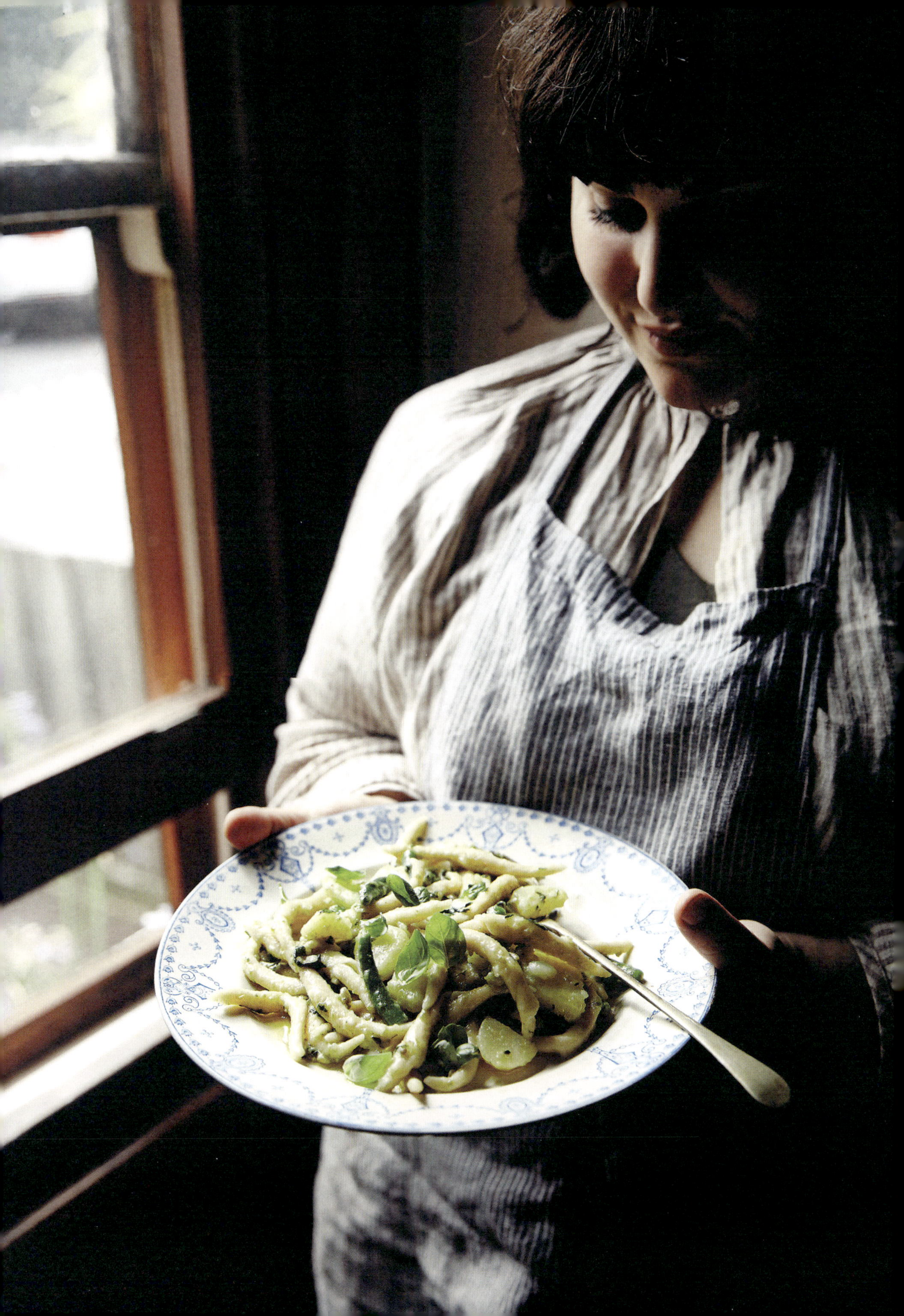

TAGLIATELLE WITH BEEF SHORT-RIB RAGÙ

·❈· SERVES 4–6 ·❈·

Beef short ribs can be bought in racks cut across the bone, asado style, or cut between the bones into individual ribs. Either is fine; however, if you're using the former, simply cut the rack into more manageable pieces for browning. Ribs benefit from a long, slow cook – they will be incredibly rich, tender and full of flavour. Fresh pasta is a perfect match for this ragù – cooked briefly in the sauce, it will take on all of the richness.

60 ml (¼ cup) extra-virgin olive oil

1 onion, finely chopped

1 celery stalk, finely chopped

1 small carrot, finely chopped

sea salt

800 g beef short ribs, cut into individual ribs if necessary

250 ml (1 cup) red wine

3 garlic cloves, roughly chopped

680 g tomato passata

2 fresh bay leaves

2 oregano sprigs

large handful of basil leaves

black pepper

grated parmesan, to serve

TAGLIATELLE

300 g tipo 00 flour

100 g semolina flour (see page 13), plus extra for dusting

generous pinch of sea salt

4 eggs

RECIPE CONTINUED OVERLEAF ·⟶

Heat 2 tablespoons of the olive oil in a large heavy-based saucepan over a low heat. Add the onion, celery, carrot and a pinch of salt and sauté for 10–15 minutes until soft and caramelised. Transfer to a large bowl and wipe the saucepan clean. Heat the remaining olive oil over a high heat and brown the ribs on all sides. Transfer to the bowl and discard any oil left in the saucepan. Return to the heat, add the wine and simmer for a minute or two, scraping any bits stuck to the bottom. Return the vegetables and ribs to the saucepan, add the garlic, passata and 300 ml of water and stir so it's all nicely combined. Add the bay leaves and oregano. Bring to the boil, then reduce the heat to low and cover. Cook for 3–4 hours until the meat is tender and falling away from the bone.

To make the dough for the tagliatelle, tip the flours and salt onto a clean work surface and combine. Create a well in the centre and crack in the eggs. Gently whisk the eggs using a fork, then slowly bring in the flour and incorporate until you have a shaggy dough. You'll have to ditch the fork after a little while and use your hands instead. Knead for about 8 minutes until the dough is soft but not at all sticky.

Cover with a damp cloth or plastic wrap and allow to rest at room temperature for at least 30 minutes.

Divide the pasta dough into four pieces. Cover three of the pieces and set aside. On a lightly floured work surface, roll the dough using a rolling pin into a rough disc shape about 5 mm thick. Roll the dough through a pasta machine set to the widest setting, then roll again through the next two narrower settings, dusting with a little flour between each roll if needed. Fold the dough back in on itself so it's a bit narrower than the width of the machine and use a rolling

PASTA AND GRAINS 113

RECIPE CONTINUED ⟶

pin to flatten slightly. Set the machine back to the widest setting and roll back through the first three settings again, folding and flattening the pasta dough before each roll. Repeat this process three more times, so in total you've rolled the dough through the three widest settings, folding between each roll, four times in total. This makes the pasta nice and strong, and you can now roll the dough through the settings until the pasta is around 1.5 mm thick. Dust the pasta sheet with semolina flour. Repeat the process with the remaining pieces of dough. Allow the pasta sheets to dry out slightly for 10 or so minutes. Now, gently roll up each pasta sheet from the shortest end. With a sharp knife, cut the pasta into ribbons about 8 mm wide. Unravel the pasta and dust with a little flour. You could also arrange the pasta in small mounds – just be sure that it is well dusted to avoid sticking. If not using immediately, I hang my pasta on the back of our chairs at home, but you can use proper racks for hanging pasta, which are available at most kitchenware stores. Otherwise, a clothes-drying rack works well, too.

Remove the ribs from the ragù and shred the meat, discarding any bones. Return the meat to the sauce, along with most of the basil leaves. Simmer, uncovered, for about 10 minutes until slightly reduced. Remove and discard the bay leaves, season to taste and keep the ragù warm over a low heat while you cook the pasta.

Bring a large saucepan of generously salted water to the boil and cook the pasta for 2–3 minutes or until al dente. Transfer the tagliatelle to the ragù and toss to combine, adding 60–125 ml (¼–½ cup) of the pasta water as needed to thin the sauce. Serve into bowls and scatter with freshly grated parmesan and the remaining basil leaves.

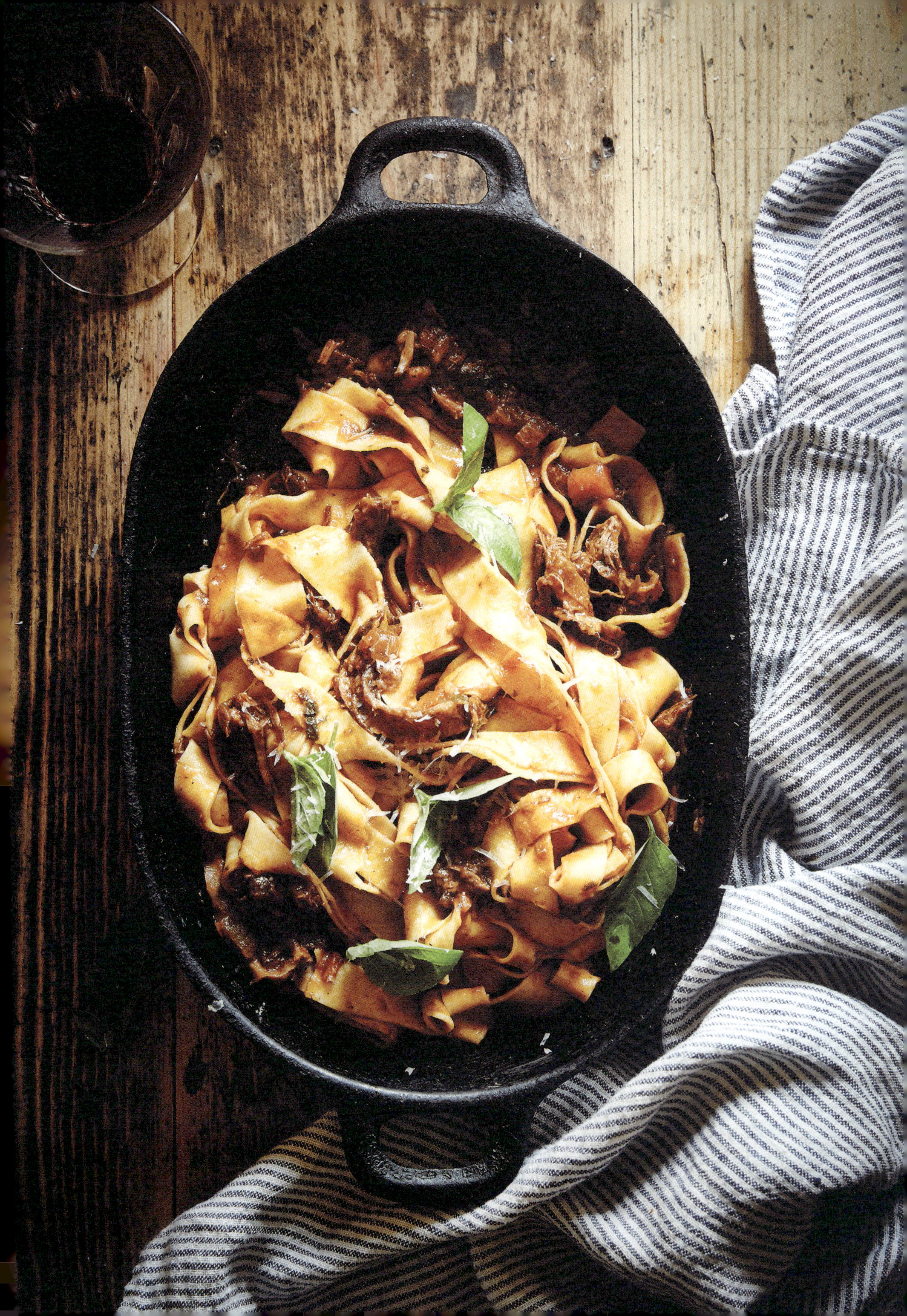

HANDMADE PICI WITH MEATBALLS IN SAUCE

· ❖ SERVES 4–6 GENEROUSLY ❖ ·

Pici is one of the simplest types of pasta to make, even if they are a little time consuming. The pasta has the most wonderful texture and it doesn't require any special equipment to make – just your hands. In fact, irregularities in the length and thickness are more than acceptable, so they don't even need to be made by the same pair of hands, which means there are often a few of us around the table getting the job done. I like to make them rather thick, but you can roll them a little thinner if you prefer. Pici originate from the areas surrounding Siena, Tuscany, and are often made simply with flour and water, but I've added eggs here too. Pici is also a great pasta to serve with the beef short-rib ragù on page 112 or the meat ragù on page 132.

I suppose I would say this my 'desert island dish' because meatballs, sauce and pasta really can't be beat. A short dried pasta, like penne or rigatoni, would be wonderful with this too, or you can skip the pasta altogether and dish up the meatballs with some crusty bread. Any leftover meatballs are eaten the next day with great delight.

2 tablespoons olive oil

1 onion, finely chopped

pinch of dried chilli flakes

2 garlic cloves, roughly chopped

sea salt

1 basil sprig, plus extra leaves to serve

1 rosemary sprig

1.4 kg tomato passata

1 × 400 g can peeled whole tomatoes, roughly chopped

1 tablespoon balsamic vinegar

grated parmesan, to serve

MEATBALLS

100 g stale white bread, crusts removed, roughly torn

80 ml (⅓ cup) full-cream milk

60 g pine nuts

500 g pork mince

500 g beef mince

50 g parmesan, finely grated

60 g pancetta, finely chopped

1 tablespoon finely chopped rosemary leaves

1 tablespoon finely chopped flat-leaf parsley leaves

1 tablespoon finely chopped oregano leaves

2 garlic cloves, finely chopped

1 egg plus 1 yolk, lightly beaten

generous pinch of freshly grated nutmeg

pinch of sea salt

PICI

200 g tipo 00 flour

200 g semolina flour (see page 13), plus extra for dusting

pinch of fine sea salt

4 eggs

2 tablespoons olive oil

1–2 tablespoons lukewarm water

To prepare the meatballs, place the bread in a bowl, cover with the milk, leave to soak for 10 minutes then drain any excess milk. Lightly toast the pine nuts in a dry frying pan over a low–medium heat for 1–2 minutes until just coloured. Cool slightly then combine with the soaked bread and the remaining ingredients in a large bowl. Mix really well using your hands, squeezing everything together to incorporate. Roll the mixture into golf ball-sized balls, place onto a baking tray, cover and rest in the fridge for 30 minutes.

To make the pici dough, tip the flours and salt onto a clean work surface and combine. Create a well in the centre and crack in the eggs. Gently whisk the eggs using a fork, mix in the olive oil, then slowly bring in the flour and mix to incorporate. When the dough becomes too stiff to work, add 1–2 tablespoons of water and bring the dough together using your hands. Knead the dough for about 8 minutes until it is smooth and elastic. It should be quite soft, but not sticky. Cover with a damp cloth or plastic wrap and allow to rest at room temperature for at least 30 minutes.

Meanwhile, heat the olive oil in a large heavy-based saucepan over a medium heat and cook the onion, chilli and garlic with a pinch of salt for 10–15 minutes until soft. Add the basil, rosemary, passata, tomatoes and a little water if needed. Bring to a simmer, reduce the heat to low and cook for 30 minutes.

Preheat the oven to 180°C.

Bake the meatballs for 15–20 minutes, turning once, until golden but still tender. Stir the balsamic vinegar into the sauce, then add the meatballs and cook for 15–20 minutes. Remove the basil and rosemary stalks and season to taste. Keep warm over a low heat until the pasta is ready.

Divide the pasta dough into four pieces. Cover three of the pieces and set aside. On a lightly floured work surface (ideally a wooden one), roll the dough out into a rectangle about 5 mm thick using a rolling pin. Cut the dough into strips around 8 mm wide and, using the palms of your hands, roll each strip into a long, thin shape, about 5 mm wide. Dust the pici with plenty of semolina flour and repeat the process with the remaining pasta dough.

Bring a large saucepan of generously salted water to the boil and cook the pici for 5–6 minutes until al dente. They take a little longer than regular fresh pasta, but the cooking time will really depend on the flour you've used and the thickness of the pici, so check them at around the 4 minute mark – they should be a little chewy but not chalky. Drain the pici, reserving some of the pasta water. In a new pan, place the pasta and enough meatballs and sauce to coat. You may not need all of the meatballs and sauce, depending on which pasta you are using. Stir gently to coat, being careful not to break the meatballs. Add 60–125 ml (¼–½ cup) of pasta water to help loosen the sauce, if needed. Simmer for a minute or two then serve in bowls topped with parmesan and basil.

PICTURED ON PAGE 119

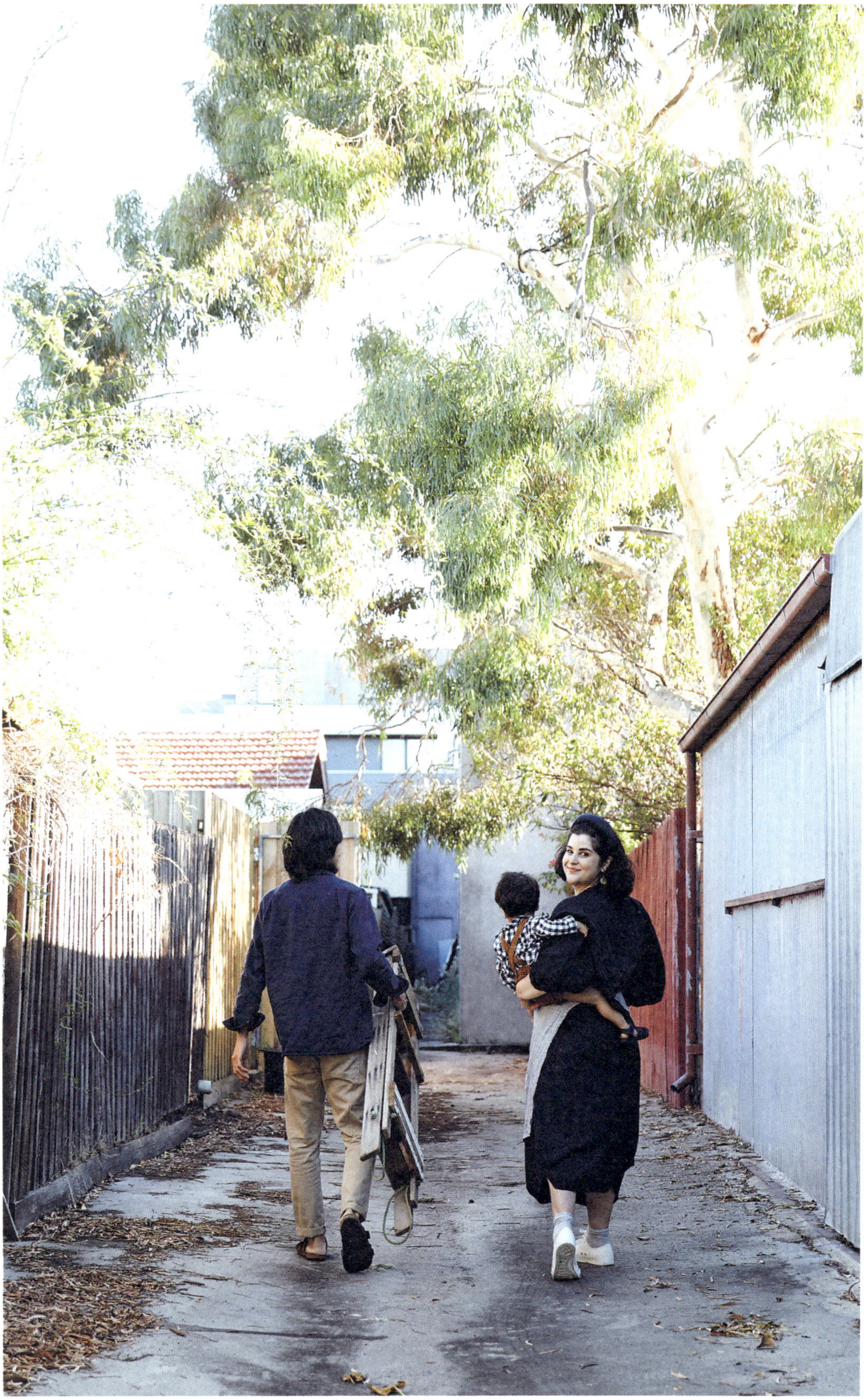

Handmade pici with meatballs in sauce (page 116)

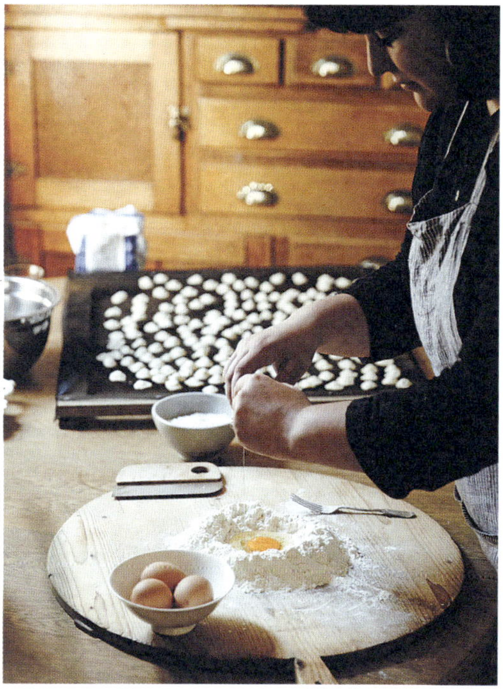

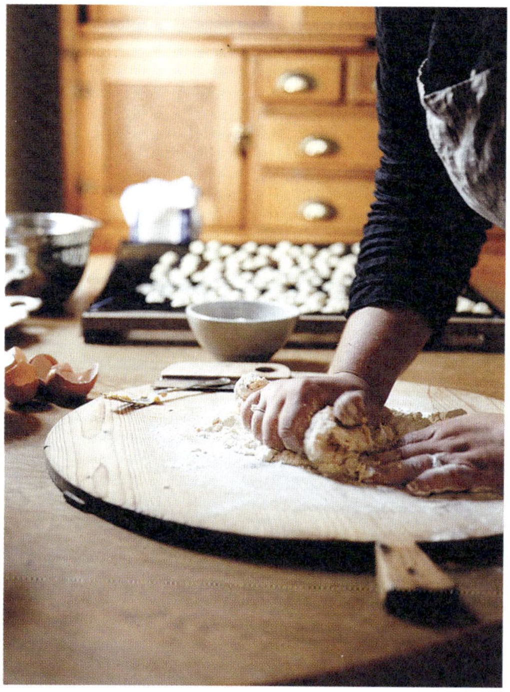

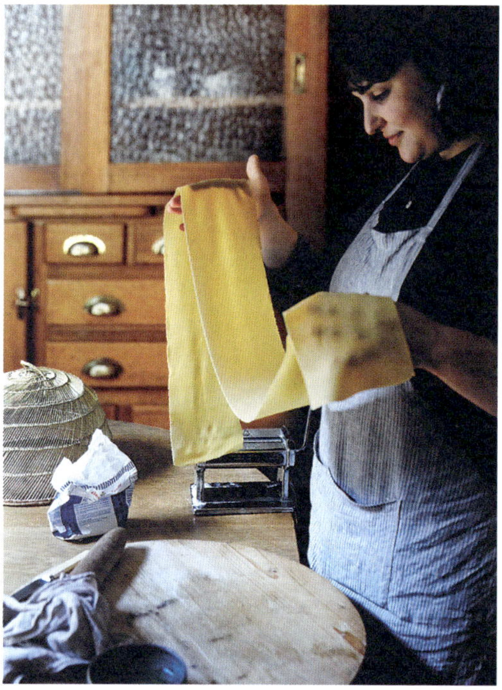

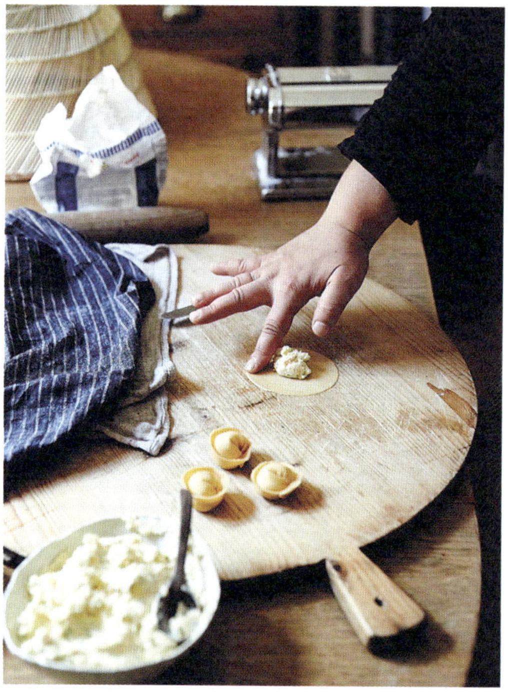

RICOTTA TORTELLONI WITH BUTTER, SAGE AND HAZELNUTS

SERVES 4

Filled pasta takes a little time to make, but is well worth your efforts. Rolling, filling and folding pasta is really meditative and a great way to calm a busy mind. The filling is simple, but really lovely and subtle, especially with the buttery sauce. You could make tortellini, the more common, smaller version of this pasta, but they do take a lot longer to prepare. You can make the tortelloni either beginning with a square or a circle to give a slightly different shape. I like to make them from a circle, which results in nice round, plump tortelloni, but do as you prefer. Usually, I would use whole eggs for pasta – at a ratio of 1 egg per 100 g flour – but for filled pasta, it's better to enrich the dough with a little more egg yolk instead, resulting in a finer pasta with better structure.

1 egg white, lightly beaten

100 g lightly salted butter

small bunch of sage, leaves picked

40 g (¼ cup) hazelnuts, roughly chopped

grated parmesan, to serve

TORTELLONI DOUGH

300 g tipo 00 flour, plus extra for dusting

pinch of sea salt

2 eggs, plus 2 yolks

1–2 tablespoons lukewarm water, if needed

RICOTTA FILLING

350 g fresh full-fat ricotta

100 g parmesan, finely grated

2 egg yolks

pinch of freshly grated nutmeg

small handful of flat-leaf parsley leaves, finely chopped (optional)

sea salt and black pepper

RECIPE CONTINUED OVERLEAF ⟶

To make the tortelloni dough, tip the flour and salt onto a clean work surface and combine. Create a well in the centre and crack in the eggs and yolks. Gently whisk the eggs using a fork, then slowly bring in the flour and mix to incorporate. When the dough becomes stiff, use your hands to mix until the dough is soft and malleable. Depending on the type of flour you've used, you may need to add the water to bring the dough together – if so, start with one tablespoon and only add the second tablespoon if you need to. Knead for about 10 minutes until the dough is smooth and elastic. Flatten into a disc, cover with a damp cloth or plastic wrap and allow to rest at room temperature for at least 30 minutes.

To make the filling, mix all of the ingredients together until smooth. Season with salt and pepper and set aside in the fridge until ready to use.

Divide the pasta dough into four pieces. Cover three of the pieces and set aside. On a lightly floured work surface, roll out the dough using a rolling pin into a rough disc shape around 3 mm thick. Roll the dough through a pasta machine set to the widest setting, then roll again through the narrower settings, dusting with a little flour between each roll if needed, until the pasta sheet is about 30 cm long. Fold the dough back in on itself so it's a bit narrower than the width of the machine and use a rolling pin to flatten slightly. Set the machine back to the widest setting and roll back through the first settings again, folding and flattening the pasta dough before each roll. Repeat this process two more times, so in total you've rolled the dough through the widest settings, folding between each roll, three times in total. This makes the pasta nice and strong, and you can now roll the dough through the settings until the pasta is around 1–1.5 mm thick.

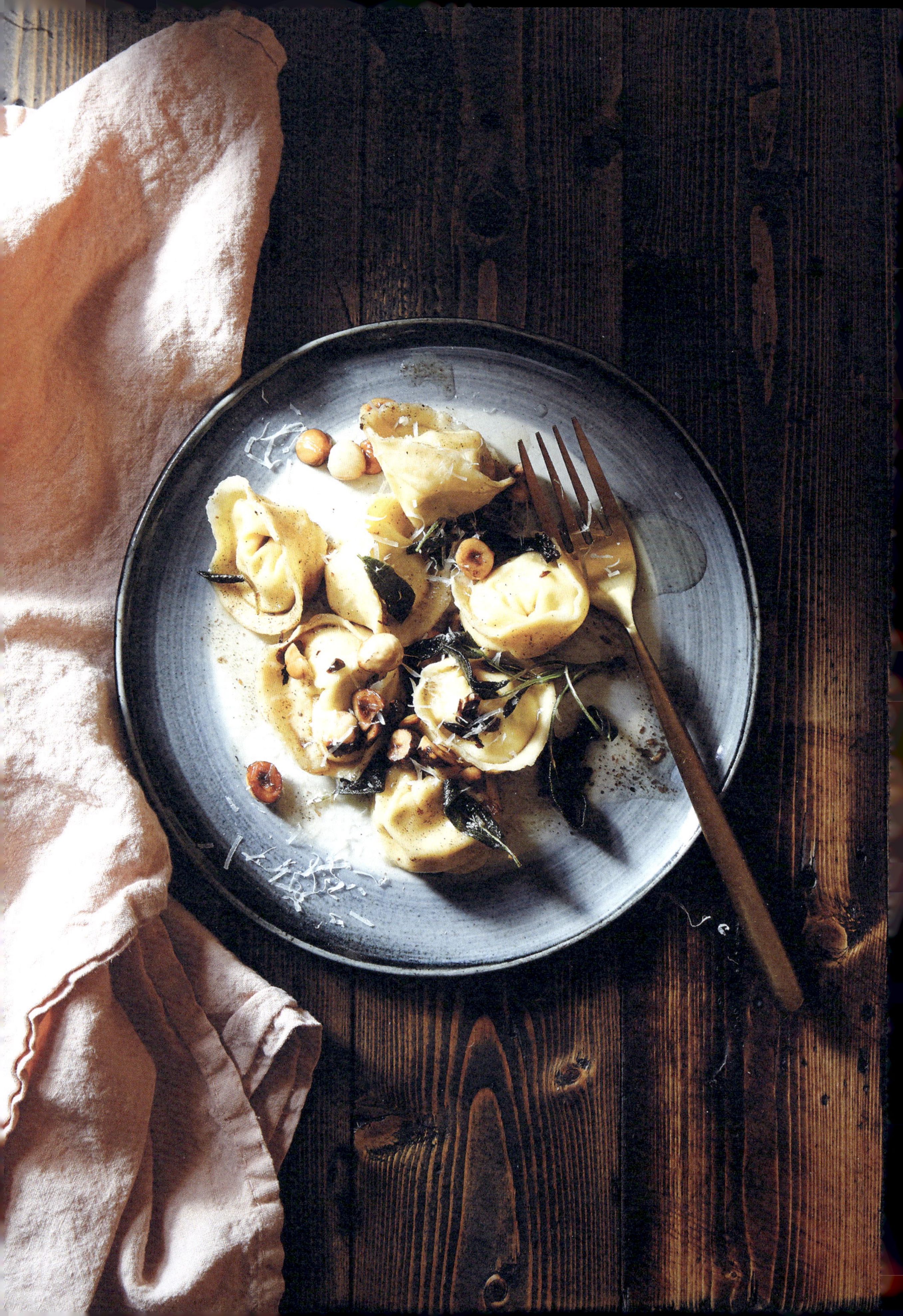

RECIPE CONTINUED ⟶

Cut into rounds using a 7 cm circle cutter and place 1 teaspoon of filling into the centre of each round. Working quickly so the pasta doesn't dry out, brush a little egg white around the edge of the circle, then fold into a half-moon shape, pressing the edges to seal. With the straight edge facing you, bring the corners together (so the straight edge curves) and press them together gently with your thumb and index finger. Set aside on a lightly floured tray and repeat with the remaining dough and filling, re-rolling any scraps of pasta. It is better to cut and shape the tortelloni just a few at a time, keeping any rolled pasta sheets or dough under a damp tea towel to prevent them drying out.

Bring a large saucepan of generously salted water to the boil and cook the tortelloni for about 2 minutes, until they have floated to the surface and are al dente. While the pasta is cooking, melt the butter with the sage and hazelnuts in a large frying pan over a low heat. Add 60–125 ml (¼–½ cup) of pasta water as needed and swirl the pan around to combine. I like the butter to be golden brown, rather than 'burnt', but if you prefer a nuttier sauce, cook the butter for a minute or two longer. Transfer the tortelloni to the sage butter using a slotted spoon and stir gently to coat. Serve immediately topped with parmesan.

ORECCHIETTE THREE WAYS

· ❊ SERVES 4 ❊ ·

Orecchiette is perhaps my most loved of all the pasta shapes. A big call, I know, but I think it's true. Fresh orecchiette, made by hand, is a wonderful thing. It is not only a pleasure to eat, but my favourite to make. The repetitive action of cutting, rolling and flicking gives me time to think clearly. It slows me right down, puts me in that moment – cutting, rolling, flicking. It requires few ingredients and is very capable of feeding hungry guests. Hailing from Puglia, in Italy's south, *orecchiette* translates as 'little ears', and they are the ultimate sauce-catchers. Overleaf, you will find three of my favourite sauces to pair with orecchiette – they are all very simple and quick to make, which means that once that pasta has been made, the meal is almost ready. The walnut and herb sauce is a regular in my kitchen – the flavour, texture and adaptability, depending on which herbs or nuts you have at hand, makes it the perfect staple. The pea and ricotta sauce is just so lovely in spring when peas are in season, while the chicory, raisins and garlic crumbs are a great comfort when winter has set in.

200 g tipo 00 flour

200 g semolina flour (see page 13), plus extra for dusting

generous pinch of fine sea salt

130–150 ml lukewarm water

Tip the flours and salt onto a clean work surface and combine. Create a well in the centre and slowly pour in enough of the water, mixing with your hands, to make a soft but not sticky dough. Knead well for 10 minutes until smooth and elastic, adding a little more flour if the dough is too sticky. Cover with a damp cloth or plastic wrap and allow to rest at room temperature for at least 30 minutes.

Divide the pasta dough into four pieces. Cover three of the pieces and set aside. On a lightly floured work surface, roll the dough into a long sausage shape about 1 cm in diameter, then cut into 1.5 cm lengths. Take one length and, using a flat, non-serrated butter knife, place the knife on top of the piece of dough and drag it towards you, with the knife at a 30 degree angle – the dough should curl up a bit as you drag it and slightly stick to the knife. Using your index finger and thumb, gently invert the orecchiette and pull it away from the knife. This is best done on a wooden surface – so that the dough grips a little – so if you don't have a wooden bench, use a large wooden cutting board. The orecchiette should have a rough exterior and plump edges. Place the shaped orecchiette onto a board or tea towel that is generously dusted with semolina flour. Continue the process with the rest of the pasta dough, arranging the orecchiette in a single layer.

Bring a large saucepan of generously salted water to the boil and cook the orecchiette for about 5–6 minutes or until al dente.

RECIPE CONTINUED OVERLEAF · →

PASTA AND GRAINS 125

RECIPE CONTINUED ⟶

ORECCHIETTE WITH PEAS AND RICOTTA

This is a lovely fresh sauce that is very quick to prepare and particularly wonderful when made with the homemade ricotta on page 24. The pasta water is crucial to creating a silky sauce, so don't be hasty and throw it down the drain.

150 g peas (preferably fresh, but frozen are fine too)

375 g fresh full-fat ricotta

2 tablespoons extra-virgin olive oil, plus extra to serve

sea salt and black pepper

1 × Orecchiette (see recipe on page 124)

large handful of mint leaves, roughly chopped

Blanch the peas in a small saucepan of boiling water for 1–2 minutes or until just cooked. Refresh in cold water and drain. Place the ricotta in a large bowl, drizzle with the olive oil and season generously. Stir until smooth and combined and add the peas.

Drain the orecchiette, reserving the pasta water. Add the orecchiette immediately to the ricotta, along with 60–125 ml (¼–½ cup) of pasta water as needed, a little at a time – just enough to thin the sauce. It shouldn't be too thick but should coat the orecchiette nicely, so don't be shy. Stir through the mint and serve immediately with a generous drizzle of extra-virgin olive oil.

PICTURED ON PAGE 131

ORECCHIETTE WITH CHICORY, RAISINS AND GARLIC CRUMBS

I love the bitterness of the chicory paired with the sweetness of the raisins, and the crunchy, salty, garlicky crumbs that adorn this dish. Another simple, but rewarding, partner for your orecchiette.

60 g butter

1½ tablespoons extra-virgin olive oil, plus extra to serve

2 onions, roughly chopped

sea salt

200 g chicory, roughly chopped

small handful of flat-leaf parsley leaves, roughly chopped

60 g (½ cup) raisins

juice of ½ lemon

1 × Orecchiette (see recipe on page 124)

black pepper

GARLIC CRUMBS

1½ tablespoons extra-virgin olive oil

2 garlic cloves, bruised with the heel of a knife

60 g (¾ cup) toasted breadcrumbs

sea salt

Heat the butter and oil in a large frying pan over a low heat. Gently cook the onions with a pinch of salt for 10–15 minutes or until soft and sweet.

Meanwhile, prepare the garlic crumbs. Gently warm the olive oil in a frying pan over a low heat with the garlic. After a few minutes, remove the garlic and increase the heat to medium. Add the breadcrumbs, stirring to coat. Fry for 2–3 minutes until crisp and golden. Season with salt and set aside to cool.

Add the chicory, parsley and raisins to the onions and stir to coat, cooking for just a minute or two, until the chicory has begun to collapse. Transfer to a large bowl and squeeze over the lemon juice. Drain the orecchiette and mix with the chicory. Season to taste and serve immediately, drizzled with a little extra olive oil and topped with the garlic crumbs.

PICTURED ON PAGE 130

RECIPE CONTINUED •⟶

PASTA AND GRAINS 128

ORECCHIETTE WITH WALNUT AND HERB SAUCE

I can't get enough of this punchy, herby and creamy sauce. The bread soaked in milk might seem an unlikely addition to a pasta sauce, but it's extremely delicious and quite common in Italy. You could use woody herbs in this sauce, too, but they will require a little more force to break down. This sauce could also be served with gnocchi or spaghetti.

1 thick slice of day-old crusty white bread, crusts removed, roughly torn

100 ml full-cream milk

130 g (1¼ cups) walnuts

3 garlic cloves, peeled

pinch of sea salt

large handful of leaves from different soft herbs, such as mint, flat-leaf parsley, dill and basil

finely grated zest of 1 lemon

80 ml (⅓ cup) olive oil

3 teaspoons red wine vinegar

1 × Orecchiette (see recipe on page 124)

grated parmesan, to serve

Place the bread in a bowl and cover with the milk. Leave to soak for 10 minutes. Lightly toast the walnuts in a dry frying pan over a low–medium heat for 1–2 minutes until just coloured.

Using a mortar and pestle, pound the garlic and salt into a paste. Add the herbs and break them down in a circular motion until smooth and combined. Add the walnuts and continue to bash with the pestle to make a nice chunky paste. Add the soaked bread and any remaining milk. Pound a little more to break up the bread and combine. Stir in the lemon zest, olive oil and red wine vinegar. Alternatively, you can pulse everything together in a food processor until smooth. Transfer to a large bowl.

Drain the orecchiette, reserving the pasta water. Add the pasta to the pesto, along with 60–125 ml (¼–½ cup) of pasta water – enough to create a silky sauce. Serve immediately sprinkled with parmesan.

PICTURED ON PAGE 131

CLOCKWISE FROM LEFT: Orecchiette with chicory, raisins and garlic crumbs (page 127), Orecchiette with walnut and herb sauce (page 129) and Orecchiette with peas and ricotta (page 127)

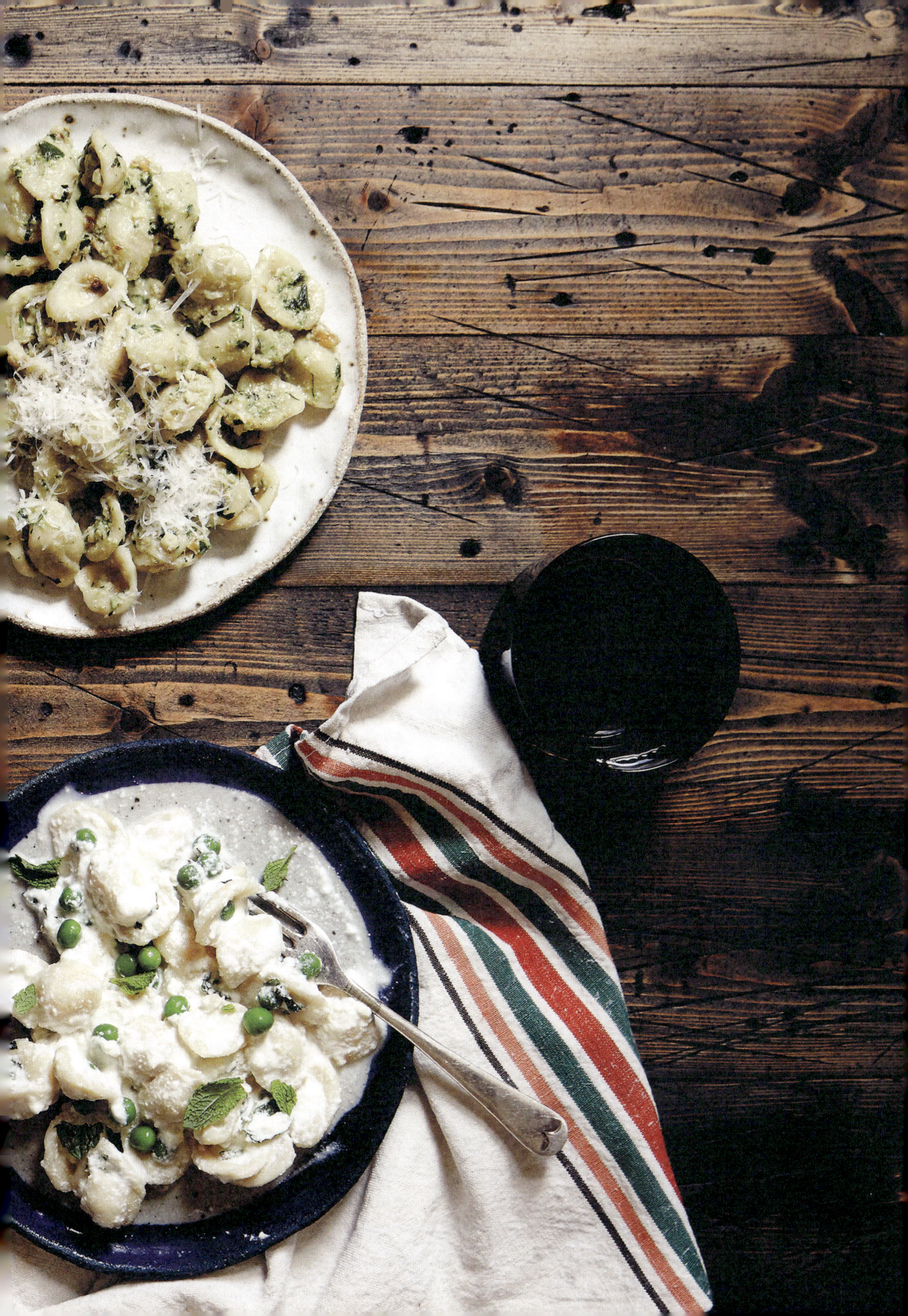

SAFFRON GNOCCHETTI WITH RAGÙ

· SERVES 4–6 ·

Gnocchetti sardi or malloreddus are tiny ridged dumplings originating from Sardinia. Saffron enriches the dough with such a lovely golden hue, you could be mistaken to think that the pasta is full of egg yolks instead. While traditionally rolled on a wicker basket, a ridged gnocchi board (see Note on page 138) is now most commonly used. If you don't have a gnocchi board at home, you could use a sushi mat or the tines of a fork to create the ridges. A sauce made with pork sausages is often served with these gnocchetti, but I've paired them with my classic ragù – a reliable sauce that I never tire of.

60 ml (¼ cup) extra-virgin olive oil

1 onion, finely chopped

2 garlic cloves, finely chopped

1 small carrot, finely chopped

1 celery stalk, finely chopped

sea salt

250 g beef mince

250 g pork mince

2 rosemary sprigs

3 fresh bay leaves

680 g tomato passata

1 tablespoon good-quality balsamic vinegar

grated pecorino, to serve

basil leaves, to serve

GNOCCHETTI SARDI

generous pinch of good-quality saffron threads

sea salt

250 ml (1 cup) warm water

200 g tipo 00 flour

200 g semolina flour (see page 13), plus extra for dusting

To make the gnocchetti dough, pound the saffron and a pinch of salt using a mortar and pestle. Place in a small bowl with the water and steep for 5–10 minutes. Tip the flours and another pinch of salt onto a clean work surface and combine. Create a well in the centre and slowly pour in enough of the saffron water, mixing with your hands, to make a soft but not sticky dough. You may not need all of the water, but don't throw it away as it can be added to the sauce. Knead vigorously for 10 minutes until smooth and elastic, adding a little more flour if the dough is too sticky or more water if too dry. Cover with a damp cloth or plastic wrap and allow to rest at room temperature for at least 30 minutes.

Break away large pieces of the dough and roll into thin sausage shapes, dusting your work surface with extra semolina flour. Cut these into 1 cm lengths and roll each piece over a ridged gnocchi board to form the gnocchetti. Use your fingers to create a little pressure as you roll, which will make an indentation as you shape the pasta – perfect for catching the sauce. Place the shaped gnocchetti onto a board or tea towel that is generously dusted with semolina flour. Continue the process with the rest of the pasta dough, arranging the gnocchetti in a single layer.

RECIPE CONTINUED OVERLEAF ·⟶

PASTA AND GRAINS 133

RECIPE CONTINUED • →

For the ragù, warm the olive oil in a large frying pan over a low heat. Add the onion, garlic, carrot, celery and a pinch of salt and cook for about 15–20 minutes until translucent and fragrant. Increase the heat to high and add the minces, stirring until browned. Add the rosemary and bay leaves and stir for a few more minutes to perfume the oil. Pour in the passata and about 300 ml of water along with any remaining saffron water. (For the water, I usually half-fill the passata bottle with water, shake and then add to the sauce, which ensures all the tomato bits stuck in the jar go into the sauce, too.) Bring to the boil, add the vinegar, then reduce the heat to medium and simmer for around 1 hour with the lid half on, until thick and rich, adding a little more water if the sauce becomes too dry.

Bring a large saucepan of generously salted water to the boil and cook the gnocchetti for 3–5 minutes until al dente. They take a little longer than regular fresh pasta, but the cooking time will really depend on the flour you've used, so check them at around the 3 minute mark – they should be a little chewy but not chalky. Drain the gnocchetti, reserving some of the pasta water, and add to the ragù along with 60–125 ml (¼–½ cup) of pasta water as needed. Stir the gnocchetti until well coated, simmer for a minute or two and season to taste. Serve immediately topped with a liberal scattering of pecorino and a few basil leaves.

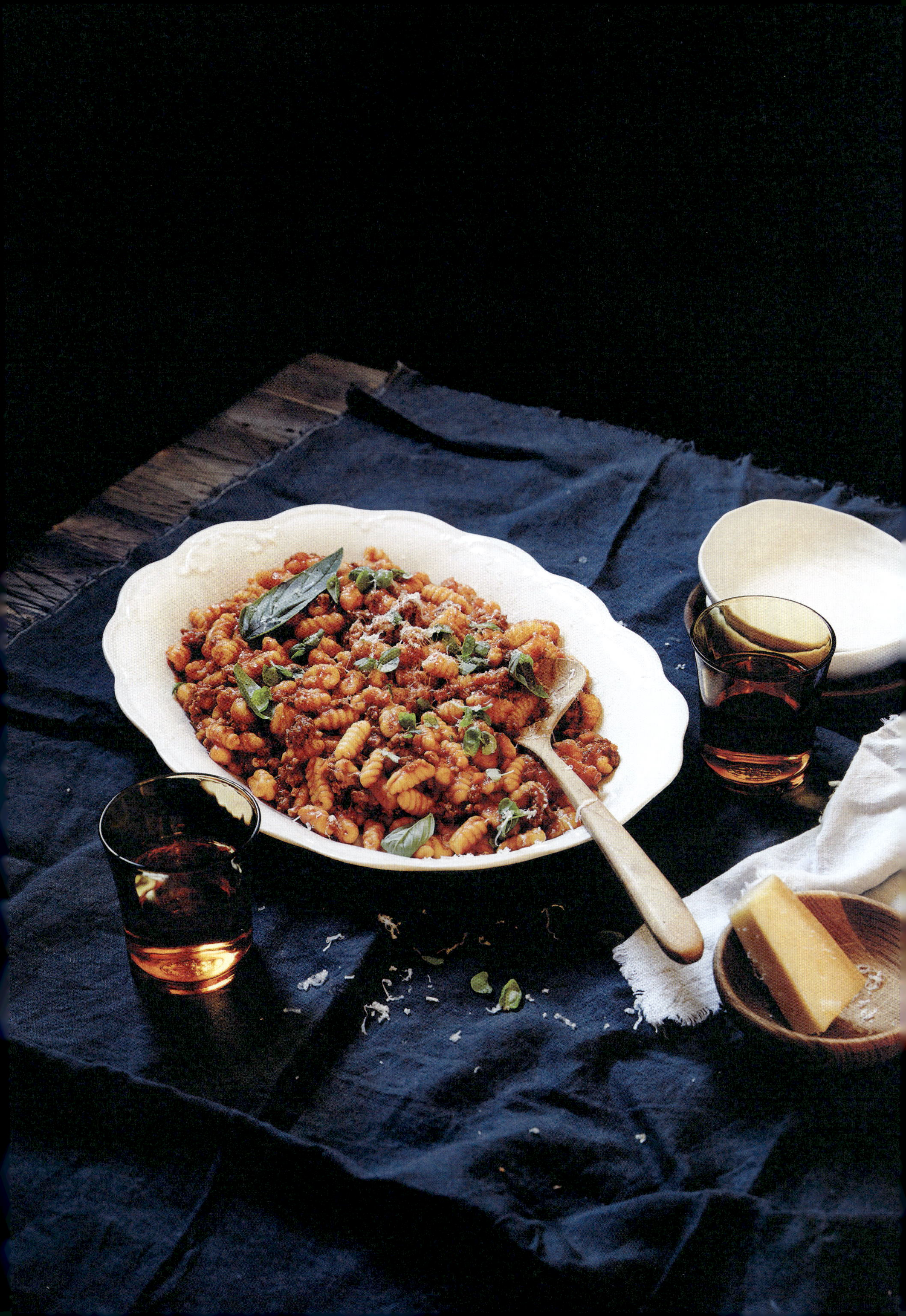

GARGANELLI WITH PANCETTA AND ZUCCHINI

SERVES 4–6

Garganelli hail from Emilia-Romagna, the home of other culinary treasures, such as tortellini, mortadella, parmesan, prosciutto and balsamic vinegar, to name just a few. It is one of my favourite regions for food, and I have fond memories of carting bags of tortellini back with me on the train to Florence after staying in Bologna for a weekend, as well as a most glorious meal of quill-shaped garganelli with peas and prosciutto cotto. These ridged beauties are similar to penne in shape, but have distinct edges along the seam where they are rolled onto themselves. They are a little more time consuming to prepare than most of the pasta I tend to make at home, and you'll need a gnocchi board and dowel to make them (see Note overleaf) – but the results are rather stunning. Garganelli would also be wonderful with the ragù on page 132, but here I've paired it with pancetta, zucchini and cream.

30 g butter

150 g zucchini, cut in half lengthways and cut into 3 cm slices

100 g flat pancetta, cut into lardons

150 ml pure cream

pinch of freshly grated nutmeg

sea salt and black pepper

grated parmesan, to serve

GARGANELLI

300 g tipo 00 flour

100 g semolina flour (see page 13), plus extra for dusting

pinch of sea salt

2 eggs, plus 2 yolks

1 tablespoon extra-virgin olive oil

50–80 ml warm water

RECIPE CONTINUED OVERLEAF ⟶

To make the garganelli, tip the flours onto a clean work surface and scatter over the salt. Make a well in the centre and crack in the eggs. Gently whisk the eggs using a fork and drizzle in the olive oil. Slowly bring in the flour and mix to incorporate. When the dough becomes stiff, use your hands to bring it together – it shouldn't be too crumbly, but also not sticky. Add a little of the water if it needs it – every flour is different, so go by feel. Knead for about 10 minutes until the dough is smooth and elastic. Flatten into a disc, cover with a damp cloth or plastic wrap and allow to rest at room temperature for at least 30 minutes.

Divide the pasta dough into four pieces. Cover three of the pieces and set aside. On a lightly floured work surface, roll the dough out using a rolling pin into a rough disc shape around 3 mm thick. Roll the dough through a pasta machine set to the widest setting, then roll again through the narrower settings, dusting with a little flour between each roll if needed, until the pasta sheet is about 30 cm long. Fold the dough back in on itself so it's slightly narrower than the width of the machine and use a rolling pin to flatten slightly. Set the machine back to the widest setting and roll back through the first settings again, folding and flattening the pasta dough before each roll. Repeat this process two more times, so you've rolled the dough through the widest settings, folding between each roll, three times in total. This makes the pasta nice and strong, and you can now roll the dough through the settings until the pasta is around 1.5 mm thick. Dust the pasta sheet with semolina flour and cut into 4 cm squares.

PASTA AND GRAINS 137

RECIPE CONTINUED ·⟶

Place a pasta square diagonally on a gnocchi board. Using an 8 mm dowel, roll up the garganelli, applying a little pressure to create the ridges. You may need to flour your board and dowel if the dough becomes sticky. Place the shaped garganelli onto a board or tea towel that is generously dusted with semolina flour. Repeat the rolling, cutting and shaping with the remaining dough pieces.

In a large frying pan, melt the butter over a medium heat until foaming, then add the zucchini. Fry gently for a few minutes, then add the pancetta and continue to cook for 2–3 minutes until the pancetta is golden and the zucchini tender. Bring a large saucepan of generously salted water to the boil and cook the garganelli for 3–4 minutes until a little under al dente (it will continue to cook in the sauce). When the pasta is nearly ready, add the cream and nutmeg to the frying pan and simmer for a few minutes until it begins to thicken. Drain the pasta, reserving some of the pasta water, and add to the sauce. Stir to coat, add 60–125 ml (¼–½ cup) of pasta water as needed, and cook for another minute or two until the pasta is al dente and the sauce is thick and creamy. Season to taste and serve topped with parmesan.

NOTE: A gnocchi board is a small wooden board with deep ridges available from most kitchenware stores. The boards usually come with a dowel, but if not you can buy one from a craft or hardware store (or use the handle of a wooden spoon or a pencil). An old butter paddle is also a fine substitute for a gnocchi board, but if you don't have either of these you can simply roll the garganelli on a flat surface, which will give you the same shape, just with a different texture.

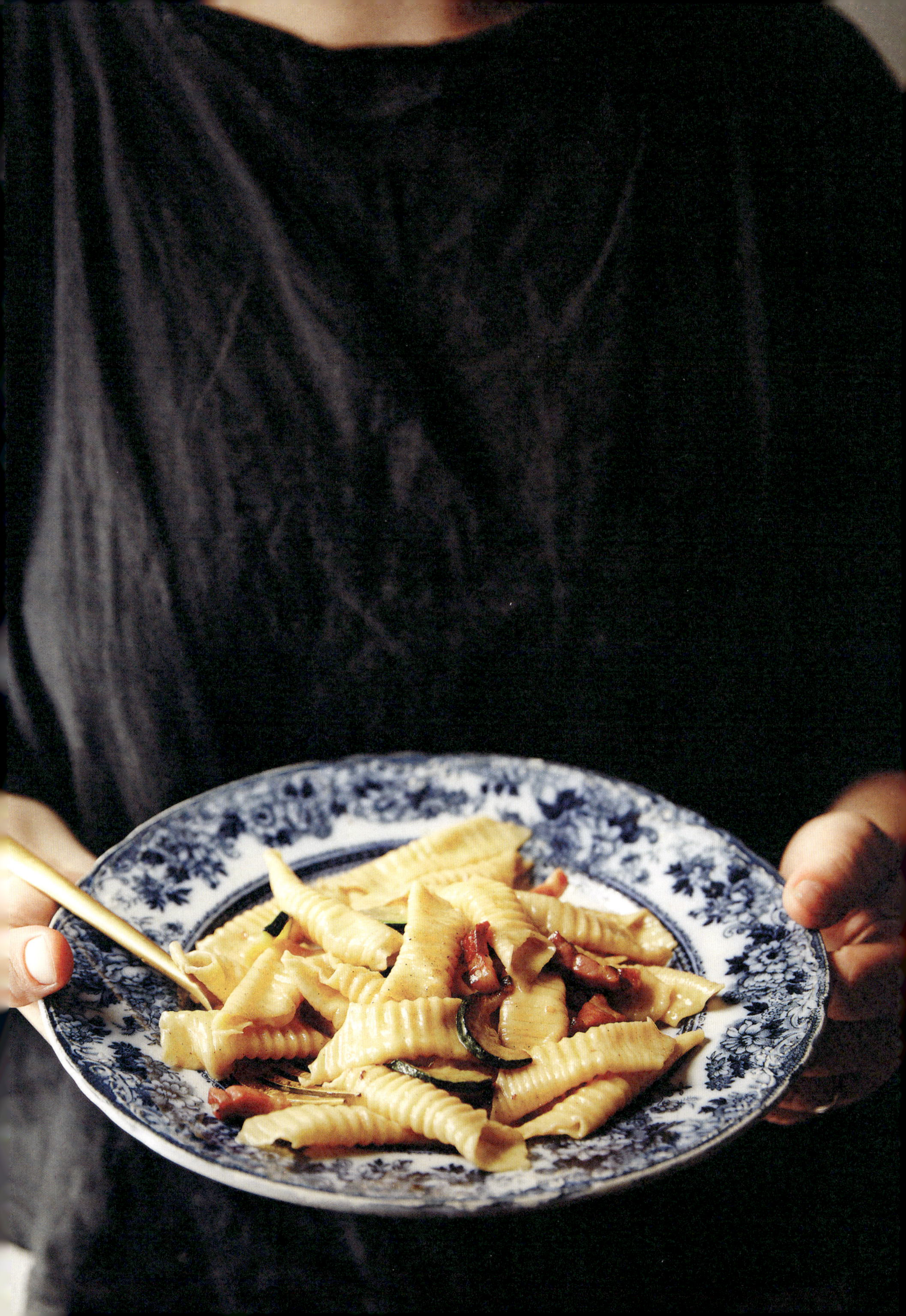

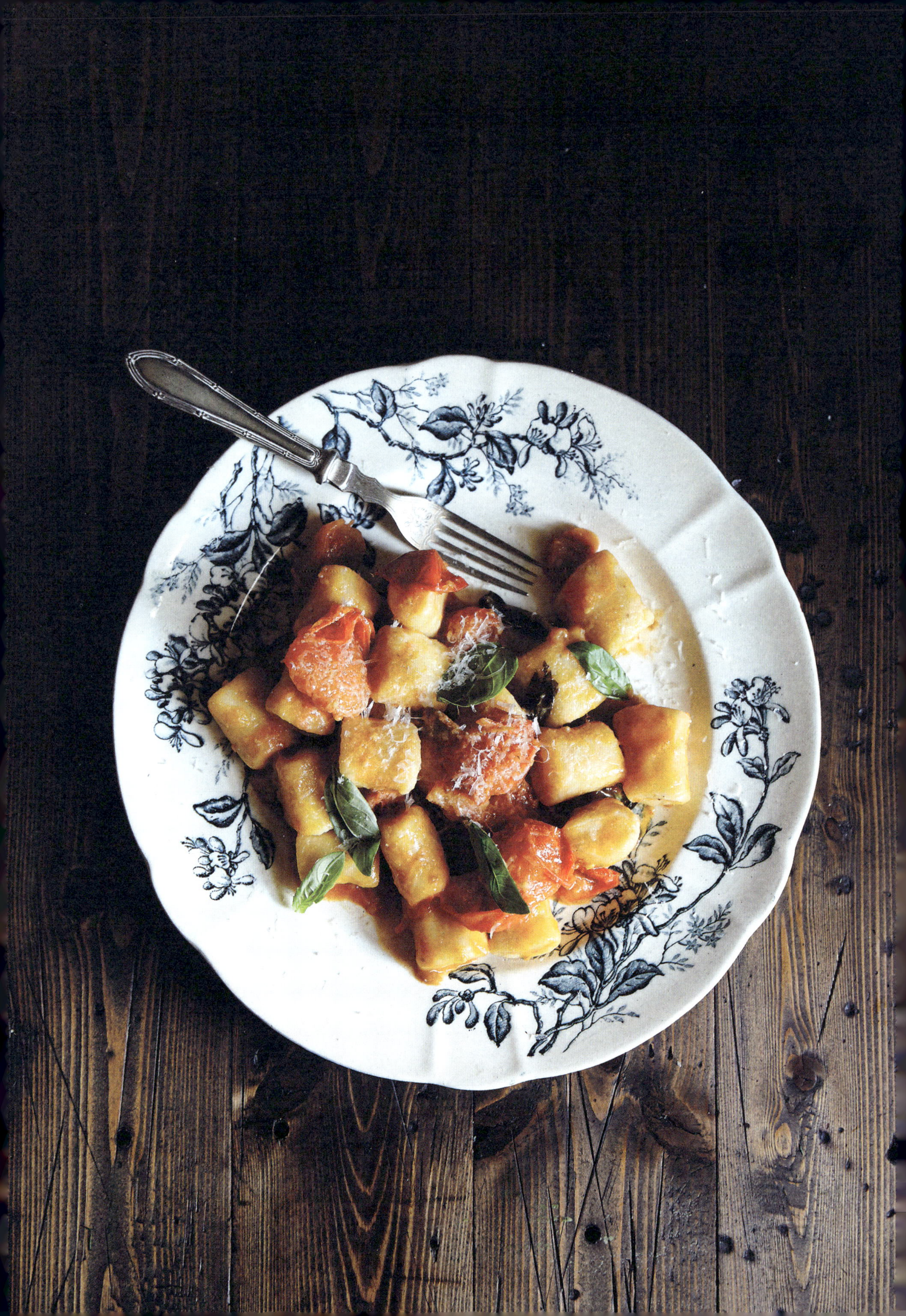

RICOTTA GNOCCHI WITH A SUMMER TOMATO SAUCE

SERVES 4

Little ricotta dumplings served in a bright, summery sauce made from cherry tomatoes is pure heaven to me. The gnocchi are quick to make, and the sauce requires very little attention – which makes it a great option on warm days. Buy the reddest and most flavourful tomatoes you can find, or better still, use homegrown. I would also recommend making your own ricotta for the gnocchi, but if you're short on time, buy good-quality firm ricotta. Anything labelled 'smooth' that comes in a container will be far too watery. This sauce is not only great with gnocchi, but also with spaghetti, penne or paccheri (a large tubular pasta from Campania and Calabria), as we ate it in Italy. I sometimes use it as pizza sauce, too.

750 g cherry tomatoes

3 garlic cloves, finely chopped

large handful of basil leaves

60 ml (¼ cup) extra-virgin olive oil

sea salt

grated parmesan, to serve

RICOTTA GNOCCHI

400 g fresh full-fat ricotta

2 egg yolks

pinch of freshly grated nutmeg

45 g parmesan, grated

100–200 g tipo 00 flour, plus extra for dusting

sea salt and black pepper

To make the gnocchi dough, combine the ricotta, egg yolks, nutmeg and parmesan in a large bowl and mix with your hands or a wooden spoon to combine. Gradually add the flour, mixing well after each addition, until the mixture comes together into a soft ball. If the dough is too sticky, add more flour, a little at a time, until you have the right consistency. Season well with salt and pepper. Cut the dough into quarters and, working with one piece at a time, roll into a sausage shape about 1.5 cm in diameter, dusting the bench with a little flour as needed. Using a knife or a pastry scraper, cut the dough into 2 cm lengths to form the gnocchi. Set the gnocchi on a tray lightly dusted with flour and repeat with the remaining dough.

For the sauce, place the cherry tomatoes, garlic and basil in a large frying pan. Drizzle over the olive oil and season generously with salt. Place the pan over a low heat and cook for 30–40 minutes or until the tomatoes have completely collapsed. During the first 5 minutes, stir quite regularly, as there won't be any liquid in the pan yet. Soon enough, the tomatoes will burst their skins and release their juices. If there are some stubborn tomatoes that haven't burst after 20 minutes or so, help them along by squishing them against the side of the pan using the back of a wooden spoon.

Bring a large saucepan of generously salted water to the boil and, when the sauce is nearly ready, cook the gnocchi for 2–3 minutes or until cooked through. Once they float to the top, I allow them to cook for a further 30 seconds before removing them. Test one after 2 minutes – if it's still dense and floury, cook for a little longer, then test again. Drain the gnocchi, reserving the pasta water, and add to the sauce. Add 60–125 ml (¼–½ cup) of pasta water as needed, stir to coat and simmer for a few minutes. Season to taste and serve immediately, topped with grated parmesan.

POTATO GNOCCHI WITH A WINTER TOMATO SAUCE

SERVES 4–6

I really struggle going without tomatoes during winter. When I taste that first summer fruit, however, I'm reminded that the wait is definitely worth it. Thankfully, I have this easy, comforting sauce that provides me with my winter tomato hit without having to sacrifice flavour. Of course, you can make this all year round, but I especially like it with winter-friendly potato gnocchi – a simple meal of simple ingredients when comfort is required. This sauce is also great to use on pizza, spooned over the bases then topped with mozzarella and basil before cooking.

It takes a little practice to master gnocchi – it's all about the feel of the dough and choosing the right potato for the job. You need a waxy yellow potato – I find white-fleshed floury potatoes not at all suitable for making gnocchi.

60 ml (¼ cup) extra-virgin olive oil

1 onion, finely chopped

2 garlic cloves, finely chopped

1 dried chilli, crumbled

sea salt

680 g tomato passata

1 × 400 g can good-quality whole peeled tomatoes (such as San Marzano)

1 fresh bay leaf

small handful of basil leaves

1 marjoram sprig

grated pecorino or parmesan, to serve

POTATO GNOCCHI

750 g yellow-fleshed waxy potatoes, well scrubbed

1 egg

sea salt

150–250 g tipo 00 flour, plus extra for dusting

RECIPE CONTINUED OVERLEAF →

Warm the olive oil in a large heavy-based saucepan over a low heat. Add the onion, garlic, chilli and a pinch of salt and cook for 15–20 minutes until very soft and fragrant. Add the passata, canned tomatoes and herbs and simmer over a low–medium heat for about 45 minutes until thick and rich, pressing the tomatoes against the pan with the back of a wooden spoon to break them up during the cooking. Season with salt and set aside.

To make the gnocchi dough, place the potatoes in a saucepan and cover with water. Bring to the boil and cook for 20–25 minutes until tender. The cooking time will of course depend on the size of your potatoes. Try not to poke and prod the potatoes too often; the less water they draw in the better. Drain the potatoes and leave to dry in the colander for 5 minutes. Lightly flour your work surface and, when the potatoes are just cool enough to handle, pass them through a potato ricer directly onto the floured bench. If you don't have a ricer, peel the potatoes and coarsely grate them. Leave the potato to cool down a little more – this makes it easier to work with your hands and also helps to remove as much moisture as possible. Add the egg and a large pinch of salt and mix gently with your hands to combine. Begin adding the flour, a little at a time, as you bring the dough together. Don't overwork the dough, just mix it enough so it can be shaped. Add just enough flour for a nice, soft, workable dough. If you're unsure about the quantity of flour, err on too little, then break off a small piece of dough and test in a pot of gently boiling water. As soon as the piece floats to the surface, remove with a slotted spoon and taste. It should be light and pillowy. If the dough disintegrates, add a little more flour.

PASTA AND GRAINS 143

RECIPE CONTINUED · →

To shape the gnocchi, take about a quarter of the dough, and flatten it into a rough rectangle about 3 cm thick. Cut into strips about 2 cm wide and, working with one strip at a time, roll into long sausage shapes, about 1.5 cm in diameter. Repeat with the other strips of dough and then line them all up in rows and dust with a little flour (this is so you can cut many gnocchi at once), all while working the dough as little as possible. Cut the dough into 1.5 cm lengths to form the gnocchi. You can either leave the gnocchi as they are, or shape using a gnocchi board or the back of a fork to create ridges. Transfer the gnocchi to a clean tea towel or board dusted with flour and repeat with the remaining dough.

When you're ready to cook the gnocchi, return the sauce to the stove over a low heat. Keep at a gentle simmer. Bring a large saucepan of generously salted water to a gentle boil. It is important that the water is not boiling rapidly as this will encourage the gnocchi to break in the water – a gentle simmer will suffice. Cook the gnocchi in batches, otherwise the water will cool too quickly and the gnocchi will turn to mush. As soon as the gnocchi rise to the top, remove with a slotted spoon and stir through the sauce. Serve the sauce-coated gnocchi on warmed plates, topped with extra spoonfuls of the tomato sauce and grated pecorino or parmesan.

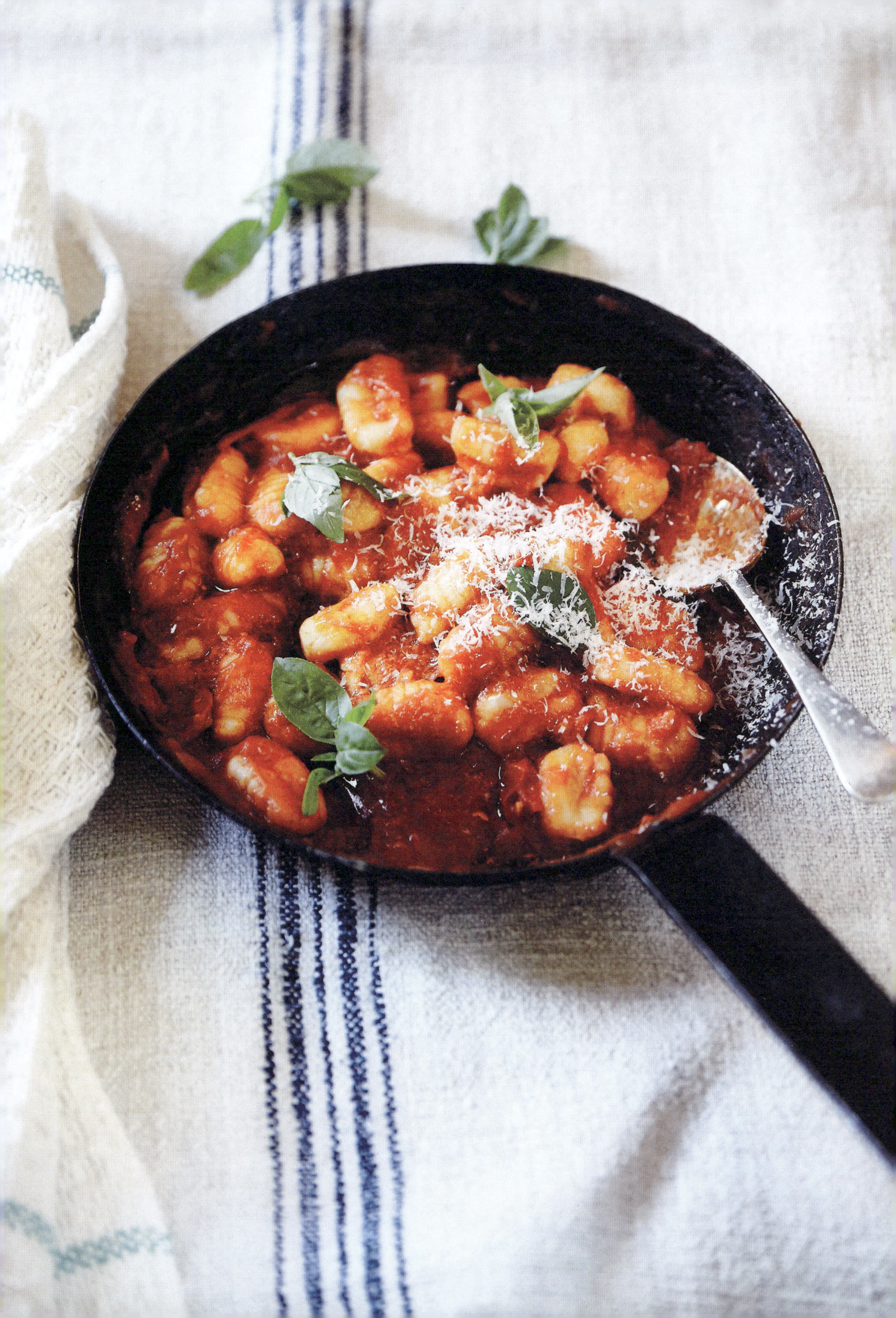

SPAGHETTI WITH PANCETTA AND VONGOLE

SERVES 4

Vongole, or clams, are such good eating, especially when paired with some pancetta and spaghetti, and cooked just right. They taste of the sea and take me back to my childhood, when we would collect pipis from a nearby beach. This dish is more about timing then anything – the pasta should be almost cooked when the vongole go in, ensuring that they both finish cooking at the same time. I sometimes add a pinch of crushed dried chilli towards the end, too, which can give the whole dish a nice kick. Undercook the pasta a little before draining, as it will continue to cook in the sauce for a minute or two as you ladle the pasta water into the sauce.

700 g vongole (clams), scrubbed

1 tablespoon extra-virgin olive oil

70 g flat pancetta, cut into lardons

500 g tomatoes, roughly chopped

100 ml dry white wine

400 g dried spaghetti

4 garlic cloves, thinly sliced

juice of ½ lemon

sea salt

handful of flat-leaf parsley leaves, finely chopped

Place the vongole in a large bowl and cover with cold water. Leave to soak for 30 minutes, then rinse well and drain. This helps to remove any sand.

Gently heat the olive oil in a large frying pan over a low heat. Add the pancetta and cook for about 3 minutes until golden. Add the tomatoes, increase the heat to medium and let them happily simmer away for 2–3 minutes, stirring occasionally. Pour in the wine, cover and simmer for 5–8 minutes until the tomatoes have collapsed and the sauce is thick.

Meanwhile, bring a large saucepan of generously salted water to the boil and cook the spaghetti according to the packet instructions, until a minute or two under al dente.

A few minutes before the pasta is ready, add the vongole and garlic to the sauce and cover with the lid to steam the clams open, which should only take a few minutes. Discard any clams that haven't opened. Drain the spaghetti, reserving the pasta water, and add to the sauce. Add the lemon juice and 60–125 ml (¼–½ cup) of pasta water as needed, and stir to coat. Let it all come together on the heat for a minute or two, adding more pasta water if the sauce seems dry. The sauce should be thick and luxurious but not watery. Season to taste, remembering that the vongole and pancetta will bring saltiness. Stir the parsley through and serve.

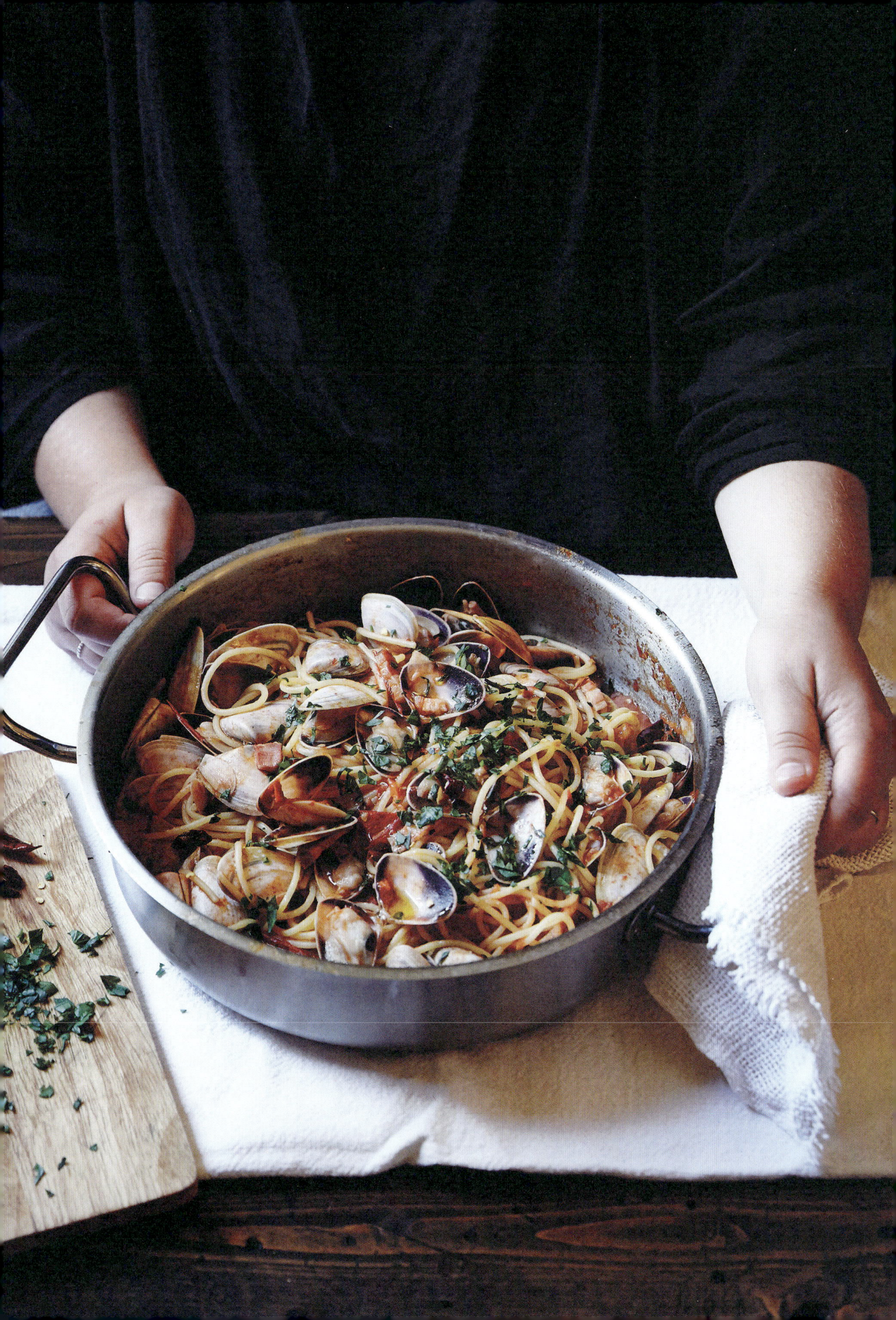

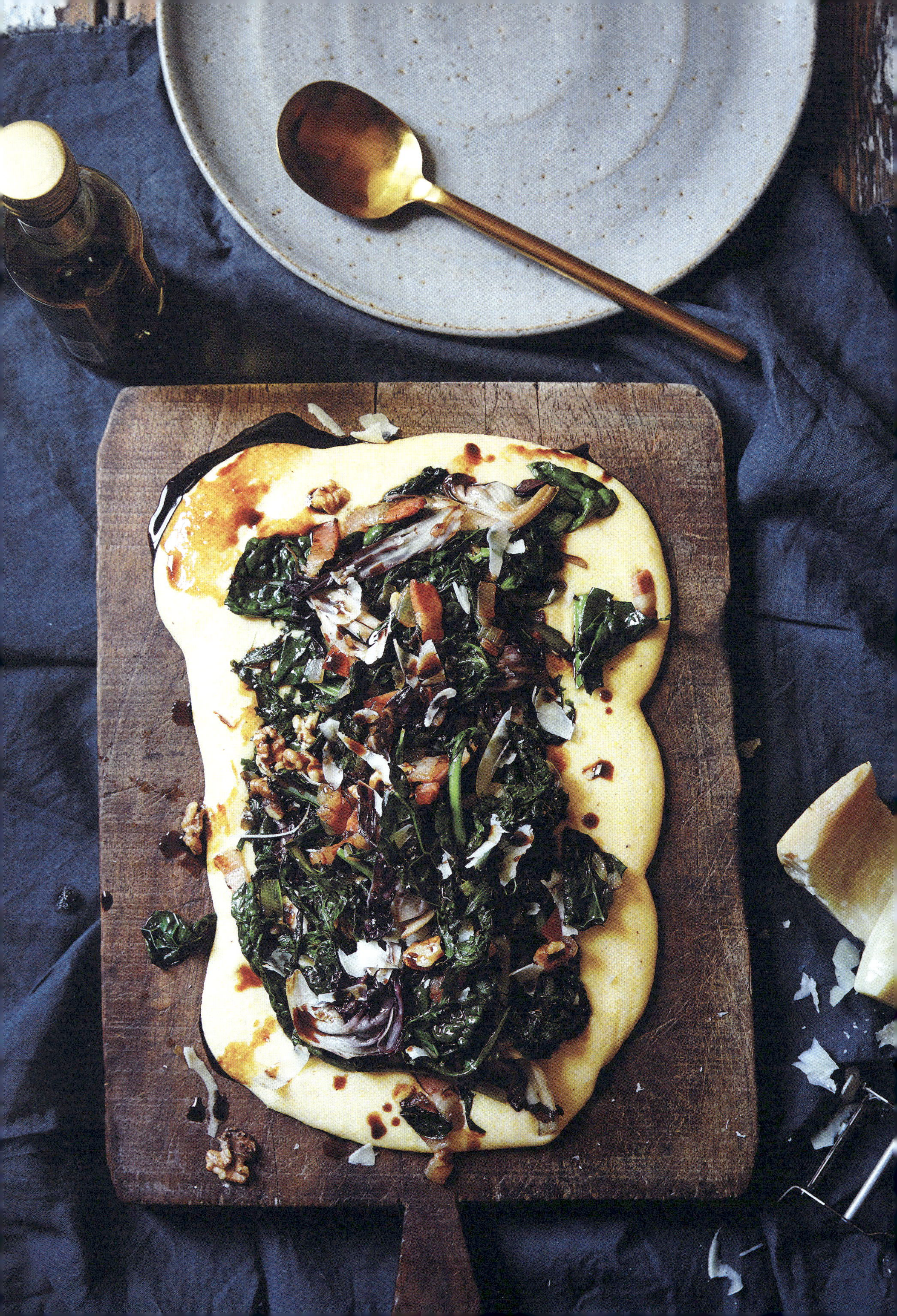

SOFT POLENTA WITH BITTER GREENS AND WALNUTS

❈ SERVES 4–6 ❈

While polenta is now viewed almost as a national treasure by many Italians – especially those in the north – it came from very humble beginnings. Initially brought to Italy from the Americas in the sixteenth century, it was considered peasant food; food that served a purpose – filling the bellies of hardworking Italians.

Although polenta is delicious just boiled in lightly salted water, I love cooking it in milk and enriching it with parmesan, butter and cream for a truly decadent meal. Polenta needs constant stirring and hardens rather fast on cooling, so I recommend cooking the onion first, then attending to the polenta. You can then gently reheat the onion and add the remaining ingredients, which only take a few minutes – this way the polenta will stay nice and creamy. If you ever come across *polenta taragna* – polenta combined with buckwheat – it has an amazing earthiness, which would be perfect here. Buy the best balsamic vinegar you can afford for this dish; it should be sweet but still sharp.

40 g (⅓ cup) walnuts

40 g unsalted butter

1 tablespoon extra-virgin olive oil

1 onion, roughly chopped

70 g flat pancetta, cut into lardons

300 g bitter leaves, such as radicchio or chicory

150 g cavolo nero, tough stems removed, leaves washed thoroughly and roughly chopped

1½ tablespoons good-quality aged balsamic vinegar

sea salt

grated parmesan, to serve

POLENTA

750 ml (3 cups) full-cream milk

1 teaspoon sea salt

250 g (1⅔ cups) polenta

80 g parmesan, finely grated

50 g unsalted butter, roughly chopped

150 ml pure cream

Lightly toast the walnuts in a dry frying pan over a low–medium heat for 1–2 minutes until just coloured. Set aside until needed.

Heat the butter and olive oil in a large frying pan over a low heat. When the butter is foaming, add the onion and cook gently for 10–15 minutes until soft and fragrant. Remove from the heat and set aside until the polenta is cooked.

To make the polenta, combine the milk with 750 ml (3 cups) of water in a large heavy-based saucepan and bring to the boil. Reduce the heat to a simmer and add the salt. Pour in the polenta in a thin, steady stream, whisking to prevent lumps. Cook for 30–40 minutes, stirring constantly with a wooden spoon, until the polenta is smooth and silky. You may need to add a little extra water if the polenta becomes too thick. Stir in the parmesan, butter and cream and continue to stir until incorporated. Season to taste and keep warm.

Place the frying pan with the onions back over a medium heat and add the pancetta. Fry for 3–4 minutes until golden. Add the bitter leaves and the cavolo nero and cook for about 3 minutes until just collapsed. Stir the walnuts through and remove from the heat. Season to taste.

Serve the creamy polenta on a wooden board topped with the greens or on individual plates. Drizzle with the balsamic vinegar and sprinkle generously with parmesan.

ORZOTTO OF MUSHROOMS WITH MASCARPONE

SERVES 8–10

Orzotto is a portmanteau of the words *orzo* ('pearl barley' in Italian – not to be confused here with the pasta of the same name) and *risotto*. It is essentially pearl barley cooked in the style of a risotto, where stock is slowly added to the grains, allowing it to be fully absorbed before adding more. This results in a much creamier texture, due to the starch released during the stirring and cooking, than if the barley was simply boiled. My favourite way to cook orzotto is with a mixture of mushrooms, which complement the nuttiness of the barley very well.

200 g pearl barley

2 tablespoons extra-virgin olive oil, plus extra to serve

1 onion, finely chopped

1 celery stalk, finely chopped

sea salt

1 litre vegetable stock (see recipe page 104)

10 g dried porcini

125 ml (½ cup) dry white wine

400 g mixed mushrooms, larger mushrooms roughly torn or chopped

60 g unsalted butter, roughly chopped

3 garlic cloves, roughly chopped

black pepper

large handful of flat-leaf parsley leaves, finely chopped

grated parmesan, to serve

mascarpone (see recipe page 238), to serve

Preheat the oven to 180°C.

Cook the pearl barley in a saucepan of boiling water for 15 minutes. Drain and set aside.

Heat the olive oil in a large heavy-based saucepan over a low heat and fry the onion and celery with a pinch of salt for about 10 minutes until soft and fragrant.

Combine the stock and porcini in a saucepan over a medium heat. Bring to a gentle simmer.

Add the pearl barley to the saucepan with the onion and celery and cook for a minute or two, stirring to coat and toast the grains. Increase the heat, add the wine and bring to a simmer. Once the barley has absorbed the wine, add one ladle of the hot stock. Keep stirring and allow the barley to absorb the liquid before adding more. Keep adding stock, simmering and stirring until the barley is almost al dente – this should take about 25 minutes and should use up most of the stock.

Meanwhile, arrange the mushrooms in a tray and scatter with the butter and garlic. Bake for 15 minutes until the mushrooms have collapsed and the garlic is soft.

Add the mushrooms and any of the garlicky butter left in the tray to the barley and cook, stirring, for another 5 minutes. You can add the porcini from the stock now too, if you like. Season to taste. Remove from the heat and stir the parsley through. Serve in shallow bowls topped with a scattering of parmesan, a generous dollop of mascarpone and a drizzle of olive oil.

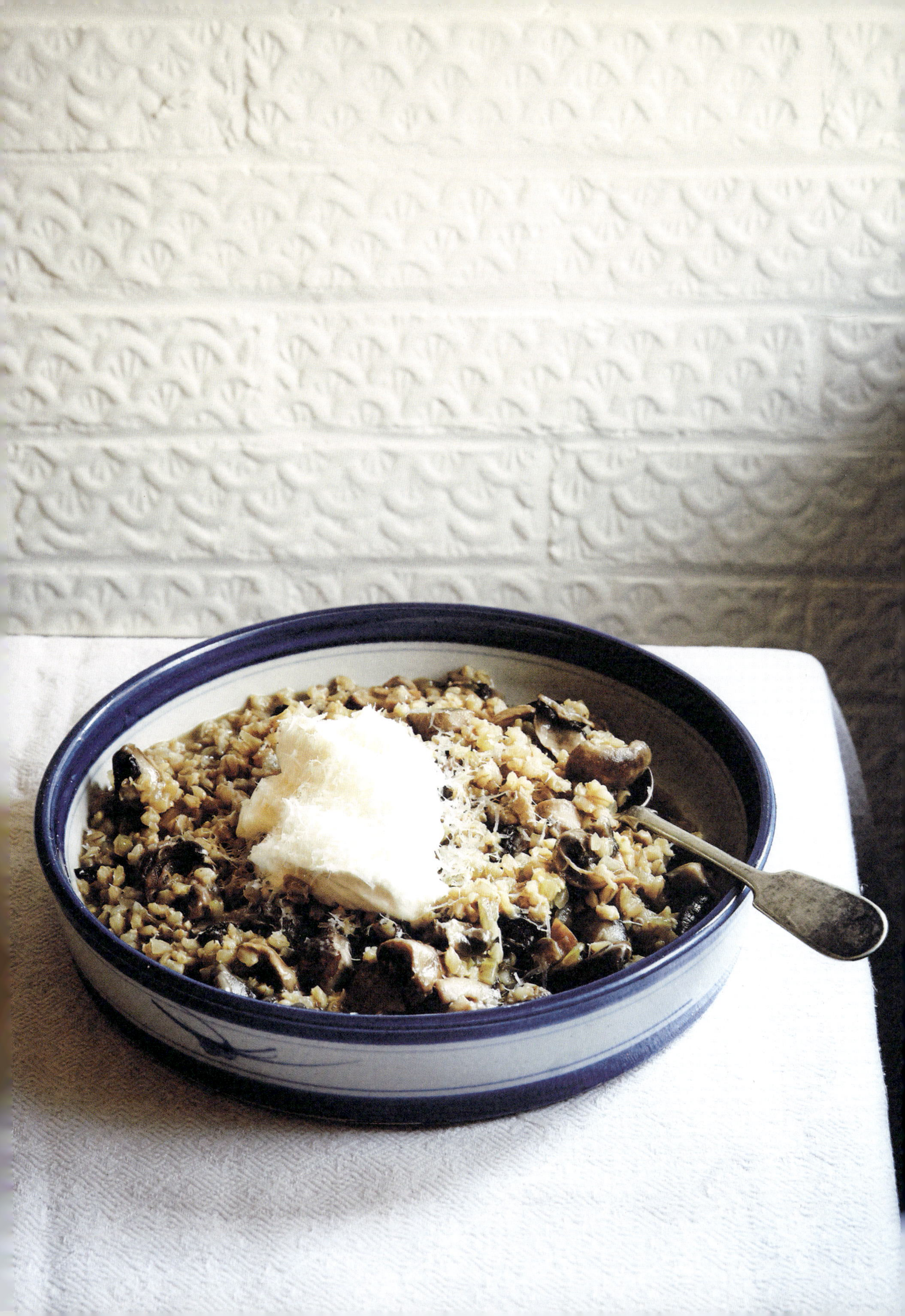

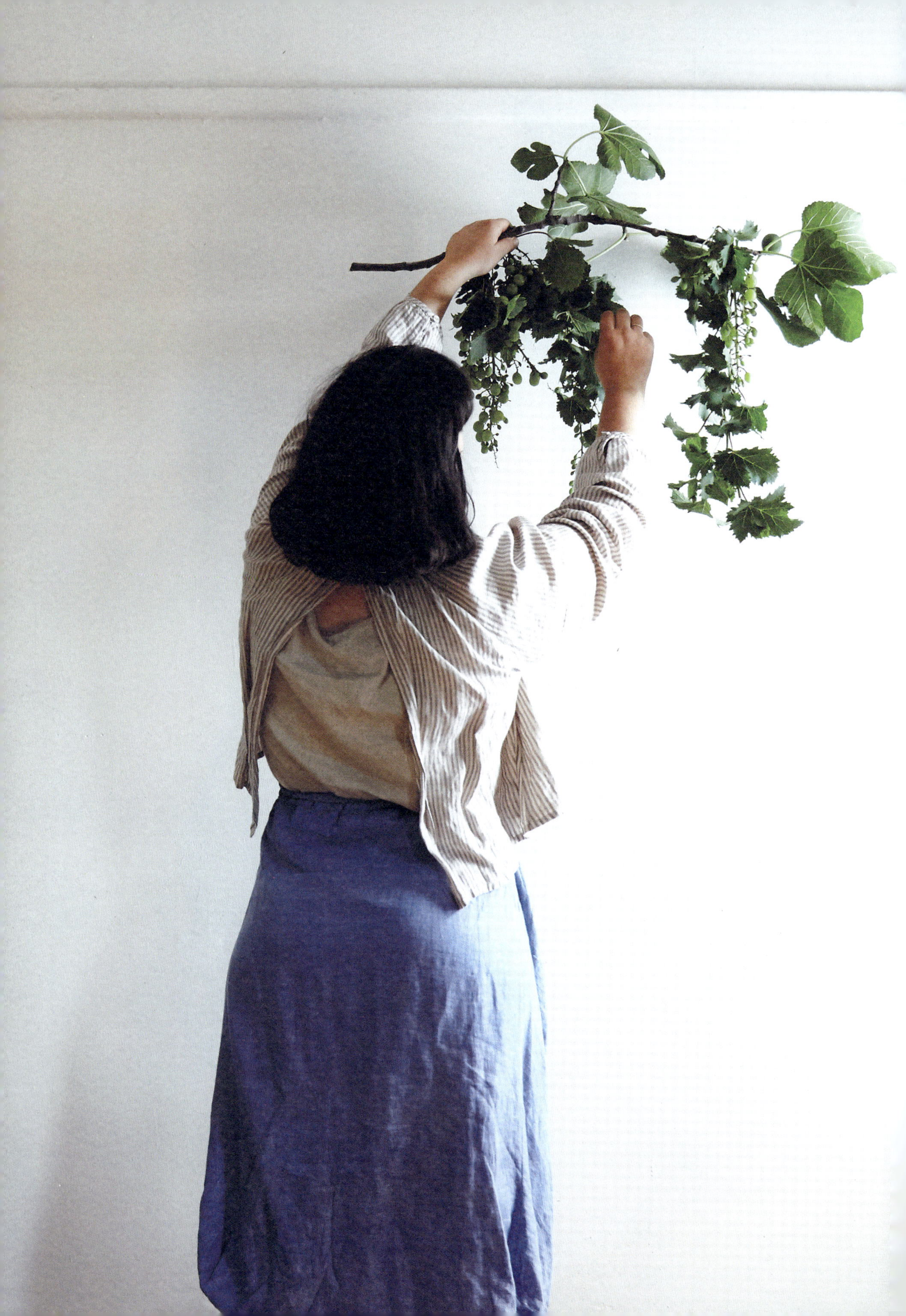

SEAFOOD AND MEAT

There is no moment in the kitchen when I feel more grateful than when I am preparing meat or seafood for a meal. In our house, it is something that is reserved more for weekends and special occasions, when I can go to the market or butcher and seek out good-quality and ethically raised meat and fish. If we ate it every day, that level of care would become unattainable. I also prefer to buy cuts of meat that require time and effort in the kitchen to bring them to their best for eating. Aside from being more affordable, these cuts are usually the most flavourful, too.

GRILLED SQUID WITH NDUJA, GARLIC AND ALMONDS

❖ SERVES 4 ❖

Nduja is a spicy and smoky spreadable salami, hailing from Calabria in the south of Italy. I love adding it to seafood dishes, especially squid – something I ate often growing up. Topped with garlic, almonds and herbs all pounded together, this dish is full of flavour. I've suggested using 15 g of nduja, which doesn't seem like a lot, but it really is rather potent stuff. Feel free to add more or less as you see fit. You can find it at most good Italian grocers.

2 large squid (about 900 g in total), cleaned (see Note) or 500 g squid tubes, cut on the diagonal into large pieces

2 tablespoons extra-virgin olive oil, plus extra for drizzling

sea salt

2 garlic cloves, peeled

40 g (¼ cup) almonds

large handful of flat-leaf parsley leaves

large handful of mint leaves

15 g nduja, or to taste

juice of 1 lemon

Mix the squid, olive oil and a pinch of salt in a bowl and set aside for 5–10 minutes.

Meanwhile, pound the garlic and a pinch of salt to a paste using a mortar and pestle. Add the almonds and continue to pound. Now add the parsley and mint and incorporate, pounding and mixing until you have a crumbly mixture. Alternatively, you can pulse everything together in a food processor. Set aside.

Heat a large frying pan over a high heat and fry the squid for 2–3 minutes until just cooked. Add the nduja, breaking it up with the back of a wooden spoon, and the lemon juice. Cook for a further minute, stirring to coat the squid. Sprinkle over the garlic–almond mixture, drizzle over a little more olive oil and serve.

NOTE: To clean whole squid, first pull out the guts, separating them from the tentacles. Remove the beak and discard. Pull away any of the outer purple skin, then slice each squid hood on one side so you can lay them flat. Using the back of the knife, scrape away any membrane.

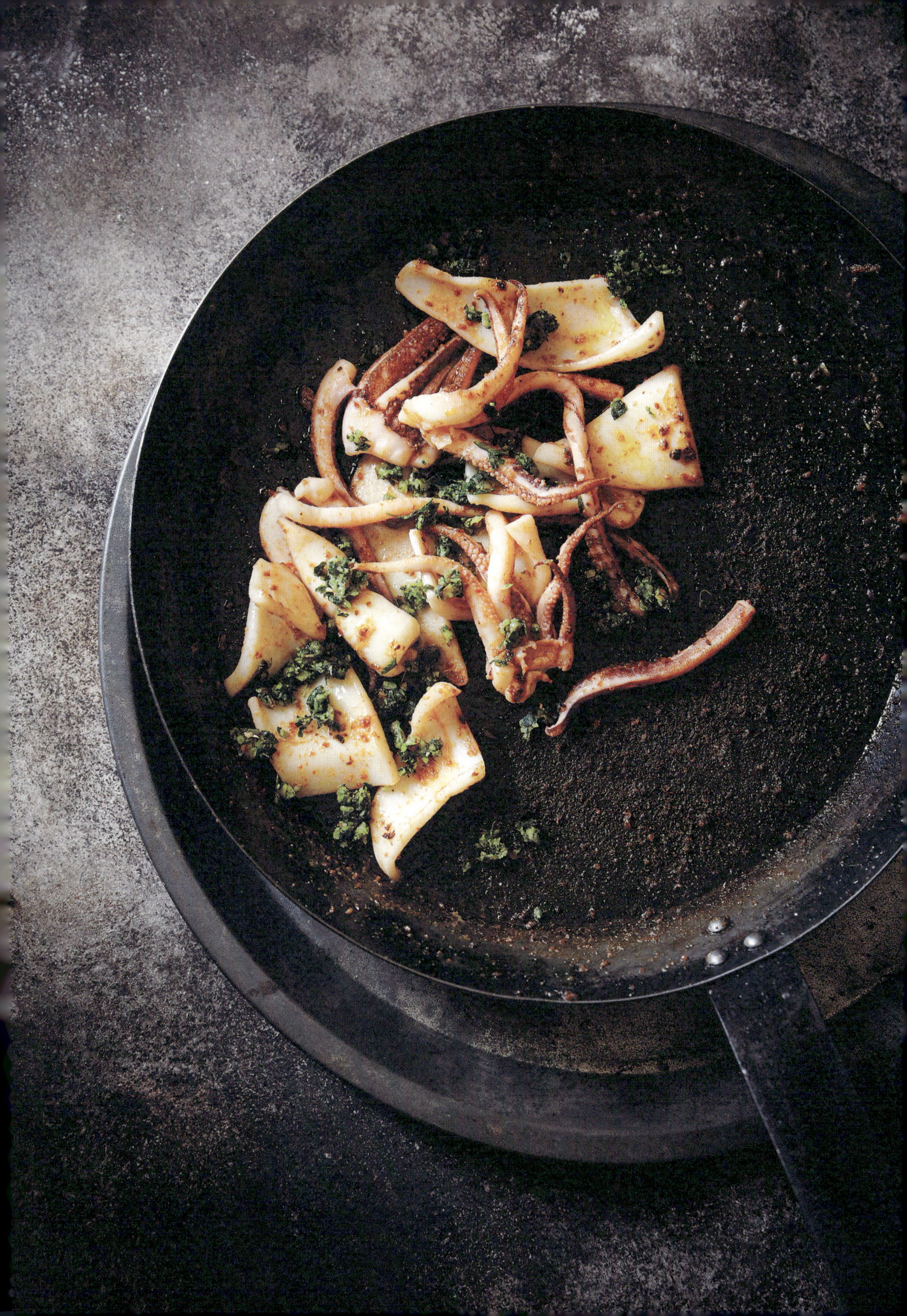

CRISPY SCHOOL PRAWNS WITH FENNEL SALT AND AIOLI

❈ SERVES 6 ❈

Crispy prawns, eaten whole, are a real treat – especially served with an ice-cold beer on a summer's day. School prawns are small prawns, usually about 4 cm in length. They are sweeter than their larger counterparts and are especially delicious fried – if you can't find them, try using whitebait, which are perfect prepared this way too. While traditional aioli is made without egg, I've added a yolk here for a creamier accompaniment to the prawns. Try making the aioli using a mortar and pestle – although it's a bit of a workout, I find it easier than using a whisk and bowl.

vegetable oil, for deep-frying

150 g (1 cup) plain flour

sea salt and black pepper

500 g school prawns, left whole

lemon wedges, to serve (optional)

FENNEL SALT

1 tablespoon fennel seeds

2 tablespoons sea salt flakes

AIOLI

2 garlic cloves, sliced

sea salt

1 egg yolk

70 ml extra-virgin olive oil

70 ml vegetable oil

lemon juice (optional), to taste

To make the fennel salt, lightly toast the fennel seeds in a dry frying pan over a low–medium heat for 1–2 minutes until fragrant. Cool slightly, crush lightly using a mortar and pestle, then combine with the salt flakes. Set aside.

To make the aioli, pound the garlic and a generous pinch of salt to a smooth paste using a mortar and pestle. Mix in the egg yolk, stirring until emulsified. Slowly pour in the oils, just a little at a time, stirring with the pestle until you have a thick emulsion. Season with some lemon juice, if desired, and a little more salt. If the aioli is too thick, stir in a little warm water. Keep refrigerated until ready to serve.

Heat the vegetable oil in a heavy-based saucepan or deep-fryer to 180°C, or hot enough that a cube of bread dropped into the oil turns golden brown in 15 seconds.

Place the flour in a dish and season well with salt and pepper. Toss the prawns in the flour to coat and shake off any excess. Deep-fry, in batches, for about 3 minutes until crispy, a little golden and cooked through. Drain on paper towel and serve immediately sprinkled with the fennel salt and with the aioli alongside. You might like some lemon wedges for squeezing, too.

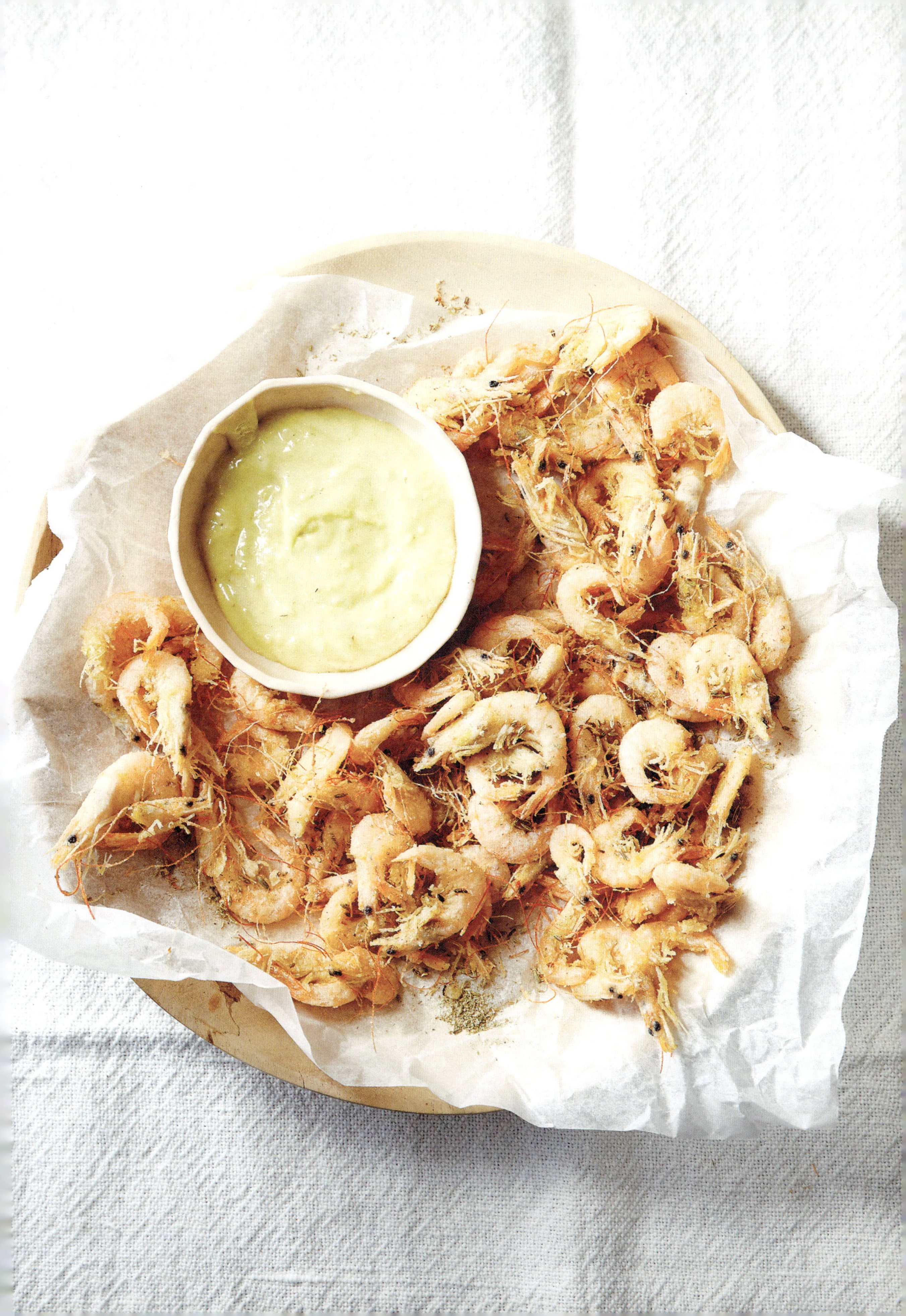

SEAFOOD STEW

SERVES 4

When I was a child I was astonished that my mum could turn a fish head and some scrappy vegetables into this amazing stew, bulked out with rice to feed our big family. For us, making use of ends and scraps was normal – and, in fact, a celebration of how resourceful a cook could be, to create something satisfying and nourishing for the family out of so little.

My version is a little more dressed up, but could easily be made as my mum did, with basic fish offcuts. Similarly, other seafood can be used, like blue swimmer crab, mussels or scallops; just be aware of cooking times. Served with grilled baguette, rubbed with olive oil and garlic, this dish is generous and such a pleasure to eat. Sometimes, I do as my mum would do and scatter some uncooked rice into the stew during the last 15 minutes of the cook. It soaks up all the goodness of the broth and makes for a heartier meal.

250 g pipis

2 tablespoons extra-virgin olive oil, plus extra for drizzling

1 small fennel bulb, finely diced, fronds reserved

1 onion, finely diced

1 carrot, finely diced

2 celery stalks, finely diced

1 teaspoon fennel seeds

4 garlic cloves, 3 roughly chopped, 1 cut in half

sea salt

250 ml (1 cup) dry white wine

500 ml (2 cups) fish stock (see recipe page 104) or water

250 g (1 cup) tomato passata

300 g raw prawns, shelled and deveined, tails intact

1 × 400 g piece of rockling or other firm white fish, bones and skin removed, cut into 3 cm pieces

2 small squid (about 450 g in total), cleaned (see Note on page 154) or 250 g squid tubes, sliced into rings

8 slices of baguette

handful of flat-leaf parsley leaves, roughly chopped

handful of mint leaves, roughly chopped

lemon wedges, to serve

Place the pipis in a large bowl and cover with cold water. Leave to soak for 30 minutes then rinse well and drain. This helps to remove any sand.

Heat the olive oil in a large heavy-based saucepan over a low heat. Add the fennel bulb, onion, carrot, celery, fennel seeds, chopped garlic and a pinch of salt. Cook for 10–15 minutes until soft and fragrant. Add the wine and simmer for 5 minutes, scraping any bits from the bottom of the pan. Stir in the stock or water and the passata. Simmer for 15–20 minutes to allow the broth to reduce and the flavours develop. Add the pipis, prawns, fish and squid to the stew and gently stir to coat. Cover with a lid and simmer for 5 minutes or until the seafood is just cooked through and the pipis have opened.

Meanwhile, preheat a grill to hot. Drizzle a little olive oil over the baguette slices and arrange on a baking tray. Place under the grill and toast for 2–3 minutes, flipping the slices halfway, until golden on both sides. Rub the oiled side of the toasts with the cut sides of the remaining garlic clove.

Discard any unopened pipis from the stew, season to taste and serve into individual bowls. Top with the reserved fennel fronds, herbs and the toasted baguette slices, with the lemon wedges alongside.

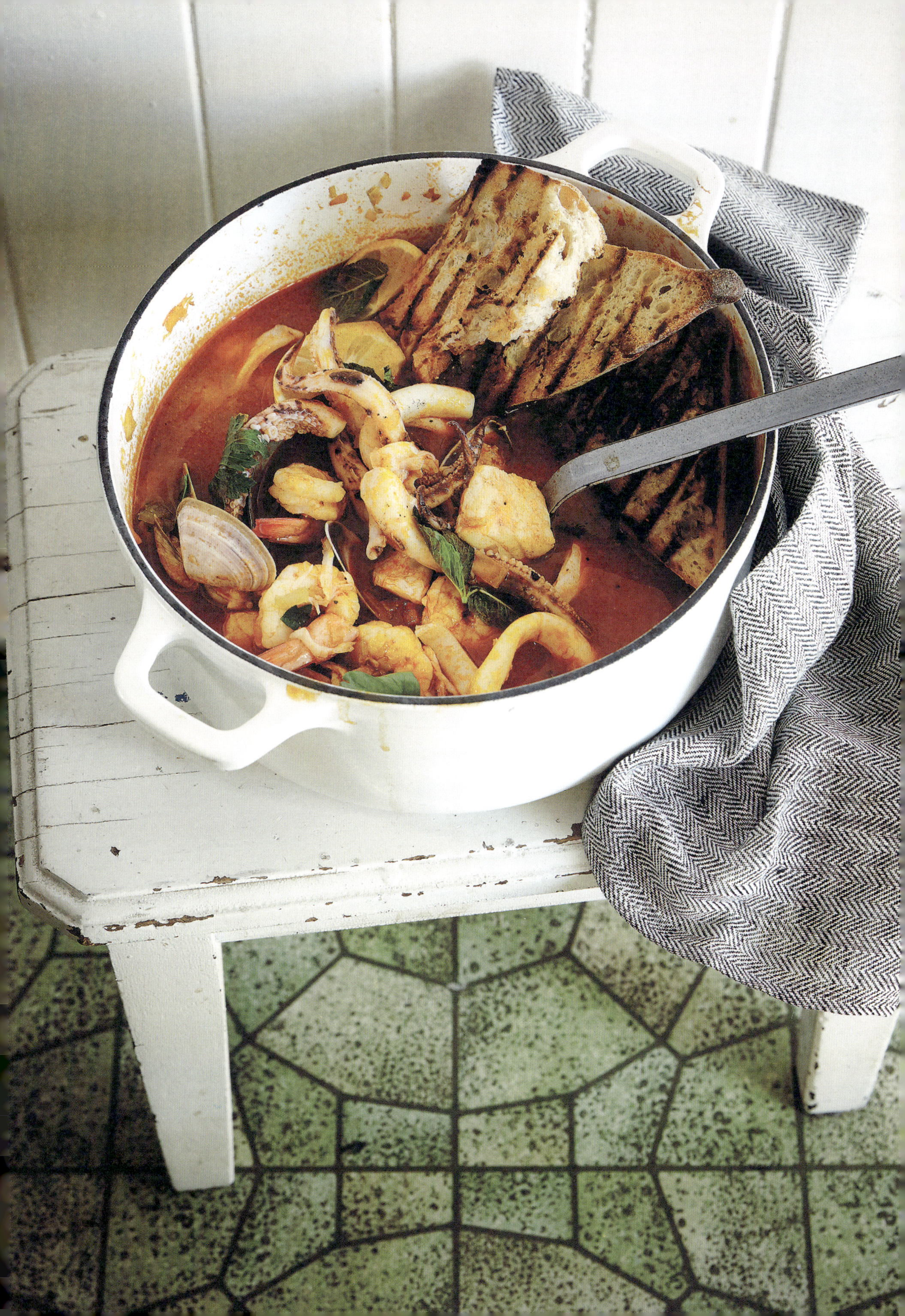

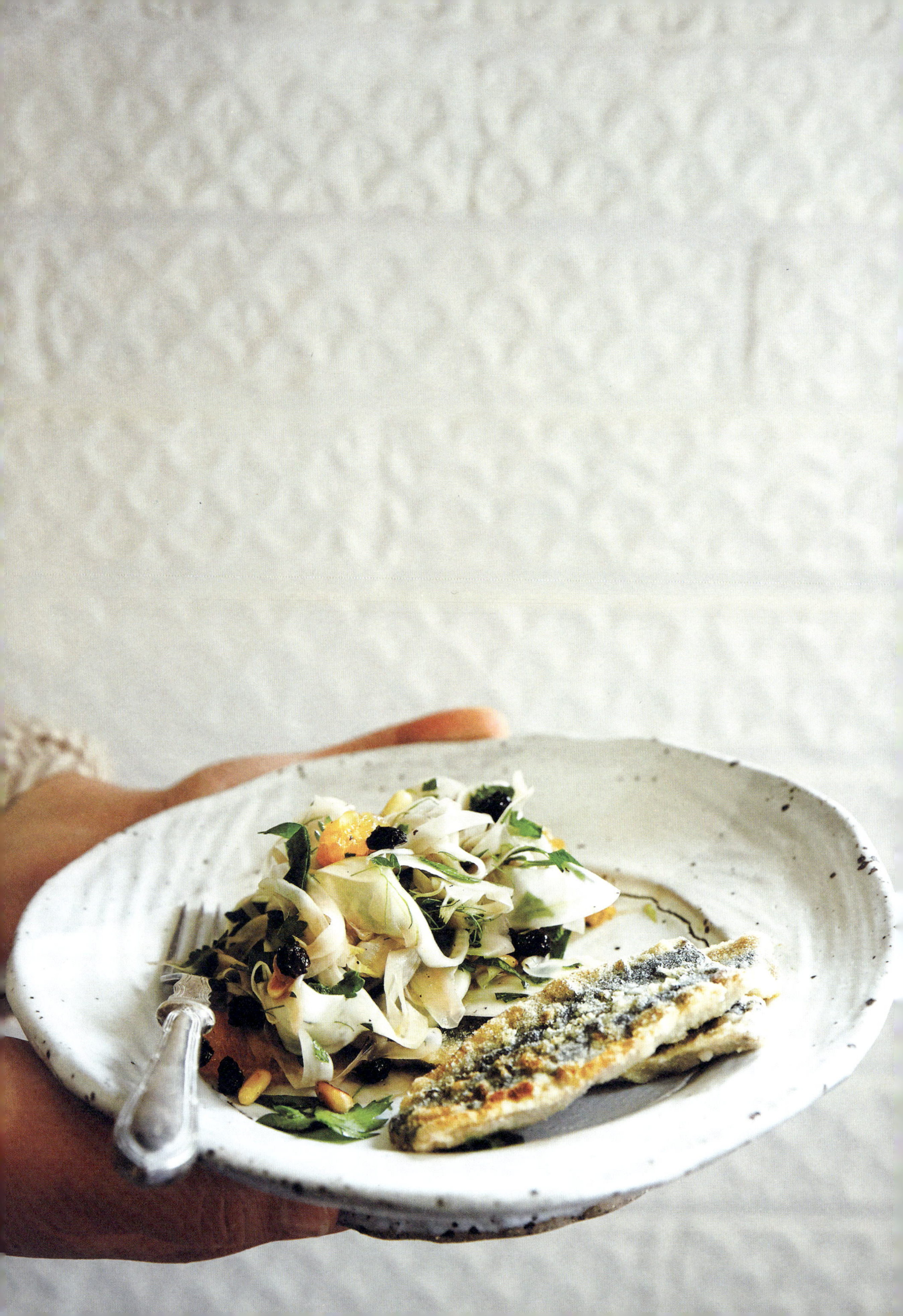

SARDINES WITH PINE NUTS, FENNEL AND ORANGE

· SERVES 4 ·

Oily fish like sardines are perfectly matched with something sharp to cut through their lovely richness. Adding some sweetness helps, too. You can buy sardines already filleted, but doing it yourself is quite straightforward, if a little fiddly – see the note at the end of the recipe for instructions.

30 g (¼ cup) currants

2 tablespoons red wine vinegar, plus extra if needed

2½ tablespoons pine nuts

1 orange, peeled and cut into segments

1 fennel bulb (about 300 g), thinly sliced, fronds reserved

small handful of flat-leaf parsley, roughly chopped

80 ml (⅓ cup) extra-virgin olive oil, plus extra if needed

sea salt and black pepper

16 good-sized sardine fillets (about 500 g in total) or 1 kg whole sardines, cut into fillets (see Note)

fine semolina, for dusting

Mix the currants and vinegar in a non-reactive (glass or ceramic) bowl and let stand for 10 minutes.

Lightly toast the pine nuts in a dry frying pan over a low–medium heat for 1–2 minutes until just coloured. Set aside to cool.

Combine the orange segments, pine nuts, fennel bulb and fronds and parsley in a bowl. Add the currants and vinegar, drizzle with 2 tablespoons of the olive oil and toss to combine. Season to taste and adjust the balance of vinegar and oil if needed – it should be rather sharp, but still well rounded. Set aside while you cook the sardines.

Season the sardine fillets and then lightly dust them with the semolina. Heat the remaining olive oil in a large frying pan over a medium–high heat and fry the sardines, skin-side down, for 2 minutes. Turn over and cook ever so briefly, 20–30 seconds. Arrange the sardines on a serving plate and top with the fennel salad, drizzling any of the dressing over the top.

NOTE: To fillet the sardines, assuming they have already been scaled and gutted, first remove the heads and tails. Flatten the fish by pressing down on the backbone – so the inside of the fish is flat on your cutting board – then turn the sardine over and remove the main bone. Trim the sardines as necessary. You'll need to buy about double the weight of whole fish to yield the desired fillet amount.

TRAY-ROASTED CHICKEN WITH GRAPES, OLIVES AND WALNUTS

SERVES 4–6

A meal that can be prepared in just a few minutes is sometimes very necessary and much appreciated in the middle of the week. Nice free-range chicken from a reputable source will ensure this dish really sings. You really must use skin-on chicken thighs to prevent them from drying out. I like to use good-quality Italian olives, with their pits still in, for the best result.

6 boneless chicken thigh fillets (about 800 g in total), skin on
120 g red grapes
50 g (¼ cup) olives
2 garlic cloves, roughly chopped
30 g (¼ cup) walnuts
1 rosemary sprig, leaves picked
1 lemon
2 tablespoons extra-virgin olive oil
sea salt

Preheat the oven to 180°C.

Arrange the chicken thighs, skin-side up, in a deep roasting pan. Scatter around the grapes, olives, garlic, walnuts and rosemary. Halve the lemon, squeezing the juice into the pan, then nestle the lemon halves into the grapes and olives. Drizzle with the olive oil, season with sea salt and roast, uncovered, for 40–45 minutes until the chicken is cooked through and golden. If there is too much liquid in the pan, increase the oven temperature to 200°C. Remove the chicken from the pan, keep warm and return the tray to the oven for 5–10 minutes to reduce the liquid. Return the chicken to the pan and serve.

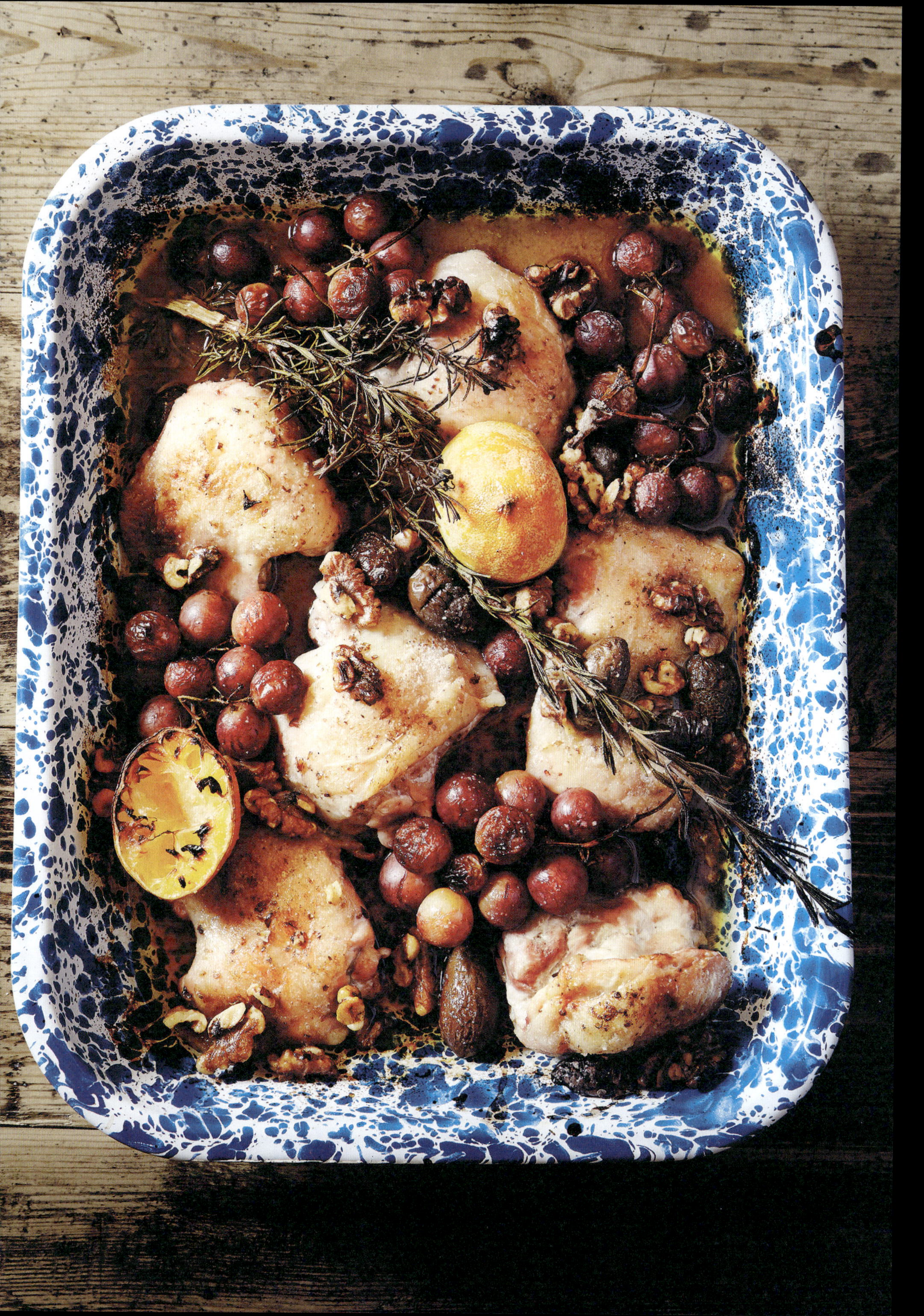

FRIED CHICKEN WITH FENNEL SLAW AND CAPER MAYONNAISE

· SERVES 4–6 ·

I prefer to use only chicken thighs when making fried chicken – a mixture of different cuts will require different cooking times, which can make it tricky to have all of the pieces cooked perfectly. Frying the chicken twice and leaving it to rest between cooking also helps to give you an even cook. The marinade perfumes the chicken and cuts through the richness.

3 garlic cloves, finely chopped

1 rosemary sprig, leaves picked and roughly chopped

1 tablespoon extra-virgin olive oil

2 tablespoons red wine vinegar

sea salt

800 g boneless, skinless chicken thigh fillets

vegetable oil, for deep-frying

200 g cornflour

CAPER MAYONNAISE

2 egg yolks

1 teaspoon dijon mustard

1 tablespoon white wine vinegar

150 ml light olive oil

1 tablespoon salted capers, rinsed and roughly chopped

sea salt

FENNEL SLAW

2 fennel bulbs, finely sliced, fronds reserved

¼ white cabbage (about 200 g), finely sliced

1 red shallot, finely sliced

large handful of dill, roughly chopped

large handful of flat-leaf parsley leaves, roughly chopped

juice of ½ lemon

sea salt and black pepper

Combine the garlic and rosemary with the olive oil, vinegar and a generous pinch of salt in a non-reactive (glass or ceramic) bowl. Add the chicken, mix to coat and leave to marinate for 30 minutes at room temperature.

To make the caper mayonnaise, whisk the egg yolks, mustard and vinegar in a bowl. Add a few drops of the olive oil, whisk to emulsify, then continue to whisk while pouring in the remainder of the oil in a thin, steady stream, until the mayonnaise is thick. Stir in the capers, season to taste and refrigerate until needed.

For the slaw, mix all of the ingredients in a large bowl with about 70 g (¼ cup) of the caper mayonnaise. Season to taste and set aside while you fry the chicken.

Heat the vegetable oil in a heavy-based saucepan or deep-fryer to 180°C, or hot enough that a cube of bread dropped into the oil turns golden brown in 15 seconds.

Drain the excess marinade from the chicken and toss the chicken in the cornflour to coat. Fry, in batches, for 3 minutes. Drain on paper towel and rest for 4 minutes. Return the chicken to the hot oil and cook again, in batches, for just 30–60 seconds more – the outside of the chicken should be crunchy and lightly golden. Season with salt and serve with the fennel slaw and an extra dollop of the caper mayonnaise, if desired.

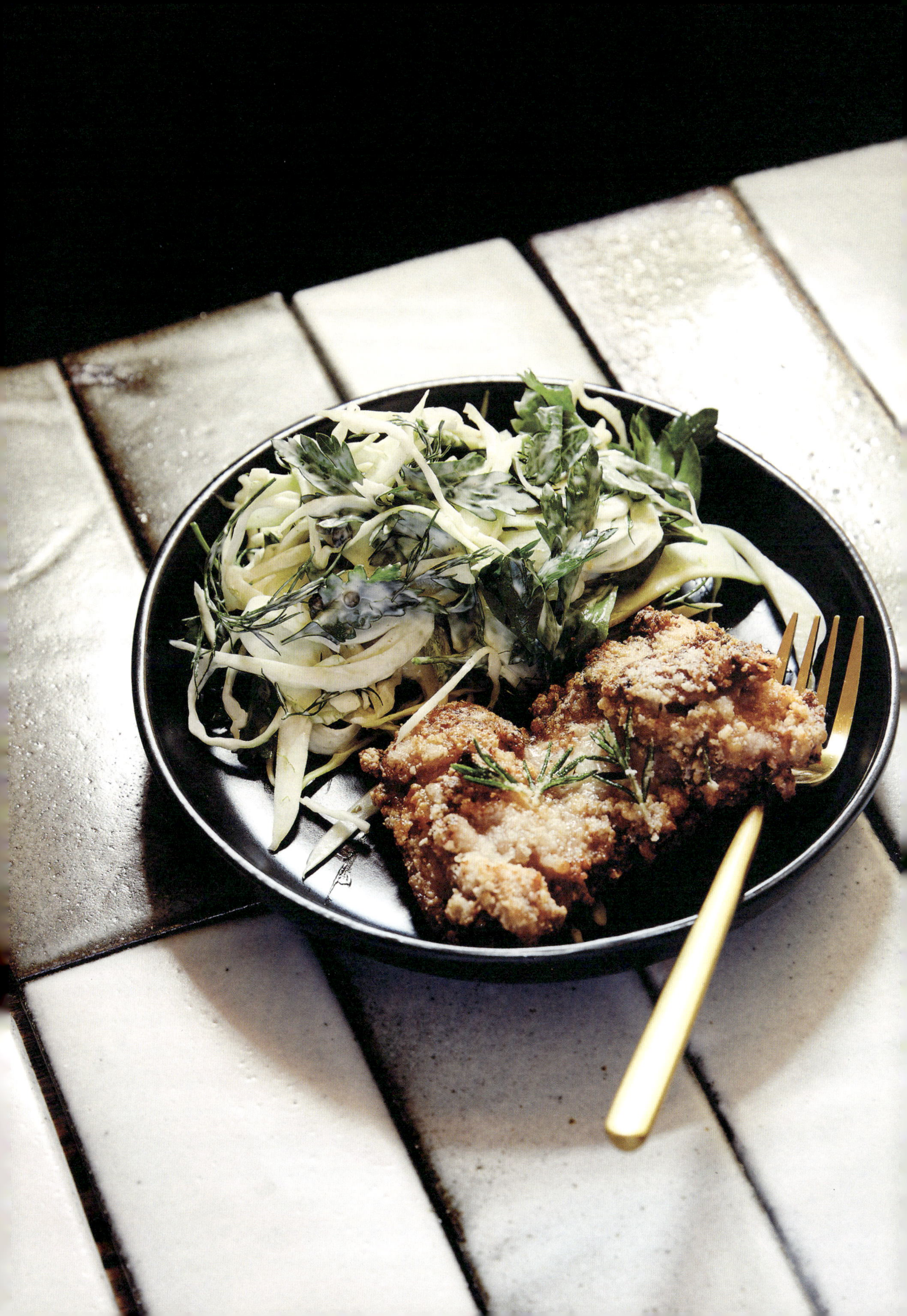

SLOW-ROASTED CHICKEN AND STOVETOP POTATOES

· ❈ SERVES 4 ❈ ·

I like to roast my chicken slowly at a low temperature and then slather it in butter and finish it off in a super-hot oven. The reward for your patience is wonderfully tender chicken with a burnished buttery skin. The stovetop potatoes are a great alternative to oven-roasted, and have the added benefit of not having to coordinate oven space while the chicken is roasting. Perfumed with rosemary and garlic, they are crunchy on the outside and soft in the middle. Serve the chicken and potatoes with the house salad on page 70 for a complete meal.

1 × 1.5 kg chicken

large handful of woody herbs such as sage, tarragon, oregano and thyme

1 lemon, cut in half

6 garlic cloves

2 onions, cut in half

1 tablespoon extra-virgin olive oil

200 ml dry white wine

sea salt

40 g butter, softened

STOVETOP POTATOES

80 ml (⅓ cup) extra-virgin olive oil

700 g yellow-fleshed waxy potatoes, scrubbed and cut into 1.5 cm cubes

2 garlic cloves

1 rosemary sprig

sea salt

Ensure your chicken is completely dry, either by patting it down with paper towel or leaving it uncovered in the fridge for at least 1 hour.

Preheat the oven to 110°C.

Place the chicken in a roasting pan. Fill the cavity of the chicken with the herbs and the lemon halves. Tie the legs together with kitchen string, if desired. Scatter the garlic and onion around the chicken. Drizzle the chicken with the olive oil and pour the wine around the base. Season everything generously with salt. Roast for 1½ hours.

Remove the chicken and increase the oven temperature to 220°C. Rub the butter all over the chicken and cook for 15–20 minutes until golden, basting the chicken with the buttery juices during the first 5 minutes. Allow to rest for 10 minutes before carving.

Meanwhile, for the stovetop potatoes, heat the olive oil in a large frying pan over a low–medium heat and add the potatoes, along with the garlic and rosemary. Cook for 20–30 minutes, stirring every few minutes, until the potatoes are cooked and crunchy. Season generously with salt and serve alongside the chicken.

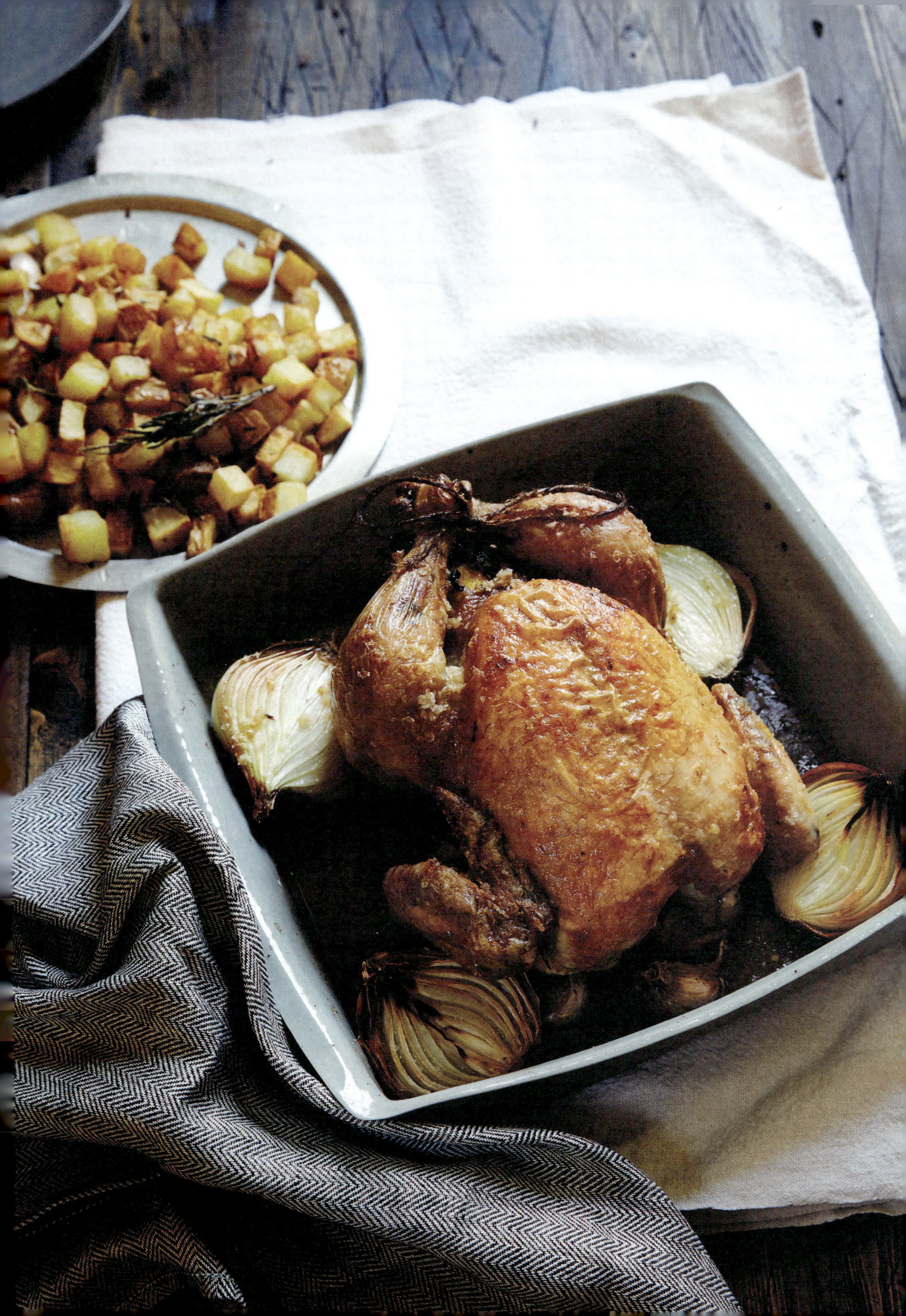

LENTILS WITH CAVOLO NERO AND SAUSAGE

SERVES 6

This recipe is inspired by a dish of lentils and cotechino (a fatty Italian sausage made from gelatinous parts of the pig) traditionally eaten together on New Year's Eve. The lentils are said to bring good fortune and that is a tradition I stick to. Cavolo nero – possibly my favourite leafy green – really brightens up this version, and I've replaced the cotechino with pork sausages, which are much leaner and easier to find. Choose a good-quality sausage; something like a nice Italian pork and fennel would be lovely. You can make the salsa verde in advance, as well as the lentils, which will just require reheating as you cook the sausages. Be sure to sort through your lentils before cooking them – small rocks and debris are often easily disguised.

1½ tablespoons extra-virgin olive oil, plus extra if needed

1 carrot, finely diced

1 onion, finely diced

sea salt

100 ml dry white wine

1 fresh bay leaf

1 tomato, roughly chopped

3 garlic cloves, roughly chopped

350 g French green (puy) lentils

1 litre chicken stock (see recipe page 105)

1 bunch of cavolo nero, tough stems removed, leaves roughly chopped

6 good-quality pork sausages

SALSA VERDE

1 thick slice of day-old white crusty bread, crust removed, roughly torn

full-cream milk, for soaking

1 garlic clove, peeled

pinch of sea salt

1 tablespoon salted capers, rinsed

3 anchovy fillets

large handful of flat-leaf parsley leaves

finely grated zest and juice of ½ lemon

60 ml (¼ cup) extra-virgin olive oil, or enough to loosen the mixture

Heat the olive oil in a large heavy-based saucepan over a low heat and cook the carrot and onion with a pinch of salt for about 10 minutes, until soft and translucent. Add the wine, increase the heat to medium and simmer for 1–2 minutes. Throw in the bay leaf, tomato, garlic and lentils and cover with the chicken stock. Bring to the boil then simmer, covered, for 40 minutes or until the lentils are al dente. Add the cavolo nero, stir for a minute or two, then cover and remove from the heat. Season to taste.

Meanwhile, for the salsa verde, first place the bread in a small bowl, add just enough milk to cover and leave to soak for 10 minutes. Squeeze out the excess milk and set aside. Finely chop the garlic with the salt. Add the capers and anchovies and continue to chop. Now add the parsley and chop until everything is fine and amalgamated. Add the bread and keep chopping until everything is nicely combined. Transfer to a bowl, add the lemon zest and juice and enough olive oil to loosen the mixture.

Cook the sausages in a pan or on a grill, with a little olive oil if needed, until nicely browned and cooked through. Serve with the lentils alongside and topped with salsa verde.

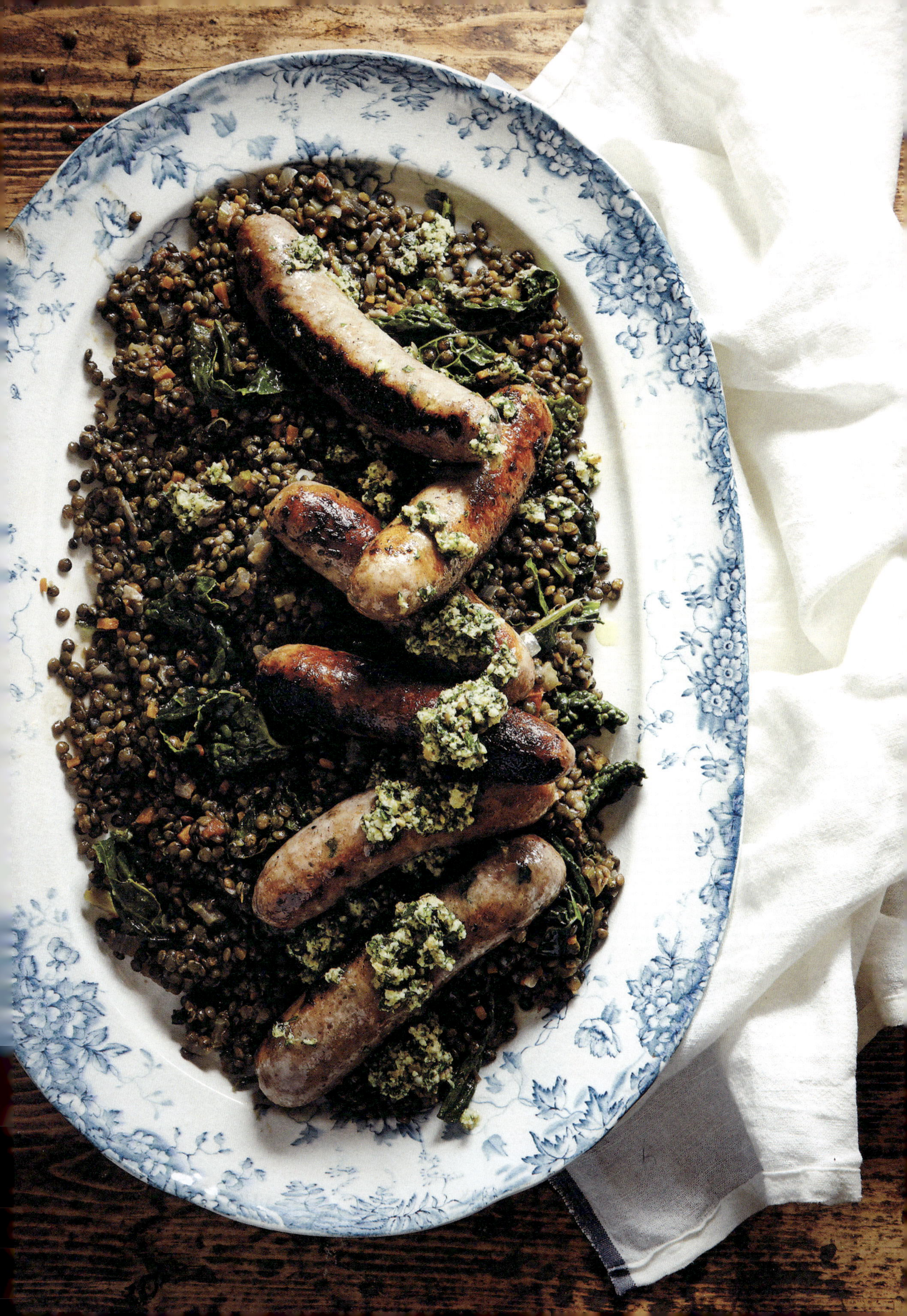

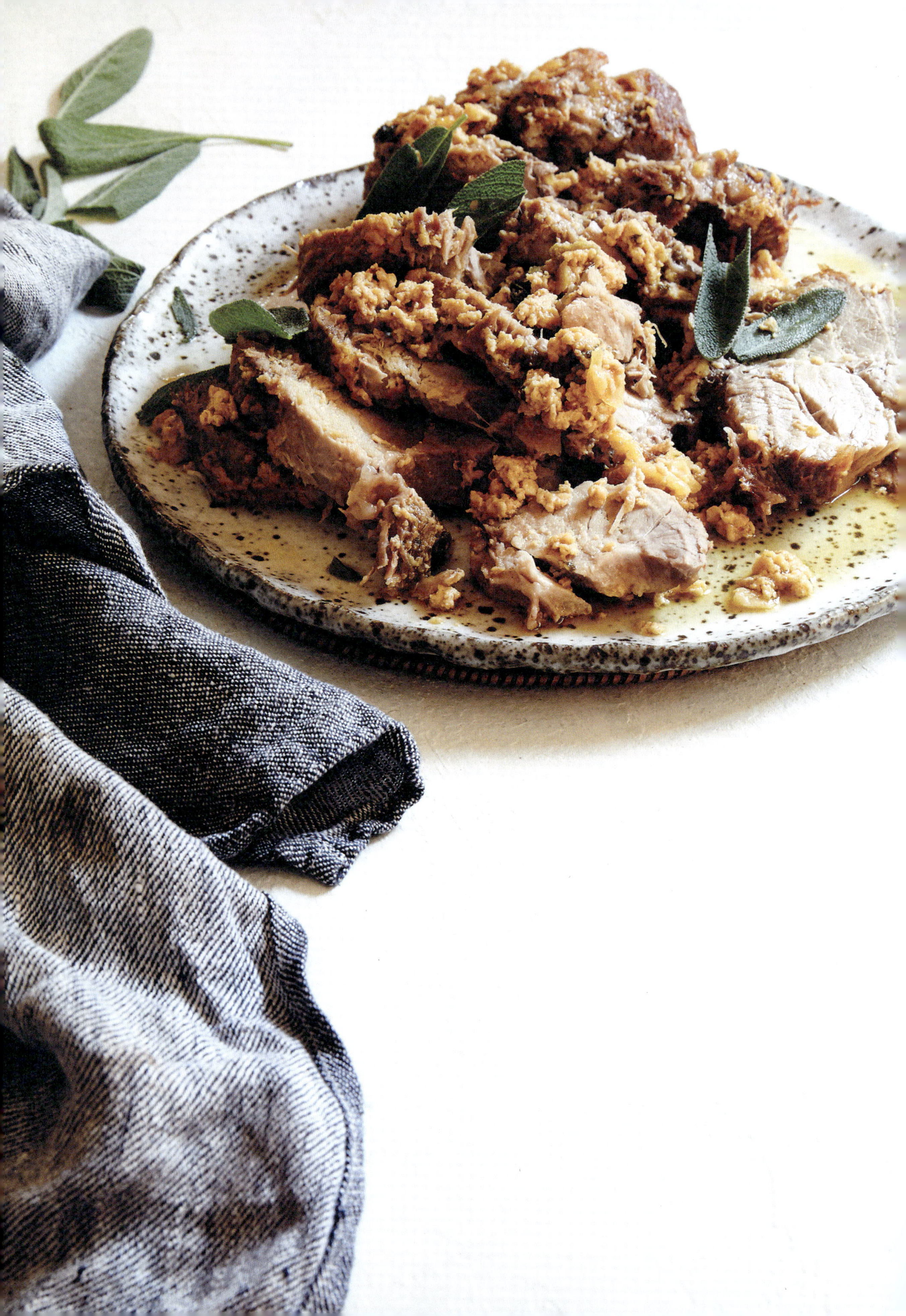

PORK COOKED IN MILK

SERVES 4–6

While this certainly isn't the prettiest of dishes, it really doesn't matter when something tastes this good. The lactic acid in the milk tenderises the pork as it cooks and then turns into wonderful golden curds thanks to the lemon. I learned to make this dish from Roberta, a wonderfully generous lady in Italy who is like family. She would use turkey, but traditionally pork is the meat of choice. You can use pork loin, but I find the neck is much nicer. Serve with some blanched greens dressed simply in olive oil and lemon juice, or buttered new potatoes.

2 tablespoons extra-virgin olive oil

1 × 1 kg piece of pork neck, excess fat trimmed

8 garlic cloves, peeled

handful of sage leaves

1 litre full-cream milk, plus extra if needed

peeled zest of 2 lemons

sea salt and black pepper

Heat the olive oil in a large heavy-based saucepan over a medium heat. Add the pork and brown on all sides. Remove from the pan and set aside. Throw in the garlic and sage and stir for a minute to coat in the oil. Return the pork to the pan, pour in the milk and add the lemon zest. Cook over a medium heat, partially covered with a lid, for 2½–3 hours, turning the pork occasionally. Resist the urge to skim the sauce as it's cooking – the foaming milk is important to create the rich sauce you are left with at the end. The pork should be extremely tender, and the milk should be a lovely thick sauce with golden curds. If you find that the sauce hasn't reduced enough, simply take the lid off and simmer uncovered and, if it seems to be reducing before the pork is tender, top up with some warmed milk. Season to taste and slice the pork, arranging it on a serving dish. Spoon the sauce over and serve.

PORK AND WHITE BEANS

SERVES 4–6

Any cut of pork suitable for braising would be perfect for this dish. I use the neck, a secondary cut, but you could also use the shoulder or belly – anything with enough fat and connective tissue for the long cooking time is ideal. Try to source dried beans that aren't too old – old ones will need far more cooking time than the pork. I don't always soak my beans before cooking, but due to the low cooking temperature here it's very necessary. You'll need to soak them overnight.

350 g dried cannellini beans

1½ tablespoons extra-virgin olive oil

1 onion, finely diced

1 carrot, finely diced

2 celery stalks, finely diced

2 garlic cloves, roughly chopped

1 teaspoon fennel seeds

pinch of dried chilli flakes

sea salt

2 fresh bay leaves

4 thyme sprigs

small handful of sage leaves

1 tablespoon tomato paste

250 ml (1 cup) dry white wine

1 × 1 kg piece of pork neck, cut into three large pieces

finely grated zest of 1 lemon

Place the cannellini beans in a bowl and cover with cold water. Leave to soak overnight, then drain and rinse.

Preheat the oven to 160°C.

In a large heavy-based ovenproof saucepan, heat the olive oil over a low heat. Add the onion, carrot, celery, garlic, fennel seeds, chilli and a pinch of salt and cook gently for 10–15 minutes or until soft and translucent. Stir in the herbs, then add the tomato paste and white wine and stir to combine. Add the cannellini beans and 600 ml of water. Increase the heat and bring to the boil. Add the pork, ensuring it is immersed in the liquid, and season with salt. Simmer for 10 minutes then cover with a lid and cook in the oven for 3–3½ hours, checking every hour or so to make sure the beans and pork haven't dried out – you may need to add a little more water during cooking. When ready, the beans should be tender and the pork falling apart.

Season to taste and scatter the lemon zest over the top. Serve in shallow bowls, spooning the braising liquid over the pork and beans.

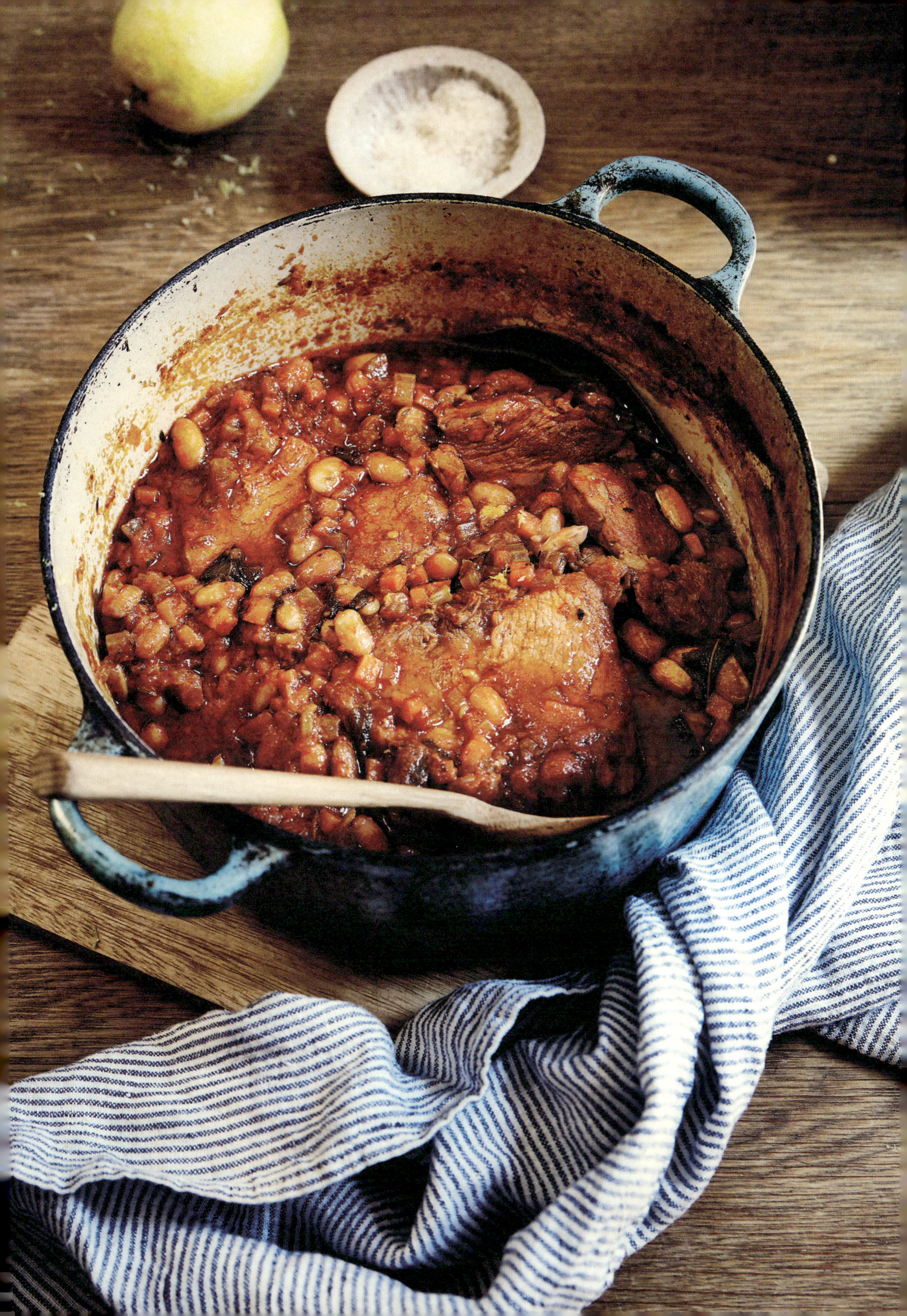

ROAST PORK WITH APPLE, FENNEL AND SAGE

SERVES 4–6

This is my very favourite Sunday roast. By adding the apples to the roasting pan with the pork you are rewarded with the most amazing caramelised apples – the best substitute for apple sauce, and with hardly any effort. Look for pork with nice marbling, and be sure to ask your butcher to score the skin for you – it can be difficult to do unless your knife is extremely sharp.

1 × 1.2 kg rack of pork, rind scored with a sharp knife

extra-virgin olive oil, for drizzling

sea salt

3 apples, cut in half horizontally

1 onion, cut into quarters

2 fennel bulbs, trimmed and roughly chopped

handful of sage leaves

finely grated zest of ½ lemon

Preheat the oven to 200°C.

Place the pork in a large roasting pan, drizzle with a little olive oil and season generously with salt. Rub the salt into the pork, ensuring that everything is evenly covered. Arrange the apple, onion and fennel around the pork and dress with a little more olive oil and salt, tossing to coat. Roast for 25–30 minutes until the skin begins to crackle.

Reduce the oven temperature to 180°C and cook for another 30–40 minutes, until the juices run clear when the pork is pierced with a skewer. Cover and allow to rest for 20 minutes before carving. Scatter the pork with the sage leaves and lemon zest and serve.

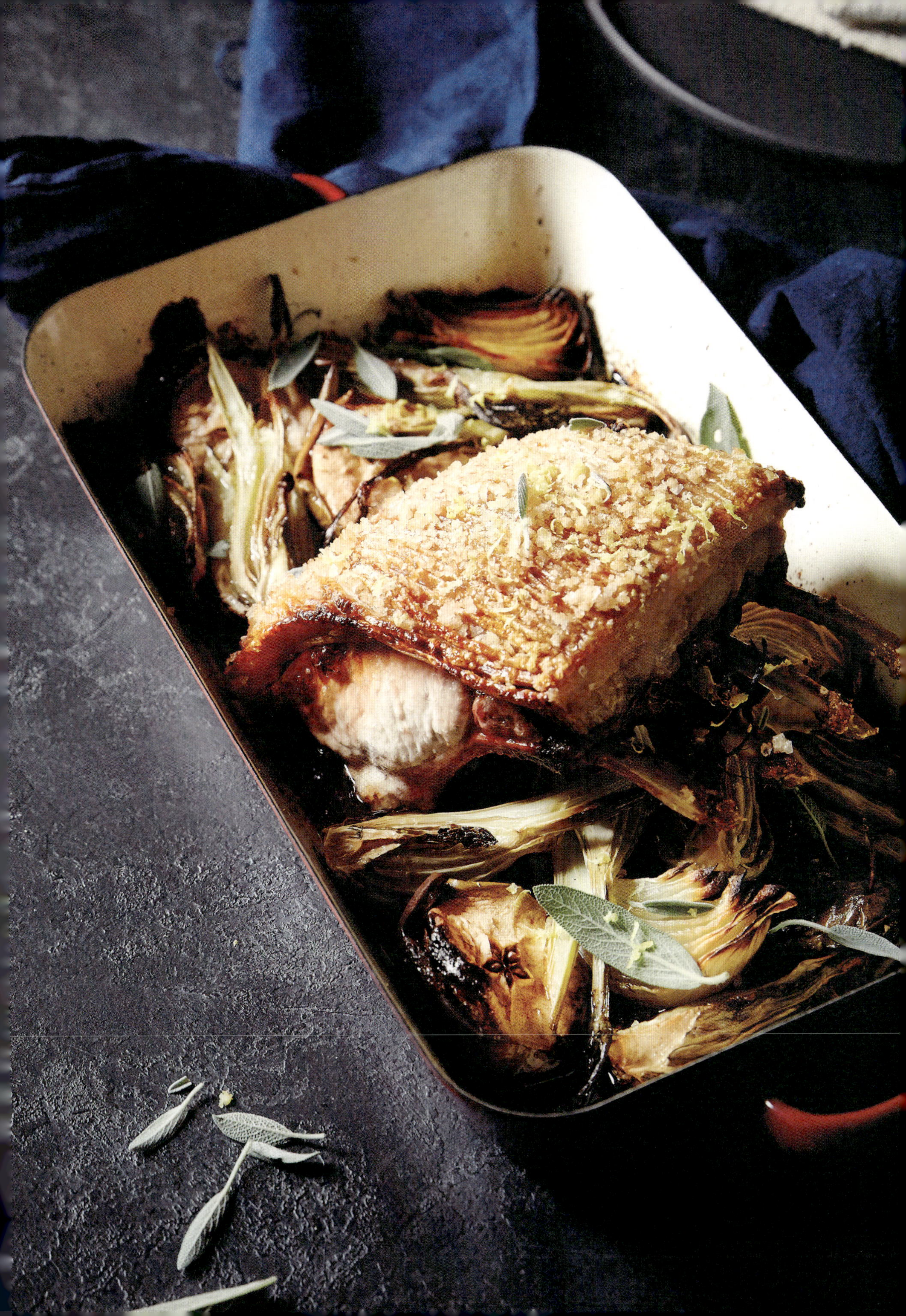

RABBIT PIE

· SERVES 4–6 ·

Growing up, we didn't eat meat that often, but when we did, it was often rabbit. Usually we would eat it braised in a rich tomato stew with, from memory, many, many peas. The rabbit would be removed and we would eat the sauce with spaghetti, and then the rabbit separately, with vegetables or just some crusty bread. My dad's friend would bring us freshly killed and skinned rabbits for eating. Sometimes Mum would fry it, in a little bit of butter and olive oil, with sage, or turn the rabbit stew into a pie. All delicious options, really.

My rabbit pie is much lighter than the traditional Maltese version. I braise the rabbit in wonderful aromatics and top it all off with a lid of really good homemade rough puff pastry. Rabbit is notorious for being dry and tough, which is why I recommend using just the marylands – that is the thigh and leg – which are much more tender than the very lean saddle, which is great for quicker cooking. Many butchers do sell them separately if you ask, but, if unavailable, use the whole rabbit, cut into pieces.

15 g dried porcini mushrooms

500 ml (2 cups) boiling water

60 ml (¼ cup) extra-virgin olive oil

1 kg rabbit marylands or
1 × 1 kg rabbit, jointed

sea salt and black pepper

1 onion, finely chopped

1 celery stalk, finely chopped

1 carrot, finely chopped

250 ml (1 cup) dry white wine

3 garlic cloves, roughly chopped

1 tomato, roughly chopped

1 oregano sprig

1 rosemary sprig

3 thyme sprigs, plus a small handful of leaves, finely chopped

500 ml (2 cups) chicken stock (see recipe page 105)

1 teaspoon plain flour

small handful of sage leaves, finely chopped

small handful of flat-leaf parsley leaves, finely chopped

small handful of tarragon leaves, finely chopped

½ × rough puff pastry (see recipe page 56)

1 egg, lightly beaten

Place the porcini in a bowl and cover with the water. Leave to soak for 15 minutes.

Meanwhile, heat the olive oil in a large heavy-based saucepan over a medium–high heat. Season the rabbit generously and fry, in batches if necessary, until lightly golden. Set the rabbit aside, and reduce the heat to low. Cook the onion, celery and carrot with a pinch of salt for 10–15 minutes, until soft and fragrant. Add the wine and scrape up any bits stuck to the pan. Bring to a simmer and let the wine bubble away for a minute or two. Add the garlic, tomato and the sprigs of oregano, rosemary and thyme. Stir to coat and nestle the rabbit back in the pan.

Simmer for a few minutes then pour in the stock, along with the porcini and soaking liquid. Bring to the boil, then reduce the heat to low. Cover with a circle of baking paper, pressing it onto the surface of the braising liquid, then cover with a lid. Braise for 2 hours or until the rabbit is tender and falling away from the bone.

Preheat the oven to 200°C. Lightly grease a 24 cm pie dish.

Strain the rabbit cooking liquid into a medium-sized saucepan. Simmer over a high heat until it has reduced to about 300 ml. Allow to cool briefly and skim any fat that rises to the surface. Whisk in the flour until smooth.

Meanwhile, pick the rabbit meat away from the bones, placing the meat in a large bowl and discarding the bones and the herb stalks. Add the vegetables, the chopped herbs and the reduced braising liquid, season to taste and mix well. Spoon the filling into the prepared pie dish.

On a lightly floured work surface, roll the pastry dough out to a circle about 5 mm thick, large enough to cover the pie dish. Whisk 1 teaspoon of water into the egg. Brush the edge of the pie dish with the egg wash, then cover with the pastry. Gently press the pastry onto the pie dish, then trim around the dish to remove any overhanging pastry. Gently score the top of the pastry using a small, sharp knife and poke a hole in the middle to allow steam to escape. Brush with the egg wash and bake for 40–45 minutes until the pastry is puffed and golden.

PICTURED ON PAGE 179

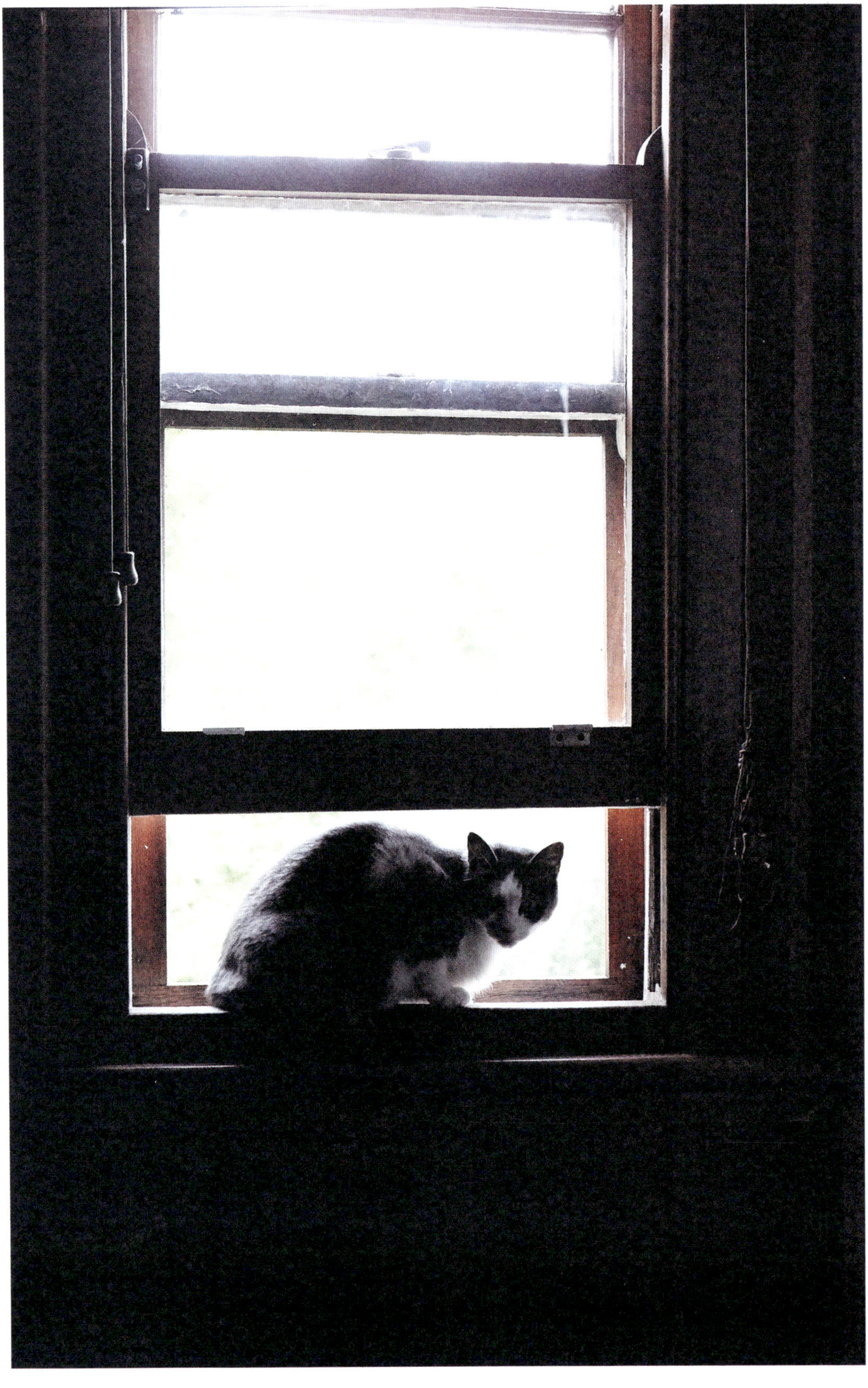

Rabbit pie (page 176)

LAMB MEATBALLS WITH BROAD BEANS

SERVES 4

When broad beans are in season, I love to eat them a few times a week. They remind me of my childhood – we would pod kilos of them at a time to dry out and use in various Maltese dishes throughout the year. During the short window when they were available, we would eat them fresh, often braised with other spring vegetables like artichokes and peas, and sometimes with meatballs, usually pork. Here I've teamed the broad beans with lamb, mint and pecorino – a wonderful combination.

1 thick slice of day-old bread, crust removed, roughly torn

100 ml full-cream milk

500 g lamb mince

3 garlic cloves, finely chopped, plus 2 extra garlic cloves, finely chopped

1 egg

handful of finely chopped herbs, such as parsley, mint, oregano and dill, plus extra to serve

4 anchovy fillets, finely chopped

pinch of dried chilli flakes

2 small onions, finely chopped

sea salt

2 tablespoons extra-virgin olive oil

250 g shelled broad beans

100 g podded peas

100 ml chicken stock (see recipe page 105)

juice of ½ lemon

grated pecorino, to serve

Place the bread in a small bowl, cover with the milk and leave to soak for 10 minutes. Squeeze out the excess milk and place the bread in a large bowl, crumbling it with your fingers. Add the mince, garlic, egg, herbs, anchovies, chilli and half of the onion. Season, then mix with your hands, squeezing so everything is well incorporated. Cover and rest in the fridge for 30 minutes.

Roll the meat into golf ball–sized balls, about 30 g each. Heat half of the olive oil in a frying pan over a medium heat and brown the meatballs in batches.

Meanwhile, bring a saucepan of water to the boil. Add the broad beans, boil for a few minutes, then drain (keep the water) and set aside to cool. Peel off and discard the outer layer of the beans. Bring the water to the boil again and blanch the peas. Drain.

Heat the remaining olive oil in large frying pan over a low heat and gently fry the remaining onion with a pinch of salt for 10 minutes, or until soft and fragrant. Add the extra garlic, the browned meatballs and the chicken stock and simmer for 15 minutes. Add the broad beans, peas and lemon juice and stir to coat. Serve with a generous scattering of grated pecorino and the extra herbs.

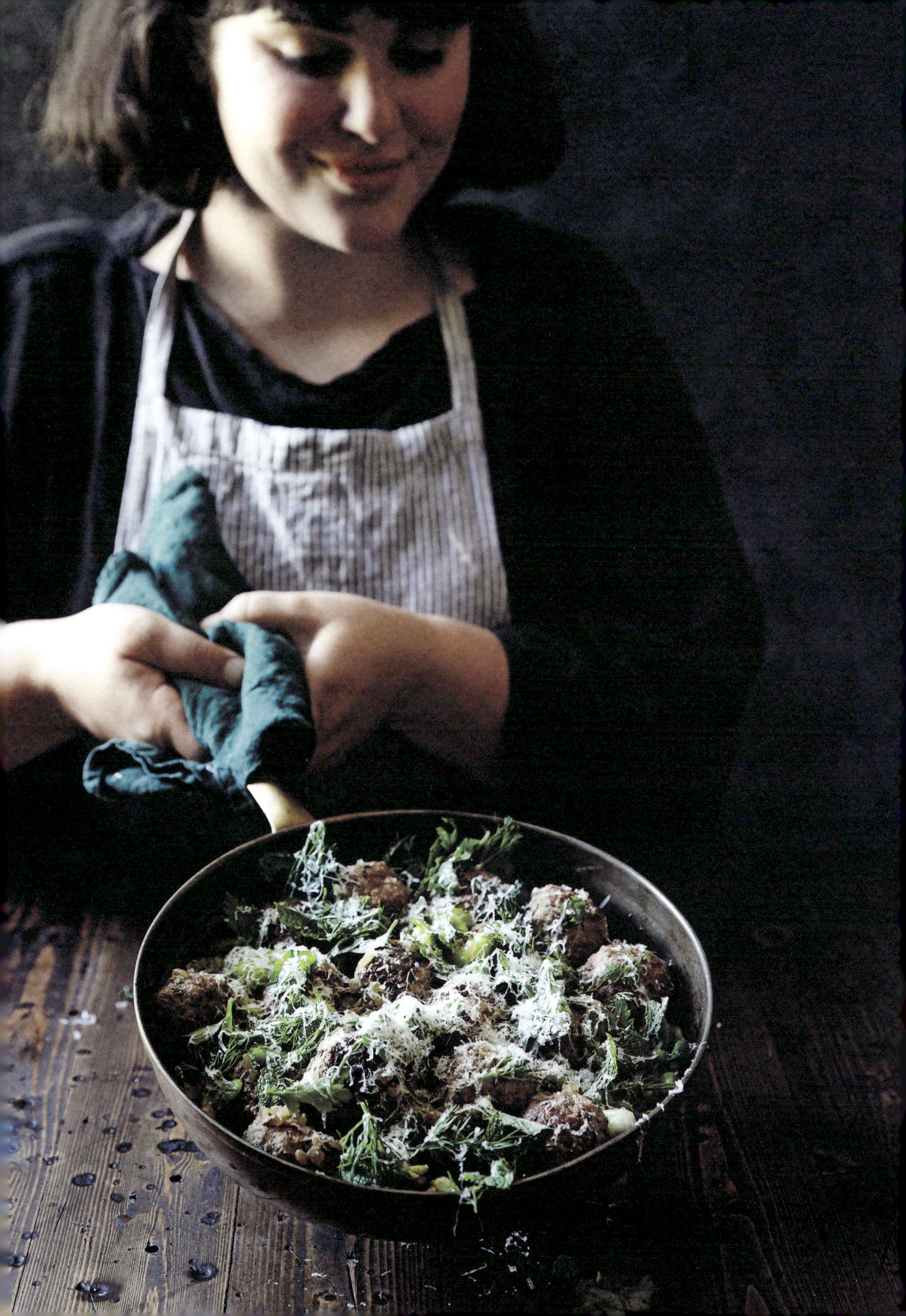

BRAISED LAMB WITH CHICKPEAS

SERVES 4–6

Lamb shoulder is perfect for braising and goes particularly well with tomatoes, as the acid cuts through the richness of the meat. With the addition of chickpeas, this braise is a one-pot dish that will both satisfy and nourish.

200 g dried chickpeas

1½ tablespoons extra-virgin olive oil

1 kg boneless lamb shoulder, cut into 4 cm pieces

sea salt

1 onion, finely chopped

600 g roma tomatoes, roughly chopped

2 garlic cloves, roughly chopped

1 fresh bay leaf

150 ml dry white wine

800 ml vegetable stock (see recipe page 104), chicken stock (see recipe page 105) or water

handful of flat-leaf parsley leaves, roughly chopped, to serve

juice of 1 lemon

Place the chickpeas in a bowl and cover with cold water. Leave to soak overnight, then drain.

Heat the olive oil in a large heavy-based saucepan over a medium–high heat. Season the lamb with salt and sear in the pan in batches, ensuring the pieces are golden all over. Remove the lamb and set aside, and drain most of the oil from the saucepan. Return the pan to a low heat, add the onion and cook for 10 minutes until soft and fragrant. Add the tomatoes and fry for 2–3 minutes until soft, then add the garlic, bay leaf, wine and chickpeas. Return the lamb to the pan and cover with the stock or water. Simmer, covered, over a low heat for 2½–3 hours or until the lamb is tender and the chickpeas are cooked. Season to taste. To finish the dish, scatter with the parsley and squeeze over the lemon juice.

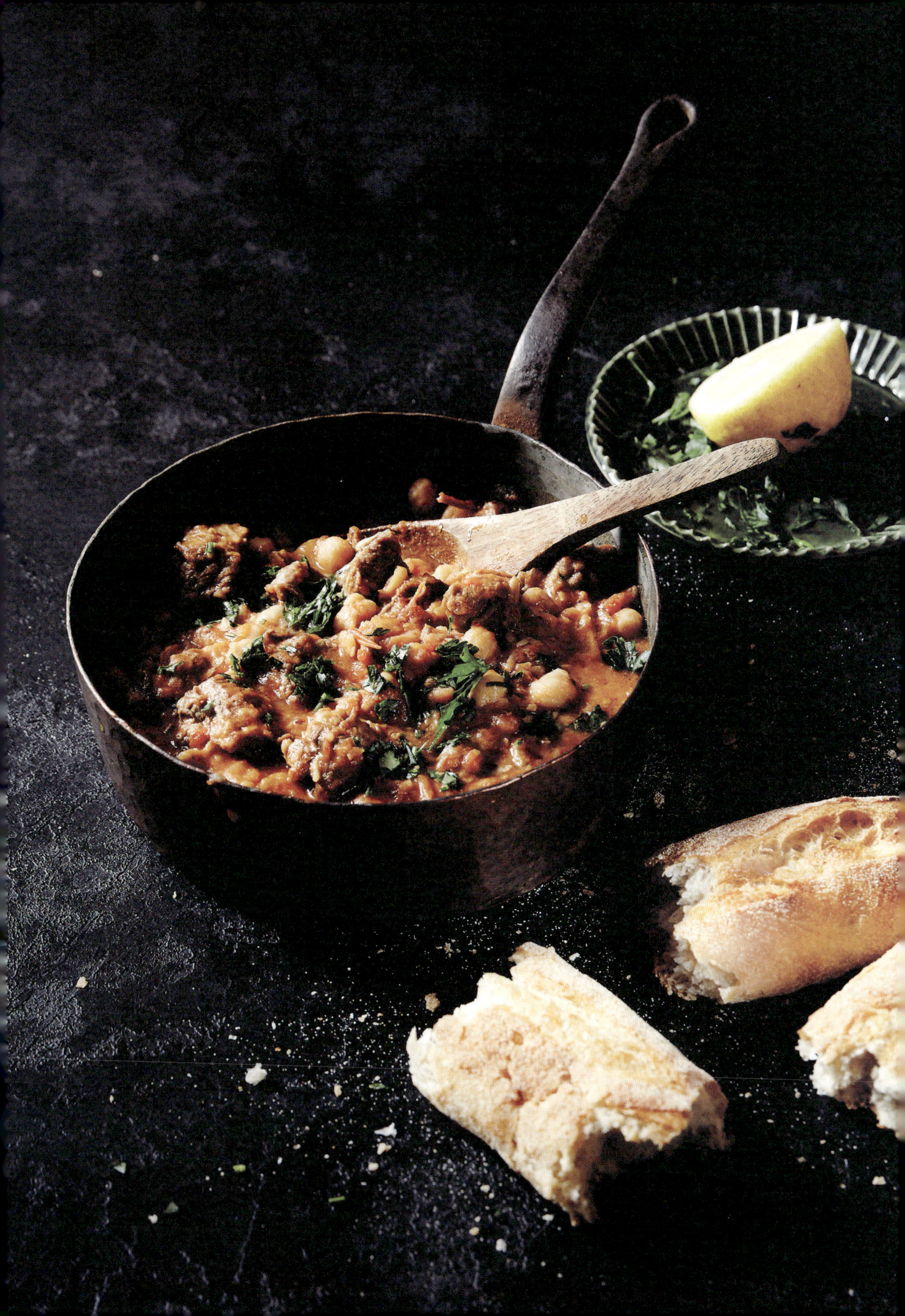

LAMB SHOULDER WITH PEAS AND ANCHOVIES

SERVES 4–6

A lamb recipe for the springtime when peas are plentiful. Here, anchovies are used as seasoning – they impart a subtle saltiness, which intensifies during the slow cook.

3 garlic cloves, peeled

1 rosemary sprig, leaves picked

sea salt

4 anchovy fillets

2 tablespoons extra-virgin olive oil

1 × 1.2 kg bone-in lamb shoulder

250 ml (1 cup) dry white wine

200 g peas, fresh or frozen

large handful of mint leaves, roughly chopped

large handful of dill, roughly chopped

2 tablespoons red wine vinegar, or to taste

Using a mortar and pestle, pound the garlic and rosemary with a pinch of salt until you have a rough paste. Add the anchovies and bash a little to combine. Drizzle in the olive oil and stir. Rub all over the lamb and leave to marinate in the fridge for at least 1 hour.

Preheat the oven to 200°C.

Place the lamb in a deep roasting pan and season. Pour in the wine and roast for 20 minutes, then cover with foil and reduce the oven temperature to 120°C. Cook for 4–5 hours until the meat is falling away from the bone. Remove the lamb from the tray and keep warm.

Skim any fat from the pan and transfer the juices to a small saucepan. Simmer over a medium heat until reduced slightly. Keep warm while you prepare the peas.

Blanch the peas in boiling water until tender, then drain and refresh under cold water. Place the peas in a bowl, then add the mint, dill and vinegar. Season to taste, adding more vinegar if desired. Pour the braising juices over the lamb and top with the peas to serve.

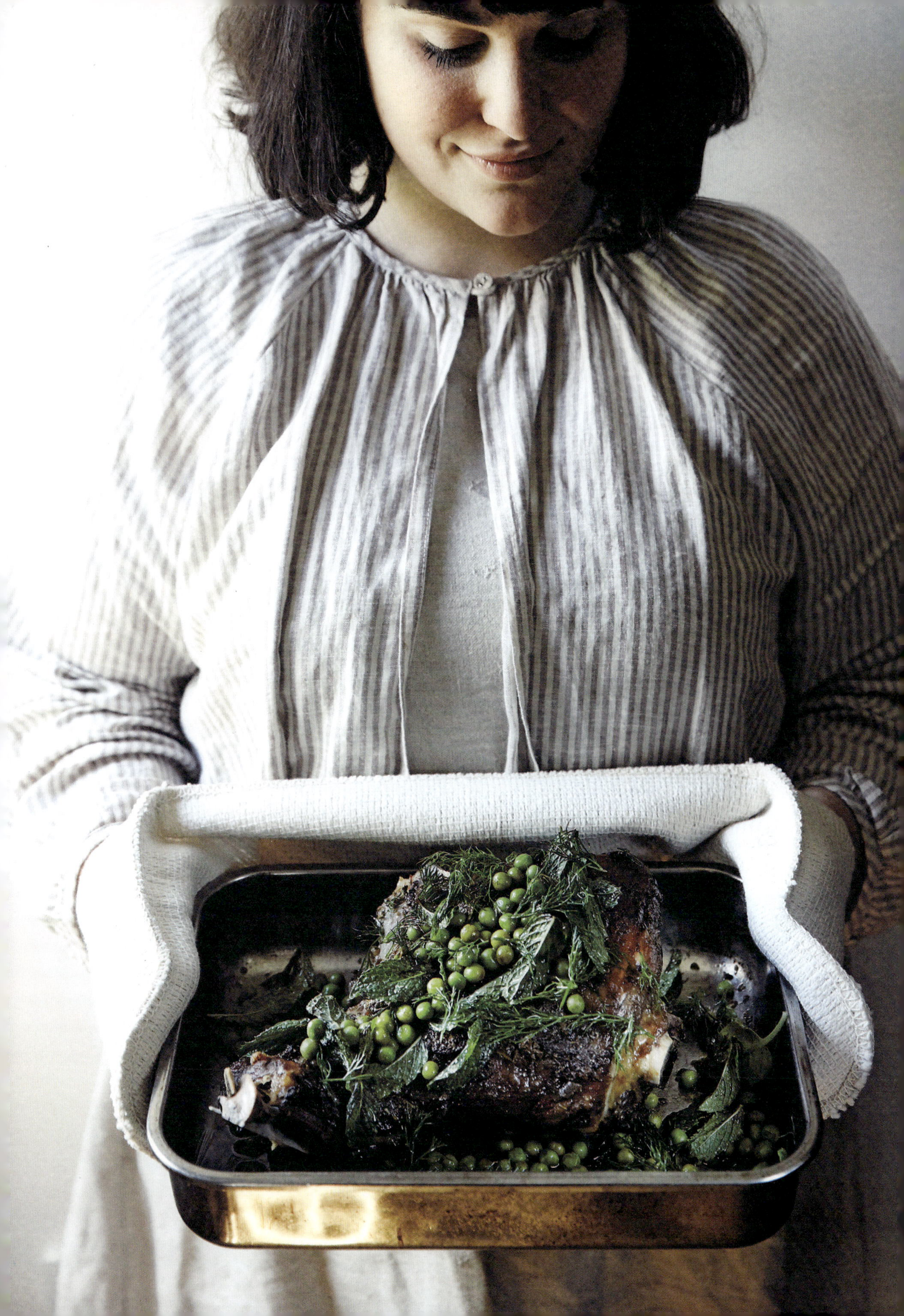

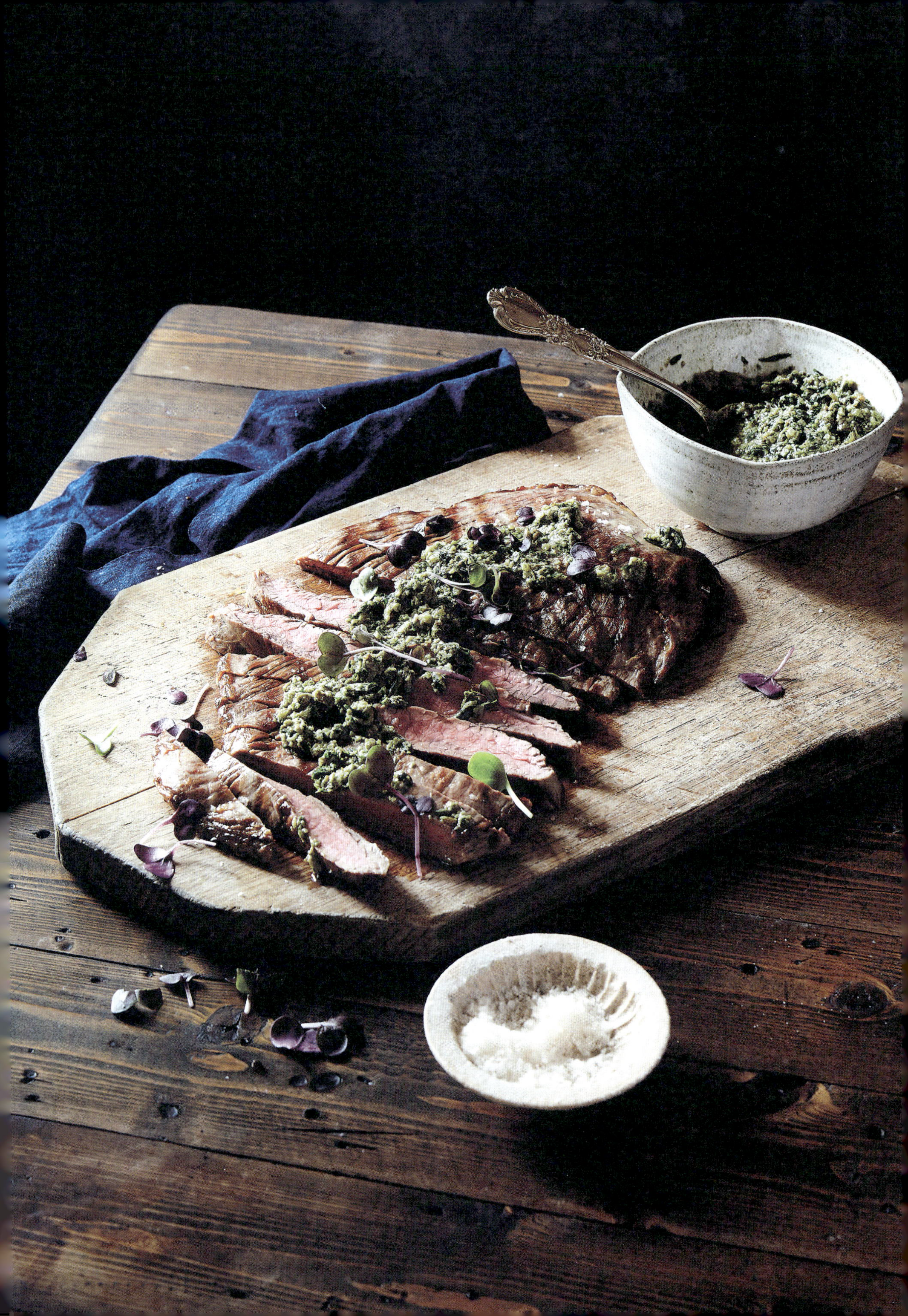

SEARED SKIRT STEAK WITH SALSA VERDE

· ❊ SERVES 4 ❊ ·

Salsa verde, which translates to 'green sauce', is extremely versatile and can be made with almost any herb, although traditionally only parsley is used. Sometimes I soak bread in milk (such as in the recipe on page 168) or add some hard-boiled egg yolks, which gives the sauce a lovely texture. Here, I use toasted walnuts for creaminess. Skirt steak has such wonderful flavour and is thin enough to be cooked in one whole piece, making it a great choice when preparing steak at home. Cooking the steak over charcoals on a barbecue is the best method, but a searing hot pan, as I've suggested, works well too. Just be sure to rest the steak really well, and slice across the grain. If you can't find skirt steak, ask your butcher for hanger or flank, which are also wonderful eating.

1 × 650 g piece of skirt steak

extra-virgin olive oil, for coating

sea salt

micro herbs, to serve (optional)

SALSA VERDE

60 g (½ cup) walnuts

1 garlic clove, peeled

sea salt

large handful of herb leaves, including flat-leaf parsley, basil and mint (about 80 g in total)

3 anchovy fillets

1 tablespoon salted capers, rinsed

finely grated zest and juice of ½ lemon

about 60 ml (¼ cup) extra-virgin olive oil, or enough to loosen the mixture

1 tablespoon red wine vinegar

To make the salsa verde, lightly toast the walnuts in a dry frying pan over a low–medium heat for 1–2 minutes until just coloured. Using a mortar and pestle, pound the garlic with a pinch of salt. Add the herbs and bash until you have a rough but cohesive paste. Pound in the walnuts and anchovy fillets, then the capers. Stir in the zest and juice and pour in enough olive oil to make the sauce like a thick dressing. Stir in the vinegar and taste to see if more salt is needed. Set aside while you prepare the steak.

Rub the steak all over with olive oil. Season generously with salt.

Preheat a large frying pan until very hot. For medium–rare, cook the steak for 8–10 minutes, flipping over halfway. Rest on a rack or plate in a warm place for 10 minutes. Slice across the grain and serve with the salsa verde and a scatter of micro herbs, if desired.

VEAL COTOLETTA WITH CAPERS AND ROSEMARY

SERVES 4

Cotoletta alla milanese is a veal cutlet, bone in, that is breaded and fried in clarified butter. It is also my mum's favourite thing to eat, so, in turn, I love preparing it for her. It is, as the name suggests, typical of Milan, a city I love for its aperitivo and breathtaking duomo, among many other things. I've added some capers and rosemary, which, along with the lemon, brighten up the cotoletta. If you can't find veal on the bone, you can use thin boneless pieces of veal, which will require a shorter cooking time, or you can even use pork chops. I like panko breadcrumbs, a Japanese variety that, although certainly not in keeping with tradition, yields a wonderfully crunchy coating.

4 × 250 g veal cutlets, bone in

50 g (⅓ cup) plain flour

2 eggs, lightly beaten

150 g (2½ cups) panko or other breadcrumbs

about 200 ml clarified butter (see Note)

sea salt

2 tablespoons salted capers, rinsed

2 tablespoons rosemary leaves, roughly chopped

lemon wedges, to serve

Lightly flatten the veal chops using a mallet to about 1.5 cm thick. Place the flour in one bowl, the egg in another and the breadcrumbs in a third. Dip each cutlet in the flour, then in the egg and finally in the breadcrumbs, packing the crumbs as firmly onto the veal as possible.

Heat the clarified butter in a large frying pan over a medium heat and fry the cutlets for 5–6 minutes on each side. They should be golden and just cooked through. This can be done in batches, and, if the cutlets are thick, you can finish cooking them in an oven set at 180°C. Remove the veal, season lightly with salt and set aside to rest. Meanwhile, keep the pan on a medium heat, add the capers and rosemary and stir to coat in some of the butter, just for 30 seconds. Remove and spoon over the veal, and serve with the lemon wedges alongside.

NOTE: To make 200 ml clarified butter, melt 280 g butter in a small saucepan over a low heat. Leave the pan still, so you don't unsettle any of the solids. Once the butter has melted, increase the heat to medium and simmer for 3–4 minutes, or until there is a foamy layer on top. Skim the milk solids that rise to the top. Allow to stand for 5 minutes or so, then carefully pour the skimmed, melted butter into a bowl through a fine-mesh sieve lined with muslin or cheesecloth. Stop pouring once you reach the bottom, where most of the white solids should have settled. The golden liquid in your bowl is now clarified butter, which will keep very well in a container or jar in the fridge for up to 4 months.

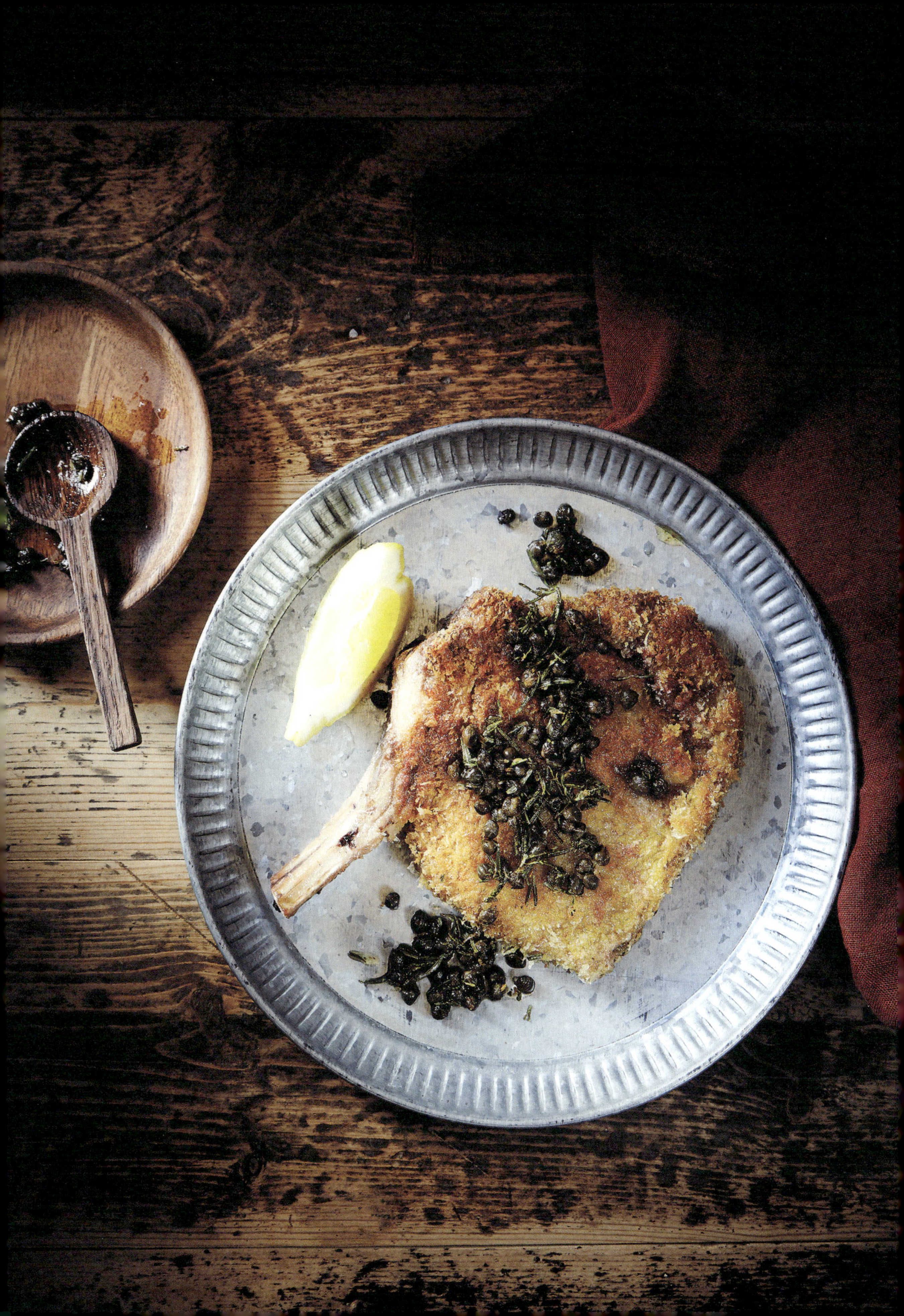

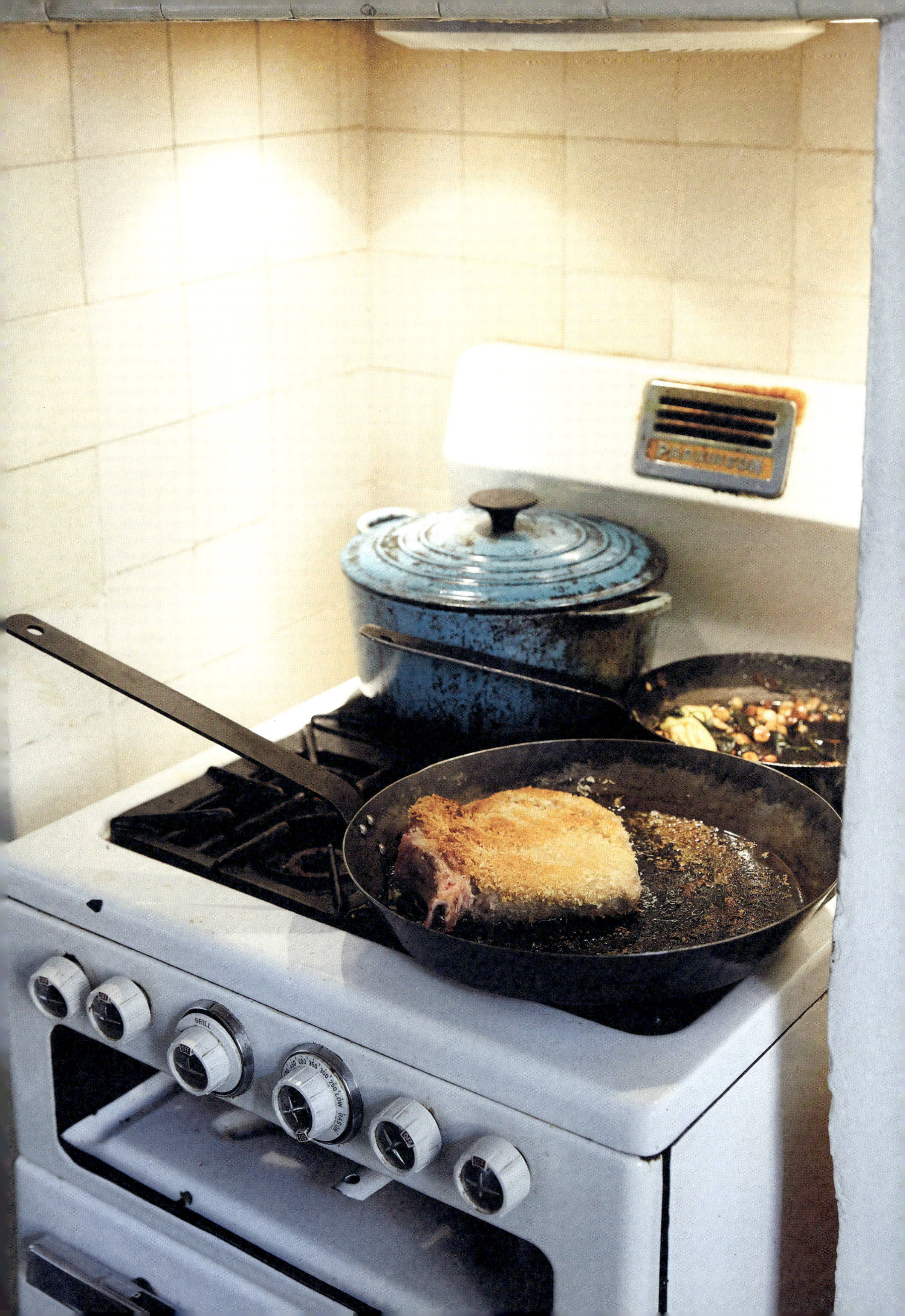
GRILL

SEAFOOD AND MEAT 191

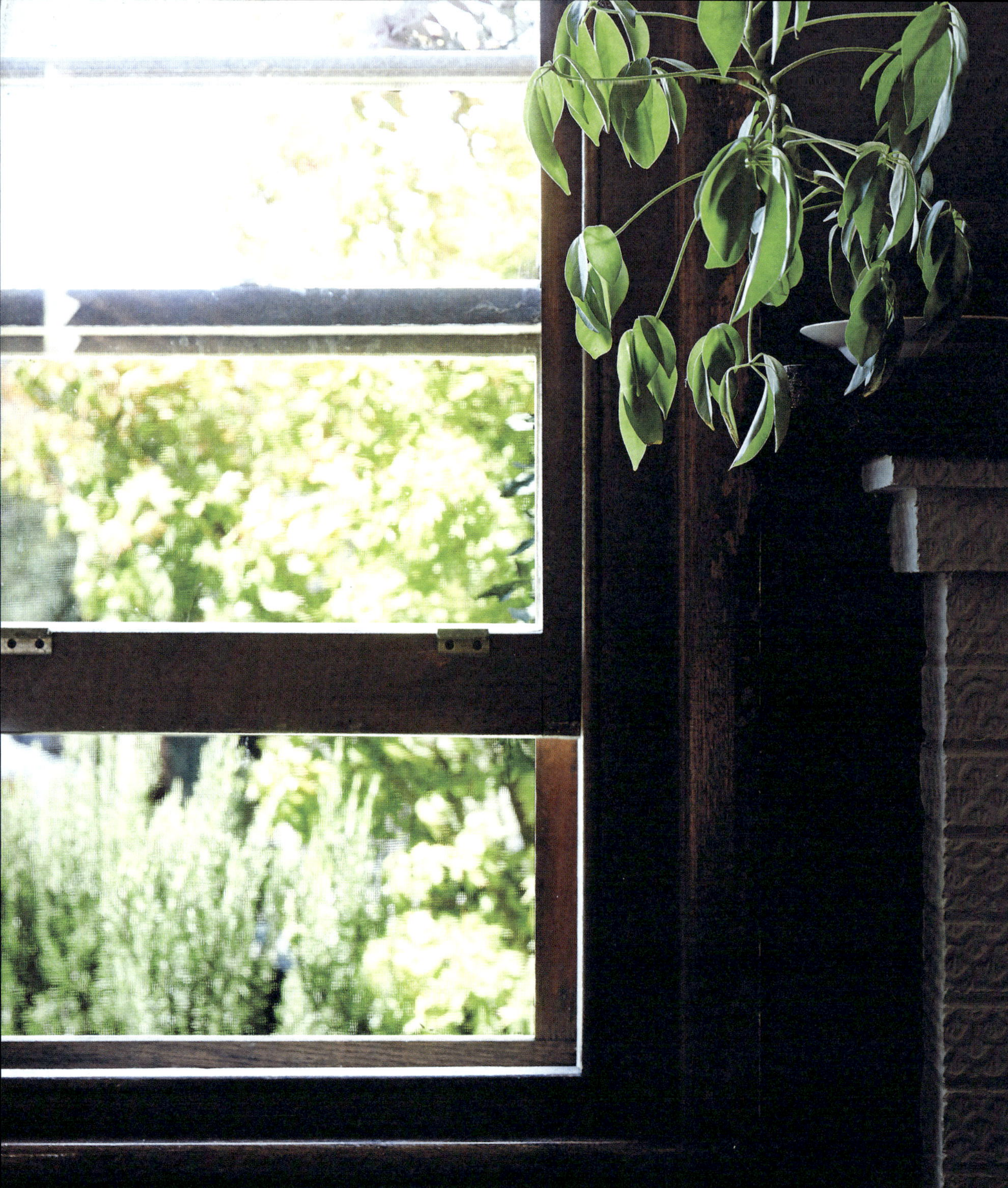

BISCUITS, LOAVES AND CAKES

A bowl and a whisk — my baking essentials. When I'm making a cake, I try to bring it back to basics. I don't feel the need for fancy equipment or long-winded recipes. It just isn't necessary. Instead, my cakes are ones that you will make over and over again because not only do they taste wonderful, but they can be made with ease and pleasure. Many of these recipes have been committed to my memory: the ingredients, the method, the taste. I've included a few more elaborate cakes for celebrations, and some biscuits too. All of the recipes are perfect for sharing or for savouring on your own in a quiet moment of the afternoon. Regardless of the occasion, there is no greater happiness than enjoying a cake made by hand.

RICCIARELLI

MAKES ABOUT 20

Ricciarelli are gorgeous Italian biscuits that date back to the fifteenth century. They were once considered so precious they were only sold in apothecaries. Hailing from Siena, these sweet, chewy almond biscuits covered in icing sugar now fill the windows of Tuscan cake shops all year round – most prominently over the Christmas period, when they are bought by the kilo. I have fond memories of making these biscotti when I lived in Italy. The aroma of bitter almonds would linger for hours, making it difficult not to eat them all at once.

125 g caster sugar

finely grated zest of 1 lemon or orange

100 g icing sugar, plus extra for coating

300 g (3 cups) ground almonds (see Note on page 212)

2 egg whites

sea salt

½ teaspoon vanilla extract

½ teaspoon almond extract or aroma of bitter almonds (optional)

Preheat the oven to 160°C. Line a baking tray with baking paper.

Place the caster sugar and zest in a large bowl. Rub the zest together with the sugar until fragrant and the citrus oils have released into the sugar. Sift in the icing sugar and add the ground almonds. Mix to combine.

Place the egg whites and a pinch of salt in a mixing bowl and whisk to stiff peaks. Add the egg whites to the almond mixture along with the vanilla and almond extract, if using, and gently fold in until the mixture becomes a firm but moist paste. Tip some extra icing sugar onto a plate or your work surface, then roll the dough into walnut-sized balls and coat in the icing sugar. Flatten the balls ever so slightly to form oval-shaped biscuits, and pinch the ends slightly into points, creating a leaf shape. Place on the prepared tray. Leave the ricciarelli to sit at room temperature for at least 30 minutes to form a slightly dry exterior.

Bake for approximately 12–15 minutes until only just coloured. The biscuits will still be soft, but they firm up as they cool. It's important not to overcook them, as the chewiness is what makes ricciarelli so special, so be sure to keep on checking the biscuits as they cook. Once cool, dust generously with extra icing sugar. Store in an airtight container for up to a week, although they are usually eaten the same day by family and friends.

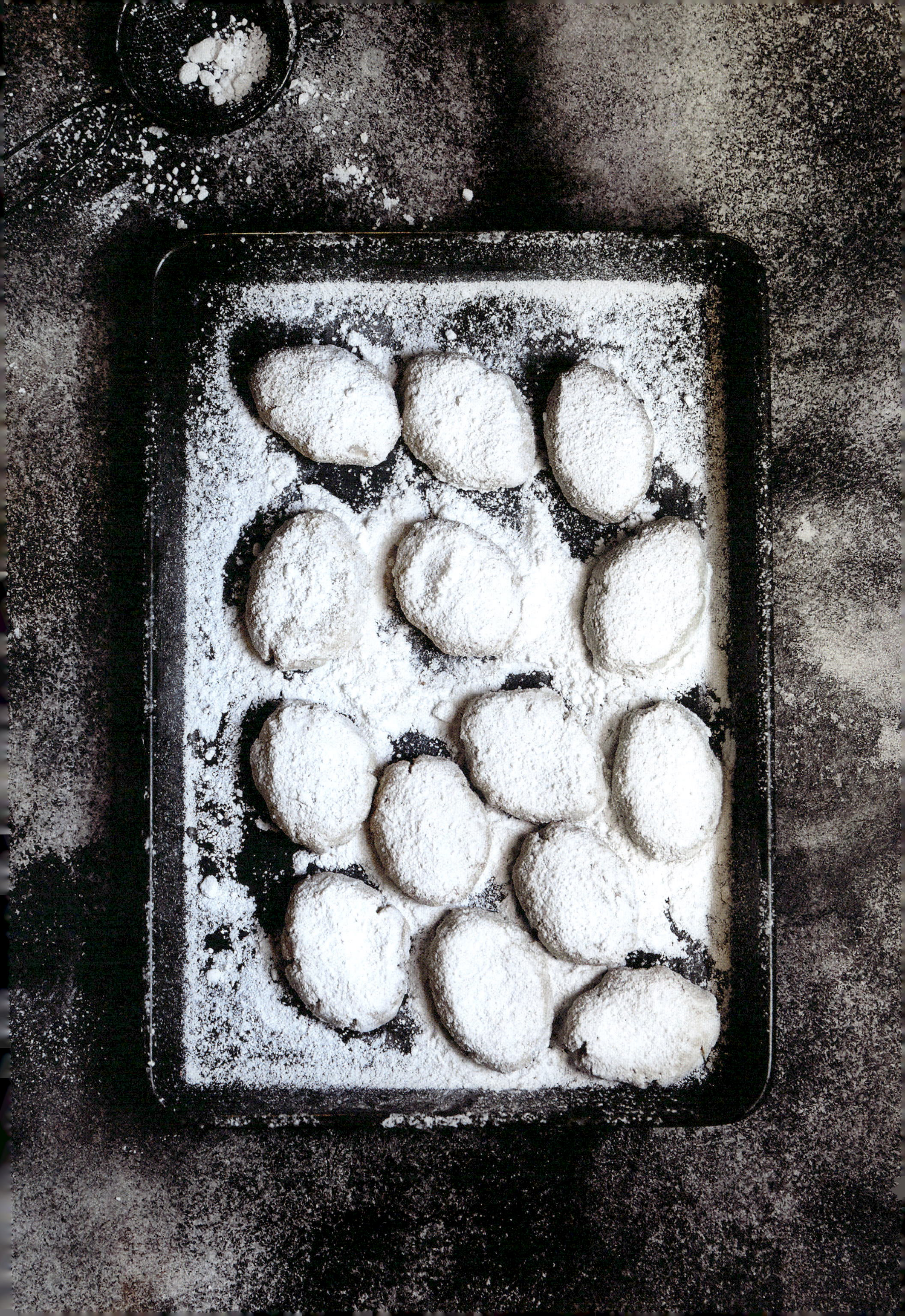

AN OAT BISCUIT FOR DUNKING

MAKES ABOUT 35

This is my ideal biscuit for dunking into hot tea – crunchy and buttery, with a thin coating of chocolate. They remind me of the biscuits that were kept in a tin with a rusty lid on the top shelf of our kitchen cupboard when I was a child, far out of reach from our wanting hands and only brought out when visitors came over.

300 g (2 cups) plain flour, sifted

300 g (3 cups) quick-cooking oats

150 g (⅔ cup, firmly packed) brown sugar

100 g caster sugar

1 teaspoon baking powder

1 teaspoon sea salt

270 g unsalted butter, roughly chopped

1 tablespoon golden syrup

½ teaspoon bicarbonate of soda

3–4 tablespoons full-cream milk, if needed

200 g dark chocolate (70% cocoa), broken into pieces

Preheat the oven to 180°C. Line four baking trays with baking paper.

In a large bowl, mix the flour, oats, sugars, baking powder and salt, breaking up any lumps with the back of a wooden spoon.

Melt the butter and golden syrup together in a small saucepan over a medium heat. Stir in the bicarbonate of soda and allow it to foam for a few seconds. Pour into the dry mixture and stir to incorporate. Take a piece of the mixture and roll it into a ball – if the mixture is too dry, add some milk, 1 tablespoon at a time, until it comes together. Roll tablespoonfuls of the mixture into golf ball–sized balls and flatten into discs about 6 cm in diameter and 4 mm thick. You can either do this with a rolling pin, or I find it's just as easy to simply press them. Alternatively, place the mixture between two sheets of baking paper, roll out to 4 mm thick and cut out 6 cm rounds, then gather the scraps and re-roll. Place on the prepared trays, leaving space as they will spread during cooking. Bake for 10–12 minutes until golden. Transfer to a rack to cool completely.

Once the biscuits have cooled, melt the chocolate in a heatproof bowl set over a saucepan of simmering water, stirring occasionally until smooth. Let the chocolate cool for 5 minutes, then, working with one biscuit at a time, spread a layer of chocolate over the flat side, setting them aside to set with the chocolate sides facing up. Once the chocolate is dry to touch, the biscuits can be stored in an airtight container in the fridge for up to 4 days.

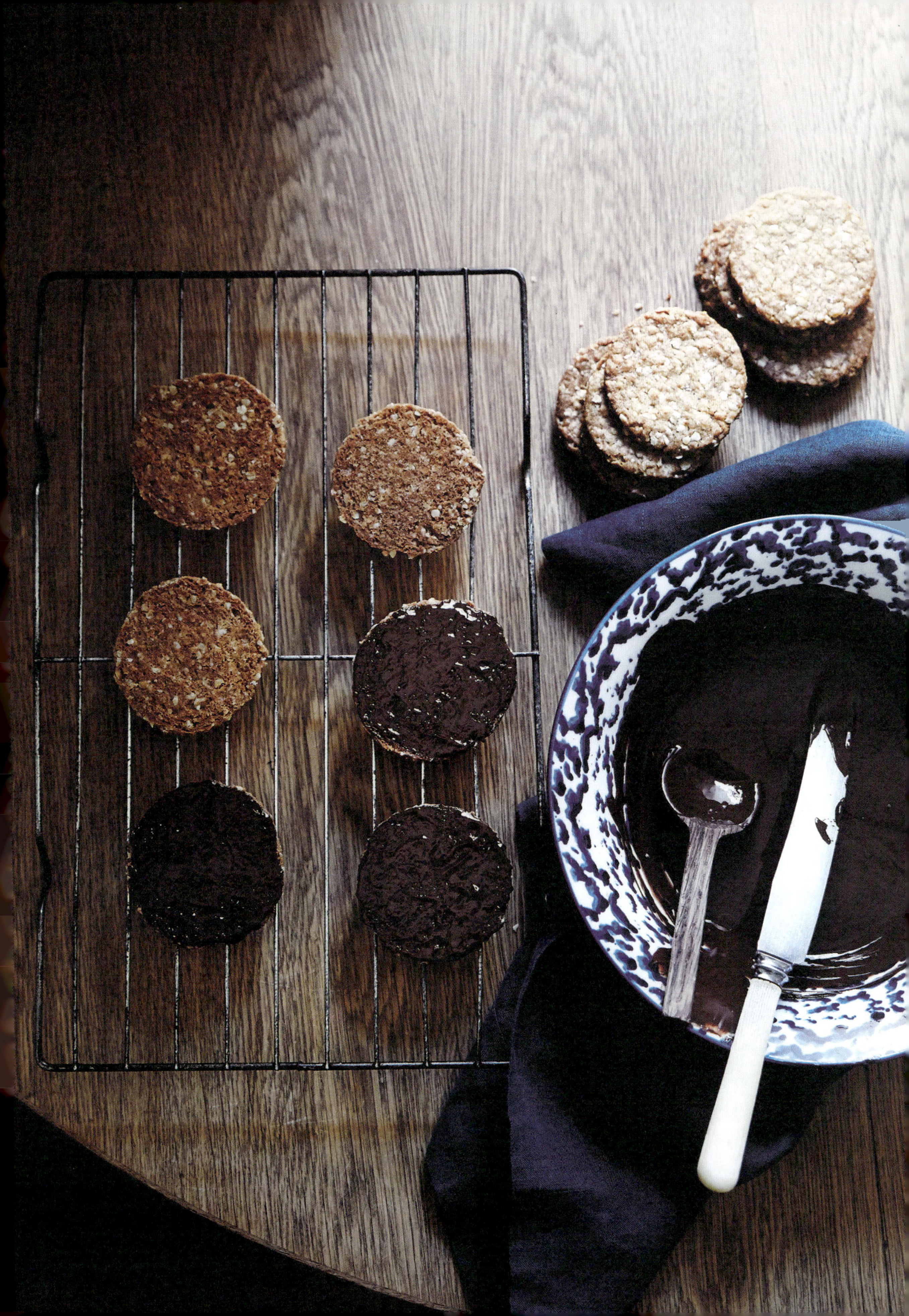

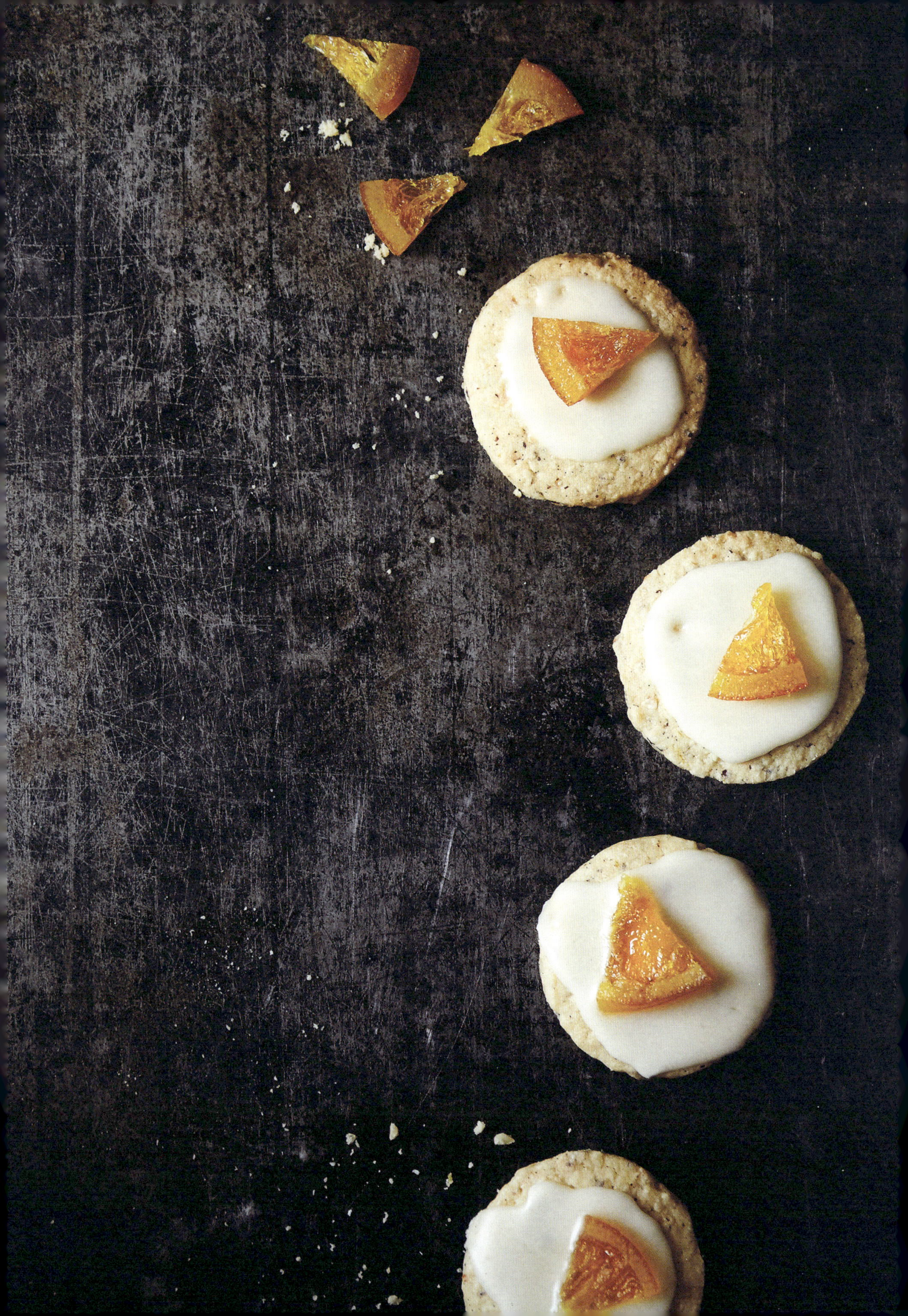

ORANGE–HAZELNUT SHORTBREAD

MAKES ABOUT 30

These orange-scented shortbreads are so buttery and soft, and are usually made around Christmas time in our home. They make a perfect treat served with coffee at the end of a feast or wrapped as a beautiful homemade gift for loved ones. You can make the dough in advance of cooking; it will keep for up to three days in the fridge. If you want to skip the icing, they are wonderful simply dusted with icing sugar.

80 g (⅔ cup) icing sugar

150 g unsalted butter, softened

1 egg yolk

100 g hazelnuts

finely grated zest of 1 orange

1 vanilla pod, split and seeds scraped

1 teaspoon orange-blossom water

150 g (1 cup) plain flour, sifted

1 teaspoon baking powder

pinch of sea salt

candied orange peel, cut into small triangles (optional)

ICING

60 g icing sugar, sifted

2–3 tablespoons freshly squeezed orange juice

Beat the icing sugar and butter together until pale and fluffy. Add the egg yolk and mix to combine.

Grind the hazelnuts using a mortar and pestle or a food processor. They should be finely ground, but not to a powder, and some larger pieces are good, too. Add the hazelnuts to the butter mixture, along with the orange zest, vanilla seeds, orange-blossom water, flour, baking powder and salt. Mix gently until just combined, being careful not to over-beat. Wrap the dough in plastic wrap, forming a log about 6 cm in diameter. Refrigerate for at least 30 minutes to firm up slightly.

Preheat the oven to 170°C. Line two baking trays with baking paper.

Cut the dough into rounds and transfer to the prepared trays, allowing a little space between them as they will spread.

Bake the biscuits for 15–18 minutes, until lightly golden. Allow to cool completely on the trays.

Meanwhile, make the icing by mixing the icing sugar with the orange juice.

Spread the icing over the cooled biscuits and top each with a piece of candied orange peel, if using. Store in an airtight container for up to a week.

EVERYDAY BANANA LOAF WITH HOMEMADE BUTTER

MAKES ONE 24 CM LOAF

I'm not saying that this loaf should be eaten every day – more that it is a simple loaf, one that can be made with the most basic ingredients and a few neglected bananas. In fact, the more ripe the bananas, the more natural sweetness they will bring to this loaf. It is perfect eaten warm, by the slice, with a thick slather of butter. When I have excess crème fraîche in the fridge, I often turn it into butter for spreading on fresh crusty bread or, in this case, slices of banana loaf. My suggested quantity of crème fraîche for making the butter yields approximately 200 g of butter and 200 ml of buttermilk, which is a very manageable amount. You can use pure cream instead of crème fraîche to make the butter or, of course, buy some butter instead. Sometimes, when I'm in the mood, I add chunks of dark chocolate to the batter or slice an extra (not so ripe) banana lengthways and press it into the top of the loaf before baking. Sometimes I do both.

2 eggs

150 g raw sugar

100 ml extra-virgin olive oil

2½ tablespoons full-cream milk (or you can use buttermilk from making the butter)

2 very ripe bananas (about 250 g in total)

150 g (1 cup) self-raising flour

½ teaspoon ground cinnamon

OPTIONAL EXTRAS

2½ tablespoons Dutch-process cocoa

100 g dark chocolate (70% cocoa), roughly chopped

50 g (½ cup) walnuts, roughly chopped

1 banana, cut in half lengthways

BUTTER

500 ml (2 cups) crème fraîche

pinch of sea salt

Preheat the oven to 180°C. Grease a 24 cm loaf tin with butter and line with baking paper.

In a large bowl, whisk together the eggs and sugar until pale. Pour in the olive oil and milk and whisk to combine. In a separate bowl, mash the bananas until smooth, then mix them into the batter. Sift in the flour and cinnamon. Stir gently, being careful not to overwork the mixture. If you wish to add the cocoa, chocolate and/or walnuts, add them to the mixture now. The cocoa will need to be sifted in, but just stir the chocolate and walnuts through.

Pour the mixture into the prepared tin and, if using, top with the halved banana. Bake for approximately 45 minutes or until a skewer inserted into the middle comes out clean.

For the butter, whisk the crème fraîche in the bowl of an electric mixer fitted with a whisk attachment. Beat until the solids separate, which will take around 7 minutes. Strain through a fine-mesh sieve over a bowl and press on the solids to release all of the liquid. That liquid is buttermilk, which you can keep to use for another purpose. Return the solids to the mixer and beat again for another 3–4 minutes to remove more buttermilk, and repeat the straining process. Fill a large bowl with very cold water and, working quickly, knead the butter in the water, squeezing out as much buttermilk as you can. Drain and repeat until the water is clear. Buttermilk left in the solids will make the butter sour, so it is important to remove as much as possible. Mix in the salt – this flavours the butter, but it also helps it keep for a little longer. It is now ready to use, or you can wrap the butter tightly in baking paper and, as long as you have removed all of the buttermilk properly, it will keep in the fridge for up to 3 weeks. If there's buttermilk still in the butter, it will sour quite quickly and will only last for about 1 week.

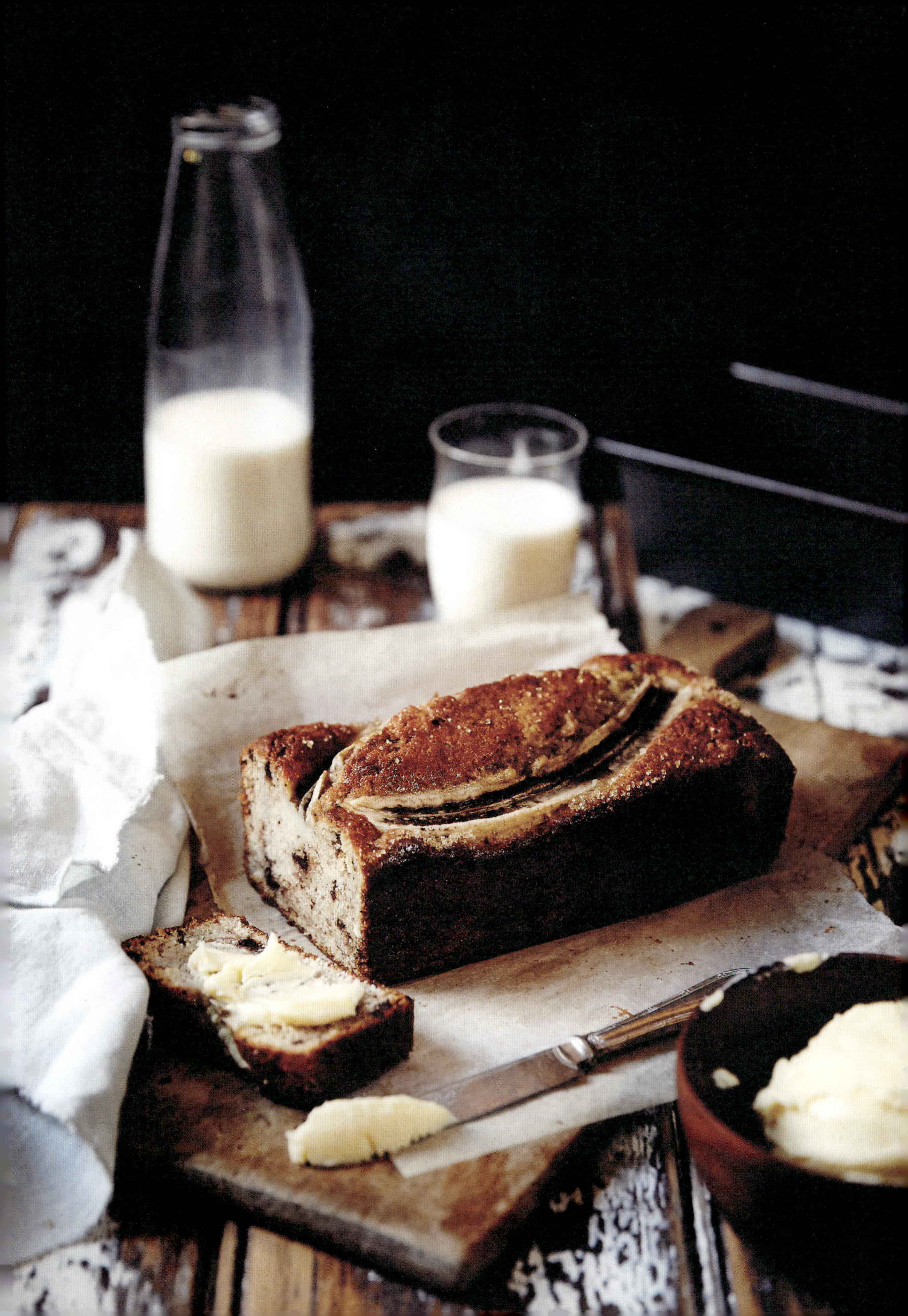

TANGELO POLENTA DRIZZLE CAKE

MAKES ONE 20 CM CAKE

Polenta gives this simple cake a wonderful texture, as well as a vibrant colour. If you can't find tangelos, you can replace them with any other citrus fruit, such as oranges or lemons. This is the kind of cake that should sit on the bench, with a knife at the ready, to be nibbled at throughout the day.

170 g caster sugar

3 eggs

1 vanilla pod, split and seeds scraped

150 g plain yoghurt

150 ml extra-virgin olive oil

finely grated zest and juice of 2 tangelos (about 100 ml juice), plus 2–3 tablespoons extra juice

150 g (1 cup) polenta

150 g (1 cup) self-raising flour

250 g icing sugar, sifted

Preheat the oven to 180°C. Grease a 20 cm round cake tin with butter and line with baking paper.

In a large bowl, whisk the caster sugar, eggs, vanilla seeds, yoghurt, olive oil and tangelo zest and juice together until combined. Stir in the polenta and sift in the flour, and stir until just combined. Pour into the prepared cake tin and bake for 45–50 minutes or until a skewer inserted into the middle comes out clean. Leave to cool in the tin for a few minutes, then invert onto a rack to cool completely. The bottom is now the top of your cake, providing a nice smooth surface for the icing.

Mix the icing sugar with enough of the extra tangelo juice to make a thick, pourable icing. You may not need all of the 2 tablespoons, so begin adding the juice slowly. Drizzle the icing over the cake, set aside while the icing hardens, then serve.

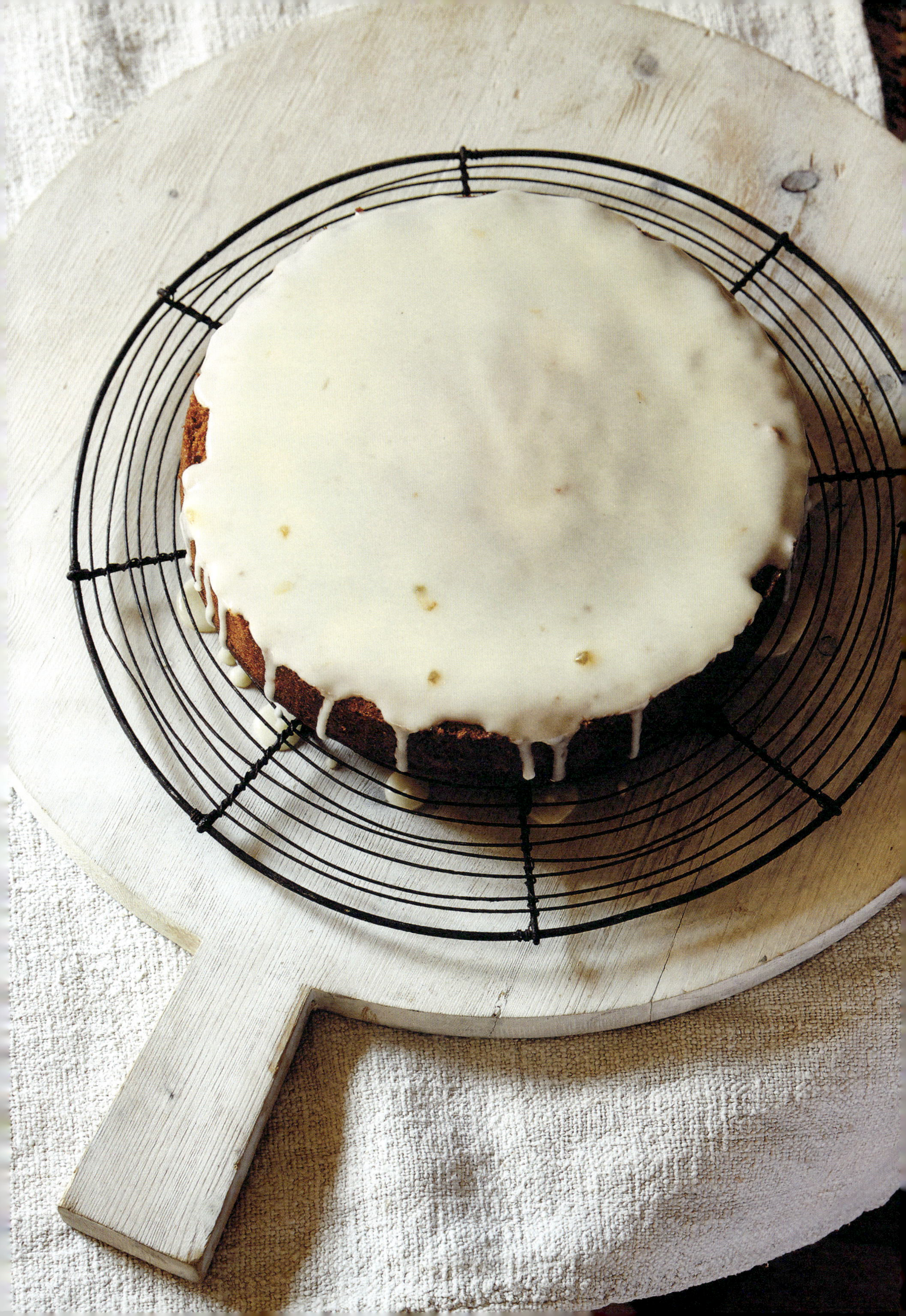

RICOTTA AND APPLE HAZELNUT CAKE

MAKES ONE 20 CM CAKE

This cake is simple to make, but the layers of ricotta and apples hiding between the hazelnut cake make it something pretty special. I used to make this in Italy, with ricotta so fresh it was still warm from being made only hours before. Sometimes we would add sultanas to the ricotta or use orange zest instead of lemon. It is truly wonderful served warm, but also quite satisfying for breakfast straight from the fridge with an espresso in hand.

120 g unsalted butter, softened

200 g caster sugar

2 eggs

125 ml (½ cup) full-cream milk

225 g (1½ cups) self-raising flour

80 g ground hazelnuts
 (see Note on page 212)

RICOTTA FILLING

250 g fresh full-fat ricotta

2 egg yolks

1½ tablespoons caster sugar

1 teaspoon vanilla extract
 or 1 vanilla pod, split and
 seeds scraped

finely grated zest of 1 lemon

APPLE FILLING

1 large (or two small) granny
 smith apples, peeled, cored
 and thinly sliced

juice of ½ lemon

1½ tablespoons caster sugar

HAZELNUT TOPPING

1 tablespoon softened
 unsalted butter

1 tablespoon caster sugar

80 g (⅔ cup) chopped hazelnuts

Preheat the oven to 170°C. Grease a 20 cm round cake tin with butter and line with baking paper.

Beat the butter and sugar until pale and creamy. Add the eggs one at a time, mixing between each addition. Add the milk and mix well. Don't be alarmed if the mixture seems lumpy or like it's not coming together; once the dry ingredients are added, the batter will become smooth. Sift in the flour, add the ground hazelnuts and gently fold into the batter until well incorporated. Pour three-quarters of the cake batter into the prepared tin.

For the ricotta and apple fillings, combine the ingredients in separate bowls. Spread the ricotta filling over the cake batter almost to the edges. Press the apple into the ricotta mixture, leaving any extra juice and sugar in the bowl. Spread the remainder of the cake batter over the top.

For the hazelnut topping, mix the butter and sugar until smooth. Combine with the chopped hazelnuts and scatter over the cake.

Bake for 45–50 minutes, until the cake springs back when touched. Leave to cool slightly in the tin and then turn out and serve warm. If you're not serving immediately, keep the cake in the fridge and bring to room temperature before serving.

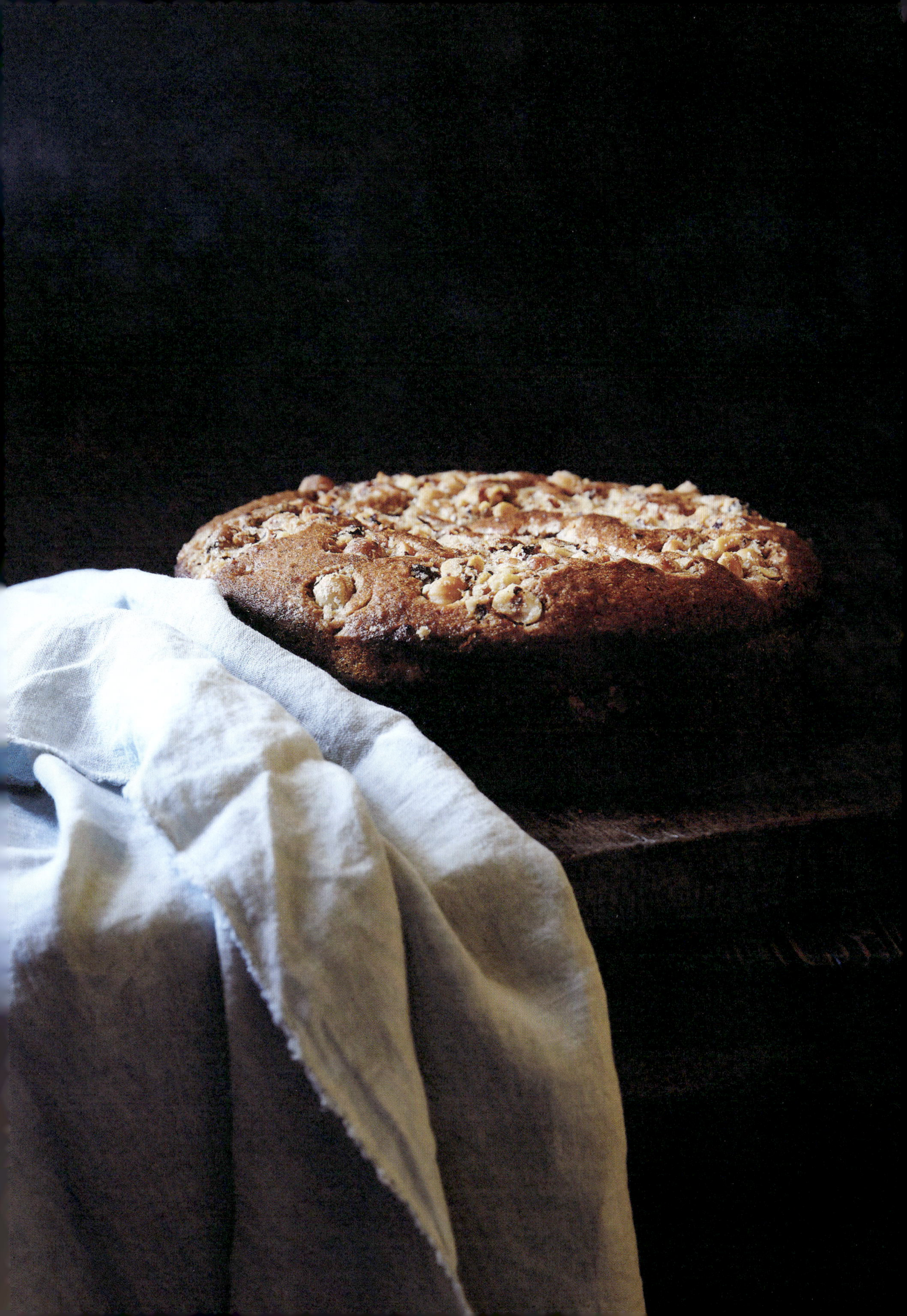

CHOCOLATE, RHUBARB AND WALNUT CAKE

MAKES ONE 35 CM × 13 CM CAKE

The tartness of rhubarb works beautifully in cakes – it mellows as it cooks and balances the sweetness. I make this cake in a shallow tart tin so the rhubarb sinks in and becomes one with the batter. The fluted edges give the cake a lovely shape, too. If you don't have a fluted rectangular tart tin, use a 24 cm loaf tin and increase the cooking time by 5–10 minutes. I have also made this in a 20 cm round cake tin with great success, so feel free to experiment.

150 g (⅔ cup) caster sugar

2 eggs

150 ml extra-virgin olive oil

150 ml full-cream milk

250 g (1⅔ cups) self-raising flour

150 g dark chocolate (70% cocoa), roughly chopped

70 g (⅔ cup) walnuts, roughly chopped

about 4 rhubarb stalks (200 g in total)

demerara sugar, for sprinkling

Preheat the oven to 180°C. Grease a loose-bottomed 35 cm × 13 cm rectangular tart tin with butter.

In a large bowl, whisk the caster sugar, eggs, olive oil and milk until combined. Sift in the flour and stir in the chocolate and walnuts. Pour into the prepared tin. Arrange the rhubarb stems on top of the batter, pressing them in gently so they are partially submerged. If the stalks are too long for the tin, just trim them to fit. Similarly, if the rhubarb stalks are very thick or woody, roughly slice them before placing onto the cake batter. Sprinkle with the demerara sugar and bake for 40–45 minutes or until the cake springs back when touched. Cool completely in the tin before serving.

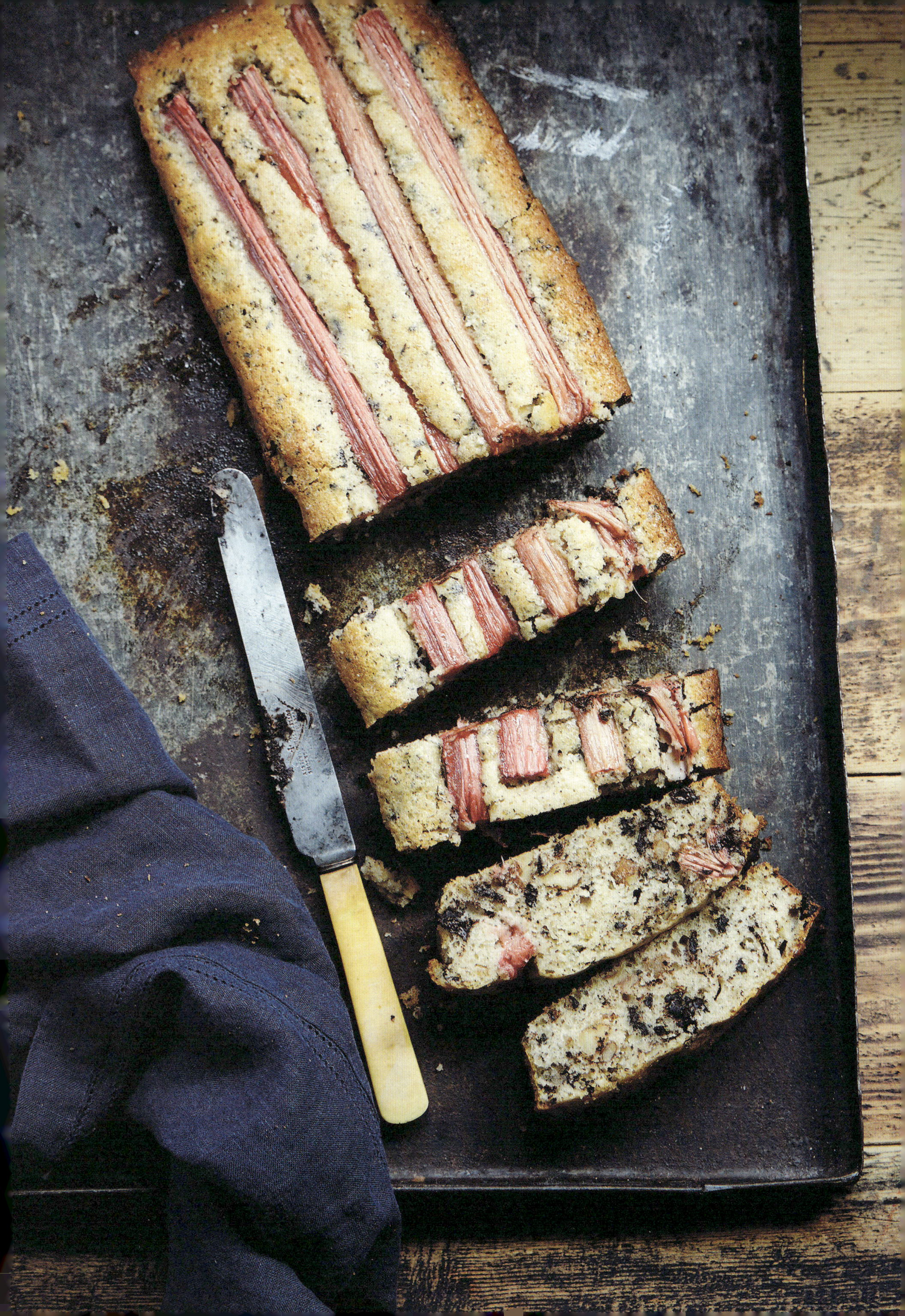

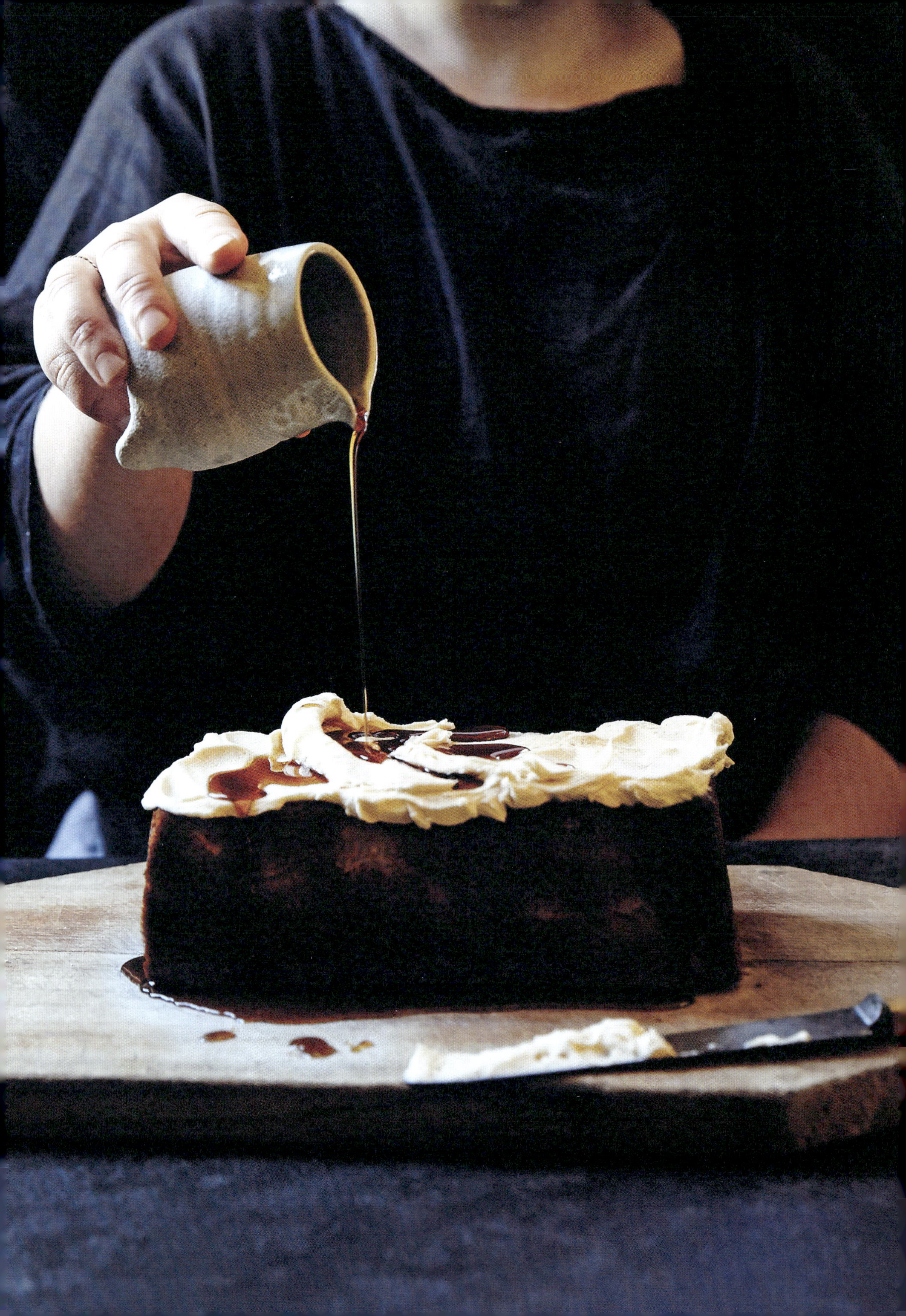

PEAR AND DATE CAKE WITH MAPLE BUTTERCREAM

MAKES ONE 24 CM LOAF

This is a comforting cake – one for cooler days when being at home in the warmth with a slice of cake and a cup of tea is the best place to be. The maple buttercream complements the cake's caramel notes perfectly. The extra maple syrup drizzled over the cake just before serving is the finishing touch. This cake can be made in a round or square cake tin, too; however, this will require a slightly longer cooking time.

100 g pitted dates, roughly chopped

½ teaspoon bicarbonate of soda

60 ml (¼ cup) boiling water

100 g unsalted butter, softened

125 g (⅔ cup, lightly packed) brown sugar

2 eggs

100 ml extra-virgin olive oil

150 g plain yoghurt

finely grated zest of 1 lemon

200 g (1⅓ cups) self-raising flour

1 heaped teaspoon ground ginger

2 pears (about 400 g in total), peeled, cored and roughly chopped

maple syrup, for drizzling

MAPLE BUTTERCREAM

50 g unsalted butter, softened

90 g (¾ cup) icing sugar, sifted

1½ tablespoons maple syrup

Preheat the oven to 180°C. Grease a 24 cm loaf tin with butter and line with baking paper.

Mix the dates in a small bowl and sprinkle with the bicarbonate of soda. Cover with the water and allow to stand for 10 minutes.

Cream the butter and sugar together in a large bowl until pale and fluffy. Add the eggs one at a time, beating well between each addition. Mix in the olive oil, yoghurt, lemon zest and the dates and soaking water. Sift in the flour and ground ginger, stirring until just combined. Gently stir in the pear and spoon the batter into the prepared tin. Bake for 45–50 minutes or until a skewer inserted into the middle comes out clean. Leave to cool in the tin for a few minutes, then turn out onto a rack to cool completely.

For the maple buttercream, beat the butter and icing sugar together in a bowl until pale and fluffy. Slowly drizzle in the maple syrup and continue beating until combined.

Spread the buttercream over the cooled cake and drizzle a little maple syrup over the top to finish.

LEMON OLIVE OIL CAKE

MAKES ONE 20 CM CAKE

The secret to this wonderfully simple cake is rubbing the lemon zest into the sugar. The citrus flavour intensifies and permeates through the whole cake, which stands impressively tall. I learned to make this cake in Italy – originally with oranges – using the freshest olive oil, made at the property where I lived. A huge vat of the golden liquid was hidden behind a wall in the kitchen. It poured out through a beautiful brass tap in what seemed like a never-ending supply. The simple quantities of the ingredients for this cake make them easily committed to memory.

finely grated zest and juice of 2 lemons

300 g caster sugar

3 eggs

300 ml full-cream milk

300 ml extra-virgin olive oil

300 g (2 cups) self-raising flour, plus extra if needed

Preheat the oven to 180°C. Grease a 20 cm round cake tin with butter and line with baking paper.

In a large bowl, rub the lemon zest and sugar together until the sugar is fragrant and damp. Add the eggs and whisk until pale and thick. Add the milk, olive oil and lemon juice and whisk well to combine.

Sift the flour into a separate bowl and make a well in the centre. Slowly pour in the wet ingredients, mixing until just incorporated. The batter should be quite wet – the consistency of a thick pouring cream. If the batter is runnier than that, mix in a little more flour.

Bake for 45–50 minutes until golden and a skewer inserted into the middle comes out clean. Leave to cool in the tin for a few minutes, then turn out onto a rack to cool completely.

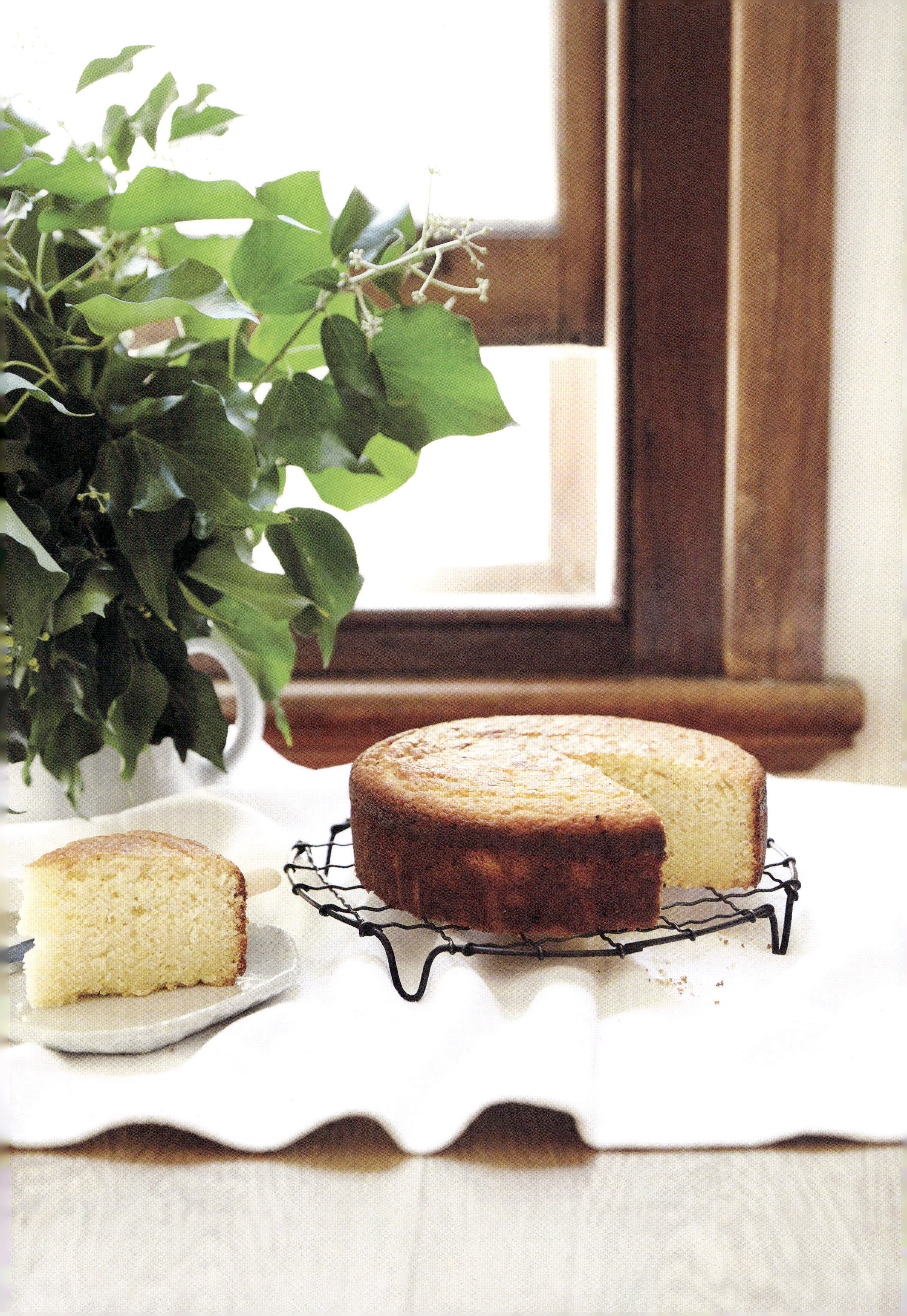

ALMOND CHOCOLATE CAKE

MAKES ONE 20 CM CAKE

This is one of my favourite cakes to make and is a real crowd pleaser. I used to eat a similar cake when I lived in Florence – it was sold in thin slices and sat on a marble bench-top in the window of the cutest little cake shop at the end of my street. I would often pick up a slice on my way home from class and eat it for breakfast with an espresso the following morning. The richness and fudge-like texture is really the best part of this cake. Try and buy the best dark chocolate you can afford – it makes all the difference. Dust the cake with the cocoa powder just before serving.

180 g good-quality dark chocolate (70% cocoa), broken into pieces

150 g unsalted butter, cut into cubes

1 tablespoon almond liqueur (such as Amaretto)

200 g caster sugar

7 eggs, 5 separated

180 g ground almonds (see Note)

50 g unsweetened cocoa powder, plus extra for dusting

1 vanilla pod, split and seeds scraped

pinch of sea salt

crème fraîche, to serve

Preheat the oven to 150°C. Grease a 20 cm round cake tin with butter and line with baking paper.

Place the chocolate, butter and liqueur in a heatproof bowl set over a saucepan of simmering water. Stir occasionally until melted and smooth, then remove from the heat. Set aside to cool.

Beat the sugar, the 2 whole eggs and the 5 egg yolks until the mixture is pale, thick and glossy. Gently fold the ground almonds, cocoa powder and vanilla seeds into the egg mixture. Add the melted chocolate mixture and stir until combined.

In a clean bowl, whisk the egg whites with a pinch of salt until stiff peaks form. Gently fold into the chocolate mixture, a little at a time. The chocolate mixture will be quite heavy, but try to be as gentle as possible. Pour the batter into the prepared tin and bake for 40–45 minutes until just cooked. Leave to cool completely in the tin before turning out.

Dust the cake lightly with cocoa powder and serve with a dollop of crème fraîche.

NOTE: For ground almonds or hazelnuts, if you don't wish to grind them yourself, simply purchase some almond or hazelnut meal. This is quite finely ground and will result in a refined, smooth texture. I prefer a slightly coarser texture, so I like to grind them myself – simply place the required quantity of blanched nuts in a mortar or food processor and grind to your desired texture.

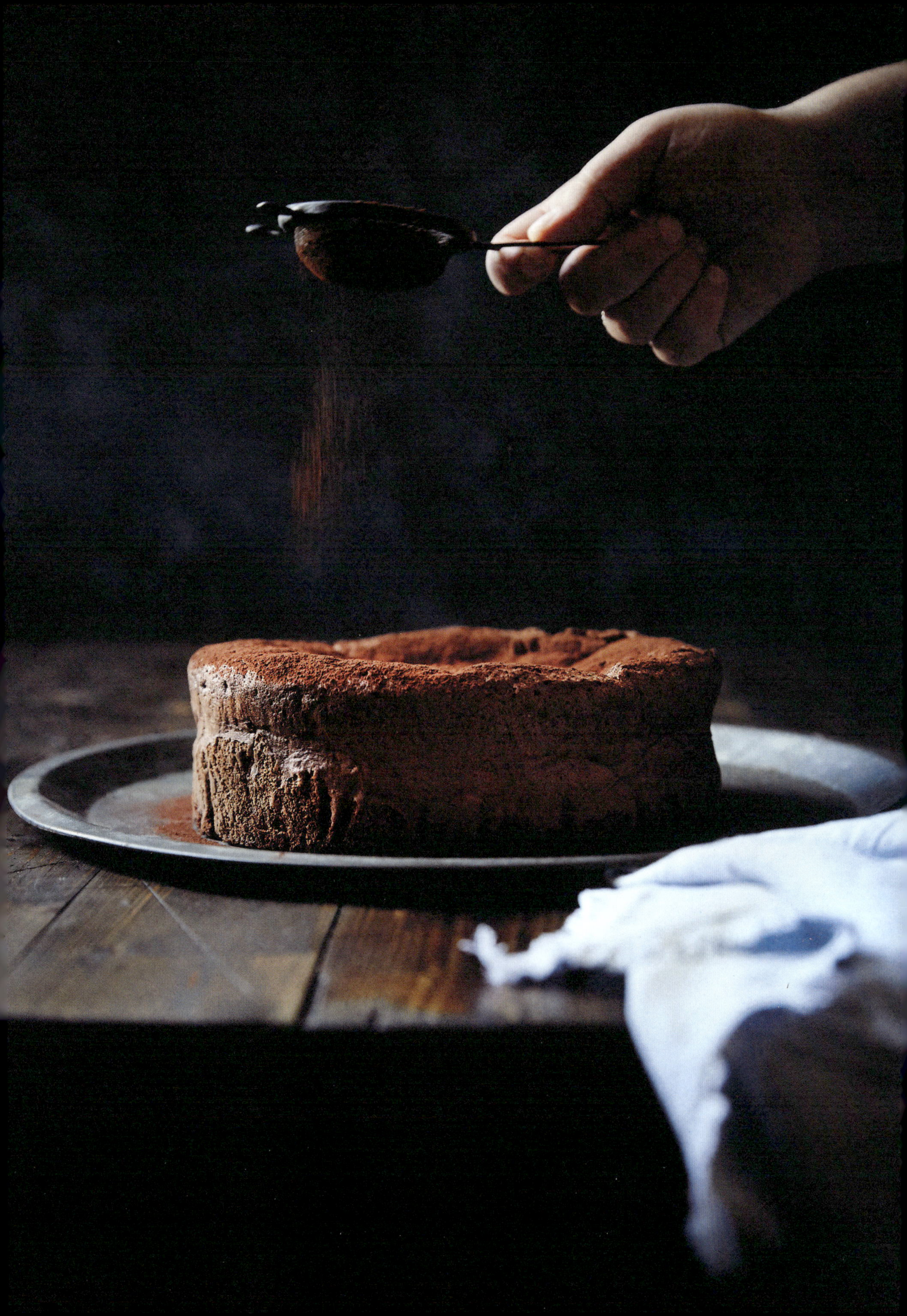

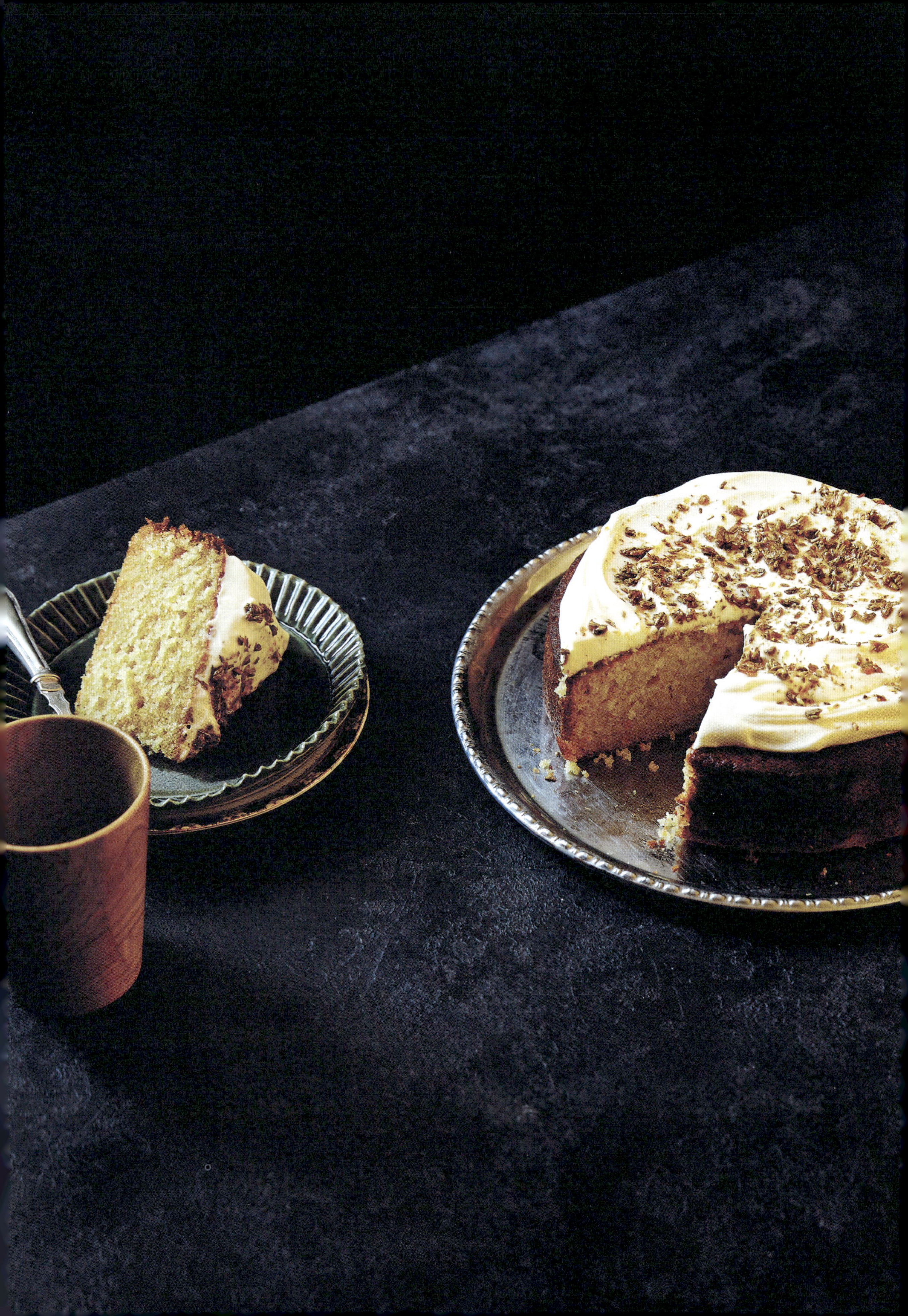

WHOLE ORANGE CAKE WITH CANDIED FENNEL SEEDS

MAKES ONE 20 CM CAKE

Puréed oranges give this cake a subtle bitterness, something I absolutely adore. You can experiment with using different citrus fruit, such as blood oranges, Seville oranges or even one lemon and one orange to increase the bitterness. I love that you can use the whole oranges here without having to boil them for hours on the stove first – a perfect cake if you're short on time. Serve the cake as is, simply dusted with icing sugar, or as I have done, with a simple frosting and candied fennel seeds, which pair beautifully with citrus.

2 oranges (about 300 g in total), ends trimmed, cut into quarters and seeds removed

300 g caster sugar

3 eggs

250 ml (1 cup) extra-virgin olive oil

250 g (1⅔ cups) self-raising flour

CANDIED FENNEL SEEDS

1 tablespoon fennel seeds

2 tablespoons icing sugar

FROSTING

250 g (1 cup) crème fraîche

50 g icing sugar

Preheat the oven to 180°C. Grease a 20 cm round cake tin with butter and line with baking paper.

Blitz the oranges in a food processor, skin and all, until you have a purée. Set aside. Beat the sugar with the eggs until pale and thick. Add the olive oil and puréed oranges and whisk until combined. Sift in the flour and gently whisk until you have a smooth batter. Pour into the prepared cake tin and bake for 45 minutes or until a skewer inserted into the middle comes out clean. Leave to cool in the tin for a few minutes, then turn out onto a rack to cool completely.

For the candied fennel seeds, combine the fennel seeds and icing sugar in a small bowl and toss to coat. Tip the mixture into a small frying pan over a low–medium heat, and stir continuously until the icing sugar melts and turns a deep amber colour. Remove from the heat and spoon the fennel seeds onto baking paper to cool.

To make the frosting, simply whisk the crème fraîche and icing sugar together until thick.

Spread the frosting over the cooled cake and sprinkle with the candied fennel seeds.

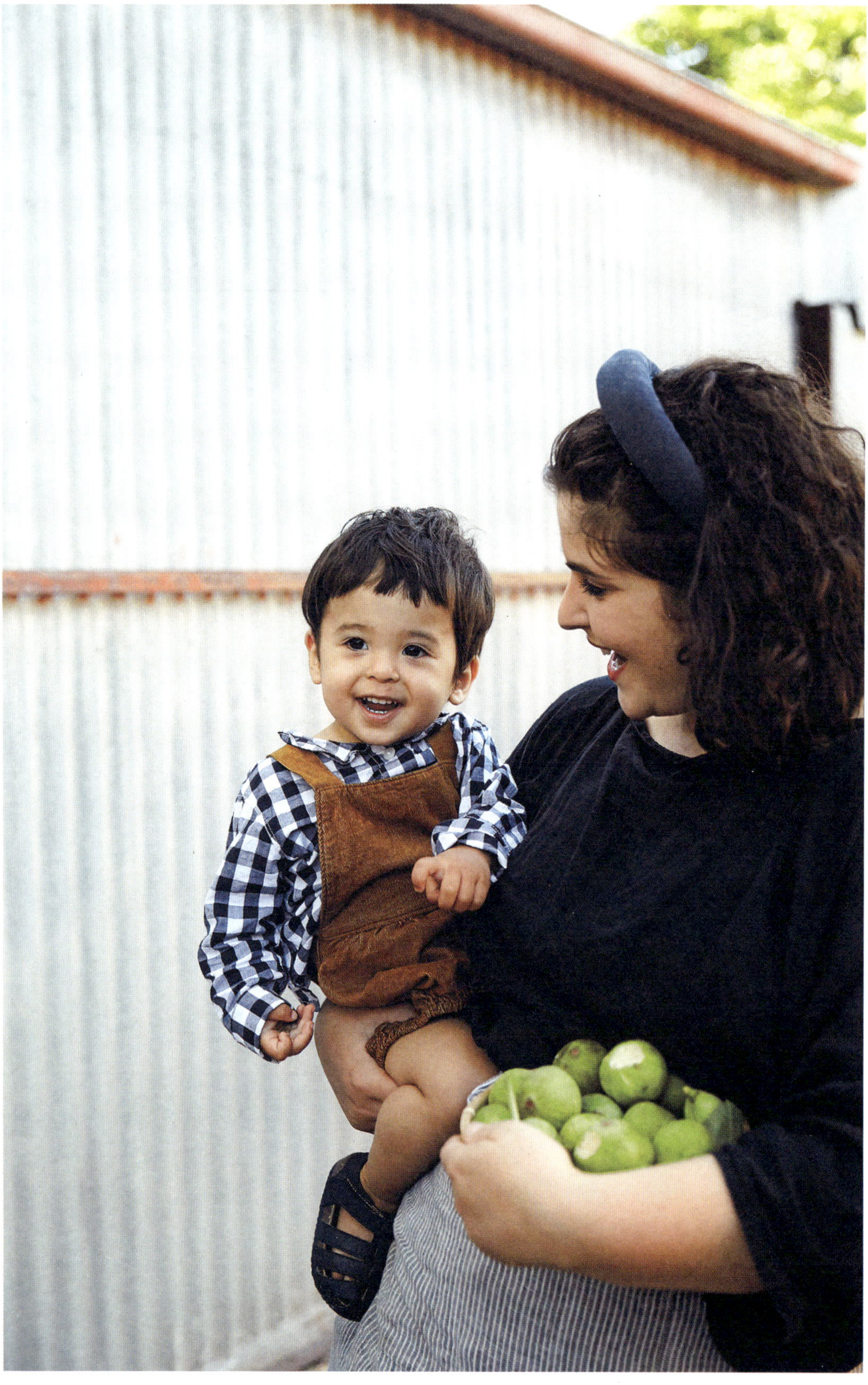

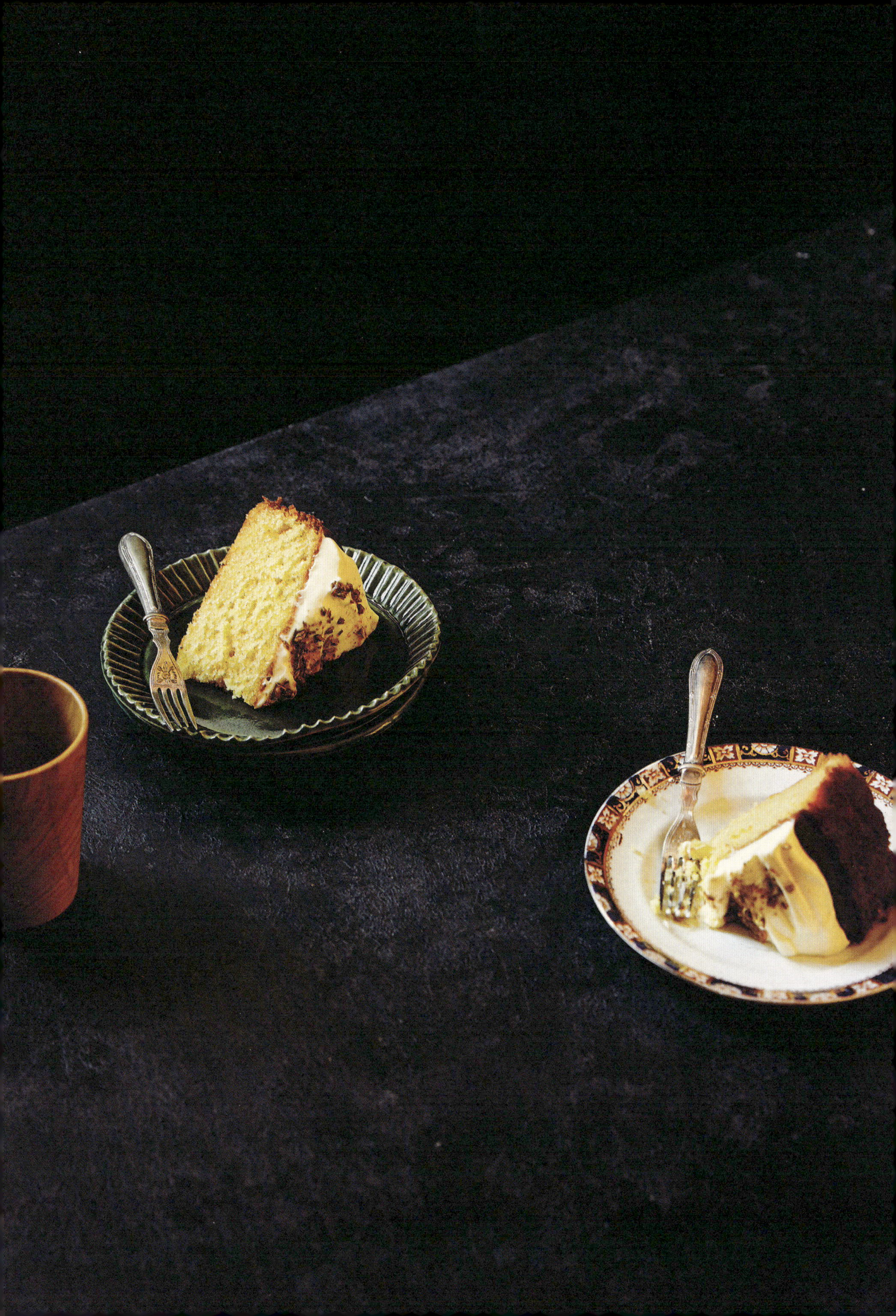

A NICE PLUM CAKE

MAKES ONE 20 CM CAKE

A nice plum cake for afternoon tea. This cake is best served with a dollop of thick cream, and eaten in admiration of the deep, rich, crimson plums that adorn its bumpy top, thanks to a lovely buttery crumble. You could use other stone fruit, such as apricots or peaches, if plums aren't at hand.

150 g (⅔ cup) caster sugar

150 g unsalted butter, softened

1 vanilla pod, split and seeds scraped

2 eggs

100 g ground almonds (see Note on page 212)

100 ml full-cream milk

1 teaspoon baking powder

150 g (1 cup) plain flour, sifted

6 small plums (about 300 g in total), cut in half and stones removed

CRUMBLE TOPPING

40 g chilled unsalted butter

40 g (¼ cup, lightly packed) brown sugar

30 g (⅓ cup) flaked almonds

40 g plain flour

pinch of sea salt

Preheat the oven to 180°C. Grease a 20 cm round cake tin with butter and line with baking paper.

Cream the sugar, butter and vanilla seeds together until pale and fluffy. Stir in the eggs, one at a time, beating after each addition. Stir in the ground almonds (the mixture will be a little stiff, but the milk will loosen the batter). Add half of the milk and stir to incorporate, followed by the baking powder and half of the flour. Mix in the remainder of the milk, finishing with the rest of the flour, gently stirring until smooth and combined. Spoon the batter into the prepared tin and top with the plums, cut-side up, pressing them into the mixture a little.

To make the crumble topping, place all of the ingredients in a small bowl and rub together into a crumbly mixture. Scatter over the top of the cake batter and bake for 40–45 minutes or until a skewer inserted into the middle comes out clean. Leave to cool in the tin for a few minutes, then turn out onto a rack to cool completely. This cake is best eaten on the day it is made.

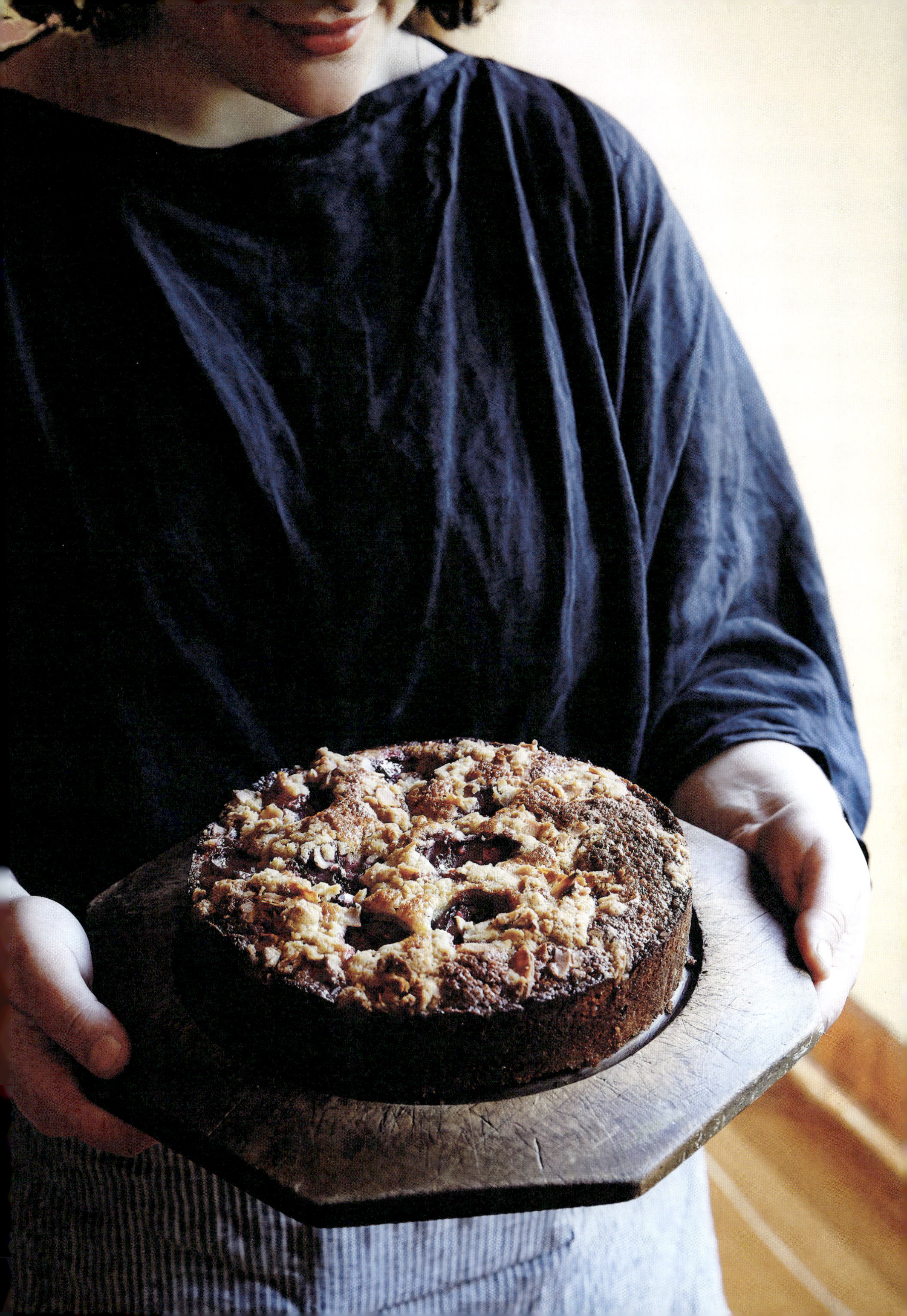

SPICED HONEY CAKE

MAKES ONE 20 CM CAKE

This cake was dreamt up after a conversation with a friend about the honey cakes she used to eat as a child. Her mother used to make them, and the subtle spices and hint of espresso have lingered in her memory. This is my version, which is incredibly moist and gently spiced. You can play around with the spices, adding a little extra if you prefer a more pronounced flavour. Sometimes I serve this cake simply dusted with icing sugar, but here I've suggested a delightful honey and mascarpone frosting.

3 eggs

100 g (½ cup, lightly packed) brown sugar

1 vanilla pod, split and seeds scraped

2½ tablespoons strong espresso, cooled

250 ml (1 cup) buttermilk

250 ml (1 cup) extra-virgin olive oil

200 g runny honey (see Note)

300 g (2 cups) self-raising flour

1 teaspoon ground cinnamon

½ teaspoon ground allspice

pinch of sea salt

toasted walnuts, for topping

HONEY FROSTING

250 g (1 cup) mascarpone (see recipe page 238)

1 tablespoon runny honey

50 g icing sugar, sifted

Preheat the oven to 180°C. Grease a 20 cm round cake tin with butter and line with baking paper.

In a large bowl, whisk together the eggs, sugar and vanilla seeds. Combine the espresso with 2½ tablespoons of water and add to the bowl along with the buttermilk, olive oil and honey. Whisk until smooth. Sift in the flour, add the spices and salt and whisk to combine. Pour the batter into the prepared tin and bake for about 50 minutes or until a skewer inserted into the middle comes out clean. Leave to cool in the tin for a few minutes, then turn out onto a rack to cool completely.

To make the frosting, place the mascarpone in a bowl and, using a spoon, gently stir in the honey. Add the icing sugar and stir until just combined. The key here is to not over-work it, as mascarpone can easily become grainy due to its high fat content.

Spread the frosting over the completely cooled cake and scatter walnuts over the top.

NOTE: If it's not the middle of summer, most likely your honey will be a little firm, or it may have crystallised. Just heat the honey on the stove in a small saucepan for 30 seconds to melt, and then bring back to room temperature before using.

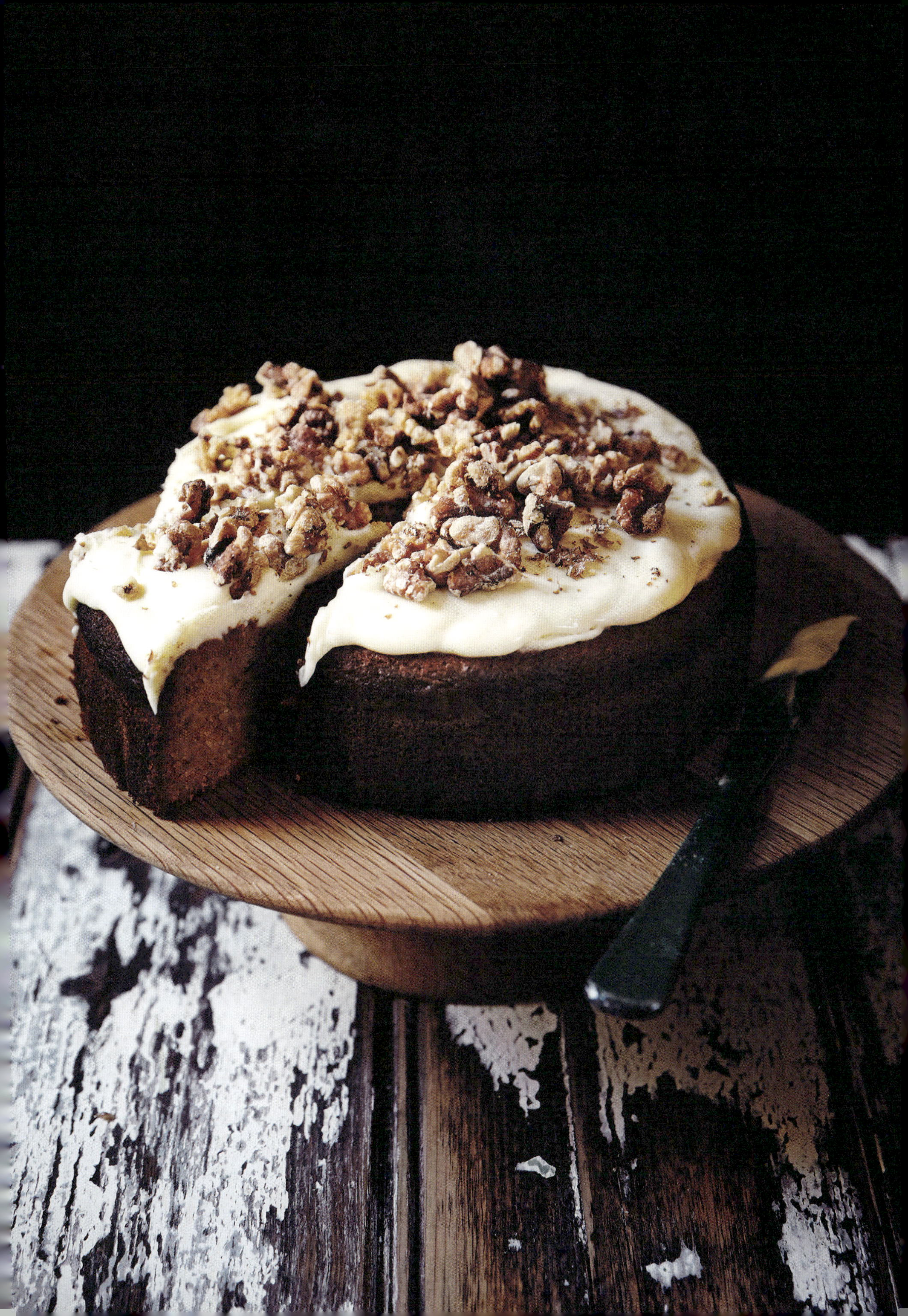

CHOCOLATE LAYER CAKE WITH ESPRESSO FROSTING AND BLACKBERRIES

MAKES ONE 20 CM ROUND DOUBLE-LAYER CAKE

A lovely rich cake for celebrating and sharing with friends. This recipe never fails me and is always much loved at birthdays and events. The espresso brings a subtle warmth to the cake, with the shiny deep blackberries balancing out the richness of the cake. While I usually use just a hand whisk when making cakes, the amount of mixture required is rather large, so an electric mixer or beaters are quite necessary here.

250 g dark chocolate (70% cocoa), broken into pieces

450 g (3 cups) self-raising flour

60 g (½ cup) Dutch-process cocoa powder

400 g unsalted butter, softened

150 g (⅔ cup) caster sugar

150 g (⅔ cup, firmly packed) brown sugar

5 eggs

200 ml full-cream milk

100 ml espresso

200 g plain yoghurt

blackberries, for decorating

BLACKBERRY JAM

250 g (2 cups) blackberries, fresh or frozen

150 g (⅔ cup) caster sugar

1 vanilla pod, split and seeds scraped

ESPRESSO FROSTING

200 g dark chocolate, (70% cocoa), broken into pieces

300 g unsalted butter, softened

200 g icing sugar, sifted

60 g (½ cup) Dutch-process cocoa powder, sifted

2½ tablespoons espresso

Preheat the oven to 180°C. Grease two 20 cm round cake tins with butter and line with baking paper.

Melt the chocolate in a heatproof bowl set over a saucepan of simmering water, stirring occasionally until smooth. Allow to cool.

Sift the flour and cocoa powder into a large bowl. Using electric beaters or an electric mixer fitted with a paddle attachment, cream the butter and sugars together until pale and fluffy. Add the eggs, one at a time, beating between each addition. Add the milk, espresso and yoghurt and beat to combine. The mixture may be a bit lumpy and look separated at this stage – but don't worry, it will come together. With the mixer on low, gradually add the dry ingredients and melted chocolate, alternating between the two and beating until smooth and combined.

Pour the batter into the prepared tins, level out the top and bake for 45–50 minutes or until a skewer inserted into the middle comes out clean. Leave to cool in the tins until just warm, then turn out onto a rack to cool completely.

Meanwhile, to make the blackberry jam, combine the blackberries, sugar and vanilla seeds in a small saucepan over a low–medium heat. Bring to the boil, stirring often in the first minute or two. Reduce the heat and simmer for 10 minutes, or until thick and reduced. Allow to cool.

For the frosting, melt the chocolate in a heatproof bowl set over a saucepan of simmering water, stirring occasionally until smooth. Allow to cool. Using electric beaters or an electric mixer fitted with a paddle attachment, beat the butter, icing sugar and cocoa powder together until pale and fluffy. Pour in the melted chocolate and the espresso and continue to beat until smooth and fluffy, about 3 minutes.

RECIPE CONTINUED OVERLEAF ⟶

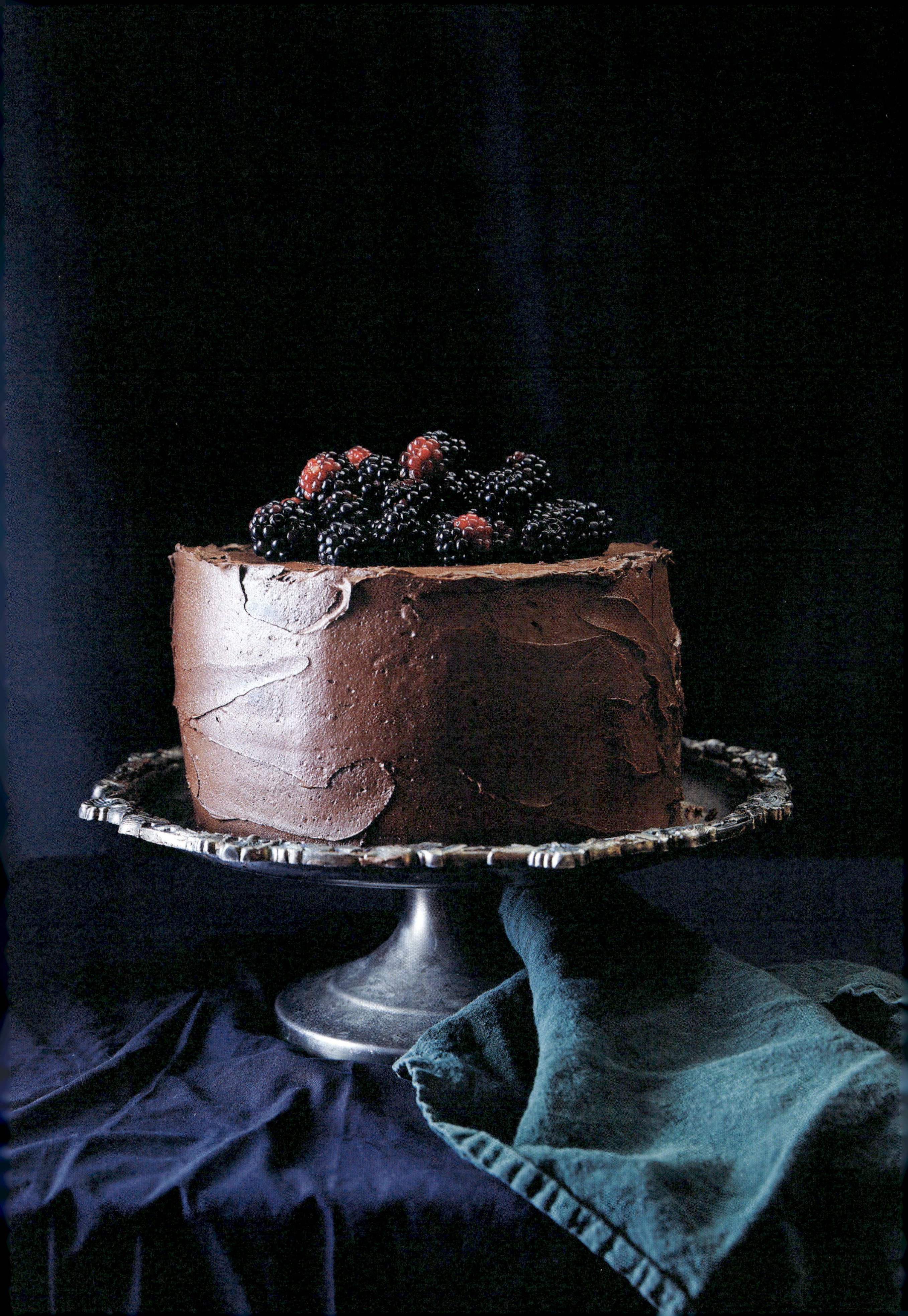

RECIPE CONTINUED ·⟶

If needed, use a long, sharp bread knife to trim off the rounded tops from the cooled cakes so they are mostly flat. Slice the cakes in half horizontally so you now have four thinner cakes. Place one cake, trimmed-side up, onto a board. Spread with a layer of frosting, spreading it out to the edges of the cake, and drizzle with one-third of the blackberry jam. Top with a cake layer and repeat, finishing with a cake layer on top, with the trimmed edge facing down. Using a palette knife, coat the top and sides of the cake with a thin layer of frosting – this is called a 'crumb coat' and will hold the crumbs in place when you do the final layer of frosting. Place the cake in the fridge for 30 minutes, then frost the cake, smoothing the frosting with the knife as you go. Top with blackberries and serve at room temperature.

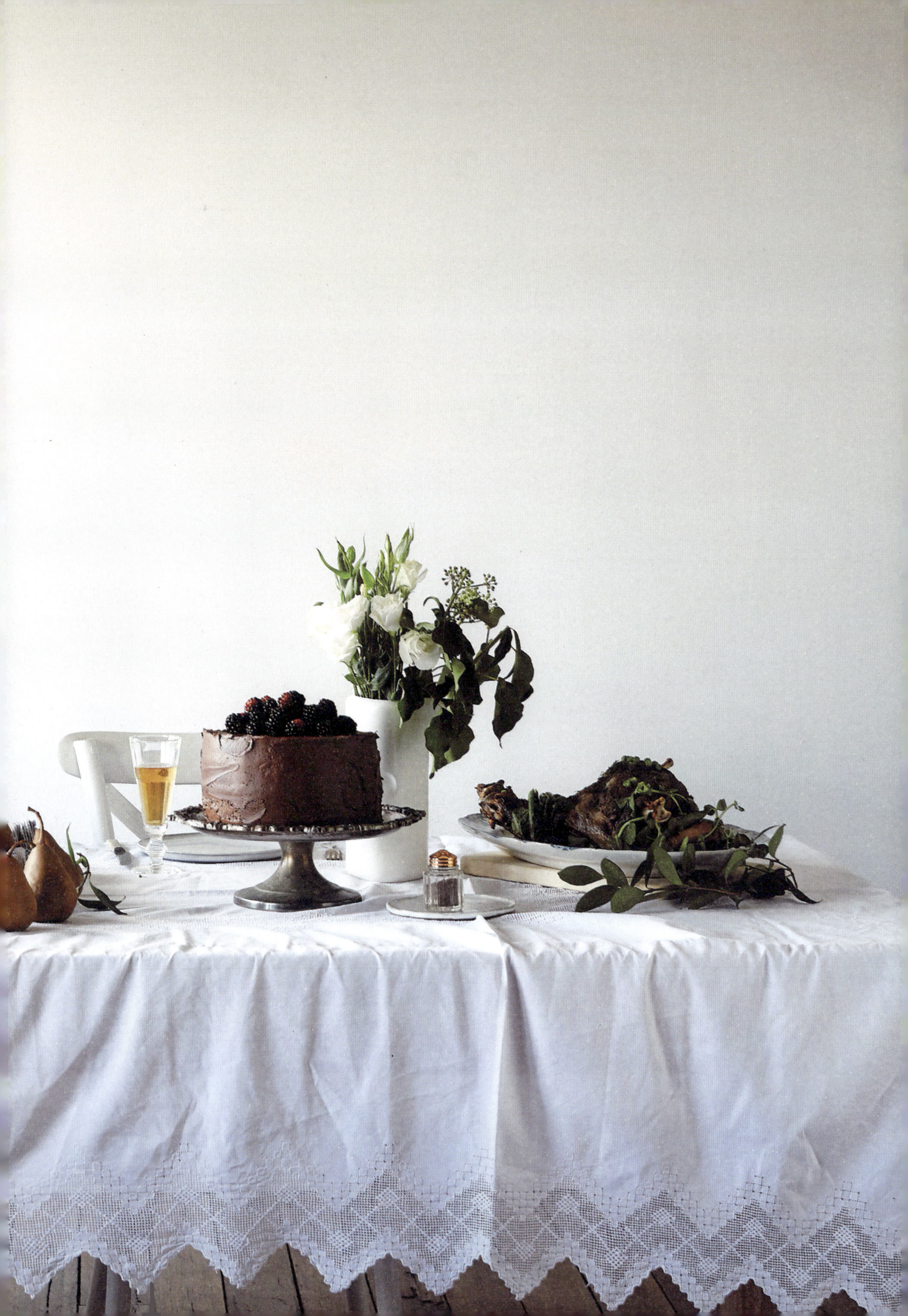

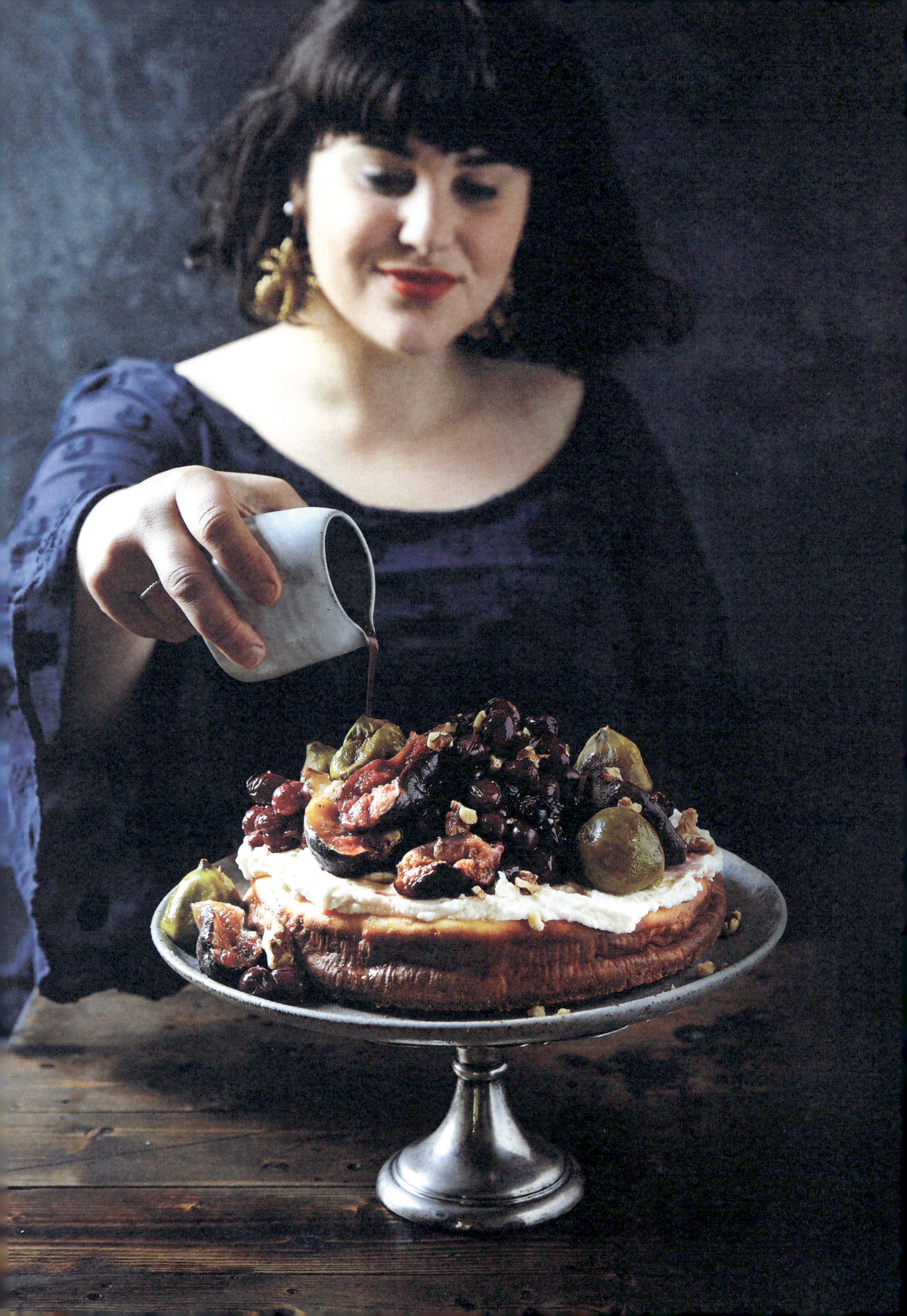

DESSERT

The first dessert I ever made was an apple-flavoured meringue dish called 'apple snow'. I was four, it was 1992 and I begged my mum to make it with me after seeing it on *Play School*. It is safe to say that my desire to cook started quite early. Most of my childhood memories are actually food memories. Meals, occasions and particular moments in the kitchen are the things I remember most clearly. While there is no apple snow here, my final chapter contains recipes for the end of a meal or for times when you feel like a sweet pick-me-up. Many of the recipes here have significant meaning — the chocolate pots are reminiscent of the Cointreau-spiked mousse my mum always made for special lunches, the cardamom buns are part of our Christmas tradition and the ice creams are steeped in family history.

CHOCOLATE AND SOUR CHERRY BRIOCHE BUNS

❈ MAKES 8 LARGE BUNS ❈

These buns are decadent – buttery brioche filled with dark chocolate, sour cherries and walnuts. They are rather simple to make, especially if you have an electric mixer. I have made them by hand on some occasions and it wasn't too difficult, just a bit of a workout! You can omit the cherries if you can't find them, and feel free to replace the walnuts with almonds, pistachios or even hazelnuts. The overnight proofing helps to make this soft and buttery dough workable. Similarly, don't try to make these on a hot day, as the dough will be far too soft to handle in the heat. These buns are best eaten on the day of baking, but they can be toasted and eaten the following day.

350 g (2⅓ cups) plain flour, sifted, plus extra for dusting

7 g active dry yeast

70 g caster sugar

100 ml full-cream milk, plus 1 tablespoon extra for brushing

4 eggs

finely grated zest of 1 orange

150 g unsalted butter, softened

CHOCOLATE AND SOUR CHERRY FILLING

50 g (½ cup) toasted walnuts

100 g dark chocolate (70% cocoa), finely chopped

1¾ tablespoons caster sugar

finely grated zest of 1 orange

40 g (⅓ cup) dried sour cherries, roughly chopped

Place the flour, yeast and sugar in the bowl of an electric mixer fitted with a dough hook attachment. Gently warm the milk in a saucepan over a low heat until tepid, about 30°C. Turn the mixer on to medium speed and pour the milk into the dry ingredients, along with three of the eggs and the orange zest. Mix for 3–4 minutes until combined into a sticky yet elastic dough. With the motor still running, add the butter, a tablespoon at a time, ensuring it is incorporated before adding more. Once all the butter has been added, mix for another 2–3 minutes until the dough is elastic. Transfer to a large bowl that has been lightly greased with butter and cover with a cloth or plastic wrap. Set aside in a warm place to rise for about 1 hour or until the dough has doubled in size. Knock back the dough, cover again and place in the fridge to prove for at least 6 hours or overnight.

Meanwhile, to make the filling, lightly toast the walnuts in a dry frying pan over a low–medium heat for 1–2 minutes or until just coloured. Allow to cool, then chop them finely and combine with the remaining ingredients. Set aside.

Preheat the oven to 190°C. Line a baking tray with baking paper.

Tip the dough onto a lightly floured bench and, using your hands or a rolling pin, push or roll the dough out to a rectangle about 40 cm × 20 cm, flouring the dough as you need. Scatter the filling evenly over the rectangle of dough, then fold the short edges in so they meet in the middle, so it looks like an open book. Then fold the dough in half along where the edges meet (like closing a book). You will now have a long, flat shape. You can cut the buns like this, or roll gently, from the longer edge, into a log shape. Trim the rough ends, then cut the log into eight pieces about 6 cm wide. Arrange on the prepared tray with 4 cm of space between each bun to allow them to expand. Leave in a warm place for 30 minutes for a final proof. Lightly whisk the remaining egg with the extra tablespoon of milk and brush over the top of the buns. Bake for 18–20 minutes until golden and risen. Allow to cool slightly on the tray before moving to a wire rack to finish cooling. Serve warm, or at room temperature on the day of baking.

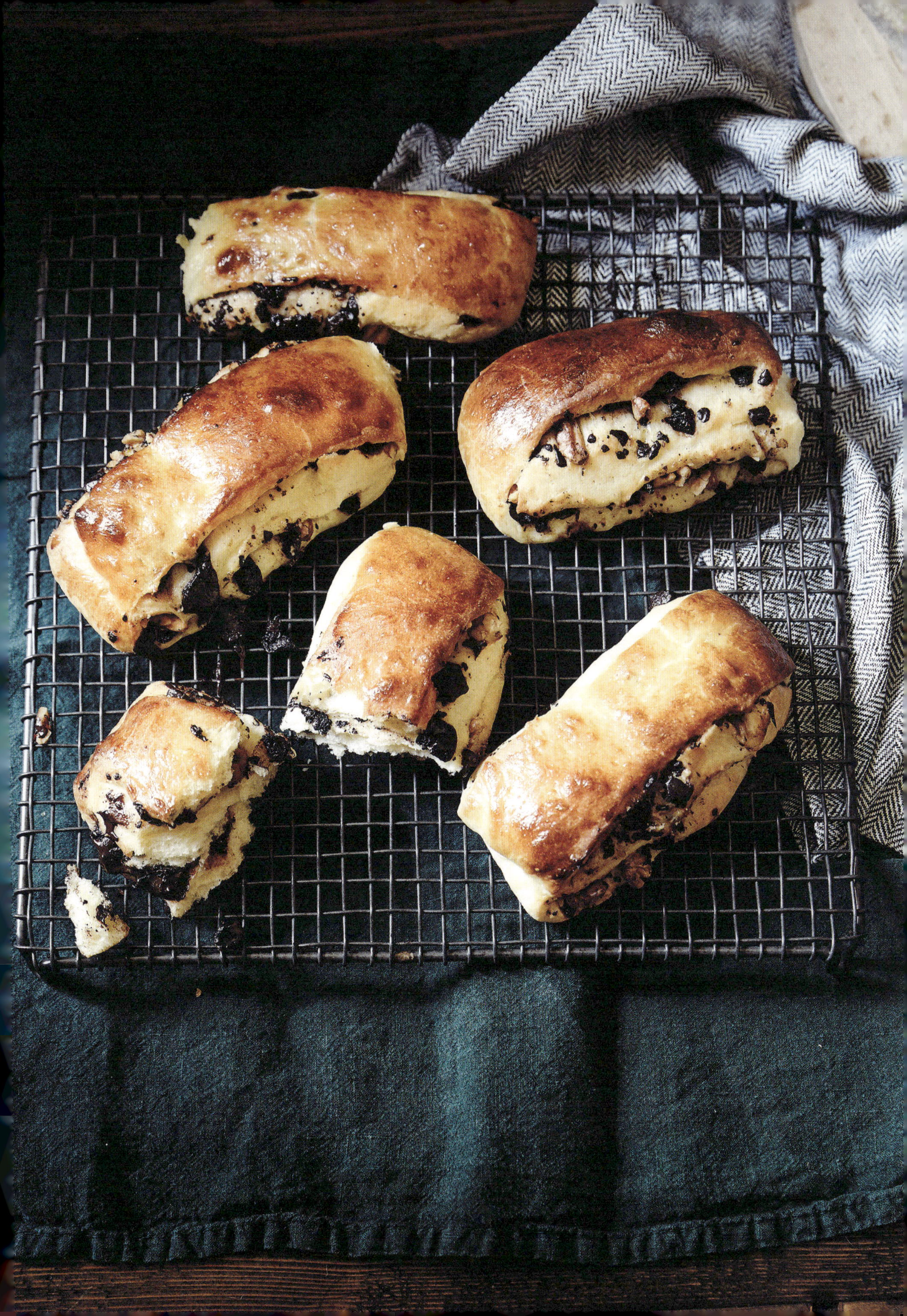

DESSERT 230

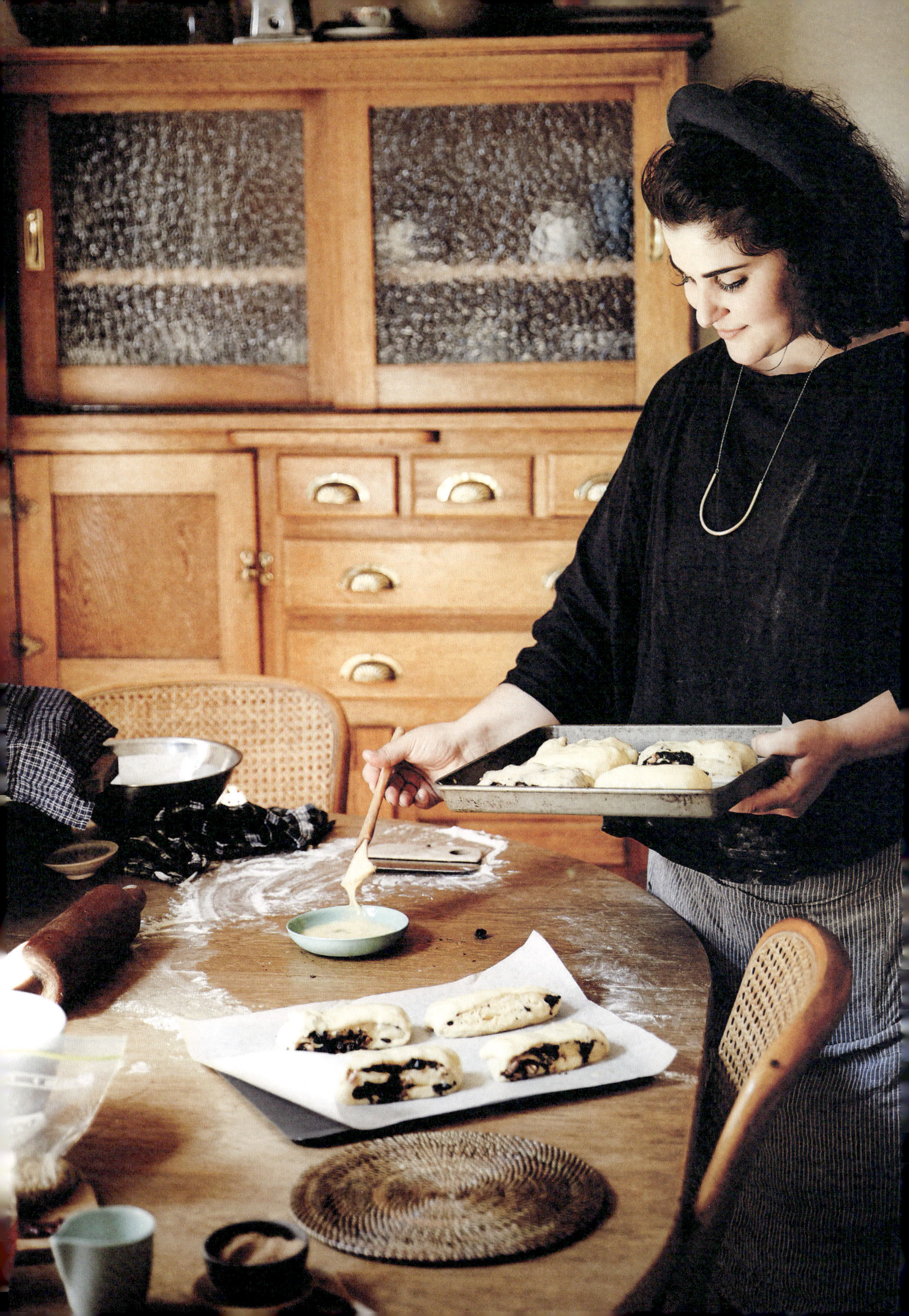

CINNAMON DOUGHNUTS WITH CUSTARD CREAM

MAKES 14

For a few years, I baked cakes and other sweets for people in Melbourne – parties, workshops and weddings. My cinnamon doughnuts were often requested and were always the first thing to be devoured. They're fluffy without being too airy and are dangerously moreish. I make them in the classic ring style with a dollop of thick custard cream, inspired by the way they are served at a small restaurant in Osaka called Bird, one of my favourite places to eat when I visit Japan.

My brother-in-law, Aurélien, hails from a town in the Loire Valley. He makes the most wonderful desserts and has a small notebook filled with his family's recipes, all carefully written out by hand. The recipe for this custard cream comes from him.

400 g (2⅔ cups) plain flour, sifted, plus extra for dusting

7 g active dry yeast

40 g caster sugar

150 ml thickened cream

100 ml full-cream milk

45 g unsalted butter, softened

1 vanilla pod, split and seeds scraped

1 egg, lightly beaten

vegetable oil, for deep-frying

CUSTARD CREAM

2 egg yolks

100 g caster sugar

20 g plain flour

20 g cornflour

500 ml (2 cups) full-cream milk

1 vanilla pod, split and seeds scraped

CINNAMON SUGAR

200 g caster sugar

1½ teaspoons ground cinnamon

RECIPE CONTINUED OVERLEAF ⟶

Place the flour, yeast and sugar in the bowl of an electric mixer fitted with a dough hook attachment. Gently warm the cream, milk and butter with the vanilla seeds and pod in a saucepan over a low heat until tepid, about 30°C. If the mixture becomes too hot, simply allow it to come to the right temperature before using. Remove the vanilla pod from the milk and mix in the egg. Turn the mixer on to medium speed and pour the cream mixture into the dry ingredients. Mix for 5–6 minutes until combined into a sticky yet elastic dough. Transfer to a large bowl that has been lightly greased with butter and cover with a cloth or plastic wrap. Set aside in a warm place to rise for about 1 hour or until the dough has doubled in size. Knock back the dough, cover again and leave to rise for another 45 minutes, until doubled in size again.

Line a baking tray with baking paper. Tip the dough onto a lightly floured work surface and roll out to about 1 cm thick. Cut into rounds using an 8 cm circle cutter, then use a 2 cm circle cutter to cut out the holes. Transfer to the prepared tray, leaving a bit of space between the doughnuts so they can expand. Re-roll any scraps and repeat, then set aside to rise for 15 minutes.

Meanwhile, to make the custard cream, whisk the egg yolks with the sugar in a large bowl until pale and thick. Sift in the flours, mix well and set aside. Warm the milk with the vanilla seeds and pod in a saucepan over a low heat until lukewarm, about 35°C. Strain the milk and add to the egg mixture, just a few tablespoons at a time to begin with, whisking between each addition. After about a quarter of the mixture has been mixed in, whisk in all of the remainder of the milk. Pour into a clean saucepan over a medium heat and bring to a simmer, whisking continuously as it can scorch very easily. Reduce the heat to low, stirring constantly, for 2–3 minutes until thick. Transfer to a bowl and cover, placing the plastic wrap directly onto the custard to stop a skin forming, and refrigerate until ready to use.

DESSERT 233

RECIPE CONTINUED ⟶

To make the cinnamon sugar, combine the sugar with the cinnamon in a shallow bowl. Set aside.

Heat the vegetable oil in a heavy-based saucepan or deep-fryer to 180°C, or hot enough that a cube of bread dropped into the oil will turn golden brown in 15 seconds. Fry the doughnuts, in batches, for 3–4 minutes, flipping halfway, until golden and puffed. Drain on paper towel or a wire rack, then toss in the cinnamon sugar.

Serve the doughnuts, each with a generous dollop of the custard cream.

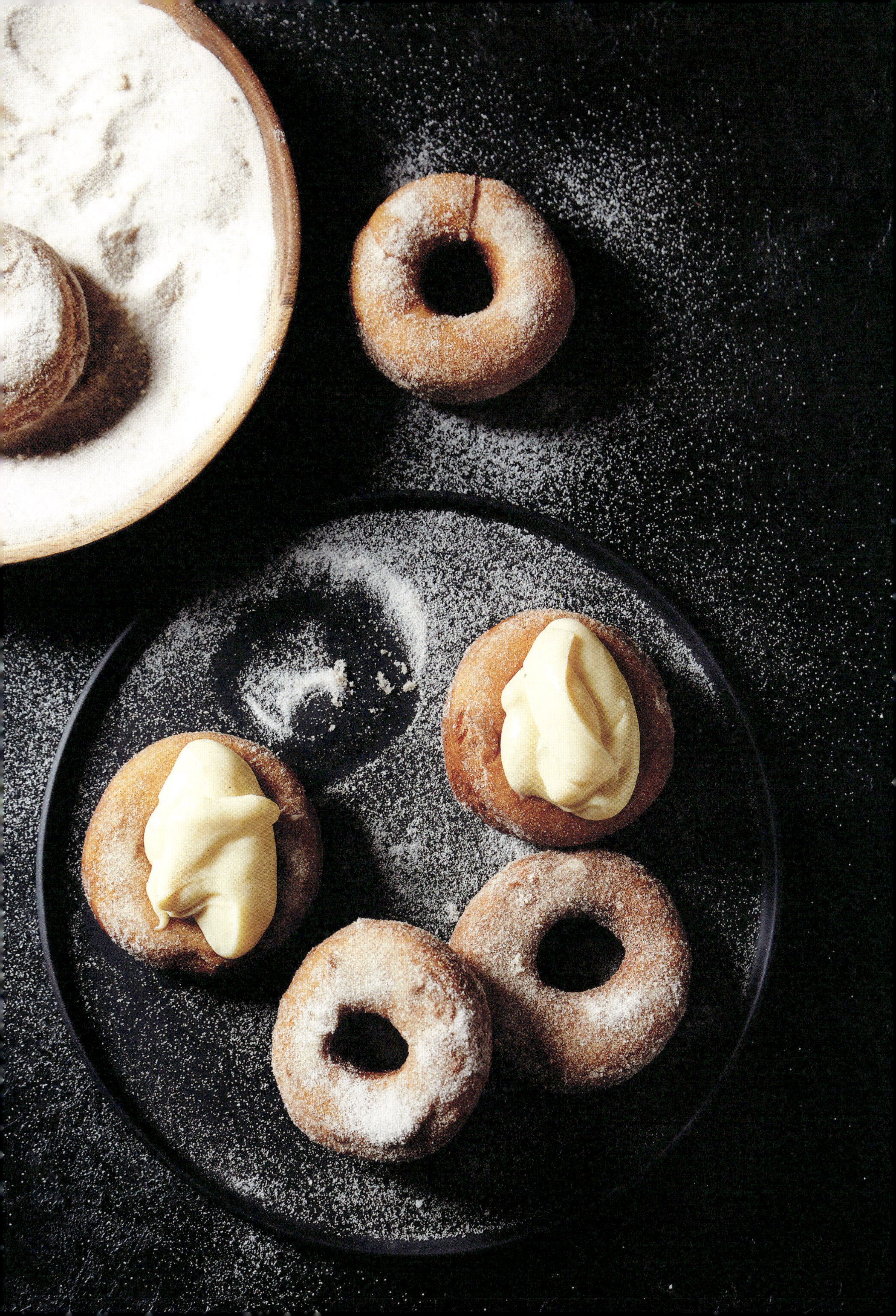

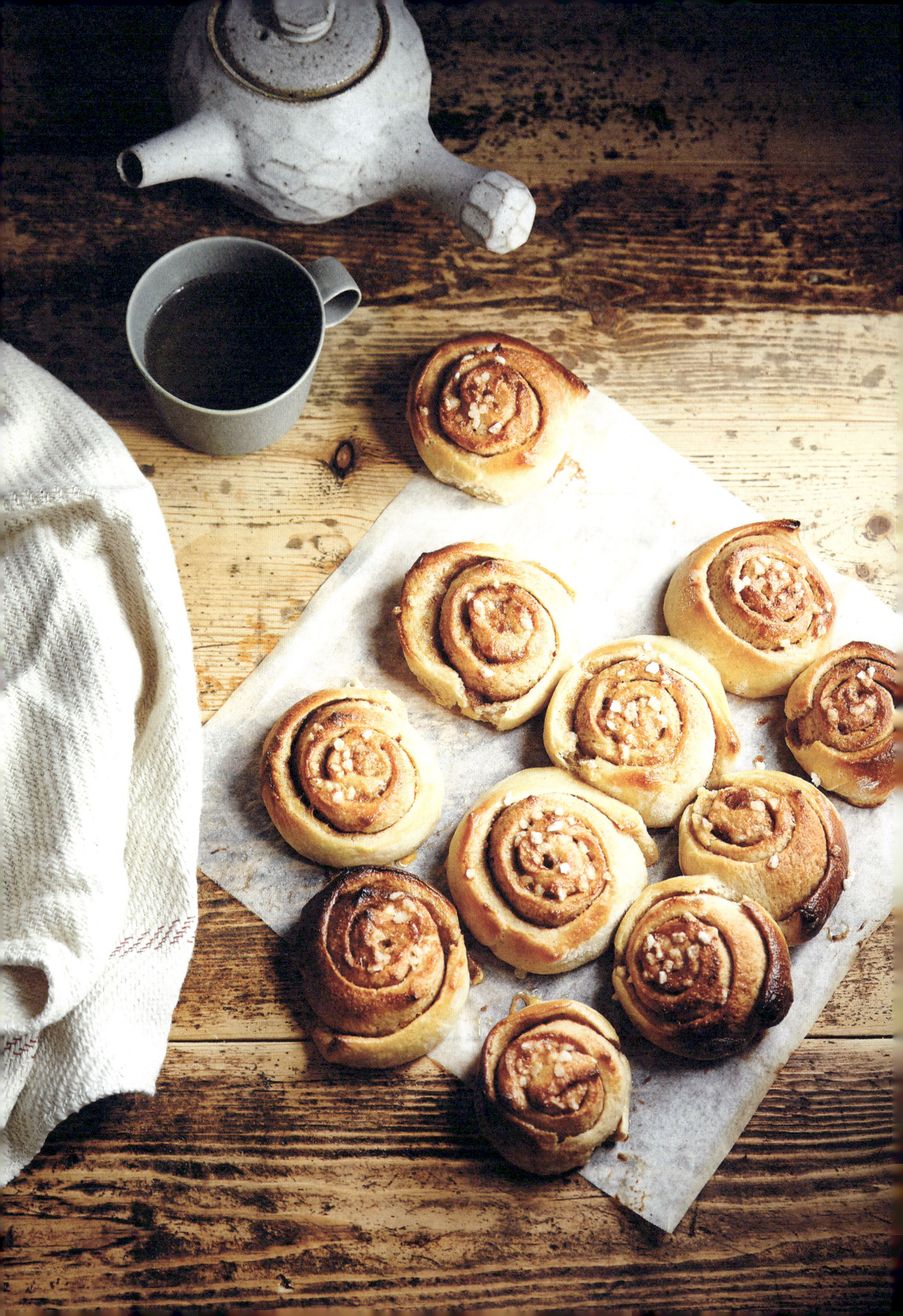

CARDAMOM BUNS

MAKES 15 BUNS

I make these buns every Christmas – we eat them for breakfast with a strong cup of coffee as we unwrap presents. It's a tradition I started when we were a new little family several years ago, and I'm glad it's stuck. The scent of the buns cooking is reason enough to make them again and again, whether it's Christmas or not.

80 g unsalted butter, softened

1¾ tablespoons caster sugar

275 ml full-cream milk, plus 1 teaspoon extra for brushing

1 teaspoon vanilla extract

10 g active dry yeast

450 g (3 cups) plain flour, sifted

1 teaspoon freshly ground cardamom

pinch of sea salt

1 egg

pearl sugar, for topping (see Note)

SPICED FILLING

100 g unsalted butter, softened

2½ tablespoons brown sugar

2½ tablespoons caster sugar

1 teaspoon freshly ground cardamom

1 teaspoon ground cinnamon

Cream the butter and sugar together until pale and fluffy. Warm the milk and vanilla in a small saucepan over a low heat until lukewarm, about 35°C. Stir in the yeast then add to the butter and sugar mixture, stirring to combine. Add the flour, cardamom and salt and mix with your hands until a shaggy dough forms. Tip out onto a clean work surface and knead for about 8 minutes or until the dough is smooth and elastic. Transfer to a clean bowl, cover with a cloth or plastic wrap and allow to prove in a warm space for 45 minutes or until doubled in size.

Meanwhile, to make the spiced filling, combine the ingredients in a small bowl and mix to a smooth paste. Set aside.

Preheat the oven to 220°C. Line two baking trays with baking paper.

Knock the air out of the dough and tip onto a lightly floured work surface. Roll out to a 40 cm × 30 cm rectangle. Spread the filling evenly over the dough, right up to the edges. Starting at the longer edge, roll the dough into a sausage shape. Using a sharp knife or pastry cutter, cut into 3 cm wide slices. Place the buns, spiral-side up, onto the prepared trays. Whisk the egg with the extra milk and brush over the buns. Sprinkle generously with the pearl sugar.

Turn the oven down to 190°C and bake for 15–20 minutes until golden and puffed. Eat warm or at room temperature on the day of baking, or on the following day lightly warmed under a grill.

NOTE: Pearl sugar, sometimes called nib sugar or hail sugar, is a coarse white sugar most commonly used in European baking. It typically doesn't melt during baking so is perfect for scattering over buns, waffles and cakes. Pearl sugar can be found in select baking supply stores; substitute demerara sugar if unavailable.

TIRAMISÙ

SERVES 8–10

Tiramisù is truly a classic, but, having apparently originated in the Veneto region in Italy's north in the 1960s, it is a rather new culinary creation by Italian standards. *Tiramisù*, meaning 'pick me up', is a great celebration dish – not only is it loved by most, but it stores well in the fridge so you can make it ahead of time. The homemade mascarpone is rich and luscious, while the savoiardi made from scratch give the dessert just the right texture. I like to add Marsala to my espresso; however, many people add rum, brandy or another liquor of their choice. I learned how to make tiramisù whilst living in Italy – my version is rich, with lots of mascarpone (which is actually surprisingly light, thanks to the addition of egg whites) and a good hit of espresso. If you prefer it a little less damp, soak your biscuits according to your preference. I usually make my tiramisù in a large, round glass serving dish, which is the traditional shape, but a rectangular or square dish works perfectly fine.

5 eggs, separated

120 g caster sugar

pinch of sea salt

300 ml espresso, cooled

80 ml (⅓ cup) Marsala

Dutch-process cocoa powder or grated dark chocolate, for sprinkling

MASCARPONE (SEE NOTE OVERLEAF)

1 litre pure cream

2 tablespoons lemon juice

SAVOIARDI (SEE NOTE OVERLEAF)

icing sugar, for dusting

4 eggs, separated

100 g caster sugar, plus extra for sprinkling

1 vanilla pod, split and seeds scraped (optional)

pinch of sea salt

100 g (⅔ cup) plain flour

60 g (½ cup) cornflour

RECIPE CONTINUED OVERLEAF ⟶

To make the mascarpone, heat the cream in a saucepan over a low–medium heat until it reaches 90°C, just before boiling point. Add the lemon juice and stir continuously for approximately 5 minutes. You don't want the milk to boil, barely simmering is fine. Remove from the heat and set aside to cool completely. Place a sieve over a bowl and line with three or four layers of clean, damp muslin or cheesecloth. Pour the milk into the lined sieve and place in the fridge for at least 8 hours or overnight to drain. You will be left with a thick, velvety mixture, which is your mascarpone. Transfer to an airtight container and store in the fridge for up to 3 days.

To make the savoiardi, preheat the oven to 180°C. Line two baking trays with baking paper and dust generously with icing sugar. In the bowl of an electric mixer fitted with a whisk attachment or by using a hand whisk, beat together the egg yolks, half of the sugar and the vanilla seeds, if using, until pale and thick. In a clean bowl, beat the egg whites and salt until stiff peaks form. Gradually add the remaining sugar and continue to beat until glossy and stiff again. You should be able to hold the bowl above your head without the egg whites falling. Fold the egg yolk mixture gently into the egg whites, then sift the flours over the mixture, a little at a time, gently incorporating before adding more. Spoon the batter into a piping bag fitted with a 2 cm round nozzle and pipe into 8 cm fingers, leaving space between each biscuit as they will spread. Dust twice with icing sugar, allowing the icing sugar to absorb into the batter between each dusting. Sprinkle a little extra caster sugar over each biscuit and bake for 10–15 minutes until golden. Leave to cool before gently removing from the trays. Store in an airtight container for up to a week.

DESSERT 239

RECIPE CONTINUED · ⟶

Using a hand whisk, electric beaters or an electric mixer fitted with a whisk attachment, beat the egg yolks with the sugar until pale and thick. Add the mascarpone and gently whisk in until combined. In a clean bowl, beat the egg whites and salt to stiff peaks. Gently fold the egg whites into the mascarpone mixture a little at a time, being careful to keep the air in the mixture. Set aside.

Mix the espresso with the Marsala, adding a little water if it's too strong for your liking.

To assemble the tiramisù, spread just enough of the mascarpone cream to cover the base of your serving dish. Working with a few savoiardi at a time, dip into the espresso mix for a few seconds until the espresso has just soaked in – any longer and the biscuit will become too soggy. Place the soaked biscuits onto the cream in a single layer. Top with more of the cream, being more generous this time, and carefully spread to cover the biscuits. Repeat with the savoiardi and then the cream again until all the savoiardi and cream have been used, making sure the final layer is the cream. Top with a little sifted cocoa or grated chocolate and place in the fridge to set for at least 2 hours before serving. This will ensure the cream and espresso-soaked biscuits meld together nicely. It will be even better the following day.

NOTES: Once you make your own mascarpone, you will never buy it again. Making it at home is the closest thing you will get to the mascarpone you can buy in Italy – creamy, rich and so luscious. Really nothing like the store-bought stuff we find here, which tends to be grainy and often dry. My recipe makes about 500 g.

Savoiardi, also known as 'lady fingers' (among other names), date back to the fifteenth century, when they were served in the court of the Duchy of Savoy to celebrate a visit from the king of France. The elongated sponge biscuits are wonderfully sweet and incredibly light. They are rather simple to make, only requiring a few ingredients and a little care. The subtleness and sponge-like texture make savoiardi perfect for tiramisù and other similar desserts, as they are a superb vessel for soaking up flavour. Some people add vanilla to the mixture and I have also made them with lemon or orange zest, which adds a lovely perfume to the biscuits. My recipe makes about 30 biscuits.

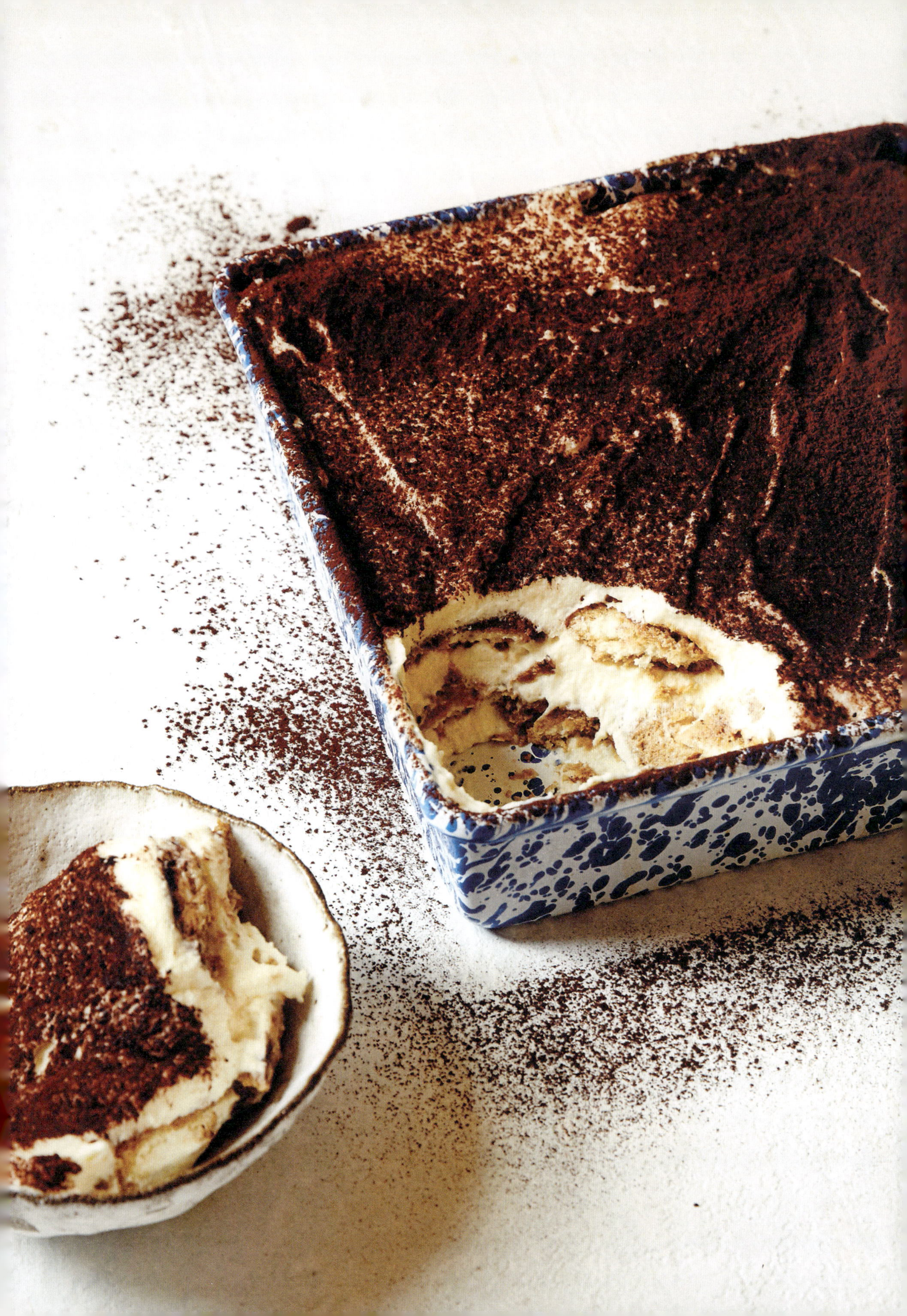

BALSAMIC RHUBARB AND STRAWBERRY PIE

SERVES 8

There is something about a proper fruit pie that is so comforting and inviting. The combination of buttery flaky pastry and seasonal fruit is undeniably classic, and for good reason. Rhubarb and strawberry make for one of my favourite pie fillings, all ruby and crimson, a little bit sour and sweet. Adjust the amount of sugar to your liking, as I prefer the sourness of the rhubarb to shine through. The addition of balsamic vinegar and black pepper here heightens the flavour of the strawberries, a combination commonly used in Italian desserts.

600 g strawberries, trimmed and cut in half

240 g caster sugar, or to taste

500 g rhubarb, trimmed and cut into 1.5 cm lengths

2 granny smith apples (about 300 g in total), peeled and grated

1 tablespoon good-quality balsamic vinegar

30 g (¼ cup) arrowroot flour

black pepper

1 egg

2 tablespoons demerara sugar

PASTRY

375 g (2½ cups) plain flour, plus extra for dusting

1 tablespoon caster sugar

large pinch of sea salt

250 g chilled unsalted butter, cut into cubes

about 150 ml iced water

1 tablespoon apple cider vinegar

To make the pastry dough, sift the flour onto a clean work surface and sprinkle the sugar and salt over the top. Toss the butter through the flour and, using a pastry scraper or butter knife, cut the butter into the flour until the mixture resembles coarse breadcrumbs. Mix the iced water with the vinegar and dribble it over the flour and butter, a little at a time, using the pastry scraper or your fingers to bring the dough together – it should be shaggy and not at all smooth, but there shouldn't be any dry floury crumbs left behind. You most likely won't need all of the liquid, so be sure not to add it all in one go. Divide the dough in two, flatten into discs and cover with plastic wrap. Refrigerate for at least 30 minutes.

Take one of the pieces of dough from the fridge and let it sit at room temperature for 10 minutes. Grease a 25 cm pie dish with butter. On a lightly floured work surface, roll the pastry out into a 3 mm thick circle that's about 6 cm larger than your pie dish. Drape the pastry into the dish, pressing gently to remove any air trapped in between the dish and the pastry. Allow 4 cm of pastry to overhang, trimming any excess if necessary. Cover and return to the fridge for 1 hour.

Remove the second piece of dough and repeat the rolling as you did with the base, this time rolling out to a rectangle about 3 mm thick. Using a pizza cutter, pastry cutter or a knife, cut the pastry into 2–3 cm width strips. Loosely cover, transfer to the tray and refrigerate for 30 minutes. (If you don't want to do a lattice top, you can skip this whole step and just roll out the pastry once you have filled the pie.) Remove from the fridge 5 minute before ready to use.

RECIPE CONTINUED OVERLEAF ⟶

DESSERT 243

RECIPE CONTINUED •⟶

Meanwhile, place the strawberries in a large bowl and gently toss with 40 g of the caster sugar. Leave to macerate for 30 minutes. Drain and then return to the bowl. Add the rhubarb, apple, vinegar, arrowroot, the remaining sugar and a few grinds of black pepper. Gently mix to combine, then tumble into the chilled pie base.

Layer the pastry strips over the top of the pie to make a lattice pattern (or roll out the second piece of pastry now, drape over the top of the pie and make a small hole in the centre for steam to escape). Roll the overhanging pastry into the inner edge of the pie dish, then crimp the edges of the pastry to seal. Refrigerate for 30 minutes.

Preheat the oven to 200°C. Line a baking tray with baking paper.

Whisk the egg with 1 teaspoon of water. Brush over the top of the pie and sprinkle with demerara sugar. Bake for 20 minutes, then reduce the temperature to 180°C and bake for another 25–30 minutes until the pastry is golden and the filling is bubbling. If the crust is browning too fast, cover it with foil. Allow the pie to stand for at least 2–3 hours before serving. The resting time is important as it allows the filling to set, avoiding a soggy-bottomed pie.

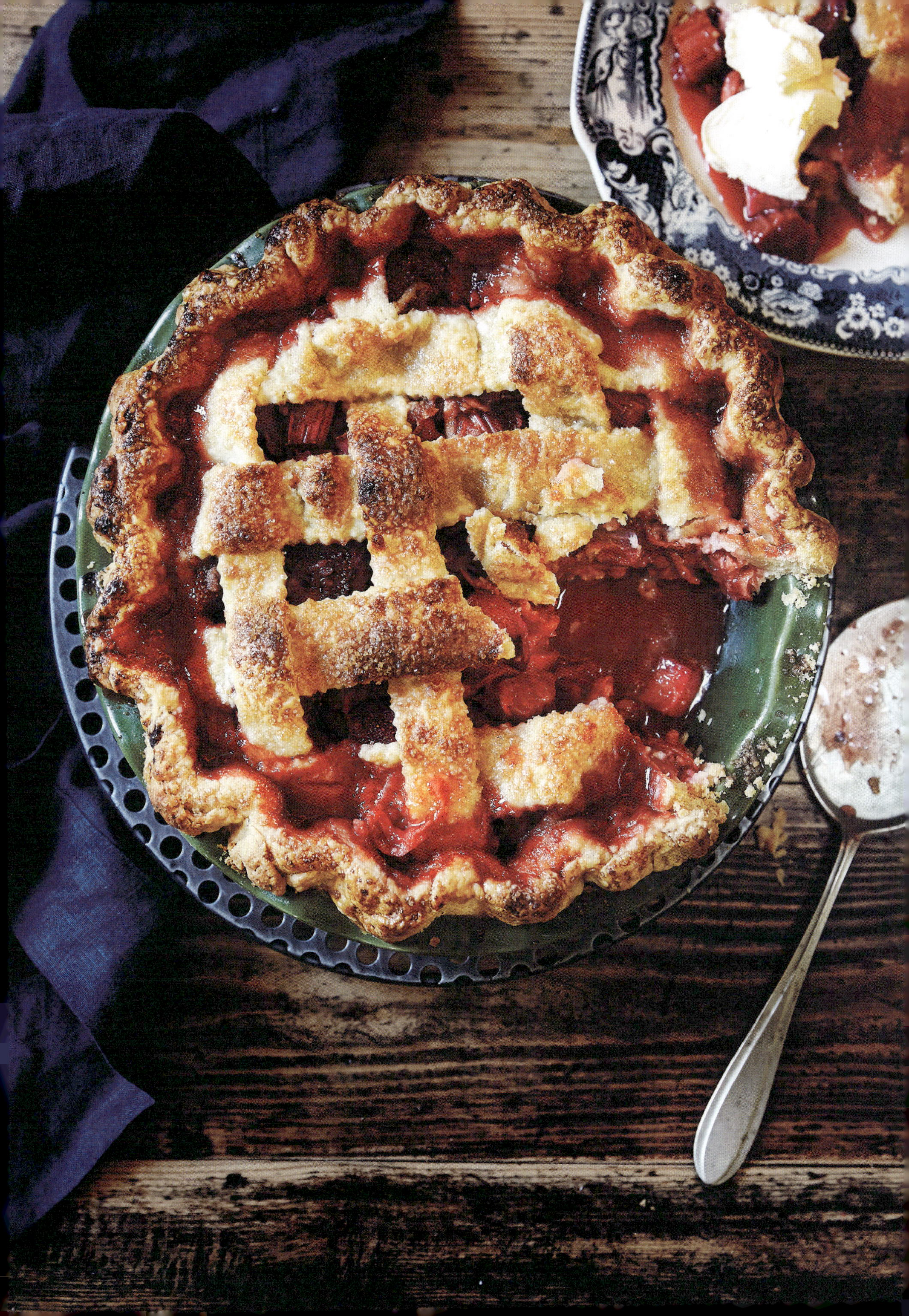

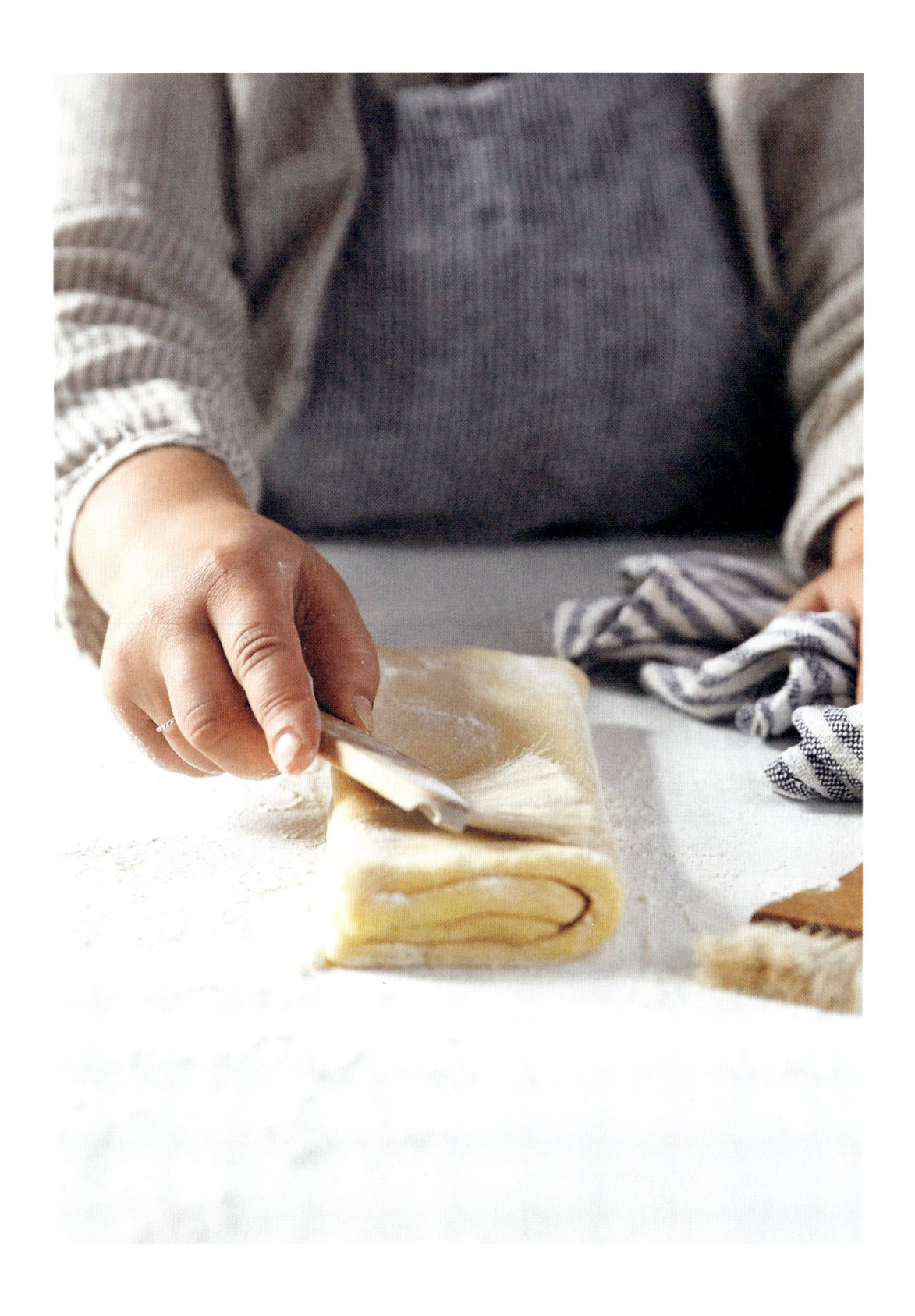

ROASTED PEACH TART

❈ SERVES 6 ❈

This recipe is incredibly versatile and can be made with any fruit that's suitable for roasting – pears, apples or plums are all wonderful. If you have a glut of berries, skip the roasting and simply scatter them over the filled tart, perhaps with some toasted flaked almonds and a dusting of icing sugar. Because all of the elements can be prepared in advance, all that needs doing is a little assembly just before serving, making it a lovely option for picnics. If you're short on time, a good-quality store-bought puff pastry would work just fine, too.

250 ml (1 cup) pure cream

250 g (1 cup) mascarpone (see recipe page 238)

45 g icing sugar, sifted

ROUGH PUFF PASTRY

250 g (1⅔ cups) plain flour

1 tablespoon icing sugar

pinch of sea salt

250 g chilled unsalted butter, cut into cubes

100–150 ml iced water

ROASTED PEACHES

4–5 yellow peaches, cut in half and stone removed

1 tablespoon honey

1 rosemary sprig, leaves picked

60 ml (¼ cup) dry white wine

1 tablespoon extra-virgin olive oil

1 vanilla pod, split and seeds scraped

RECIPE CONTINUED OVERLEAF ⟶

To make the pastry dough, sift the flour, sugar and salt onto a clean work surface. Toss the butter through the flour and, using a pastry scraper or butter knife, cut the butter into the flour until the buttery lumps are pea sized. Be careful not to overwork the butter and flour – a few larger lumps of butter are fine. Gently pour a few tablespoons of the water over the top and use the pastry scraper or your fingers to bring the pastry together, continuing to add a little water until you are able to shape the pastry into a flat square. Cover with plastic wrap and refrigerate for 20–30 minutes.

Lightly flour your work surface and roll the pastry out into a rectangle about 1.5 cm thick. Fold the short edges in so they meet in the middle, so it looks like an open book. Then fold the dough in half along where the edges meet (like closing a book). Wrap the pastry and refrigerate for 20–30 minutes. Repeat the rolling, folding and chilling steps twice more.

Preheat the oven to 180°C.

On a lightly floured work surface, roll the pastry out to about 5 mm thick. Use the pastry to line a loose-bottomed fluted tart tin, gently pressing into the edges and corners. I use a rectangular tin; however, a round or square tin would be equally fine. Trim the excess pastry and keep for another use. Refrigerate for 20–30 minutes.

Line the pastry with baking paper and fill with pie weights. Bake for approximately 30 minutes, then remove the pie weights and bake for a further 5–10 minutes until golden. Cool in the tin completely before removing.

Meanwhile, beat the cream, mascarpone and icing sugar together until stiff but luscious peaks form, being careful not to over-mix. Cover and set aside in the refrigerator until you're ready to assemble the tart.

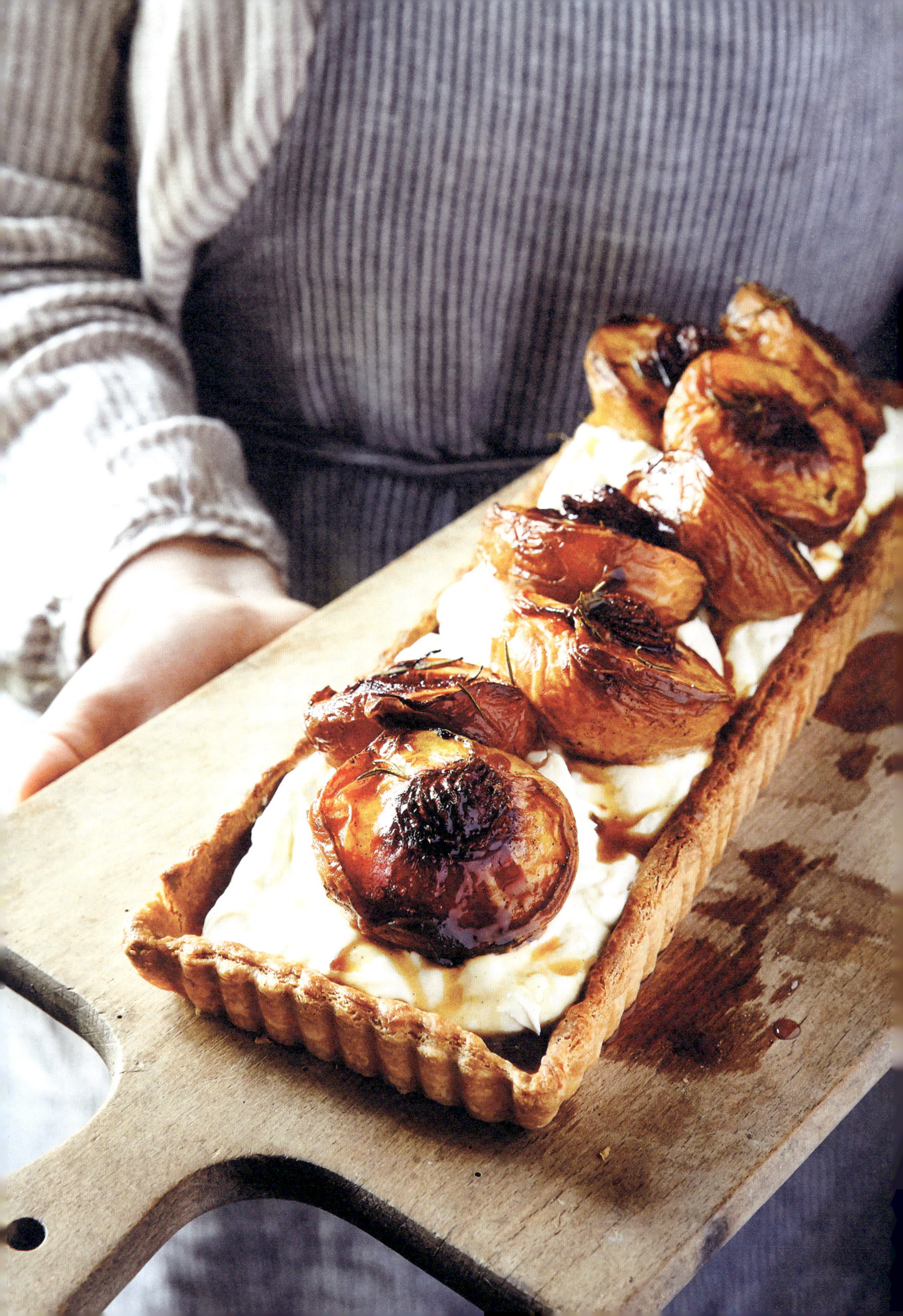

RECIPE CONTINUED ⟶

To make the roasted peaches, reduce the oven to 170°C. Arrange the peaches, cut-side up, in an ovenproof dish. In a small saucepan over medium heat, combine the honey, rosemary, wine, olive oil and the vanilla seeds and pod, and heat until just coming to the boil. Pour the syrup over the peaches and roast, basting the peaches with the juices as they cook, for 1 hour or until the fruit has just collapsed. Check on them regularly, and add a little water to the dish if they are beginning to dry out. Set aside to cool.

To assemble the tart, fill the pastry shell with the chilled cream mixture. Arrange the roasted peaches on top of the tart and drizzle with any remaining syrup. Serve immediately.

SALTED DARK CHOCOLATE POTS WITH PALMIERS

· SERVES 8 ·

These chocolate pots are my take on the French crème au chocolat, which is similar to a mousse but even more rich and decadent. They can be made ahead of time and just topped with the cream before serving, making for a perfect dinner-party dessert. I love to serve the pots with these palmiers for some crunch. Although palmiers look intricate, they are really simple to make. Traditionally, puff pastry is used, but I make a rough puff, which gives similar flaky layers without as much effort. You can substitute with a good-quality store-bought butter puff pastry, too. Feel free to experiment with different sugars, or even add a little dusting of cinnamon.

200 g crème fraîche

100 ml pure cream

sea salt flakes

cocoa powder, for dusting

PALMIERS

250 g (1⅔ cups) plain flour

1 teaspoon caster sugar

pinch of sea salt

250 g chilled unsalted butter, cut into cubes

about 150 ml iced water

demerara sugar, for sprinkling

CHOCOLATE POTS

250 g dark chocolate (70% cocoa), finely chopped

400 ml pure cream

1 vanilla pod, split and seeds scraped

4 egg yolks

60 g caster sugar

To make the dough for the palmiers, sift the flour onto a clean work surface and sprinkle the sugar and salt over the top. Toss the butter through the flour and, using a pastry scraper or butter knife, cut the butter into the flour until the buttery lumps are pea sized. Be careful not to overwork the butter and flour – a few larger lumps of butter are fine. Gently pour a few tablespoons of the water over the top and use the pastry scraper or your fingers to bring the pastry together, continuing to add a little water until you are able to shape the pastry into a flat square. Cover with plastic wrap and refrigerate for 20–30 minutes.

Lightly flour your work surface and roll the pastry out into a rectangle about 1.5 cm thick. Fold the short edges in so they meet in the middle, so it looks like an open book. Then fold the dough in half along where the edges meet (like closing the 'book'). Wrap the pastry and refrigerate for 20–30 minutes. Repeat the rolling, folding and chilling steps twice more.

Preheat the oven to 190°C. Line two trays with baking paper.

On a lightly floured work surface, roll the dough out into a rectangle about 5 mm thick. Sprinkle the pastry generously with demerara sugar. Now fold each long end in so that the edges meet in the middle and sprinkle with more sugar. From the long edge again, fold the pastry in along where the edges meet, so the pastry almost forms a log. Transfer to one of the prepared trays, loosely cover and refrigerate for 30 minutes.

RECIPE CONTINUED OVERLEAF ·⟶

DESSERT 251

RECIPE CONTINUED •⟶

Trim the pastry log, then cut into about 16 slices, 2 cm thick. Place on the prepared trays with the cut sides facing up, leaving about 4 cm between each palmier as they spread a lot during cooking. Sprinkle with more sugar. Bake for about 20 minutes or until golden brown and puffed. Allow to cool completely before transferring to an airtight container. The palmiers will keep for up to 3 days, but they are best eaten as soon as they've cooled down.

For the chocolate pots, place the chocolate in a heatproof bowl. Heat the cream with the vanilla seeds and pod in a saucepan over a low heat until it just begins to simmer. Don't let it boil. Pour the cream mixture over the chocolate and allow to sit for 5 minutes, stirring a few times, until the chocolate is melted. Meanwhile, place the egg yolks and sugar in a heatproof bowl set over a saucepan of simmering water and whisk continuously for 4–5 minutes or until thick, pale and doubled in volume. I usually use the bowl from my mixer for ease later on. Combine the chocolate cream mixture with the eggs and beat, using electric beaters or an electric mixer fitted with a whisk attachment, for about 5 minutes until thick and cooled. You can do this by hand; however, it will take longer and will require a little elbow grease. Divide the mixture equally among eight serving glasses. Refrigerate, covered, for 2 hours or until set. The chocolate pots will keep in the fridge for up to 2 days.

To serve, whip the crème fraîche and cream together to form soft peaks. Sprinkle the tops of the chocolate pots with a little salt, top with dollops of the whipped cream and dust with cocoa powder. Serve with a palmier (or two) on the side.

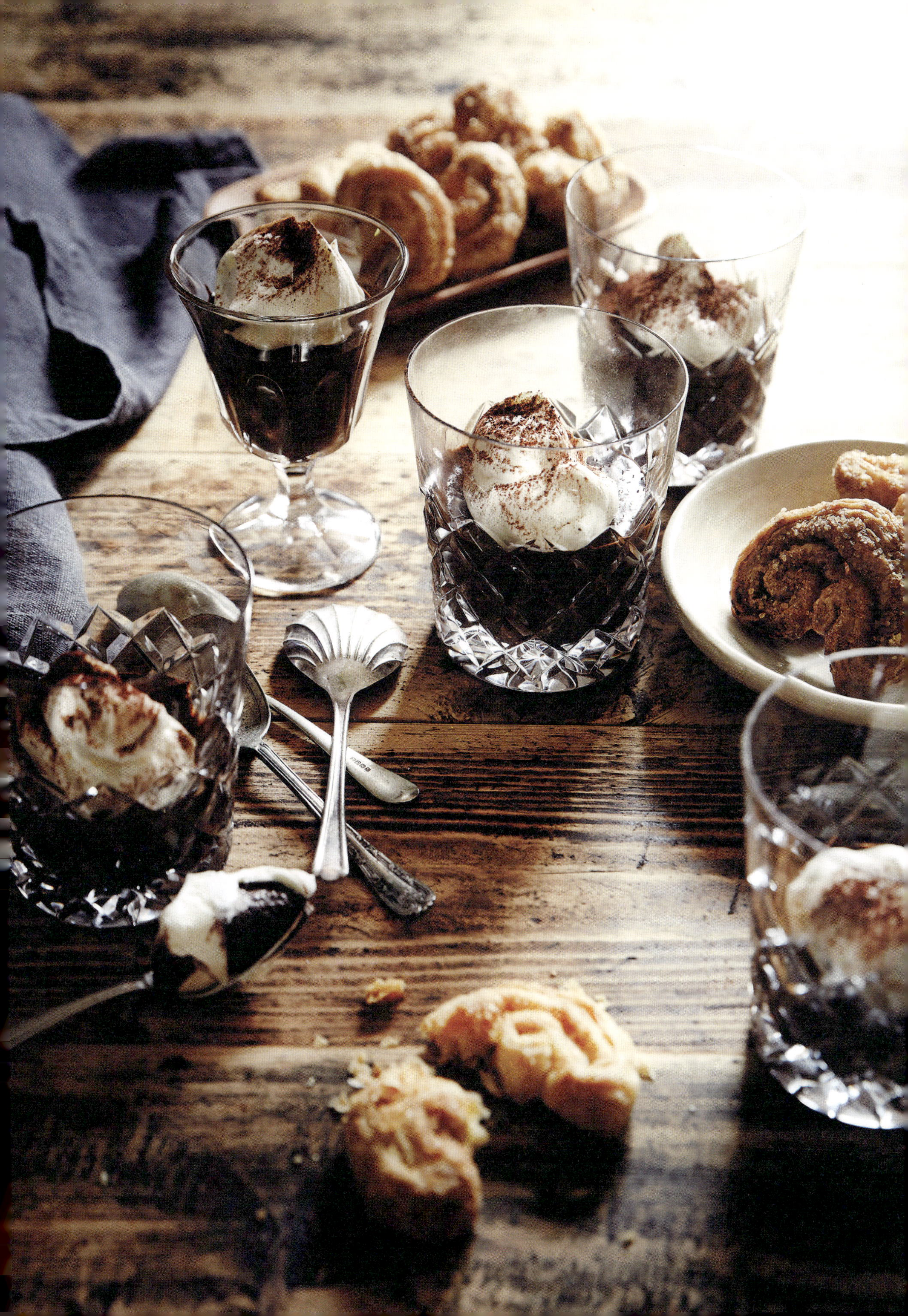

NECTARINE AND ALMOND CROSTATA

· ❈ SERVES 8 ❈ ·

A crostata (or galette, as it is known in France) is an often free-form tart, and the perfect recipe to celebrate a bounty of nectarines (which we are lucky enough to get from our neighbour's tree). Homegrown fruit in all its motley glory is perfect in a rustic tart, which, apart from the resting of the pastry, can be pulled together in a matter of minutes. Other stone fruit, such as plums or apricots, as well as berries can be substituted for the nectarines – and in autumn, figs are great here, too.
This is wonderful for dessert, served just warm with a dollop of double cream.

about 8 nectarines (1 kg in total), stones removed and sliced into 1 cm thick wedges

30 g (¼ cup) ground almonds (see Note on page 212)

2 tablespoons demerara sugar, plus extra for sprinkling

1 vanilla pod, split and seeds scraped

1 tablespoon unsalted butter

1 egg

1 tablespoon flaked almonds

PASTRY

250 g (1⅔ cups) plain flour

large pinch of caster sugar

large pinch of sea salt

160 g chilled unsalted butter, cut into cubes

100 ml iced water

1 tablespoon apple cider vinegar

To make the pastry dough, sift the flour onto a clean work surface and sprinkle the sugar and salt over the top. Toss the butter through the flour and, using a pastry scraper or butter knife, cut the butter into the flour until the mixture resembles coarse breadcrumbs. Mix the iced water with the vinegar, and dribble over the flour and butter, a little at a time, using the pastry scraper or your fingers to bring the dough together (you most likely won't need all the liquid). Flatten the dough to form a disc and cover with plastic wrap. Refrigerate for at least 30 minutes.

Place the nectarines in a bowl with the ground almonds, sugar and vanilla seeds. Mix gently to combine. Set aside while you roll out the pastry.

On a lightly floured work surface, roll the pastry out into a rough 30 cm circle about 3 mm thick. Transfer the pastry to the prepared tray. Pile the nectarine mixture in the centre of the pastry and spread it out a little, leaving a 4 cm border of pastry around the fruit. Working with a small section at a time, fold the edges over towards the middle, pleating the pastry as you work your way around the circle. Loosely cover and refrigerate for 1 hour.

Preheat the oven to 190°C. Line a baking tray with baking paper.

Dot the butter on top of the nectarines. Whisk the egg with 1 teaspoon of water and brush over the pastry. Scatter the flaked almonds on top of the pastry; some on the fruit is fine, too. Bake on the bottom shelf of the oven for 30–35 minutes, until the nectarines are cooked and the pastry is golden. Serve warm or at room temperature.

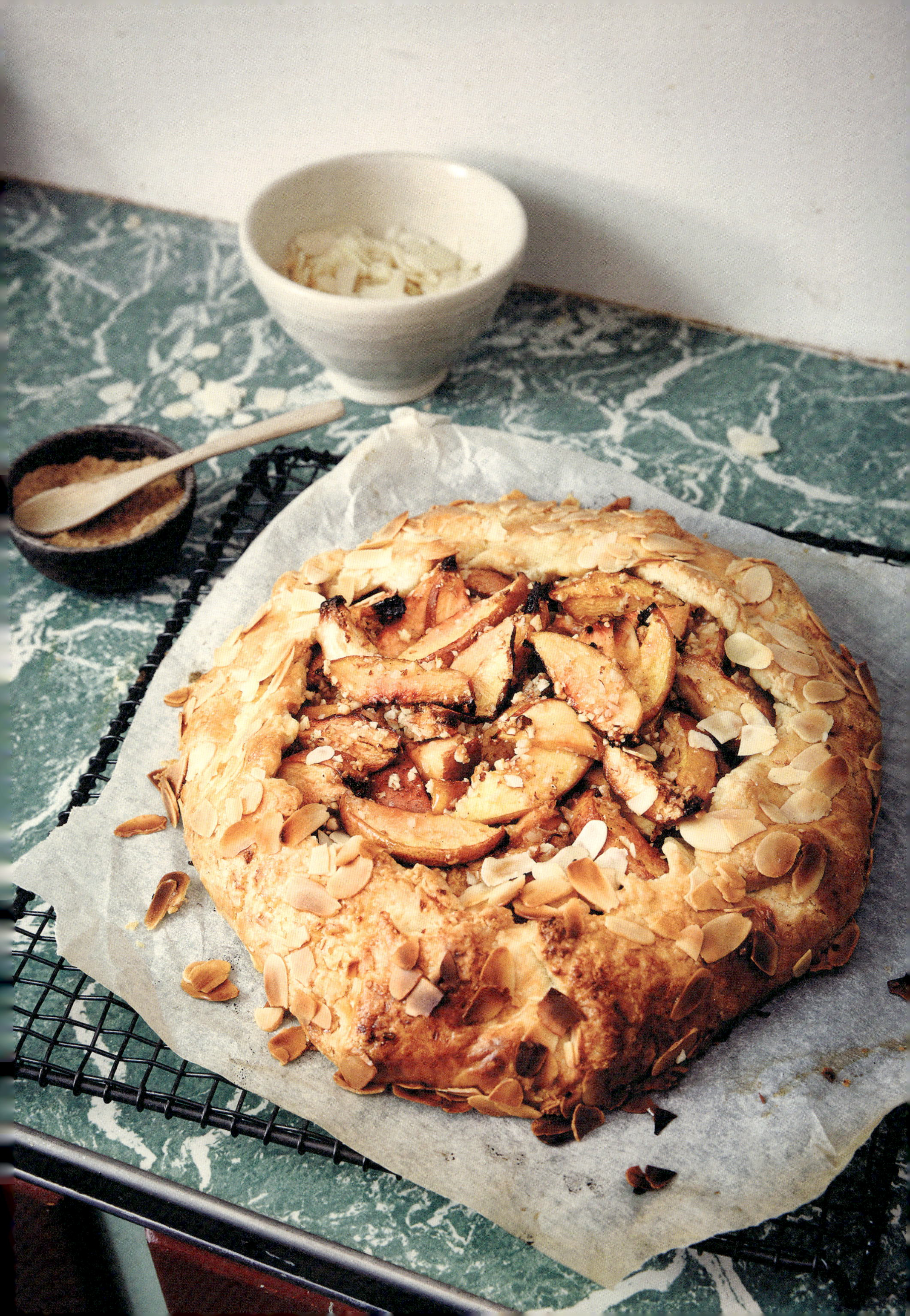

BREAD PUDDING

SERVES 6–8

A cross between bread and butter pudding and an Italian bread cake called *miascia*, my bread pudding is incredibly inviting and makes for perfect comfort food when it's cold outside. By using good-quality crusty bread, the pudding is tender and custardy but also golden and crunchy. It is best served soon after it emerges from the oven, with a drizzle of cream or a scoop of ice cream.

100 g raisins

70 ml Marsala

3 eggs

150 g (⅔ cup) caster sugar

½ teaspoon ground cinnamon

100 ml full-cream milk

600 ml pure cream

finely grated zest of 1 lemon

40 g (¼ cup) pine nuts

1 × 500 g loaf crusty ciabatta bread, roughly torn

cream or ice cream, to serve

Place the raisins in a bowl and cover with the Marsala. Set aside to soak for at least 1 hour.

Preheat the oven to 180°C. Grease a 30 cm × 20 cm rectangular baking dish with butter.

In a large bowl, whisk the eggs with the sugar and cinnamon until pale and thick. Pour in the milk and cream and add the lemon zest, pine nuts and raisins, as well as any Marsala remaining in the bowl. Whisk until combined. Add the bread, stirring gently to ensure that the pieces are well soaked in the liquid. Arrange the mixture in the prepared dish and bake for 40–45 minutes until the custard is set and the top is crunchy and golden.

Serve with cream or ice cream.

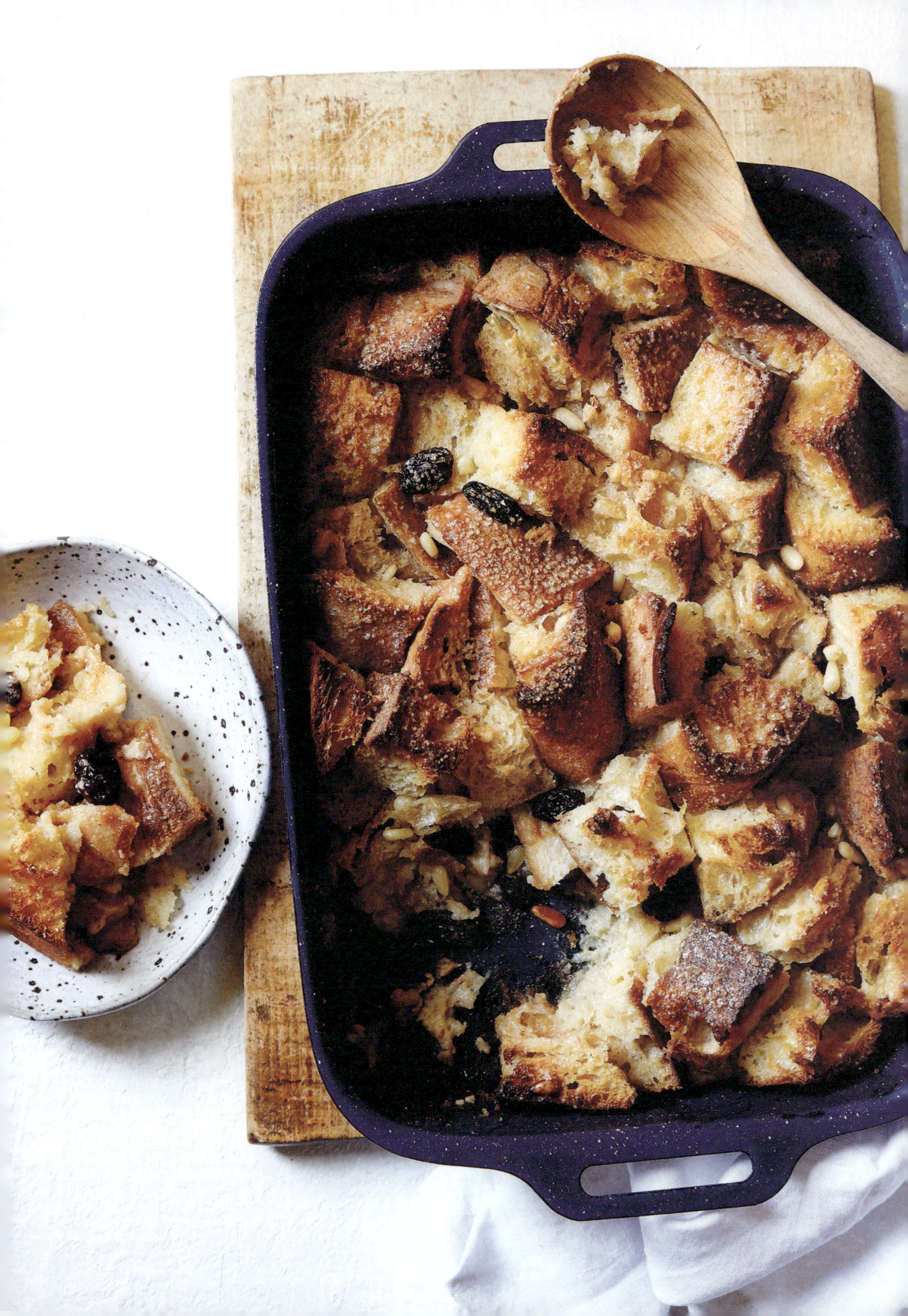

BAKED RICOTTA CHEESECAKE WITH FIGS AND GRAPES

·❖· MAKES ONE 23 CM ROUND CAKE ·❖·

I am very fond of a baked cheesecake, especially when it's filled with ricotta and topped with roasted fruits. You could substitute the grapes and figs for what is in season; just adjust the cooking time accordingly. I make my own biscuits for the base, but if you prefer to use bought ones, ginger snaps would be ideal. While I know it's tempting to eat the cheesecake as soon as it cools, it really does benefit from a good stint in the fridge before serving. Smoothing a layer of ricotta cream over the cooled cheesecake hides any cracks or bumps on top of the cake.

pinch of sea salt

80 g unsalted butter, melted, plus extra if needed

500 g fresh full-fat ricotta

250 g cream cheese, softened

120 ml pure cream

4 eggs

150 g (⅔ cup) caster sugar

40 g plain flour

1 vanilla pod, split and seeds scraped

finely grated zest of 1 lemon

toasted walnuts, for topping

BROWN SUGAR SPICED BISCUITS

50 g chilled unsalted butter, cut into cubes

100 g (⅔ cup) plain flour, sifted

50 g (¼ cup, lightly packed) brown sugar

½ teaspoon baking powder

½ teaspoon ground ginger

½ teaspoon ground cinnamon

½ teaspoon ground cardamom

½ teaspoon allspice

pinch of sea salt

1 egg, lightly beaten

1–2 tablespoons full-cream milk, if needed

ROASTED GRAPES AND FIGS

1½ tablespoons honey

1 tablespoon extra-virgin olive oil

250 g red or black grapes

about 5 figs (350 g in total), cut in half

RICOTTA TOPPING

200 g fresh full-fat ricotta

100 ml pure cream

finely grated zest of ½ lemon

½ teaspoon ground cinnamon

1 tablespoon caster sugar

To make the biscuits, preheat the oven to 180°C and line two baking trays with baking mats or baking paper. Rub the butter into the flour until the mixture is the texture of coarse breadcrumbs. Add the sugar, baking powder, ginger, cinnamon, cardamom, allspice and salt. Add the egg and mix until the dough comes together into a nice smooth ball. If the dough doesn't come together easily, add a little milk as required. On a lightly floured work surface, roll out the dough to 4 mm thick. If it's a really hot day, you should chill the dough for about 30 minutes before rolling. Cut into 4 cm squares using a knife or cutter and arrange on the prepared trays. Re-roll any scraps and repeat. Bake for 12–15 minutes or until golden. Cool completely.

Reduce the oven temperature to 170°C. Butter and line a 23 cm springform tin with baking paper.

Crush the biscuits in a food processor or by hand using a mortar and pestle, so they are mostly the texture of fine breadcrumbs – a few slightly larger bits are fine though – and place in a mixing bowl with the salt. Pour in the melted butter and mix to combine. The crumb should hold together when squeezed in your hands. If the mixture is too crumbly, add a little extra melted butter. Press firmly and evenly into the base of the prepared tin.

Whisk the remaining ingredients, except the walnuts, together until smooth and pour over the biscuit base. Bake in the preheated oven for 45–50 minutes until just set. Allow to cool completely before removing from the tin. Refrigerate for at least 3 hours, preferably overnight.

Meanwhile, to make the roasted grapes and figs, preheat the oven to 180°C. Mix the honey and olive oil in a small bowl until combined. Place the grapes, preferably in just one or two bunches, in an ovenproof dish. Drizzle with the honey and olive oil and roast for 15 minutes or until the grapes are just starting to blister. Add the figs and continue to roast for 5 minutes. Set aside to cool completely.

For the ricotta topping, whisk all of the ingredients together in a bowl until smooth.

Spread the ricotta topping over the chilled cheesecake, arrange the roasted fruits on top and scatter with walnuts.

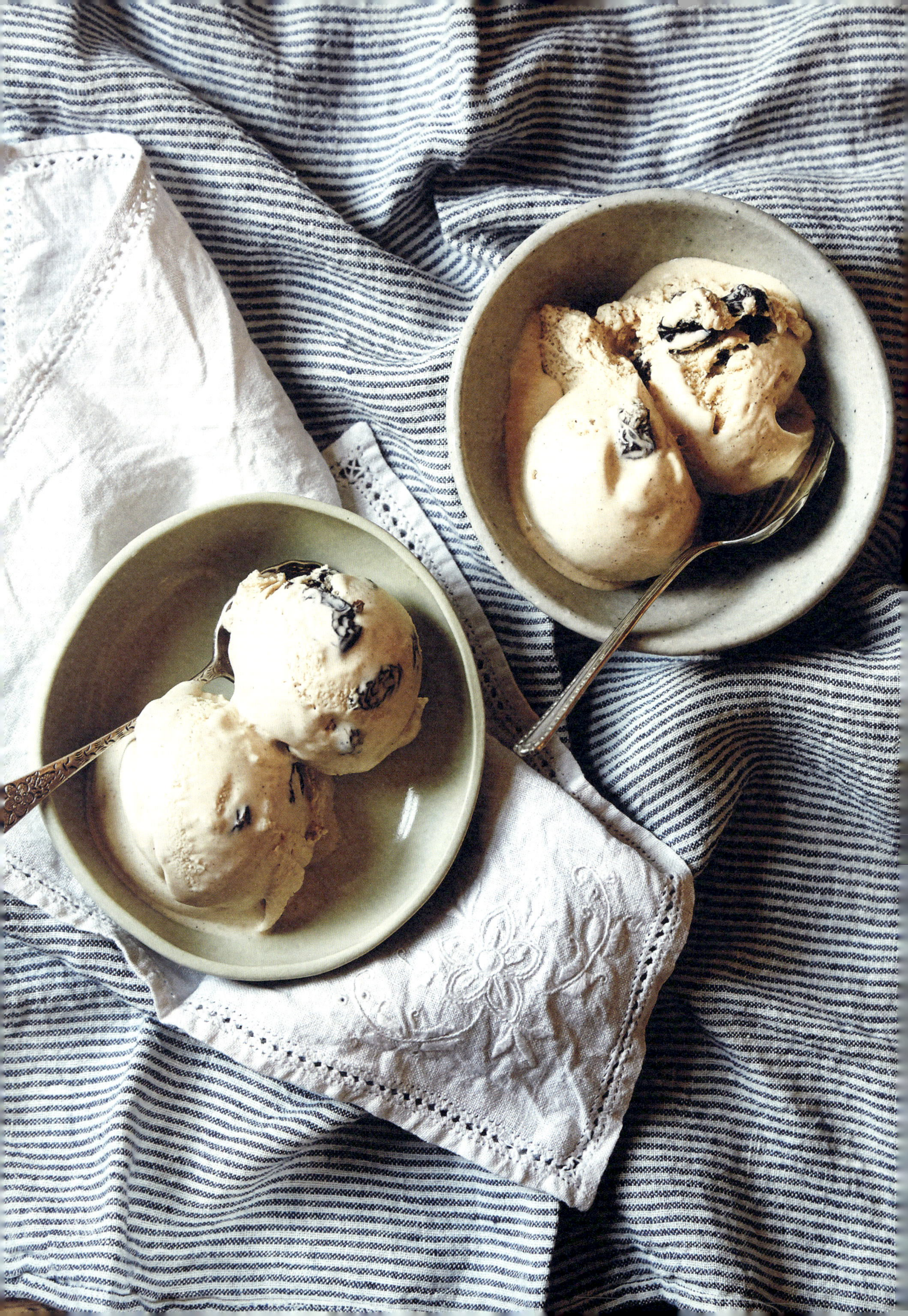

CINNAMON–RAISIN ICE CREAM

MAKES 1 LITRE

Ice cream goes back generations in my family, with my great uncle having opened one of the first ice-cream shops in Adelaide after immigrating to Australia from Malta in 1915. As a child, I would listen to my mum tell stories of afternoons in his shop, sneaking spoonfuls of ice cream from the metal tubs. This ice cream is beautifully fragrant and is traditionally served at Maltese weddings or at other times of celebration – it reminds me so much of my childhood. I like to add Marsala-soaked raisins, but you can leave them out if you prefer.

100 g raisins

70 ml Marsala

6 egg yolks

1 teaspoon ground cinnamon

130 g caster sugar

2 cinnamon sticks

600 ml pure cream

200 ml full-cream milk

Combine the raisins and Marsala in a small saucepan and place over a medium heat. Simmer for 2–3 minutes. Set aside to soak for at least 1 hour, then drain.

Place the egg yolks, cinnamon and sugar in a large bowl and whisk for a few minutes until pale and thick. Set aside.

Break the cinnamon sticks by pounding briefly using a mortar and pestle, then place in a large saucepan along with the cream and milk. Heat over a medium heat, stirring to avoid the mixture catching on the bottom, until just before the mixture breaks into a simmer (you don't want it to boil). Remove from the heat and leave to infuse for 5 minutes. Strain and discard the cinnamon sticks.

Slowly pour the milk mixture over the egg mixture, whisking to combine. It is really important that you don't add the hot milk all at once, otherwise you'll end up with scrambled eggs. Return the mixture to a clean saucepan and cook over a low heat, stirring continuously, for about 4–6 minutes or until the mixture thickens enough to coat the back of a spoon. Stir in the raisins, then cool the mixture completely, either by pouring it into a bowl set over some ice, or by placing it in the fridge. Transfer to an ice-cream machine and churn according to the manufacturer's instructions, then freeze for 2–3 hours before serving.

BURNT HONEY AND THYME ICE CREAM

MAKES 1 LITRE

Inspired by a honey and fig gelato I ate once in Rome, this ice cream has the most amazing creamy texture and flavour thanks to the honey. While you're not exactly burning the honey, by simmering it on the stove before adding the milk and cream, it changes from pale gold to a deep amber, transforming the ice cream. The thyme is subtle, understated and good pairing with honey, but rosemary or bay leaves could be used instead.

6 egg yolks

1¾ tablespoons caster sugar

180 g mild-flavoured honey

600 ml pure cream

180 ml full-cream milk

6 thyme sprigs

In a large bowl, whisk the egg yolks and sugar together until combined.

Place the honey in a large saucepan and bring to a simmer over a medium–high heat. Swirl the pan around to keep the honey moving and simmer for 4–5 minutes until the honey has changed colour to a deep amber. Remove from the heat and whisk in the cream, milk and thyme, being careful as the mixture may spit. The honey may go clumpy, but will melt again once on the heat. Return the pan to the heat and continue to whisk until smooth. Just before the mixture breaks into a simmer, remove from the heat and leave to infuse for 5 minutes. Strain and discard the thyme.

Slowly pour the milk mixture over the egg mixture, whisking to combine. It is really important that you don't add the hot milk all at once, otherwise you'll end up with scrambled eggs. Return the mixture to a clean saucepan and cook over a low heat, stirring continuously, for about 4–6 minutes or until the mixture thickens enough to coat the back of a spoon. Cool the mixture completely, either by pouring it into a bowl set over some ice, or by placing it in the fridge. Transfer to an ice-cream machine and churn according to the manufacturer's instructions, then freeze for 2–3 hours before serving.

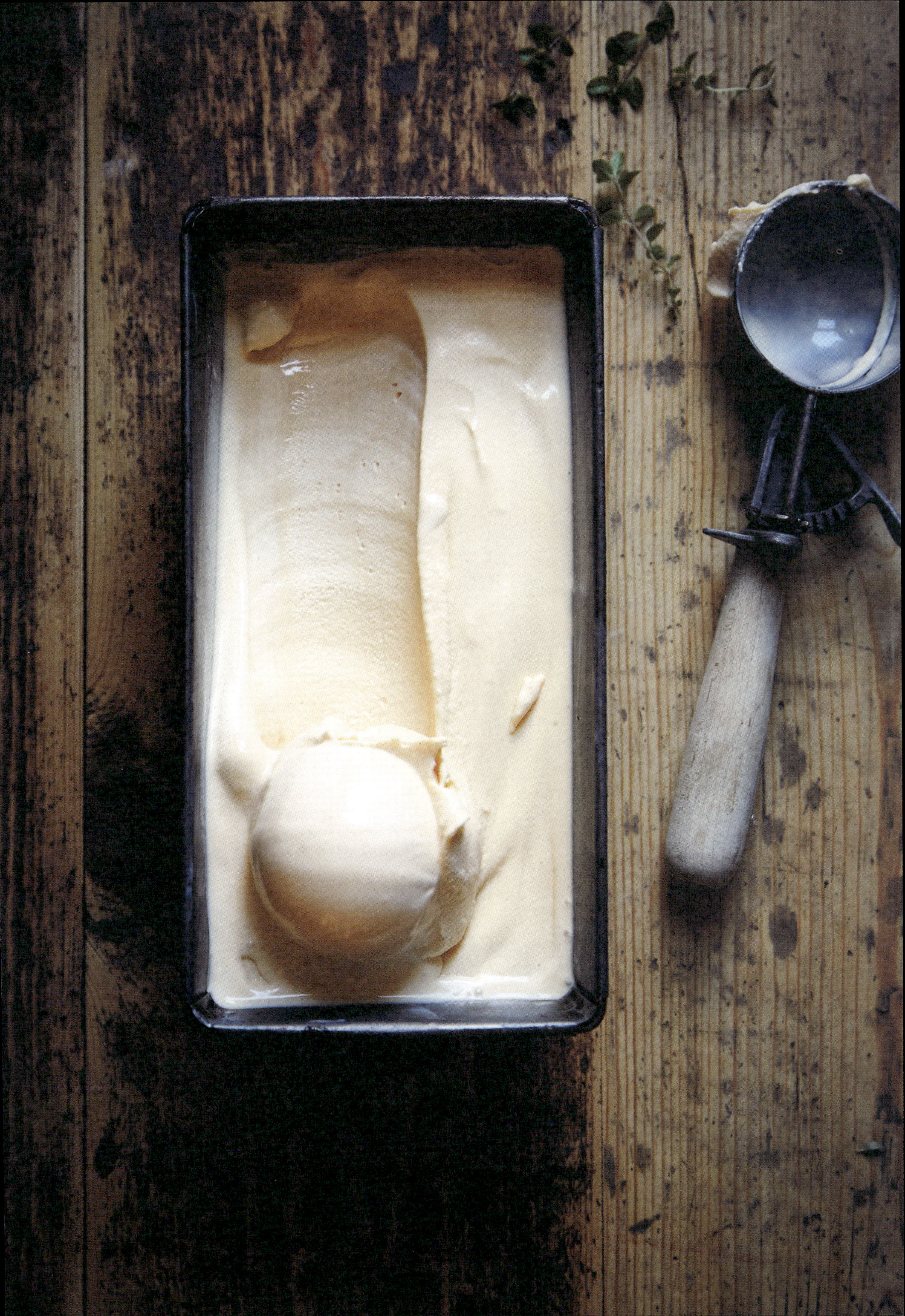

YELLOW PEACH AND SHISO SORBET

MAKES 1 LITRE

Shiso, sometimes called perilla, is a fragrant herb common in Japanese cooking. We grow red shiso at home, but it can often be found at produce markets or specialty grocery stores. It is somewhat similar to mint, so use that as a substitute if you can't get your hands on shiso. The combination of peach and shiso in a sorbet is so refreshing and a perennial favourite.

200 g caster sugar

5–6 large shiso leaves, roughly chopped

1 kg yellow peaches

juice of 1 lemon

micro shiso leaves, to serve (optional)

Combine the sugar with 200 ml of water in a saucepan over a high heat. Bring to the boil, then reduce the heat so the syrup is just simmering. Add the shiso and cook for 4–5 minutes until the syrup reaches 100°C (use a candy thermometer to measure). Remove from the heat and set aside to cool completely.

Meanwhile, bring a large saucepan of water to a simmer. Using a sharp knife, cut a cross into the base of each peach. Gently place the peaches in the simmering water and poach over a low–medium heat for 15 minutes or until tender. The poaching time will depend on how ripe the peaches are, with firmer ones taking longer. Drain, and when cool enough to handle, peel off the skins and roughly chop the flesh. Combine with the lemon juice in a bowl and leave for 10 minutes, then blend to a fine purée using a food processor.

Mix in 150 ml of the shiso sugar syrup. Taste the mixture for sweetness and add more syrup if needed. Depending on the peaches, you may need to add more – remembering that the frozen sorbet will not be as sweet as the liquid mixture. Transfer to an ice-cream machine and churn according to the manufacturer's instructions, then freeze for 2–3 hours before serving. Serve topped with the micro shiso leaves, if using.

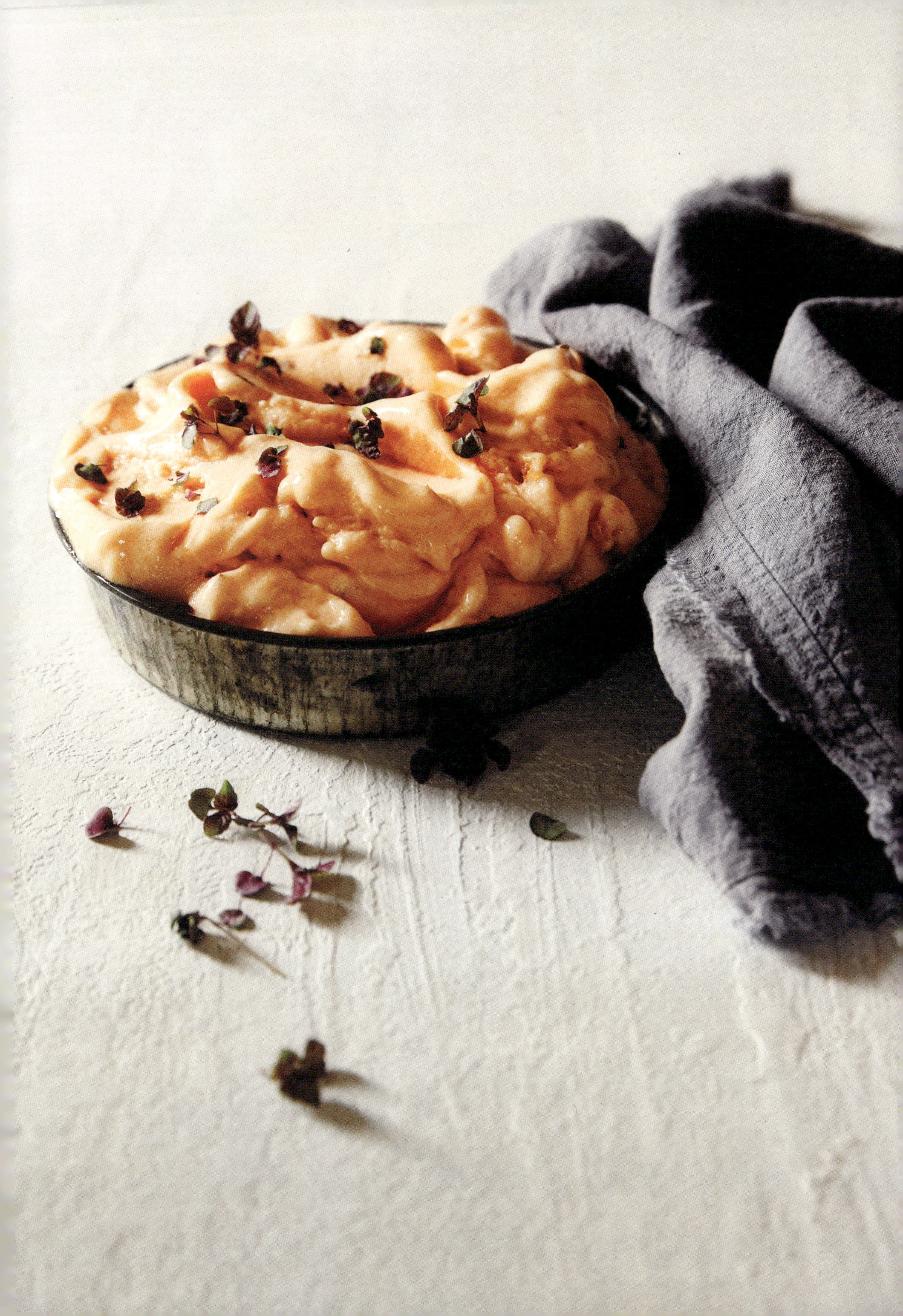

ACKNOWLEDGEMENTS

A genuine and heartfelt thanks to my wonderful family at Plum, who have made this book so special.

To Mary Small, my publisher, who many years ago approached me at a farmers' market, for believing in my food and in me. Your vision, honesty and friendship are so valued.

To Clare Marshall, my project editor, for your support, enthusiasm and expertise. I am so grateful for all of your hard work on this book.

To Armelle Habib, my warm and talented photographer – it has been the greatest privilege to work with you. Thank you for capturing my food and family so genuinely.

To Stephanie Rooney, thank you for your effortless photography assistance on the shoot.

To Karina Duncan, for styling my food with attention to detail and care. You are such a talent.

To Michelle Mackintosh, my amazing book designer, who understood what I was all about before even meeting me. I so admire your work ethic and generous spirit. Thank you for making this book so beautiful.

To Emma Warren, my irreplaceable food assistant on the shoot. When I heard that you were a real chef, I was so nervous to meet you, but after five minutes it really felt like we were old friends. Thank you for your wisdom, patience and calmness. And for your respect and laughter in the kitchen throughout the making of this book. You are a very special person, and I feel honoured to have worked with you.

To Sebastien Nichols, thank you for helping out in the kitchen during shoot. You were such fun to work with.

To Hannah Koelmeyer, thank you for your superb and thorough editing of my work. Your suggestions and edits have added so much to this book.

To Charlotte Ree, for encouraging me to get out there and make this happen. Much love to you.

Thanks to the Melbourne Fire Brick Company for loaning an amazing pizza oven for our shoot.

Thank you to my second family in Italy – Roberta, Luca and Benedetta. The months spent living with you all changed my life, and for that I am so grateful. You opened up your home and kitchen to me, and this book wouldn't be the same without you.

To my fellow Plum author Hetty McKinnon, for encouraging and inspiring me to make this book. Your words of support over that glass of wine will not be forgotten.

To Belinda Jeffery, for your reassuring advice when I really had no idea about this whole publishing world.

Thank you to Lucy Feagins, for always being a huge supporter of my food and sharing it with such a large audience all those years ago – I so appreciate it!

To all my dear friends, for your support, kind words and honest feedback, always. I love you all and I'm so thankful.

To the wonderful people who took the time to test recipes for this book – your comments and notes were immensely helpful in polishing and fine-tuning the book. Thank you.

To all of my followers on Ostro and Instagram for cooking from my recipes. This book would not be here if it weren't for you.

To all of my family. Thank you for supporting me unconditionally. Knowing you're all behind me means so much to me.

To my mum, Rachel, for always encouraging me to cook and travel, taste and eat. Even though we had very little, you gave me freedom in the kitchen to experiment from a very young age. Thank you for picking up ingredients for me late at night when I'd run out of something. Thank you for being so giving of your time during the shoot and always. I'm eternally grateful, Mum.

Thank you to my sweet son, Haruki – you are simply the loveliest and constantly inspire and motivate me to work harder and be better. Thank you for always keeping me company in the kitchen.

The biggest thanks is reserved for my dear husband, Nori. Always patient, kind and generous of time, love and knowledge. Thank you for always doing my dishes, eating my food and sharing in this with me. You teach me so much.

INDEX

A
aioli 156
Aljotta – my grandmother's fish soup 92
Almond chocolate cake 212
almond meal 212
anchovy
  Crostini of anchovy, butter and mozzarella 18
  Lamb shoulder with peas and anchovies 184
  Roast potatoes with tomato and anchovies 54
  Roasted broccoli with lemon, garlic and anchovy crumbs 52
apple
  apple, pancetta and sage topping 103
  apple filling 204
  caramelised 174
  Ricotta and apple hazelnut cake 204

B
Baby beetroots with burrata and walnuts 50
baked beans, Slow 65
Baked ricotta cheesecake with figs and grapes 258–259
Balsamic rhubarb and strawberry pie 242–244
banana loaf, Everyday, with homemade butter 200
basil pesto 108–110
beans *see* legumes and beans
beef
  Barley, cavolo nero and beef broth 96
  Beef stock 105
  Seared skirt steak with salsa verde 187
  Tagliatelle with beef short-rib ragù 112–114
beetroots, Baby, with burrata and walnuts 50
biscuits
  An oat biscuit for dunking 196
  brown sugar spiced biscuits 258–259
  Orange–hazelnut shortbread 199

Ricciarelli 194
savoiardi 238–240
blackberry jam 222–224
Borlotti bean soup with maltagliati 98–100
bread *see also* crostini; focaccia
  Bread and onion soup with gruyere 90
  Bread pudding 256
  Ribollita 84
  Roasted onion and bread salad 47
  Rosemary grissini 28
breadcrumbs
  anchovy crumbs 52
  garlic crumbs 127
  making 52
brioche buns, Chocolate and sour cherry 228
broccoli, Roasted, with lemon, garlic and anchovy crumbs 52
Buffalo mozzarella, guanciale and zucchini pizza 41
buns
  Cardamom buns 237
  Chocolate and sour cherry brioche buns 228
burrata, Baby beetroots with, and walnuts 50
butter
  clarified 188
  homemade 200
  maple buttercream 209

C
cabbage salad, A dependable 74
cakes and loaves
  A nice plum cake 218
  Almond chocolate cake 212
  Baked ricotta cheesecake with figs and grapes 258–259
  Chocolate, rhubarb and walnut cake 206
  Chocolate layer cake with espresso frosting and blackberries 222–224
  Everyday banana loaf with homemade butter 200
  Lemon olive oil cake 210
  Orange cake, Whole, with candied fennel seeds 215

Pear and date cake with maple buttercream 209
Ricotta and apple hazelnut cake 204
Spiced honey cake 220
Tangelo polenta drizzle cake 202
caper mayonnaise 164
capsicum, Roasted, with basil and capers 62
Cardamom buns 237
cauliflower, Roasted, and wheat salad 68
cavolo nero
  Barley, cavolo nero and beef broth 96
  Lentils with cavolo nero and sausage 168
  Ribollita 84
Cheese and onion pie 80
cheesecake, Baked ricotta, with figs and grapes 258–259
cherries: Chocolate and sour cherry brioche buns 228
chicken
  Chicken broth with wheat and spring vegetables 86
  Chicken stock 105
  Fried chicken with fennel slaw and caper mayonnaise 164
  Slow-roasted chicken and stovetop potatoes 166
  Tray-roasted chicken with grapes, olives and walnuts 162
chickpeas
  Braised lamb with chickpeas 182
  Pasta and chickpea soup 89
  pasta e ceci 89
chicory
  Chicory, provolone and salami pizza 40
  Orecchiette with chicory, raisins and garlic crumbs 127
chocolate
  Almond chocolate cake 212
  Chocolate, rhubarb and walnut cake 206
  Chocolate and sour cherry brioche buns 228
  Chocolate layer cake with espresso frosting and blackberries 222–224

Salted dark chocolate pots with palmiers 250–252
cinnamon
  Cinnamon doughnuts with custard cream 232–234
  cinnamon sugar 232–234
  Cinnamon–raisin ice cream 261
clams: Spaghetti with pancetta and vongole 146
clarified butter 188
cook's notes 13–14
cream 13
crème au chocolat 250–252
crostini
  Crostini of anchovy, butter and mozzarella 18
  Crostini of cannellini beans, black olives and mint 21
  Crostini of zucchini and basil 20
crumble topping 218
custard cream 232–234

D
date, Pear and, cake with maple buttercream 209
deep-frying 13
dessert
  Baked ricotta cheesecake with figs and grapes 258–259
  Balsamic rhubarb and strawberry pie 242–244
  Bread pudding 256
  Cinnamon doughnuts with custard cream 232–234
  Nectarine and almond crostata 254
  Roasted peach tart 247–249
  Salted dark chocolate pots with palmiers 250–252
  Tiramisù 238–240
doughnuts, Cinnamon, with custard cream 232–234
dressings and sauces
  aioli 156
  caper mayonnaise 164
  herb oil 86
  honey dressing 76
  pesto alla Genovese 108–110
  ragù 132–134

salsa verde 168, 187
sauce for meatballs 116–117
tahini dressing 68
tomato sauce, summer 141
tomato sauce, winter 142–144
walnut and herb sauce 129

E
eggs 13
espresso frosting 222–224

F
fennel salt 156
fennel seeds, candied 215
fennel slaw 164
figs
  figs and grapes, roasted 258–259
  Figs with honey and labneh 76
fish *see also* seafood
  Aljotta – my grandmother's fish soup 92
  Fish stock 104
  Sardines with pine nuts, fennel and orange 161
flour 13
focaccia
  focaccia col formaggio 30
  Olive oil focaccia 32–34
  Soft cheese focaccia 30

G
Garganelli with pancetta and zucchini 136–138
garlic crumbs 127
gnocchi *see also* pasta
  Potato gnocchi with a winter tomato sauce 142–144
  Ricotta gnocchi with a summer tomato sauce 141
grapes and figs, roasted 258–259
Greens pie 60
grissini, Rosemary 28
gruyere, Bread and onion soup with 90
guanciale 41

H
hazelnut meal 212
hazelnut topping 204

herbs
  cook's notes 13
  herb oil 86
honey
  Burnt honey and thyme ice cream 262
  honey dressing 76
  honey frosting 220
  Spiced honey cake 220
House salad 70

I
ice cream
  Burnt honey and thyme ice cream 262
  Cinnamon–raisin ice cream 261
  Yellow peach and shiso sorbet 264

L
labneh 76
lamb
  Braised lamb with chickpeas 182
  Lamb meatballs with broad beans 180
  Lamb shoulder with peas and anchovies 184
leeks
  Buttery leek soup topped with apple, pancetta and sage 103
  Potato, leek and mozzarella pie 78
legumes and beans
  Borlotti bean soup with maltagliati 98–100
  Chicken broth with wheat and spring vegetables 86
  cook's notes 14
  creamy white beans 21
  Crostini of cannellini beans, black olives and mint 21
  Lamb meatballs with broad beans 180
  Pork and white beans 172
  Ribollita 84
  Slow baked beans 65
Lemon olive oil cake 210
Lentils with cavolo nero and sausage 168
loaves *see* cakes and loaves

M

maltagliati, Borlotti bean soup with 98–100
maple buttercream 209
mascarpone
   homemade 238–240
   Orzotto of mushrooms with meatballs 150
   Spiced honey cake 220
   Tiramisù 238–240
mozzarella
   Buffalo mozzarella, guanciale and zucchini pizza 41
   Crostini of anchovy, butter and mozzarella 18
   Potato, leek and mozzarella pie 78
   Zucchini and mint salad 48
mushrooms
   Mushroom and barley pie 56–58
   Orzotto of mushrooms with mascarpone 150

N

nduja 154
Nectarine and almond crostata 254

O

oat biscuit for dunking, An 196
olive oil
   cook's notes 14
   Lemon olive oil cake 210
   Olive oil focaccia 32–34
   olive oil pastry 78
onion
   Bread and onion soup with gruyere 90
   Cheese and onion pie 80
   Roasted onion and bread salad 47
   Tomato and red onion salad 72
orange
   Orange cake, Whole, with candied fennel seeds 215
   Orange–hazelnut shortbread 199
orecchiette *see* pasta
Orzotto of mushrooms with mascarpone 150
oven temperatures 13

P

palmiers 250–252
pancetta
   Garganelli with pancetta and zucchini 136–138
   Spaghetti with pancetta and vongole 146
parmesan 14
pasta *see also* gnocchi
   Borlotti bean soup with maltagliati 98–100
   cook's notes 13–14
   Garganelli with pancetta and zucchini 136–138
   Handmade pici with meatballs in sauce 116–117
   Orecchiette three ways 124–9
   Orecchiette with chicory, raisins and garlic crumbs 127
   Orecchiette with peas and ricotta 127
   Orecchiette with walnut and herb sauce 129
   Pasta and chickpea soup 89
   Ricotta tortelloni with butter, sage and hazelnuts 121–123
   Saffron gnocchetti with ragù 132–134
   Spaghetti with pancetta and vongole 146
   Tagliatelle with beef short-rib ragù 112–114
   Trofie with pesto alla Genovese 108–110
pastry
   cheddar shortcrust pastry 60
   for crostata 254
   for fruit pie 242–244
   olive oil pastry 78
   rough puff pastry 56, 247–249
   sour cream pastry 80
peach
   Roasted peach tart 247–249
   Yellow peach and shiso sorbet 264
Pear and date cake with maple buttercream 209
pearl barley
   Barley, cavolo nero and beef broth 96
   Mushroom and barley pie 56
   Orzotto of mushrooms with mascarpone 150
peas
   Lamb shoulder with peas and anchovies 184
   Orecchiette with peas and ricotta 127
pecorino 14
peppers, Roasted, with basil and capers 62
pesto alla Genovese 108–110
pici, Handmade, with meatballs in sauce 116–117
pie (savoury)
   Cheese and onion pie 80
   Greens pie 60
   Mushroom and barley pie 56–58
   Potato, leek and mozzarella pie 78
   Rabbit pie 176–177
pizza
   Buffalo mozzarella, guanciale and zucchini pizza 41
   Chicory, provolone and salami pizza 40
   Pizza four ways 38
   Pizza Margherita 40
   Taleggio and potato pizza 41
plum cake, Nice 218
polenta
   making 149
   Soft polenta with bitter greens and walnuts 149
   Tangelo polenta drizzle cake 202
pork
   guanciale 41
   Pork and white beans 172
   Pork cooked in milk 171
   Roast pork with apple, fennel and sage 174
potatoes
   Potato, leek and mozzarella pie 78
   Potato gnocchi with a winter tomato sauce 142–144
   Roast potatoes with tomato and anchovies 54
   stovetop potatoes 166
prawns: Crispy school prawns with fennel salt and aioli 156

R

Rabbit pie 176–177
rhubarb
   Balsamic rhubarb and strawberry pie 242–244
   Chocolate, rhubarb and walnut cake 206
Ribollita 84
Ricciarelli 194
ricotta
   Baked ricotta cheesecake with figs and grapes 258–259

Greens pie 60
Homemade ricotta with seed crackers and honey 24
Orecchiette with peas and ricotta 127
Ricotta and apple hazelnut cake 204
Ricotta gnocchi with a summer tomato sauce 141
Ricotta tortelloni with butter, sage and hazelnuts 121–123
risotto 150
Roast pork with apple, fennel and sage 174
Roast potatoes with tomato and anchovies 54
Roasted broccoli with lemon, garlic and anchovy crumbs 52
Roasted cauliflower and wheat 68
Roasted onion and bread salad 47
Roasted peach tart 247–249
Rosemary grissini 28

S
Saffron gnocchetti with ragù 132–134
salads
  A dependable cabbage salad 74
  Baby beetroots with burrata and walnuts salad 50
  House salad 70
  Roasted cauliflower and wheat salad 68
  Roasted onion and bread salad 47
  Tomato and red onion salad 72
  Zucchini and mint salad 48
salsa verde 168, 187
Salted dark chocolate pots with palmiers 250–252
sardines
  filleting 161
  Sardines with pine nuts, fennel and orange 161
sauces *see* dressings and sauces
savoiardi 238–240
school prawns, Crispy, with fennel salt and aioli 156
seafood *see also* fish
  Crispy school prawns with fennel salt and aioli 156

Grilled squid with nduja, garlic and almonds 154
Seafood stew 156
Spaghetti with pancetta and vongole 146
semolina flour 13
shiso, Yellow peach and, sorbet 264
Slow-roasted chicken and stovetop potatoes 166
Soft cheese focaccia 30
Soft polenta with bitter greens and walnuts 149
soup
  Aljotta – my grandmother's fish soup 92
  Barley, cavolo nero and beef broth 96
  Borlotti bean soup with maltagliati 98–100
  Bread and onion soup with gruyere 90
  Buttery leek soup topped with apple, pancetta and sage 103
  Chicken broth with wheat and spring vegetables 86
  Pasta and chickpea soup 89
  Ribollita 84
Spaghetti with pancetta and vongole 146
squid, Grilled, with nduja, garlic and almonds 154
stock
  Beef stock 105
  Chicken stock 105
  Fish stock 104
  Vegetable stock 104
strawberry and rhubarb pie, Balsamic 242–244
sweets *see* biscuits; buns; cakes and loaves; dessert; ice cream

T
Tagliatelle with beef short-rib ragù 112–114
Taleggio and potato pizza 41
Tangelo polenta drizzle cake 202
Tiramisù 238–240
tomatoes
  Aljotta – my grandmother's fish soup 92

Braised lamb with chickpeas 182
cherry tomato focaccia 32–34
cook's notes 14
Handmade pici with meatballs in sauce 116–117
Pizza margherita 40
Potato gnocchi and a winter tomato sauce 142–144
Ribollita 84
Ricotta gnocchi with a summer tomato sauce 141
Roast potatoes with tomato and anchovies 54
Saffron gnocchetti with ragù 132–134
Slow baked beans 65
Spaghetti with pancetta and vongole 146
Tagliatelle with beef short rib ragù 112–114
Tomato and red onion salad 72
Tray-roasted chicken with grapes, olives and walnuts 162
Trofie with pesto alla Genovese 108–110

V
Veal cotoletta with capers and rosemary 188
Vegetable stock 104
vongole, Spaghetti with pancetta and 146

W
wheat
  Chicken broth with wheat and spring vegetables 86
  Roasted cauliflower and wheat salad 68

Y
yeast 13

Z
zucchini
  Crostini of zucchini and basil 20
  Garganelli with pancetta and zucchini 136–138
  Zucchini and mint salad 48

A Plum book

First published in 2017 by
Pan Macmillan Australia Pty Limited

Level 25, 1 Market Street,
Sydney, NSW 2000, Australia

Level 3, 112 Wellington Parade,
East Melbourne, VIC 3002, Australia

Text copyright © Julia Busuttil
Nishimura 2017

Photography Armelle Habib
copyright © Pan Macmillan 2017

Design Michelle Mackintosh
copyright © Pan Macmillan 2017

The moral right of the author
has been asserted.

Design by Michelle Mackintosh
Edited by Hannah Koelmeyer
Index by Frances Paterson
Photography by Armelle Habib
Prop and food styling by Karina Duncan
Food preparation by Emma Warren and
    Sebastien Nichols

Typeset by Megan Ellis

Colour reproduction by Splitting Image
    Colour Studio

Printed and bound in China by 1010 Printing
    International Limited

A CIP catalogue record for this book is
available from the National Library of
Australia.

All rights reserved. No part of this book may
be reproduced or transmitted by any person
or entity (including Google, Amazon or similar
organisations), in any form or means, electronic
or mechanical, including photocopying,
recording, scanning or by any information
storage and retrieval system, without prior
permission in writing from the publisher.

The publisher would like to thank the
following for their generosity in providing
props for the book: Bridget Bodenham,
Sophie Moran and The Melbourne Fire
Brick Company.